# MANAGEMENT, WORK AND ORGANISATIONS

Series editors: **Gibson Burrell**, The Management Centre, University of Leicester
**Mick Marchington**, Manchester School of Management UMIST
**Paul Thompson**, Department of Human Resource Management, University of Strathclyde

This series of new textbooks covers the areas of human resource management, employee relations, organisational behaviour and related business and management fields. Each text has been specially commissioned to be written by leading experts in a clear and accessible way. The books contain serious and challenging material, take an analytical rather than prescriptive approach and are particularly suitable for use by students with no prior specialist knowledge.

The series is relevant for many business and management courses, including MBA and post-experience courses, specialist masters and postgraduate diplomas, professional courses and final-year undergraduate courses. These texts have become essential reading at business and management schools worldwide.

*Published*

Paul Blyton and Peter Turnbull **The Dynamics of Employee Relations** (3rd edn)
Sharon C. Bolton **Emotion Management in the Workplace**
Peter Boxall and John Purcell **Strategy and Human Resource Management**
J. Martin Corbett **Critical Cases in Organisational Behaviour**
Keith Grint **Leadership**
Marek Korczynski **Human Resource Management in Service Work**
Karen Legge **Human Resource Management**: anniversary edition
Stephen Procter and Frank Mueller (eds) **Teamworking**
Helen Rainbird (ed.) **Training in the Workplace**
Jill Rubery and Damian Grimshaw **The Organisation of Employment**
Harry Scarbrough (ed.) **The Management of Expertise**
Hugh Scullion and Margaret Linehan (eds) **International Human Resource Management**
Adrian Wilkinson, Mick Marchington, Tom Redman and Ed Snape **Managing with Total Quality Management**
Diana Winstanley and Jean Woodall (eds) **Ethical Issues in Contemporary Human Resource Management**

For more information on titles in the series please go to www.palgrave.com/busines/mwo

*Invitation to authors*

The Series Editors welcome proposals for new books within the Management, Work and Organisation series. These should be sent to Paul Thompson (p.thompson@strath.ac.uk) at the Dept of HRM, Strathclyde Business School, University of Strathclyde, 50 Richmond St, Glasgow G1 1XT

# International Human Resource Management: a critical text

Edited by

**Hugh Scullion**
and
**Margaret Linehan**

palgrave
macmillan

First published 2005 by
PALGRAVE MACMILLAN
Houndmills, Basingstoke, Hampshire RG21 6XS and
175 Fifth Avenue, New York, N.Y. 10010
Companies and representatives throughout the world.

PALGRAVE MACMILLAN is the global academic imprint of the Palgrave
Macmillan division of St. Martin's Press, LLC and of Palgrave Macmillan Ltd.
Macmillan® is a registered trademark in the United States, United Kingdom
and other countries. Palgrave is a registered trademark in the European
Union and other countries.

ISBN-13: 978-0-333-74139-9
ISBN-10: 0-333-74139-0

This book is printed on paper suitable for recycling and made from fully
managed and sustained forest sources.

A catalogue record for this book is available from the British Library.

Library of Congress Cataloging-in-Publication Data

International human resource management : a critical text / edited by
Hugh Scullion & Margaret Linehan.
    p. cm.—(Management, work and organisations)
    Includes bibliographical references and index.
    ISBN 0-333-74139-0 (pbk.)
    1. International business enterprises—Personnel management. 2. Personnel
management. I. Scullion, Hugh. II. Linehan, Margaret. III. Series.

HF5549.5.E4515773 2004
658.3—dc22                                                    2004054823

10  9  8  7  6  5  4  3  2  1
14  13  12  11  10  09  08  07  06  05

Printed and bound in China

# Contents

**Part 3   Contemporary issues in international HRM**

**Part 4   Emerging issues in international HRM**

# Notes on the Contributors

**Nancy J. Adler** is a Professor of Management at McGill University in Montreal, Canada. Dr. Adler consults with global companies and government organizations on projects in Asia, Europe, North and South America, and the Middle East. She conducts research on global leadership, cross-cultural management, and women as global managers and leaders. She has authored more than one hundred articles and produced the film, *A Portable Life*. Her books include *International Dimensions of Organizational Behaviour* (with over a quarter million copies in print), *Women in Management Worldwide*, *Competitive Frontiers: Women Managers in a Global Economy*, and *From Boston to Beijing: Managing with a Worldview*. Professor Adler is a Fellow of both the Academy of Management and the Academy of International Business.

**Jaime Bonache** is Professor of Human Resource Management at the University Carlos III of Madrid in Spain. Professor Bonache received his PhD and MBA degrees in Management from the Universidad Autonoma of Madrid, and his MA from Carleton University of Ottawa (Canada). His research interests are in the areas of international management development, expatriate management and cross-cultural management. His research work has been published in both Spanish and international journals. He has participated in a number of European and Spanish research projects in the area of international human resource management.

**Pawan S. Budhwar** is a Reader in Organisational Behaviour and Human Resource Management at Aston Business School, UK. He received his doctorate from Manchester Business School in Cross National Human Resource Management. His current research interests are in the fields of IHRM, management in developing countries, HRM in call centres and BPO, leadership and quality of life, and firms' performance. His publications include several articles in academic journals, three books and contributions to edited volumes.

**Paula Caligiuri** is Director of the Centre for Human Resource Strategy (CHRS) and an Associate Professor of Human Resources Management at Rutgers University in the School of Management and Labor Relations. Paula is also a Visiting Professor at Università Bocconi business school in Milan, Italy. Paula researches, publishes and consults in three primary areas: strategic human resource management in multinational organizations, global leadership development, and global assignee management. Paula was one of the founding members of the Global Mobility Forum, a worldwide organization dedicated to global HR research. She is also currently serving as a Senior Research Advisor for the Conference Board's research on global leadership development. Her academic publications include several articles in the *International Journal of Human Resource Management, Journal of World Business, Journal of Applied Psychology, Personnel Psychology*, and *International Journal of Intercultural Relations*. Paula is on several editorial boards and is an Associate Editor for *Human Resource Management Journal*. Paula holds a Ph.D. from Penn State University in industrial and organizational psychology.

**Yaw A. Debrah** is a Reader in Management and International Business at Brunel University, London, UK. Prior to his current appointment, he was a Senior Lecturer at Cardiff Business School, Cardiff University, Wales, UK He was also previously a lecturer at Nanyang Business School, Nanyang Technological University, Singapore. In addition, Yaw has worked in Africa, North America and Europe. He has edited five books including: *Human Resource Management in Developing Countries* (with Pawan Budhwar) (Routledge, 2001) and *Human Resource Management in Africa* (with Ken Kamoche, Frank Horwitz and Gerry Muuka) (Routledge, 2004). His publications have appeared in journals such as *Human Relations, Journal of Organizational Behaviour, International Journal of Human Resource Management, Australian Journal of Management, Asia-Pacific Business Review, Asia-Pacific Journal of Human Resources, Thunderbird International Business Review*, and *Construction Management and Economics*.

**Jacqueline Fendt** is a Researcher at the Graduate School of Business Administration, Zurich, Switzerland. Her research interests are Management Education, Management Development, and Global Management Responsibility.

**Zulima Fernández** is Full Professor of Strategic Management and Vice-Chancellor of Academics Affairs at the Universidad Carlos III de Madrid. She received her PhD in Management from the Universidad de Oviedo. Her research interests are in the areas of family business, international business, and privatisation and competitive dynamics. She has published a number of books and papers in both Spanish and international journals. She is also member of the Scientific Committees of Cuadernos de Economíay Dirección de la Empresa and Universia Business Review.

**Patrick Gunnigle** is Professor of Business Studies at the University of Limerick, Ireland, where he is also Director of the Employment Research Unit.

**Susan E. Jackson** is Professor of Human Resource Management in the School of Management and Labor Relations at Rutgers University. She also serves as Graduate Director for the Doctoral Program in Industrial Relations and Human Resources, and holds an appointment as Research Fellow at the Graduate School of Business Administration, Zurich, Switzerland. Her primary areas of expertise are the strategic management of human resources and organizational behaviour; special interests include managing team effectiveness, workforce diversity, and the design of human resource management systems to support learning and innovation. She has authored or co-authored over 100 articles and books on these and related topics. Her books include *Managing Knowledge for Sustained Competitive Advantage: Designing Strategies for Effective Human Resource Management* (with Michael Hitt and Angelo DeNisi), *Managing Human Resources: A Partnership Perspective* (with Randall Schuler), *Managing Human Resources in Cross-Border Alliances* (with Randall Schuler), *Management* (with Don Hellriegel and John Slocum), and *Diversity in the Workplace: Human Resource Initiatives*, a volume in the SIOP Practice series. In addition to her university activities, Professor Jackson has held numerous positions in professional societies. She currently serves on the editorial boards of several journals, including the *Academy of Management Journal, Human Resource Management Journal*, and *Applied Psychology: An International Review*. In the Academy of Management, she has served as a member of the Human Resources Division's Executive Committee, and is editor of the *Academy of Management Review*, a journal devoted to the publication of scholarly reviews and theory development.

**Mila B. Lazarova** is an Assistant Professor at the Faculty of Business Administration at Simon Fraser University in Vancouver, Canada. Mila received a Ph.D. degree and a Master of Science degree in Human Resources and Industrial Relations from the School of Management and Labor Relations, at Rutgers University. She also holds a Master's in International Economic Relations from the University of National and World Economics in Sofia, Bulgaria. With a background in international business and human resource management, Mila Lazarova conducts research in the areas of expatriate management (with a focus on repatriation and career impact of international assignments, female expatriates, and work/life balance issues related to assignments), global careers, and the role of organizational career development and work/life balance practices on employee retention. Mila's work has been published in outlets such as the *International Journal of Human Resource Management* and the *Journal of World Business*. She has also contributed chapters to several books on international human resource management and global leadership.

**Margaret Linehan** is a Lecturer in Human Resource Management at the Department of Adult and Continuing Education, Cork Institute of Technology, Ireland. Her main research interest is women in international management. Her work has been published in numerous refereed academic journals including *The International Journal of Human Resource Management*, *The British Journal of Management*, and *Women in Management Review*. She has authored/edited ten books, one of her, books *Senior Female International Managers: Why so Few?* (Ashgate, 2000), has been translated to Slovene (GV Publishing, 2001). She is on several editorial boards of academic journals.

**Wolfgang Mayrhofer** is Professor of Organisational Behaviour and Management at Faculty of Business Administration Vienna University, Vienna, Austria. He conducts research in the area of international leadership and human resource management, careers in organizations and systems theory and management. In addition, he regularly consults to both private and public sector organizations.

**Michael J. Morley** is Senior Lecturer in the Department of Personnel and Employment Relations at the University of Limerick, Ireland. His current research interests include convergence and divergence in European human resource management; international assignments and expatriate management; intercultural transitional adjustment, intercultural sensemaking and cross-cultural competence; and human resource management in US MNCs in Europe.

**Nancy K. Napier** (PhD, Ohio State University) is Professor of International Business and Executive Director of the Global Business Consortium at Boise State University. She was a former Associate Dean of the College of Business and Economics and Chairman of the Management Department. She also managed Boise State's nine-year involvement in an $8.5m Swedish and USAID funded capacity building project at the National Economics University in Hanoi, Vietnam. She has published three books; her most recent is *Managing Relationships in Transition Economies* (with D. Thomas), published by Praeger. Her articles appear in such journals as *Journal of Management Inquiry*, *Human Resource Management Journal*, *Human Resource Planning*, *Organisation*, *Academy of Management Review*, *Journal of Management Studies*, and *Journal of International Business Studies*.

**Emer O'Hagan** is a Senior Consultant in PricewaterhouseCoopers' Advisory Division, Belfast. Previously she held a Junior Fellowship at the Institute of Governance, Public Policy and Social Research, Queen's University, Belfast.

**Jaap Paauwe** is Professor of Business and Organization at the Rotterdam School of Economics, Erasmus University, Rotterdam. He has written and co-authored numerous books on HRM and published many articles in leading journals on industrial relations, organizational change and international HRM. His recent pathbreaking work on 'HRM and Performance: Achieving Long-Term Viability' (2004) follows on from excellent papers in this area. Jaap edited a special edition of the *International Journal of Human Resource Management* on 'HRM and Performance' and coordinates the research programme on organizational performance at Erasmus University. Jaap's field of interest include HRM, organizational change and corporate strategy.

**Randall S. Schuler** is Professor of Strategic International Human Resource Management and Director of the Masters Degree in HRM Program in the Department of Human Resource Management at Rutgers University in New Brunswick, New Jersey, and holds an appointment at the Graduate School of Business Administration, Zurich, Switzerland. His interests are global human resource management, strategic human resource management, the human resource management function in organizations and the interface of business strategy and human resource tasks. He has authored or edited over forty books including *Strategic Human Resource Management: A Reader*, *International Human Resource Management*, *Managing Human Resources through*

*Strategic Partnerships*, and *Cases in Managing Organizations and People*. In addition, he has contributed over forty-five chapters to various books and has published over one hundred articles in professional journals and academic proceedings. Presently, he is on the editorial boards of *Organizational Dynamics, Journal of World Business, Journal of Occupational and Organizational Psychology, Human Resource Planning, Human Resource Management, International Journal of Human Resource Management, Asia Pacific Journal of Human Resources, Journal of Occupational Behavior, Journal of International Management, Journal of International Management Reviews*, and *Journal of Market-focused Management*. He is a Fellow of the British Academy of Management, the American Academy of Management, American Psychological Association and the Society for Industrial/Organizational Psychology.

**Hugh Scullion** is Professor of International Business and Director of the Strathclyde International Business Unit at Strathclyde Business School, Glasgow, having previously worked at Warwick and Nottingham Business Schools. He is a Visiting Professor at the business schools of Grenoble and Toulouse and also at Limerick University. His work on international HRM strategies, the management of expatriates, women in international management and international staffing has been published in journals such as *Academy of Management Journal, Journal of World Business, International Journal of Human Resource Management*, and *International Studies of Management and Organization*. His current research interests include the role of the corporate HR function in the international firm, expatriate psychological contracts, global staffing and further work on female expatriates. He consults with a number of leading international firms including Rolls Royce plc, teaches regularly on executive development programmes in Europe, and has conducted workshops for major global corporations. He is also convenor of the Strathclyde HR directors group, which is a network of senior HR directors from Scottish and international companies. He has written several books and over fifty specialist articles in international HRM and his latest book, *Global Staffing* (Routledge) is due to be published in 2005.

**Jan Selmer** is Professor of Management at School of Business, Hong Kong Baptist University, Hong Kong. He received his doctoral degree in business administration from Stockholm University, Sweden. Living and working in Asia for almost two decades, his research interest lies in cross-cultural management with a special focus on the region. He has published nine books and numerous journal articles in refereed academic journals including *International Business Review, International Journal of Human Resource Management, International Journal of Intercultural Relations, Journal of Business Research, Journal of International Management, Journal of Organizational Behavior, Journal of World Business, Management International Review*, and *Personnel Review*. His latest book, *International Management in China: Cross-Cultural Issues*, was published in 1998 by Routledge, UK. In August 1996, he organized the world-first international academic conference on 'Cross-Cultural Management in China'. Professor Selmer is also an active consultant in cross-cultural training for multinational corporations, such as ABB, Ericsson, Esselte, Motorola, and Singapore Airlines.

**Vesa Suutari** is Professor of International Management and Head of Department in Management and Organization at the University of Vaasa, Finland. He has specialized on cross-cultural management and international HRM. His research has been published in various international journals and edited books. His current research interests include expatriation, global leadership, global careers, and international knowledge transfers.

**Marja Tahvanainen** holds a PhD in international business, and has studied various aspects of HRM in international contexts. Her PhD thesis from 1998 focused on expatriate performance management, and, after that, she conducted further research on the topic. She lectures on global HRM at the Helsinki School of Economics, and is involved in managerial training and consulting on the same subject. Currently her research focuses on non-standard international assignments.

**Ibraiz Tarique** is a researcher in the School of Management and Labor Relations at Rutgers University, New Jersey. He teaches programmes in strategic HRM and international HRM. His research interests cover training and development issues in multinational enterprises, human capital theory and cross-cultural and international HRM issues in international alliances. His work has been presented at leading conferences such as the Academy of Management meetings and his work has been published in leading journals, including the *International Journal of Human Resource Management*.

**Sully Taylor** (Ph.D. University of Washington) is Professor of International Management and Human Resource Management at Portland State University, School of Business Administration, and Director of the Master of International Management at PSU. She has also taught at Waseda University and the Instituto de Empresa, Madrid, Spain. From 1981–84, Dr Taylor worked for Sumitomo Metal Industries in Japan, in their training and development department. Dr Taylor teaches courses in human resource management, global human resource management, international management, and the Asian business environment. Her research interests include the design of global HRM systems in multinational firms, creating global learning organizations, and the management of women expatriates and global employees. Dr Taylor has consulted for numerous companies, and has authored or co-authored a number of articles on her research that have been published in *Academy of Management Review*, *Sloan Management Review*, *Human Resource Management Journal*, *Advances in International Comparative Management*, *Asia Pacific Journal of Human Resources*, and *Human Resource Planning*. With Nancy Napier, she has written a book entitled *Western Women Working in Japan: Breaking Corporate Barriers*. In 1988, she received a Fulbright Research Grant to complete her dissertation studies in Japan, and in 1997 she received a Fulbright Faculty Grant to teach and research in Chile.

**Ingeman Torbiörn** is Associate Professor at the Department of Psychology, Stockholm University. His research is generally in organizational psychology, in particular on intercultural themes at organizational and individual levels. In this field, he has authored three books and several articles, among them *Living Abroad: Personal Adjustment and Personnel Policy in the Overseas Setting* (Chichester, Wiley, 1992).

part **1**

# Strategy and international HRM

# 1

# International HRM: an introduction

*Hugh Scullion*

*International Human Resource Management: A Critical Text* covers a wide range of topics within the rapidly developing field of international HRM. The comprehensive coverage encompasses strategic and operational aspects of international HRM, and four major themes run through all the chapters. The first is the need to understand international HRM strategies and practices in relation to changing strategies of the international business firm. The second is the need to explore the links between the implementation of international strategies and international HRM policy and practices. The third is the need to develop more comprehensive frameworks to reflect the complex set of environmental factors that affect international HRM in an international context. Finally there is the need to examine international HRM activities in ways that recognize their systematic interaction (Schuler *et al.*, 2002).

This introductory chapter has four aims. First, it seeks to review some definitions of international HRM (IHRM) and to consider why IHRM is different from HRM in the domestic sphere. Second, it examines the main reasons for the growth of the field of IHRM. Third, it outlines the distinctive contribution of this volume which seeks critically to review important theoretical and empirical developments in the area of IHRM over the last decade. The final section provides a brief summary for each chapter to help the reader identify the main themes and issues covered in each of the chapters.

The last 25 years have witnessed a major growth of interest in strategy and human resource management. Both organizations and academics have increasingly explored the ways in which HRM is strategic to business success and while there have been debates over the meaning of HRM since the term emerged in the mid-1980s, it has become the most influential term referring to the activities of management in the employment relationship (Boxall and Purcell, 2003).

International HRM, on the other hand, is a field of much more recent origin and was described by a leading scholar in international management as a field in the infancy stage of development (Laurent, 1986). Until relatively recently the majority of research on multinational companies focused on activities such as international production, international marketing and international strategy. Indeed IHRM was one of the least studied areas in international business (Ondrack, 1985) and the bulk of research in this field had been conducted by US researchers from an American rather than an international perspective (Boyacigiller and Adler, 1991).

This begs the questions: why a book on IHRM and why is it now more important for students to learn about IHRM? In addition, how will this book fit in with other major areas of business management studies? These questions will be considered below but first we need to start with some definitions.

# Definitions of international HRM

There is no consensus about what the term IHRM covers although most studies in the area have traditionally focused on the area of expatriation (Brewster and Harris, 1999). IHRM has been defined as 'the HRM issues and problems arising from the internationalization of business, and the HRM strategies, policies and practices which firms pursue in response to the internationalization of business' (Scullion, 1995). Welch (1994) concluded that international HRM was essentially concerned with the four core activities of recruitment and selection, training and development, compensation and repatriation of expatriates. Similarly, Iles (1995) identifies four key areas in IHRM as recruitment and selection, training and development, managing multicultural teams and international diversity and performance management. Hendry (1994), on the other hand, argues that there are three main issues in IHRM: first, the management and development of expatriates; second, the internationalization of management throughout the organization; and finally, the need to internationalize the whole organization by creating a new corporate culture reflecting the need for greater international experience across the whole organization due to the increasing frequency of cross-cultural interactions of doing business at home as well as abroad. The advantage of such definitions is that they cover a far wider spectrum than the management of expatriates and involve the worldwide management of people (Dowling et al., 1999). They also highlight IHRM as a related but separate field from comparative employment relations which is concerned with understanding in what ways and why HRM practices differ across countries (Bamber and Lansbury, 1998).

More recent definitions emphasize a more strategic approach and consider the role and organization of IHRM functions, the relationship between headquarters and the local units as well as the actual policies and practices adopted. For example, Taylor et al. (1996) define IHRM as: 'The set of distinct activities, functions and processes that are directed at attracting, developing and maintaining an MNC's human resources. It is thus the aggregate of the various HRM systems used to manage people in the MNC, both at home and overseas'. This suggests that international HRM is concerned with identifying and understanding how MNCs manage their geographically dispersed workforces in order to leverage their HR resources for both local and global competitive advantage (Schuler *et al.*, 2002). Globalization has brought new challenges and increased complexity such as the challenge of managing newer forms of network organization. In recognition of such developments, some writers have developed new definitions where IHRM is seen as playing a key role in achieving a balance between the need for control and coordination of foreign subsidiaries, and the need to adapt to local environments (see for example Adler and Ghadar, 1990; Milliman *et al.*, 1991). Recently, definitions have been extended to cover localization of management, international coordination, global leadership development and the emerging cultural challenges of global knowledge management (Evans *et al.*, 2002). This suggests that developing future global leaders is a key priority in the management of human resources in the global firm (Gregerson *et al.*, 1998; Scullion and Starkey, 2000).

## Why is IHRM different from domestic HRM?

Not all writers have been fully convinced about the distinction between IHRM and domestic HRM, and some emphasize the basic continuities and similarities between operating in the domestic and international business environments (for example Hendry, 1994). However, given the increasing pace of internationalization and the changing forms of globalization, there is growing support for the argument of Evans *et al.* (2002, p. 14) that 'in the global era the most relevant insights into management processes will come from studying human resource management in an international context'.

We can see that in broad terms IHRM involves the same activities as domestic HRM (for example HR planning and staffing, recruitment and selection, appraisal and development, rewards, and so on) (Morgan, 1986). However, as pointed out by Dowling *et al.* (1999), domestic HRM is involved with employees *within only one national boundary*. IHRM, on the other hand, deals with three national or country categories: the parent country where the firm is usually headquartered; the host country where a subsidiary may be located; and other countries which may be the source of labour, finance or research and development. In addition, there are three types of employees of an international firm: parent-country nationals (PCNs); host-country nationals (HCNs); and third-country nationals (TCNs). For example, Shell may employ some Australian managers to work in Japan as third-country nationals.

There are two major factors therefore which differentiate domestic HRM from IHRM. First, the complexities of operating in different countries (and therefore in different cultures), and secondly employing different national categories of workers.

It is argued that these are the key variables that differentiate domestic and IHRM rather than any major differences between HRM areas or functions performed (Dowling *et al.*, 1999). This suggests that it is the knowledge of conditions in a variety of countries and how to manage them within and across borders which is the essence of IHRM. Research suggests that many firms continue to underestimate the complexities of managing human resources across borders which often results in poor performance in international operations (Schuler *et al.*, 2004). It has been argued by Dowling *et al.* (1999) that the complexity of IHRM can be attributed to six factors that differentiate international from domestic HRM. These factors are:

1   A wider range of HR activities
2   The need for a broader perspective
3   More involvement in employees' personal lives
4   Responsiveness to changes in staffing requirements as international strategy changes
5   Higher risk exposure
6   More external influences.

Each of these factors will be discussed directly or indirectly in the chapters which follow.

## Why is it more important for business management students to learn about IHRM?

There has been rapid development of the field of IHRM over the past decade (Harzing and Van Ruysseveldt, 2004), and there are a number of indicators of the growing importance of the field. First, it has been argued that the rapid pace of internationalization has led to a more strategic role for HRM and that a more strategic and systematic approach to studying IHRM is emerging. One indicator of this is the development of more sophisticated theoretical work in the area (see Chapter 2 below) including work which identifies the main determinants of IHRM policy and practice and the development of integrated frameworks which bring together the strategic and international dimensions of IHRM (Schuler *et al.*, 1993; DeCieri and Dowling, 1999). A second important indicator of the growing importance of IHRM in the past decade is the rapidly growing body of empirical research on IHRM strategies and practices of MNCs taking place outside the United States (Scullion, 2001). It is increasingly important that business and management students are aware of studies which highlight the major differences in approaches to IHRM between US, Asian and European firms (Tung, 1982; Peterson *et al.*, 1996; Harzing, 1999). While it is important for students to have a good understanding of the North American research which has pioneered developments of the field (Scullion and Brewster, 2001) it is equally important that they are exposed to the growing body of international research which questions the assumed universality of American theories and highlights the cultural diversity of values and the impact of diversity on organizational behaviour (Hofstede, 1980).

For example, the rapid growth of research on IHRM in Europe over the last decade makes the field more interesting, relevant and challenging for students in several respects. First, European MNCs were the first to enter international markets, and due to the small size of their domestic markets European companies tend to have a high percentage of revenues coming from foreign markets and have a longer history of sending managers on international assignments. This is in contrast to US MNCs which typically have huge domestic markets and tend to find it more difficult to adapt to local markets (Yip, 1997). Second, studies have found important differences in organization structure and management processes between US, European and Japanese MNCs (Kopp, 1994; Harzing, 1999). It has been argued that US MNCs tend to stress formalization of structure and process while European MNCs place more weight on normative integration or socialization to develop shared attitudes and values across the MNC (Schneider and Barsoux, 2003). Third, many European MNCs tended to operate with multi-domestic international approaches involving little coordination and integration of international activities. Fourth, foreign subsidiaries of European MNCs have often enjoyed a large degree of autonomy which sometimes led to problems for MNCs in developing and implementing globally integrated strategies (Young and Hamill, 1992). Fifth, a recent review (Scullion and Brewster, 2001) highlighted the changing nature and patterns of expatriation in Europe and revealed both similarities and differences between Europe and North America. This highlights the importance for students of IHRM to understand the importance of context. For example, Europe is very heterogeneous (Hofstede, 1980), and while there are important cultural differences between European countries (Harzing, 1999) it has been argued that there are a number of factors which make Europe distinctive compared with North America (Scullion and Brewster, 2001).

A final indicator of the development of the IHRM field has been the rapid surge in the number of specialist conferences, articles, journals and books devoted to IHRM, many of them exploring new themes and topics and many coming from Europe and elsewhere as well as from North America. This reflects the growing recognition being given to this area by managers, consultants and researchers. The growing number of business schools offering chairs in IHRM are perhaps the final indicator that the field has developed beyond the infancy stage of development.

Finally, how will this book fit in and be relevant with other areas of business management studies? First, given the growing importance of internationalization and globalization, this book on IHRM will address the growing need for students to understand the links between international strategy and the international dimensions of HRM. In particular, the book will help students to understand the links between IHRM and the implementation issues related to international strategy. As will be argued below, increased attention is being paid to the implementation of international strategy which is becoming increasingly problematic for many MNCs. This book will provide students with a better understanding of effective strategy implementation in the international context by providing a good understanding of the role of IHRM in the control and implementation strategies of MNCs.

# Reasons for the emergence of IHRM

Having examined the indicators of the growing importance of IHRM above, it is important to understand the main reasons for the rapid growth of interest in the field over the last decade and a half. These have been outlined by Scullion (2001) and are further developed below:

1  The rapid growth of internationalization and global competition have increased the number and significance of MNCs in recent years, resulting in the increased mobility of human resources (Black *et al.*, 2000).
2  The effective management of human resources is increasingly being recognized as a major determinant of success or failure in international business (Black *et al.*, 1999; Harris *et al.*, 2003). There is also a growing recognition that the success of global business depends most importantly on the quality of management in the MNC (Stroh and Caligiuri, 1998; Gooderham and Nordhaug, 2003).
3  The performance of expatriates continues to be problematic and expatriate failure or underperformance is often costly both in human and financial terms. The evidence suggests that the indirect costs of poor performance in international assignments such as loss of market share and damage to foreign customer relations may be particularly costly (Dowling *et al.*, 1999).
4  Shortages of international managers are becoming an increasing problem for international firms (Scullion, 1994). The implementation of global strategies are increasingly constrained by shortages of international management talent which constrain corporate efforts to expand abroad (Black and Gregersen, 1999; Morgan *et al.*, 2003). Also, the rapid growth of emerging markets (Garten, 1997) implies an increasing need for managers with distinctive competences and a desire to manage in these culturally and economically distant countries, and a greater competition between MNCs for managers with the context-specific knowledge of how to do business successfully in such countries (Harvey *et al.*, 1999b).
5  IHRM issues are becoming increasingly important in a far wider range of organizations partly due to the rapid growth of small and medium-sized

enterprise internationalization and the emergence of 'micromultinationals' in recent years (Dimitratos *et al.*, 2003). Recent research highlights the importance of learning and the management team's international experience on the international performance of SMEs (Dalley and Hamilton, 2000), and suggests that performance problems in these organizations are often linked to the poor management of human resources (Anderson and Boocock, 2002; Yli-Renko *et al.*, 2002).

6 The movement away from more traditional hierarchical organizational structures towards the network MNC organization has been facilitated by the development of networks of personal relationships and horizontal communication channels (Forsgren, 1990), and it has been argued that HR plays a more significant role in network organization (Marschan *et al.*, 1997).

7 There is also growing evidence that HR strategy plays a more significant role in implementation and control in the international firm (Scullion and Starkey, 2000). It has been suggested that in a rapidly globalizing environment, many MNCs have less difficulty determining which strategies to pursue than how to implement them, and it has been argued that the success of any global or transnational strategy has less to do with structural innovations than developing very different organizational cultures (Bartlett and Ghoshal, 1998).

8 Recent research suggests that growing awareness of implementation problems in the rapidly increasing number of strategic alliances and cross-border mergers and acquisitions has further increased the strategic importance of IHRM (Doz and Hamel, 1998; Schuler *et al.*, 2004), particularly as the context of strategic alliances and global business is increasingly shifting from formal, developed and mature markets to informal, emerging and culturally distant markets (Harvey *et al.*, 1999a).

9 It has been argued that the transformation of the HR system to support the process of organizational learning is the key strategic task facing the HR function in international firms, and that global organizational learning is driven by teamwork across borders and a willingness to tap into the potential of local managers (Pucik, 1988, 1992). Learning, knowledge-acquisition and adaptation have been identified as important potential sources of competitive advantage (Bjorkman and Xiucheng, 2002). It has been argued that HR should attempt to meet the key strategic challenge of learning and seize the opportunity to add value to the organization through effectively supporting the organization's strategic learning objectives (Cyr and Schneider, 1996; Glaister *et al.*, 2003).

10 There is growing recognition that, increasingly, the source of advantage for multinational firms is derived from the firm's ability to create, transfer and integrate knowledge across borders (Kogut and Zander, 1992; Mudambi, 2002). The role of subsidiary knowledge and the organizational context is

increasingly recognized (Foss and Pedersen, 2002; Berdrow and Lane, 2003), while global knowledge management more generally has emerged as a key strategic area for MNCs, with HRM playing a central role in today's challenges of knowledge management in the international firm (Desouza and Evaristo, 2003; Gooderham and Nordhaug, 2003).

11   Recent research (Harvey *et al.*, 1999a) shows the growing importance of inpatriation in international firms; that is, the practice of developing host-country managers or third-country managers through developmental transfers to corporate headquarters. Increasingly, developmental assignments for local managers provide the means for them to develop the skills and knowledge they will need to manage a global business, and reflect the growing recognition that the best and most creative ideas and practices may come from outside the parent company. Inpatriation will become increasingly important as the need for increased diversity and multiculturalism in the global workforce is heightened, and developing a multicultural international workforce is considered to be one of the primary prerequisites for competing effectively in the global marketplace (Harvey and Novicevic, 2002).

12   Finally, the problem of how to internationalize the HRM function itself has been identified as a major issue facing international organizations, and it is recognized that the same HR policies will not produce the same effects in different country contexts. A recent review of European and North American research examined the major problems MNCs face when seeking to internationalize the HR function and concluded, 'Paradoxically, then, the function in charge of implementing internationalisation is itself rather parochial. This lack of international experience and understanding no doubt helps to explain why devising the appropriate human resource strategies remains problematic for MNCs' (Schneider and Barsoux, 2003, p. 175).

## The distinctive contribution of this book?

- **Comprehensive**. A wide range of topics and themes in IHRM will be covered, going well-beyond the traditional focus on expatriation. Strategic and operational dimensions will be examined, as well as the links between international strategy and IHRM. The second part of the book presents the latest research and thinking in the critical areas covered by the international HR cycle, while the third and fourth parts examine current debates and emerging issues in the rapidly developing field of IHRM.

- **Research focus**. Each chapter has been carefully commissioned from a leading specialist in the field, and the book includes contributions from a world-class group of scholars representing a truly authoritative source of knowledge on

IHRM. Some of the contributions introduce new and innovative research methodologies and offer original analysis of key debates in the field.

- **Critical**. The title, *International Human Resource Management: a critical text*, has been chosen for several reasons. First, due to the leading-edge research contributions in each chapter this is a book which goes beyond the prescriptive approach to IHRM and simplistic models which find little reflection in the empirical realities of the real world. Second, IHRM is subjected to very close critical analysis from a wide variety of perspectives. Third, the key issues and debates in each chapter are subject to rigorous critique from a leading expert in the respective fields.

- **Integrated**. This book is also coherent across a wide range of topics and features an integrated approach to help students make connections among different concepts and debates, and highlights key themes running through the chapters. These are outlined above in the first paragraph of this chapter. The book consists of 14 chapters written by 24 authors, and has been put together after consultation with leading authorities in the field to provide a coherent overview of the field of IHRM.

- **Global perspective**. The contributors are leading specialists in Europe, Asia and North America, and in this respect the volume is highly international drawing on a variety of global perspectives. The majority of the authors (14) work in European countries including Ireland, Spain, Austria, Finland, Switzerland, Scotland and England. Eight of the authors are based in North America (USA and Canada) and one is based in Asia (Hong Kong). Authors use examples drawing on research conducted in many countries and students will learn from diverse perspectives, including those of small and medium-sized multinationals, the experience of developing countries, as well as understanding the IHRM issues and problems facing global companies. The book is therefore global in both its outlook as well as its author base.

- **Relevance**. The latest concepts and models are presented as well as considering recent developments in international management to help students relate the material to what is currently happening in the real world. New developments in the global business environment are highlighted and the book considers the implications for IHRM policy and practice.

- **Who is this book aimed at?** It is envisaged that this book will be useful to advanced undergraduate students in business management seeking to develop their understanding of the international dimensions of HRM. The book will also appeal to Masters students majoring in international business, international management and human resource management as well as MBA students. The book will help students to better understand the linkages and connections between these areas and in particular will improve understanding of the role of human resources in the formation and implementation of international strategy. Doctoral students in international management will benefit from the critical literature reviews which will help them to form a coherent view of the field, as well as the comprehensive and up-to-date references. Finally, while managers in the field may not find ready-made solutions for their real-life problems, the book offers frameworks which will allow them to better understand the nature of IHRM in relation to the changing international strategy of the firm, and also offers insights into both the strategic and operational aspects of IHRM.

# The organization of the book

The book is divided into four parts providing a modular yet integrative approach. This makes it possible for students to use a selection of sections and chapters to focus on the topics most interesting to them, without losing the sense of cohesiveness and wholeness that is critical in an area such as IHRM which has strong linkages with international business strategy, international management and HR management. Taken together, we think the four parts presents a coherent and fairly comprehensive approach to the field of IHRM. Our readers will be the judge.

## Part 1: strategy and international HRM

In contrast to several other chapters of the book, where some attention is paid to the operational aspects of IHRM, Part 1 focuses on the more strategic aspects and argues that as a firm passes through the various stages of the internationalization process, the focus of the IHRM agenda is likely to shift over time (Adler and Ghadar, 1990). The central argument is that IHRM should be linked to the international strategy of the firm and that its changing forms must be understood in relation to the strategic evolution of the international business firm (Scullion and Starkey, 2000).

Chapter 2 critically examines some important theoretical developments in the area of strategic IHRM research and highlights the need for strategic HRM systems to address the tension between global integration and local responsiveness, and also identifies the key variables which determine strategic IHRM approaches. The second part of the chapter examines the changing role of the corporate HR function in the international firm, highlighting the variation of the role in different types of international firm. Finally, the chapter also examines some key issues in relation to global management development and the challenges faced by firms who seek to develop transnational managers.

Chapter 3 offers an original and sophisticated analysis of international staffing, exploring in some depth the links between international strategy and international staffing. It is suggested that as a firm passes through the various stages of the internationalization process, the approach to international staffing is likely to shift over time. In the early stages when there is greater reliance on expatriates to manage the foreign subsidiaries, the focus would be on the recruitment and training of expatriates.

As the pace of internationalization increases, the focus may shift to the development of high-potential host-country national managers. Finally, when the pace of internationalization further accelerates the focus will shift to a much wider attempt to internationalize the organization as a whole.

The chapter critically examines the main determinants of international staffing and a key feature is the analysis of regional comparisons in staffing patterns. It argues that the varied context of European multinationals requires a selective use of parent-country nationals and host-country nationals as well as a general orientation for handling variety. Finally, the chapter highlights the need for IHRM researchers to develop wider criteria to interpret staffing patterns to reflect the wider range of options facing firms in IHRM in general and staffing policies in particular.

## Part 2: managing the International HR cycle

Here we examine in depth the key areas covered by the traditional international HR cycle (Brewster and Scullion, 1997), covering the international aspects of recruitment and selection, training and development, rewards/compensation, career development and repatriation. The final chapter will also consider industrial relations issues in an international context. The chapters in this part of the book all address one of the key challenges in international management: the need for MNCs to be globally integrated and locally responsive, while at the same time recognizing that learning, knowledge acquisition and adaptation are important sources of competitive advantage in international firms (Bartlett and Ghoshal, 1998).

Chapter 4 focuses on the role of the training and development function in the global HR system showing how training and development initiatives have evolved into strategic HR functions. At the heart of the chapter is a critical discussion of the fit between a firm's business strategy and the organization of a firm's training and development function, highlighting the complexity of managing a strategic training and development function within a multinational organization. Three particular approaches – centralized, synergistic and localized – are identified in the light of the rapidly changing landscape for international work. The second part of the chapter reviews the major training and development initiatives that multinational firms use to provide a variety of staff with the cross-cultural competences they require to perform effectively in the multinational environment. Finally, the chapter offers some interesting insights into the changing nature of global leadership programmes (the discussion on global leaders will be developed further in Chapter 13).

Chapter 5 explains the growing strategic importance of performance management (PM) in MNCs and develops the central theme in the literature of the impact of cultural differences on the implementation of PM in different country units. The chapter argues that whether a centralized or decentralized performance management system is used in MNCs is strongly linked to the business strategy and the strategic HR approach of the company. The main focus of the chapter is on the performance management of expatriates, a group that plays a critical role in global knowledge-transfer and the implementation of global strategies. The chapter outlines the scope of expatriate performance-management systems and discusses the complex issue of expatriate performance evaluation. The links between expatriate performance and performance-related pay are explored and the contextual factors influencing the existence and form of expatriate performance-management practices are identified. The importance of the mix of these factors is emphasized to explain the variation in how expatriate PM operates in different settings. Finally, the authors reject the notion of a best-practice model for expatriate performance management, and instead usefully introduce a set of key criteria for effective performance management which applies to all employee groups in the MNC.

Chapter 6 presents an interesting alternative to the traditional approach to international compensation which tends to be of a technical nature that focuses on the design details of the salary packages of expatriates. Using a more theory-based approach, the chapter offers an alternative approach to international compensation and examines the benefits of using expatriates as well as the costs. Using a transactions-cost analysis, the authors oppose conventional wisdom by arguing that expatriates are not necessarily a costly option for the company, and they use this approach to explain the higher use of expatriates in global companies in the face of huge pressures to cut costs.

The chapter highlights the importance for MNCs of considering non-salary costs such as training and monitoring costs, as well as salary costs, when making staffing decisions involving the use of expatriates or local managers for the MNC's subsidiaries, and suggests that developing relationships of mutual loyalty is the best way to ensure that the expatriates' high costs are beneficial to the company.

Chapter 7 is mainly concerned with the repatriation of international executives, which has been cited as an under-researched area in international management. Many companies tend to assume that all of the problems with an international career move are associated with moving abroad and that repatriation is non-problematic. The existing research, however, challenges this assumption. The chapter outlines various dimensions of repatriation and highlights issues such as readjusting to the home organization, readjusting psychologically and socially, and financial readjustment.

The chapter draws on the rites-of-passage work developed by the French ethnographer Arnold van Gennep to explain the difficulties associated when people move across boundaries. The authors propose that this framework can also be used to discuss the process of repatriation, and the chapter details the various rituals and rites associated with such a move. Reverse culture shock and other problems of adaptation are also discussed.

Chapter 8 critically examines a number of key issues in the management of industrial relations in MNCs. The first section considers the long-running debate on whether MNCs tend to adopt host-country industrial-relations practices when operating subsidiaries abroad, or whether they adopt practices employed in the country of origin. Reviewing the research on this issue the authors conclude that despite the growth of MNCs and the emergence of some international regulation in the employment field, industrial-relations practices are still largely rooted at the national level. The second section examines employer associations in terms of their international and national functions and shows that despite the growth of some international functions, employers generally prefer to act on a national basis and usually seek to avoid giving more power to supra-national bodies. Finally, the chapter analyses how some specific aspects of collective bargaining such as employee involvement, grievance handling and industrial relations operate within international firms and concludes that most of the developments in international industrial relations have resulted from legal developments taking place within the EU. It is suggested that further such developments could in the future shift industrial relations more onto the international stage.

## Part 3: contemporary issues in international HRM

While Parts 1 and 2 focus specifically on the links between strategy and IHRM on the one hand, and on the main areas of the international HR cycle on the other, Part 3 uses such a context to introduce the reader to a sample of current issues and controversies in the field. Indeed the chapters in this section explore in depth some of the most critical current issues in the field of IHRM. Our authors adopt a critical and research-based approach to identify and explain key trends in a number of areas and contribute to current debates in each area. Two of the chapters in this section deal with IHRM in developing countries and emerging markets, which gives the book a broader coverage than just a focus on Europe and North America.

Chapter 9 focuses on the role of women in international management and traces the research on this topic since the 1970s. The first section outlines the reasons and myths commonly held regarding the low participation of women in international management; the general assumptions held by home-country senior management regarding the scarcity of women in international management are presented and discussed. The second section discusses the issue of the dual-career couple and suggests that in order to increase the success of international assignments companies need to take a proactive approach in dealing with dual-career couples and their families. The impact of the formal and informal barriers faced by women in international management is the focus of the final section of this chapter, and the chapter concludes that women have been and can be successful international managers despite the existence of such barriers and the continued presence of the glass ceiling as a global phenomenon.

Chapter 10 examines international joint ventures (IJVs) and international mergers and acquisitions, two of the most important forms of strategic alliances in international business. The first part of the chapter deals with IJVs, and the authors introduce a four-stage model of IJVs and the HRM issues arising during each of the stages are discussed. The complexity of HRM issues in IJVs is highlighted as well as the importance of effective learning and HR activities that build trust between potential partners.

The second part of the chapter provides a comprehensive review of some key issues involved in managing human resources in international mergers and acquisitions (IM&As). The authors identify the need for MNCs to pay attention to the very different HR issues that arise throughout the different stages of the IM&A process, and show that the key HR issues that arise will vary according to the specific type of IM&A under consideration. A three-stage model of the IM&A process is introduced to identify the key HR issues that arise. In the first stage, the precombination stage, the performance of an HR due diligence is highlighted as a key HR activity which involves the complex process of assessing the human capital of an organization. The second stage involves combining and integrating the companies and four different approaches and the HRM issues which arise under each approach are discussed. The third stage of the IM&A is identified as the solidification and assessment phase, and issues related to leadership and utilizing learning and knowledge are identified as the most important HR activity in this phase.

Chapter 11 is primarily concerned with the issue of how business expatriates adjust to work and life in China, the largest and fastest growing of the emerging markets. The first section critically examines the concept of international adjustment; the second section considers the relationship between psychological adjustment and socio-cultural adjustment; while the third section focuses on the time pattern of adjustments of expatriates on the Chinese mainland to establish whether there is any evidence to support a culture-shock experience. The concept of the U-curve adjustment hypothesis is examined in relation to the experience of expatriates in China. The author draws on his own study which involved a mail questionnaire to Western expatriates in China and Hong Kong, with a key finding being that the better adjusted the expatriates are socio-culturally, the stronger is the relationship between psychological adjustment and socio-cultural adjustment. This suggests that acquiring social skills promotes the psychological adjustment of an individual, particularly in the work context. Work adjustment was highlighted as a key factor in promoting the psychological adjustment of expatriates in China, but it is also suggested that psychological adjustment may be more difficult to achieve because it involves more fundamental change than other forms of adjustment. The main lessons for MNCs and expatriates is to seek to facilitate the adjustment process, particularly through cross-cultural training and language training, and it is suggested that MNCs should use a variety of ways to retain some of the cultural knowledge gained through the experiences of their expatriates.

Chapter 12 deals with a topic which in terms of research is in the infancy stage of development – HRM in developing countries. It explains the reasons for the recent growth of research interest in this area and highlights the need to understand HRM in developing countries in the context of changing patterns of globalization. The chapter critically examines whether best-management practices evolved in the context of Western cultural values can be adopted in developing countries.

The authors highlight the extent to which external environmental factors *and* internal work cultures influence both micro and macro-level organizational policies. In their review of the impact of the main factors on HRM in 13 developing countries, the authors identify three models of influence – religious influences, traditional cultural beliefs, and Western colonial and modern influences. The authors show how existing patterns of HRM in developing countries are influenced by these factors and they also highlight the influential role of national institutions and social institutions. Having highlighted the impact of a number of factors and variables on HRM in developing countries, the authors show how their integrative framework can be useful both in analysing HRM practices in a cross-national context, and in helping to delineate the impact of different factors and variables on HRM in each country.

## Part 4: emerging issues in international HRM

Part 4 deals with some important emerging issues in IHRM, focusing on the important themes of leadership. The first theme is that of global leadership. As Adler argues, 'Business leaders have chosen to transcend national boundaries in ways that remain outside the realm of politicians and government diplomats … Global companies know more than nations, already face difficult questions involved in integrating visions based on divergent national and cultural values' (Adler, 2002, p. 167). Global leadership involves the ability to inspire and influence the thinking, attitudes and behaviour of people around the world, and it will be argued in Chapter 13 that today's global business environment demands the emergence of global leaders who can rise to the challenge of shaping history. The second theme in Part 4 is concerned with the future role of international HR leaders and seeks to stimulate thinking about the issues IHRM will have to face in the longer term. Several key trends are identified which are felt to impact on the future role, functions and activities of IHRM leaders and it is suggested that learning to identify and track such trends and think through the implications for IHRM may be required preparation for future IHRM leaders.

Chapter 13 examines the challenge of global leadership not just in economic terms, but also in the broader terms of societal well-being. The chapter adds two dimensions to the discussion of leadership: the first is a global perspective, and the second is a focus on women, traditionally neglected in studies of leadership.

The chapter highlights the growing trend towards women joining men in senior leadership in politics and business, and suggests that more women will be leading countries in the present century than have ever done so before. The chapter cites evidence suggesting an increasing number of women leading global companies and points to the important trend for women chief executives to create their own companies or take on the leadership of a family business.

The author sees the challenge for women leaders as being to develop a new style of leadership based on different values which emphasize cooperation and sustainability, and it is argued that women exhibit a wide range of leadership visions, approaches and levels of effectiveness. The author asks why countries and companies worldwide – often for the first time – are choosing women to lead them. It is suggested that it is the possibility of significant change which woman symbolize which is so attractive. When a woman is chosen to become the first female CEO, people begin to believe that other types of organizational change are possible.

Chapter 14 outlines the reasons for the growing importance of IHRM and offers a basic framework to help us think about IHRM in the future. In particular, it explains how being aware of macro trends will become increasingly important for the IHRM specialist in the future, and several key trends which will influence the role, function and activities of IHRM are discussed.

Four key macro trends are discussed. First, the changing profile of MNCs; second, the growing interdependencies in terms of the links across economics, politics, social, technological and environmental factors influencing MNCs; third, the increasing global fragmentation arising from growing divisions in ethnic, religious and social spheres; and finally, the growth of psychic-shock syndrome where individuals become unable to cope with the changes taking place in the environment both locally and globally.

It is argued that these trends will influence the future mandate of the IHRM area and a key message for those aspiring to be IHRM specialists of the future is the need to learn how to look at the wider environment in order to understand the competences which will be required to achieve successful performance of the IHRM role in the future. Indeed, the authors argue that IHRM professionals of the future will need to be knowledgeable about the world on many more levels than before in order to be an effective strategic partner in the management of the MNC.

## References

Adler, N.J. (2002) 'Global Managers: No Longer Men Alone', *International Journal of Human Resource Management*, 13(5): 743–60.

Adler, N.J. and Ghadar, F. (1990) 'Strategic Human Resource Management: A Global Perspective', in R. Pieper (ed.), *Human Resource Management: An International Comparison*. Berlin: De Gruyter, 235–60.

Anderson, V. and Boocock, G. (2002) 'Small Firms and Internationalisation: Learning to Manage and Managing to Learn', *Human Resource Management Journal*, 12(3): 5–24.

Bamber, G. and Lansbury, R.D. (1998) *International and Comparative Employment Relations*. London: Sage.

Bartlett, C. and Ghoshal, S. (1998) *Managing Across Borders: The Transnational Solution*, 2nd edn. London: Random House.

Berdrow, I. and Lane, H.W. (2003) 'International Joint Ventures: Creating Value through Successful Knowledge Management', *Journal of World Business*, 38: 15–30.

Bjorkman, I. and Xiucheng, F. (2002) 'Human Resource Management and the Performance of Western Firms in China', *International Journal of Human Resource Management*, 13(6): 853–64.

Black, J.S. and Gregerson, H.B. (1999) 'The Right Way to Manage Expats', *Harvard Business Review*, March/April: 52–63.

Black, J.S., Gregerson, H.B., Mendenhall, M.E. and Stroh, L.K. (1999) *Globalizing People Through International Assignments*. Reading, MA: Addison-Wesley.

Black, J.S., Morrison, A.J. and Gregerson, H.B. (2000) *Global Explorers: The Next Generation of Leaders*. New York: Routledge.

Boxall, P. and Purcell, J. (2003) *Strategy and Human Resource Management*. Basingstoke: Palgrave Macmillan.

Boyacigiller, N. and Adler, N.J. (1991) 'The Parochial Dinosaur: Organizational Science in a Global Context', *Academy of Management Review*, 16(2): 262–90.

Brewster, C. and Scullion, H. (1997) 'A Review and an Agenda for Expatriate HRM', *Human Resource Management Journal*, 7(3): 32–41.

Brewster, C. and Harris, H. (eds) (1999) *International HRM: Contemporary Issues in Europe*. London: Routledge.

Budhwar, P.S. (2003) 'International Human Resource Management', in M. Tayeb (ed.), *International Management: Theories and Practices*. London: Financial Times/Prentice Hall.

Cyr, D. and Schneider, S. (1996) 'Implications for Learning: Human Resource Management in East-West Joint Ventures', *Management International Review*, 1: 201–26.

Dalley, J. and Hamilton, B. (2000) 'Knowledge, Context and Learning in the Small Business', *International Small Business Journal*, 18(3): 51–9.

De Cieri, H. and Dowling, P.J. (1999) 'Strategic Human Resource Management In Multinational Enterprises: Theoretical and Empirical Developments', in P.M. Wright, L.D. Dyer, J.W. Boudreau and G.T. Milkovich (eds), *Research in Personnel and Human Resources Management: Strategic Human Resources Management in the Twenty-First Century*, Supplement 4. Stamford, CT: JAI Press.

Desouza, K. and Evaristo, R. (2003) 'Global Knowledge Management Strategies', *European Management Journal*, 21(1): 62–7.

Dicken, P. (1998) *Global Shift: Transforming the World Economy*, (3rd edn) London: Paul Chapman.

Dimitratos, P., Johnson, J., Slow, J. and Young, S. (2003) 'Micromultinationals: New Types of Firms for the Global Competitive Landscape', *European Management Journal*, 21(2): 164–74.

Dowling, P.J., Welch, D.E. and Schuler, R.S. (1999) *International Human Resource Management: Managing People in an International Context*, 3rd edn. Cincinatti, OH: South Western College Publishing, ITP.

Doz, Y. and Hamel, G. (1998) *Alliance Advantage: The Art of Creating Value through Partnering*. Boston, MA: Harvard Business School Press.

Edstrom, A. and Galbraith, J. (1977) 'Transfer of Managers as a Coordination and Control Strategy in Multinational Organizations', *Administrative Science Quarterly*, (22): 248–63.

Evans, P., Pucik, V. and Barsoux, J.L. (2002) *The Global Challenge: Frameworks for International Human Resource Management*. New York: McGraw-Hill/Irwin.

Forsgren, M. (1990) 'Managing the International Multi-Centred Firm: Case Studies from Sweden', *European Management Journal*, 8(2): 261–7.

Forster, N. (2000) 'The Myth of the "International Manager"', *International Journal of Human Resource Management*, 11(1): 126–42.

Foss, N.J. and Pedersen, T. (2002) 'Transferring Knowledge in MNCs: The Role of Subsidiary Knowledge and Organizational Context', *Journal of International Management*, 8: 49–67.

Garten, J. (1997) *The Big Ten. The Emerging Markets and How They Will Change our Lives*. New York: Basic Books.

Gates, S. (1994) 'The Changing Global Role of the Human Resources Function'. New York: The Conference Board, Report no. 1062–94–RR, 22.

Glaister, K., Husan, R. and Buckley, P. (2003) 'Learning to Manage International Joint Ventures', *International Business Review*, 12: 83–108.

Gooderham, P.N. and Nordhaug, O. (2003) *International Management: Cross-Boundary Challenges*. Oxford: Blackwell.

Gregersen, H., Morrison, A. and Black, J.S. (1998) 'Developing Leaders for the Global Frontiers', *Sloan Management Review*, Fall: 21–32.

Harris, H., Brewster, C. and Sparrow, P. (2003) *International Human Resource Management*. London: Chartered Institute of Personnel and Development.

Harvey, M. and Novicevic, M.M. (2002) 'The Co-ordination of Strategic Initiatives Within Global Organizations: The Role of Global Teams', *International Journal of Human Resource Management*, 13(4): 660–76.

Harvey, M., Speier, C. and Novicevic, M.M. (1999a) 'The Role of Inpatriation in Global Staffing', *International Journal of Human Resource Management*, 10(3): 459–76.

Harvey, M., Speier, C. and Novicevic, M.N. (1999b) 'The Impact of Emerging Markets on Staffing the Global Organization: A Knowledge Based View', *Journal of International Management*, 5: 167–86.

Harzing, A.W.K. (1999) *Managing the Multinationals: An International Study of Control Mechanisms.* Cheltenham: Edward Elgar.

Harzing, A.W.K. and Van Ruysseveldt, J. (2004) *International Human Resource Management,* 2nd edn. London: Sage.

Hendry, C. (1994) *Human Resource Strategies for International Growth.* London: Routledge.

Hofstede, G.H. (1980) *Culture's Consequences: International Differences in Work-Related Values.* Beverly Hills, CA: Sage.

Iles, P. (1995) 'International HRM', in C. Mabey and G. Salaman (eds), *Strategic Human Resource Management.* Oxford: Blackwell.

Keeley, T.D. (2001) *International Human Resource Management in Japanese Firms.* London: Palgrave Macmillan.

Kochan, T., Batt, R. and Dyer, L. (1992) 'International Human Resource Studies: A Framework for Future Research', in D. Lewin *et al.* (eds), *Research Frontiers in Industrial Relations and Human Resources.* Madison, WI: Industrial Relations Research Association.

Kogut, B. and Zander, U. (1992) 'Knowledge of the Firm's Combinative Capabilities and the Replication of Technology', *Organization Science,* 3(3): 383–97.

Kopp, R. (1994) 'International Human Resource Management Policies and Practices in Japanese, European and United States Multinationals', *Human Resource Management,* 33(4): 581–99.

Laurent, A. (1986) 'The Cross-Cultural Puzzle of International Human Resource Management', *Human Resource Management,* 25(1): 91–103.

Linehan, M. and Scullion, H. (2002) 'Repatriation of European Female Corporate Executives', *International Human Resource Management Journal,* 13(2): 254–67.

Marschan, R., Welch, D. and Welch, L. (1997) 'Control in Less Hierarchical Multinationals: The Role of Personal Networks and Informal Communication', *International Business Review,* 5(2): 137–50.

Mayrhofer, W. and Brewster, C. (1996) 'In Praise of Ethnocentricity: Expatriate Policies in European Multinationals', *International Executive,* 38(6): 749–78.

Milliman, J., Von Glinow, M. and Nathan, B. (1991) 'Organizational Life Cycles and Strategic International Human Resource Management in Multinational Companies: Implications for Congruence Theory', *Academy of Management Review,* 16: 318–39.

Morgan, G., Kelly, B., Sharpe, D. and Whitley, R. (2003) 'Global Managers and Japanese Multinationals: Internationalisation and Management in Japanese Financial Institutions', *International Journal of Human Resource Management,* 14(3): 389–407.

Morgan, P. (1986) 'International Human Resource Management: Fact or Fiction', *Personnel Administrator,* 31(9): 43–7.

Mudambi, R. (2002) 'Knowledge Management in Multinational Firms', *Journal of International Management,* 8: 1–9.

Ondrack, D. (1985) 'International Human Resource Management in European and North American Firms', *International Studies of Management and Organization,* 15(1): 6–32.

Peterson, R.B., Sargent, J., Napier, N.K. and Shim, W.S. (1996) 'Corporate Expatriate HRM Policies, Internationalization, and Performance in the World's Largest MNCs', *Management International Review,* 36(3): 215–30.

Pucik, V. (1992) 'Globalization and Human Resource Management', in V. Pucik, N. Tichy and C.K. Barnett (eds), *Globalizing Management.* New York: John Wiley.

Pucik, V. (1988) 'Strategic Alliances, Organizational Learning, and Competitive Advantage: The HRM Agenda', *Human Resource Management,* 27(1): 77–93.

Schneider, S. and Barsoux, J.L. (2003) *Managing Across Cultures,* 2nd edn. London: Financial Times/Prentice Hall.

Schneider, S. and Tung, R. (2001) '"Introduction" to the International Human Resource Management Special Issue', *Journal of World Business,* 36(4): 341–5.

Schuler, R.S. (2000) 'The Internationalization of Human Resource Management', *Journal of International Management,* 6: 239–60.

Schuler, R.S., Budhwar, P.S. and Florkowski, G.W. (2002) 'International Human Resource Management: Review and Critique', *International Journal of Management Reviews,* 4(1): 41–70.

Schuler, R.S., Dowling, P.J. and DeCieri, H. (1993) 'An Integrative Framework of Strategic International Human Resource Management', *International Journal of Human Resource Management,* 4(4): 717–64.

Schuler, R.S., Jackson, S. and Luo, Y. (2004) *Managing Human Resources in Cross-Border Alliances.* London: Routledge.

Scullion, H. (1994) 'Staffing Policies and Strategic Control in British Multinationals', *International Studies of Management and Organization,* 24(3): 18–35.

Scullion, H. (1995) 'International Human Resource Management', in J. Storey (ed.), *Human Resource Management: A Critical Text.* London: Routledge.

Scullion, H. (2001) 'International Human Resource Management', in J. Storey (ed.), *Human Resource Management*. London: International Thompson.

Scullion, H. and Brewster, C. (2001) 'Managing Expatriates: Messages from Europe', *Journal of World Business*, 36(4): 346–65.

Scullion, H. and Starkey, K. (2000) 'The Changing Role of the Corporate Human Resource Function in the International Firm', *International Journal of Human Resource Management*, 11(6): 1061–81.

Stroh, L. and Caligiuri, P.M. (1998) 'Increasing Global Competitiveness through Effective People Management', *Journal of World Business*, 33(1): 1–16.

Taylor, S., Beechler, S. and Napier, N. (1996) 'Towards an Integrative Model of Strategic International Human Resource Management', *Academy of Management Review*, 21(4): 959–85.

Tung, R.L. (1981) 'Selection and Training of Personnel for Overseas Assignment', *Columbia Journal of World Business*, 16(1): 68–78.

Tung, R.L. (1982) 'Selection and Training Procedures of U.S., European and Japanese Multinationals', *California Management Review*, 25(1): 57–71.

Tung, R.L. (2001) 'Network Capitalism: The Role of Human Resources in Penetrating the China Market', *International Journal of Human Resource Management*, 14(2): 157–73.

Welch, D. (1994) 'Determinants of International Human Resource Management Approaches and Activities: A Suggested Framework', *Journal of Management Studies*, 31(2): 139–64.

Yip, G. (1997) 'A Borderless World: Issues and Evidence', in I. Islam, and W. Shepherd (eds), *Current Issues in International Business*. Cheltenham: Edward Elgar.

Yli-Renko, Autio, A. and Tontti, V. (2002) 'Social Capital, Knowledge, and the International Growth of Technology-Based New Firms', *International Business Review*, 11: 279–304.

Young, S. and Hamill, J. (1992) *Europe and the Multinationals: Issues and Responses for the 1990s*. Aldershot: Edward Elgar.

# 2

## Strategic HRM in multinational companies

*Hugh Scullion and Jaap Paauwe*

## Introduction: the growth of research on strategic HRM in MNCs

As multinational companies have become increasingly important players in the global economy, there has been a rapid growth of research on the strategies and management practices of these firms. As the effective management of human resources is increasingly being recognized as a major determinant of success or failure in international business (Stroh and Caligiuri, 1998; Schuler *et al.*, 2002) the theoretical and empirical linkages between HRM and strategy in the international context are increasingly being explored by researchers. In their review article De Cieri and Dowling (1999) argue that over the past decade the field of strategic human resource management (SHRM) has increasingly been applied to MNCs through the developing area of research and practice identified as 'strategic international human resource management' (SIHRM) (Milliman *et al.*, 1991; Schuler *et al.*, 1993). They link the emergence of strategic HRM in multinational companies with two parallel developments. First, the growth of research on strategic HRM, issues which focuses on the link between HRM, organizational strategy and performance. Second, the increasing attention paid by international HRM specialists to macro-level issues, such as the strategic nature of international HRM and the implications for organizational performance (Schuler, 2000; Evans *et al.*, 2002).

Before outlining the aims and structure of the chapter, it is important to distinguish between international human resource management (IHRM) and strategic international human resource management (SIHRM). In defining international HRM we will follow Taylor *et al.* (1996) who draw on the work of Schuler *et al.* (1993) and Lado and Wilson (1994). They define the MNC's international HRM system as the set of distinct activities, functions and processes that are directed at attracting, developing and maintaining an MNC's human resources (Taylor *et al.*,

1996: 960). It should be noted that company headquarters are included in this definition and the MNC's IHRM system is therefore the aggregate of the various HRM systems used to manage people in the MNC. Strategic IHRM builds on the work on strategic HRM which seeks to link HRM explicitly with the strategic management processes of the organization and emphasizes coordination among the various human resource management practices in order to achieve a better and more efficient alignment with corporate strategy and/or business strategy.

Schuler *et al.* (1993), drawing on the strategy work of Prahalad and Doz (1987) and Bartlett and Ghoshal (1989), presented an integrated framework of strategic IHRM which recognizes that a fundamental issue facing the top management of MNCs is the tension between the needs for global coordination (integration) and local responsiveness (differentiation). The integrated framework is used to link IIRM explicitly with the strategy of the MNC, and strategic IHRM is defined as 'human resource issues, functions and policies and practices that result from the strategic activities of multinational enterprises and that impact the international concerns and goals of those enterprises' (Schuler *et al.*, 1993). In addition to highlighting the strategic MNC components, the integrated framework showed endogenous factors (for example MNC structure, MNC strategy, international entry mode) and exogenous factors (for example industry characteristics, country-regional characteristics, interorganizational relationships) which impact on the achievement of MNC concerns and goals. It has been argued that this framework has been very useful in bringing together the strategic and international dimensions of HRM (Taylor *et al.*, 1996). Schuler *et al.* (2002) identify several reasons to explain the evolution of IHRM to develop more of a strategic perspective. First, the more rapid pace of globalization led to a more strategic role for HRM and a greater linkage of IHRM with the strategic needs of the business (Schuler and Jackson, 1999). Second, HRM is increasingly important to the implementation of international business strategies (Bartlett and Ghoshal, 1998). Third, international HRM policies and practices can influence the achievement of the goals of MNCs. Fourth, the relationship between MNCs and IHRM is complex and therefore strategic HRM in MNCs is a challenging field of study (Dowling *et al.*, 1999).

This chapter aims to assess critically some important theoretical developments in the area of strategic IHRM research which have emerged over the last decade. In contrast to several other chapters of the book which deal with the more operational aspects of IHRM, this chapter will focus on its more strategic aspects. Following this introduction to the reasons for the growing importance of strategic HRM in multinational companies, the next section examines the links between strategy and IHRM and reviews some important models. We then consider the role of the corporate HR function in the international firm and examine recent empirical data on the required competences for the effective functioning of the HR specialist. The fourth section examines management development issues in global firms and the final section considers the challenges of developing transnational managers.

# Models of strategic HRM in multinational companies: integrating strategy and IHRM

A review of the major research issues in IHRM has suggested that most of the research in this field still had an operational and practical orientation rather than a strategic orientation and highlighted the lack of empirical research in the field of strategic IHRM (Harzing, 1999). However, while studies such as Edstrom and Galbraith (1977) which integrate IHRM and international corporate strategy are still rare (Brewster and Scullion, 1997), there is a recently emerging literature which seeks to contribute to a better understanding of the relationship between international strategy and HRM (Schuler *et al.*, 1993; Hendry, 1994; Kobrin, 1994; Welch, 1994; De Cieri and Dowling, 1999; Dowling *et al.*, 1999; Harzing, 1999; Evans *et al.*, 2002). This research not only recognizes the MNC's need to balance the pressures for integration with the pressures for local responsiveness (Doz and Prahalad, 1986; Bartlett and Ghoshal, 1989, 1998; Paauwe and Dewe, 1995), but also suggests that at the international level firms' strategic choices impose constraints or limits on the range of IHRM options (De Cieri and Dowling, 1999; Evans *et al.*, 2002; Schuler *et al.*, 2002). The argument is that there should be distinct differences in IHRM policy and practice in multi-domestic and transnational or globally integrated firms (Kobrin, 1992). Some researchers link IHRM policy and practice to strategy (Edstrom and Galbraith 1977; Scullion, 1996), while others suggest linkages between the product life-cycle stage and international strategy and HRM policy and practice (Adler and Ghadar, 1990; Milliman *et al.*, 1991). In most of these models a contingency perspective is adopted and the main focus is on the fit of the strategic IHRM system with the goals of the firm. Increasingly 'the central issue for MNCs is not to identify the best IHRM policy per se but rather to find the best fit between the firm's external environment, its overall strategy, and its HRM policy and implementation' (Adler and Ghadar, 1990: 245).

In this section we will examine three classic models of strategic IHRM:

- Adler and Ghadar's phases of internationalization
- The two logics of Evans and Lorange
- De Cieri and Dowling's model.

## Adler and Ghadar's phases of internationalization

Adler and Ghadar's model (1990) is based on Vernon's life-cycle theory (1966). Vernon distinguished three phases in the international product life-cycle: the first phase ('high-tech') focuses on the product, research and development (R&D) playing an important role as a functional area; the second phase ('growth and internationalization') concentrates on developing and penetrating markets, not only at home but also abroad, the focus therefore shifting from R&D to marketing and management control; whilst in the third and final phase ('maturity'), intense efforts are made to lower prices by implementing cost-control measures.

According to Adler and Ghadar (1990: 239), the average length of the product life-cycle shortly after the Second World War was 15–20 years. Nowadays this is three–five years, and for some products it is as short as five months. An important implication is that the various areas of emphasis in Vernon's life-cycle must increasingly be dealt with simultaneously. Adler and Ghadar saw this as sufficient reason to suggest a fourth phase (incidentally following in the footsteps of Prahalad and Doz, 1987) in which the company must achieve differentiation (as a way to develop and penetrate markets) and integration (as a way to achieve cost control).

Having introduced a fourth phase, the authors proceed to develop a model in which cultural aspects and HRM form the main focus of attention. In short, they link Vernon's phases, which concentrate largely on strategic and structural issues, to culture and HRM.

*The influence of culture*
According to Adler and Ghadar (1990), the impact of the cultural background of a country or region differs from one phase to the next. They identify these phases (Adler and Ghadar use the same terms as Bartlett and Ghoshal, 1989, but attach them to different phases, which could be confusing):

- Domestic: focus on home market and export
- International: focus on local responsiveness and transfer of learning
- Multinational: focus on global strategy, low cost and price competition
- Global: focus on both local responsiveness and global integration.

The cultural component hardly plays a role in the first phase (domestic); management operates from an ethnocentric perspective and can afford to ignore the influence of foreign cultures. The attitude towards foreign buyers – which is a somewhat arrogant one – is the following: 'We allow you to buy our product' (Adler and Ghadar, 1990: 242) By contrast, in the second phase (international) the cultural differences of each foreign market are highly important when entering into external relations. From the polycentric perspective, product design, marketing and production will concentrate on finding a good match between the product and the preferences and style of the relevant foreign market segment. That is why production is often transferred to the relevant country and/or region.

During the third phase (multinational) the product must be globalized to such an extent that competition with other 'global players' emphasizes lower cost as a way of keeping up with price competition. This has less to do with emphasizing cultural sensitivity than with the exploitation of cost advantages arising from price differences between production factors in each country and/or region, and with the exploitation of economies of scale. It is, however, important that a certain internal sensitivity or

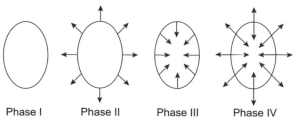

Phase I      Phase II      Phase III      Phase IV

*Source*:    Adler and Ghadar (1990: 244).

***Figure 2.1***    Location of cross-cultural interaction

awareness develops of the various cultural differences (cultural diversity) within the global concern.

Finally there is the fourth phase (global). In addition to cost advantages and low prices on world markets, the products and services must at the same time meet standards of high quality. This quality is expressed in the adaptation of the product to the tastes, preferences and/or specifications of the individual markets and market niches. Adler and Ghadar (1990: 243) describe this as follows:

> Successful corporations understand their potential clients' needs, quickly translate them into products and services, produce those products and services on a least-possible-cost basis, and deliver them back to the client in a culturally appropriate and timely fashion.

Cultural sensitivity becomes crucial, not only internally but externally as well. Figure 2.1 illustrates the relative importance of the cultural component and the direction of the interaction between organization and environment in the various phases.

*Phases and areas of focus in HRM*

Starting from the idea of a link between the phases of internationalization, the (market) environment and the influence of culture, Adler and Ghadar go on to sketch the appropriate HRM policies/instruments and the skills required of the managers involved for the various different phases. Table 2.1 illustrates their theory. For clarity's sake, we have added the terms used by Bartlett and Ghoshal (1989) to the table.

- Phase I. In this phase we can scarcely speak of IHRM in any real sense. There may be incidental brief visits to foreign agents/sales offices or a short assignment on a project basis, in which product and technical competence of the manager in question are the most important factors.
- In phase II, IHRM becomes manifest as managers are assigned to posts in foreign markets to provide general management, technical expertise and financial control. The various markets require a differentiated approach and adaptation of the product and business methods to local circumstances. In addition to

technical competence, then, selection criteria such as language skills, cross-cultural adaptability and sensitivity are also important. Since understanding of local circumstances is a requirement, host-country nationals are frequently recruited for management positions in the area of sales, marketing and personnel.

- Phase III. As it is highly important that integration and cost advantages are exploited worldwide, this phase focuses on recruiting the best managers for international positions, regardless of their country of origin. Developing a management corps in which all the members share the same organizational values and norms is one of HRM's most important tasks. After all, this will contribute to achieving the goal of integration, regardless of the fact that the company is operating in different geographical markets and its managers come from different countries. Management development, career-counselling and periodic transfers to a different assignment (every three–five years) are the spearheads of phase III HRM.
- In phase IV, a major issue for IHRM is how the company is to satisfy the requirements of global integration and national responsiveness. We can find traces of both phase II and phase III here. The large measure of cultural diversity becomes manifest both in the markets to be covered and in the organization itself. The real art is to view this cultural diversity as an opportunity rather than as a problem which has to be solved. IHRM focuses on offering promising managers the opportunity to grow so that an environment for continuous learning will be created throughout the entire organization. The degree to which such HRM can be given concrete expression determines the success or failure of the (phase IV) corporation (Adler and Ghadar, 1990: 245–54).

## The two logics of Evans and Lorange

The second contribution comes from Evans and Lorange (1989) Their main question is: 'How can a corporation operating in different product markets and diverse socio-cultural environments effectively establish human resource policies?' (1989: 144). Basing their approach on the great variety of product–market combinations to be covered and the attendant operations to be performed in settings with a wide cultural diversity, they developed two logics for shaping HRM policy.

### Product–market logic
The various phases of the product life-cycle each require a different type of manager. Cost-conscious management will be more important in the maturity phase than it would be in an emergent business, where managers with entrepreneurial skills are more appropriate. This also implies that activities such as recruitment, training and development, and assessment and compensation, will differ from one phase to the other. If we consider that a multinational organization by definition covers a wider

*Table 2.1*  Globalization and HRM

| | Phase I<br>Domestic | Phase II<br>International | Phase III<br>Multinational | Phase IV<br>Global |
|---|---|---|---|---|
| Primary orientation | Product/service | Market | Price | Strategy |
| Strategy | Domestic | Multidomestic | Multinational | Global |
| Worldwide strategy | Allow foreign clients to buy products/service | Increase market internationally, transfer technology abroad | Source, produce and market internationally | Gain global, strategic, competitive advantage |
| Staffing | | | | |
| Expatriates | None – (few) | Many | Some | Many |
| Why sent | Junket | To sell, control or transfer technology | Control | Coordination and integration |
| Who sent | | OK performers, sales people | Very good performers | High-potential managers and top executives |
| Purpose | Reward | Project 'To get job done' | Project and career development | Career and organizational development |
| Career impact | Negative | Bad for domestic career | Important for global career | Essential for executive suite |
| Professional re-entry | Somewhat difficult | Extremely difficult | Less difficult | Professionally easy |
| Training and development (language and cross-cultural management) | None | Limited (one week) | Longer | Continuous throughout career |
| For whom | No one | Expatriates | Expatriates | Managers |
| Performance appraisal | Corporate bottom line | Subsidiary bottom line | Corporate bottom line | Global Strategic positioning |
| Motivation assumption | Money motivates | Money and adventure | Challenge and opportunity | Challenge opportunity, advancement |
| Rewarding | Extra money to compensate for foreign hardships | Extra money to compensate for foreign hardships | Less generous, global packages | Less generous, global packages |

*Table 2.1*  *Continued*

|  | Phase I<br>Domestic | Phase II<br>International | Phase III<br>Multinational | Phase IV<br>Global |
|---|---|---|---|---|
| Career 'fast track' | Domestic | Domestic | Token international | Global |
| Executive passport | Home country | Home country | Home country; token foreigners | Multinational |
| Necessary skills | Technical and managerial | Plus cultural adaptation | Plus recognizing cultural differences | Plus cross-cultural interaction, influence and synergy |
| Bartlett and Ghoshal (1989) | Domestic | Multidomestic/ international | Global | Transnational |

*Source*:  Adler and Ghadar (1990: 246).

range of product–market combinations, and that these combinations will further-more differ from one another with respect to their product life-cycle phase, managing human resources would appear to be a highly complex affair, even on the basis of this logic alone. This complexity can, however, be spread out over the various management levels. Assuming that management will be split into the categories 'corporate', 'divisional' and 'business unit' levels, Evans and Lorange proposed the following duties for the corporate level:

- Key executive appointments and succession planning
- Design and management of appropriate incentive systems
- Cross-fertilization of functional and business expertise.

Given the increasing need for corporate integration – specifically with respect to the process of strategic planning – these tasks will only become more important, according to Evans and Lorange (1989: 151). The arguments the authors present to support this view are similar to those described below for the transnational company.

*Sociocultural logic*
A company that operates various business units in a wide variety of countries and regions will take on employees who differ from one another in terms of their socio-cultural backgrounds. In addition to differences in the legal (specifically employment and labour law) and educational systems, there are of course cultural differences in the sense of highly divergent values and norms (Hofstede, 1980). Taking Perlmutter

(1969) as their point of departure, Evans and Lorange identified two strategies for dealing with such extreme cultural diversity:

1  *Global approach* (Perlmutter's ethnocentrism or geocentrism). In this approach, the company's own specific culture predominates and HRM is relatively centralized and standardized. Uniform procedures and guidelines in the area of recruitment, selection, assessment, compensation and promotion define an HRM system which is applicable worldwide. Typical examples are IBM and Shell. It is true that staff are recruited globally, even for management posts, but regardless of the differences in national culture, integration into the dominant company culture is given top priority.

2  *Polycentric approach.* Here the responsibility for HRM is decentralized and devolved to the subsidiaries. Headquarters may provide certain guidelines, but each subsidiary in each country and/or region is free to interpret HRM as it sees fit. Corporate staff duties are therefore restricted to the three core tasks mentioned earlier. The adaptation to local culture is given priority. The polycentric approach loses out to the global approach when it comes down to the opportunities it presents for integration and coordination (in particular with respect to implementation of global and corporate-wide strategic objectives). On the other hand, the global approach generates higher overheads as a consequence of HRM policies aimed at selection and retention, with large expenditures for management-development activities related to indoctrination and socialization.

## DeCieri and Dowling's model

As noted earlier in this chapter, Schuler *et al.* (1993) presented an integrative framework of strategic IHRM which, in addition to identifying the strategic MNC components, also showed endogenous factors (for example MNC strategy and structure) and exogenous factors (for example industry characteristics, country-regional characteristics). De Cieri and Dowling (1999) draw on developments in theory and research since the Schuler *et al.* (1993) study to develop a revised framework. Their recent review of IHRM research trends identifies a relatively new research area, 'strategic international human resource management' (SIHRM), which has been defined earlier in the introductory section of this chapter. It considers the HRM issues and activities that result from, and impact on, the strategic activities and international concerns of multinationals (De Cieri and Dowling, 1999).

International HRM activities in MNCs are influenced by both endogeneous and exogenous factors in the revised framework of De Cieri and Dowling (1999). As shown in Figure 2.2, MNCs operate in the context of worldwide conditions, including the exogenous contexts of industry, nation and region. Dowling and De Ceiri (1999) suggest that interorganizational networks and alliances should be an additional exogenous influence, and they cite the example of the removal of internal trade barriers and integration of national markets in the EU which have led to a new range of interorganizational relationships. And, in contrast to the position of Schuler *et al.* (1993), it is argued that exogenous factors exert *direct* influence on endogenous factors, SHRM strategy and practices as well as on multinational concerns and goals, and it is further suggested that exogenous factors have a direct concern on MNC goals and concerns. An example of this influence is given as the economic impact of economic difficulties in the Asia Pacific region since the late 1990s (De Cieri and Dowling, 1999).

As indicated in Figure 2.2, endogenous factors are shown in the order of most 'tangible' to most 'intangible'. Multinational structure refers to both the structure of international operations and intraorganizational networks and mechanisms of coordination (Harzing, 1999). The life-cycle stage of the firm and the industry in which it operates are important influences for SHRM in multinationals, as are international entry modes and levels of firm strategy. The most intangible endogeneous factors are experience in international business and a headquarter's international orientation. Following developments in the literature and the integration of resource-based perspectives (for example Taylor *et al.*, 1996), the model suggests that there are reciprocal relationships between endogenous factors, SHRM and multinational concerns and goals as indicated in Figure 2.2. The relationship between organizational strategy and human resource strategy is cited as of particular relevance here. Effective SHRM is expected to assist the firm achieve its goals and objectives. This position is supported by the emerging body of SHRM literature that examines the relationships between endogenous characteristics, SHRM strategy and practices and competitive

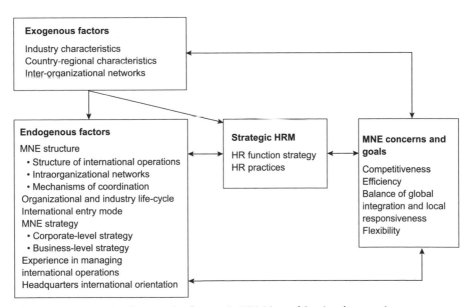

*Figure 2.2*  Integrative framework of strategic HRM in multinational enterprises

advantage or firm performance (Kobrin, 1994; Becker and Gerhart, 1996, Paauwe and Richardson, 1997).

One of the main strengths of De Cieri and Dowling's (1999) revised framework is that it is based on an expanded multidisciplinary base drawing on new theoretical developments in HRM, strategic management (including institutional theory and the resource-based view of the firm) and international business (Paauwe and Boselie, 2003). The revised framework contributes significantly to the further development of theory and empirical research in this field and it has been argued that theory-building in strategic HRM in MNCs has moved forward to a second phase (Dowling *et al.*, 1999).

In summary, the models reviewed in this section have helped to advance our theoretical knowledge of SHRM in MNCs in several ways. First, they have highlighted the links between the evolution of international strategy and the overall approach to strategic international HRM. Second, they identify the key variables which are important in determining strategic international HRM approaches. Third, they show the need for strategic HRM systems to address the tension between the dual imperatives of local responsiveness and global integration (Taylor *et al.*, 1996). Yet, surprisingly, the strategic roles and functions of the corporate HR function have been neglected. This is the topic of our next section.

## The role of the corporate HR function

While the previous section shows that there have been some attempts to integrate international corporate strategy and human resource strategy, surprisingly, given the considerable research on the roles and functions of corporate headquarters and its relationship with subsidiaries (Goold and Campbell, 1987; O'Donnell, 2000; McKern and Naman, 2003), the role of the corporate HR function has been relatively neglected, particularly in the context of the international firm. A recent review (Scullion and Starkey, 2000) suggested that HR involvement in strategic decisions in UK firms is patchy and mostly concerned with implementation rather than formulation of strategy. The review highlighted that considerable variation existed across Europe on the perceived role of HR in the formation of corporate strategy (Brewster, 1994), and noted that evidence from the USA on this question is also mixed. Kochan *et al.* (1992) suggest that in the USA the HR function remains low in influence relative to other major functions, while others have argued that the status of HR managers has increased due to the perception that its contribution to business performance has increased (Ferris *et al.*, 1991; Schuler *et al.*, 2002). A recent study which examines the role of senior HR specialists as strategic partners provides a good overall assessment on this issue, 'While there is some divergence of opinion, the dominant view in the international literature is that HR specialists, senior or otherwise, are not typically key players in the development of corporate strategy' (Hunt and Boxall, 1998: 770).

The limited empirical work on the role of the corporate HR function has led to some divergence of views. Earlier case study research suggested that the size and influence of the corporate personnel department was being reduced largely due to the trend towards decentralization (Purcell, 1985), while a study of the largest UK private-sector corporations, in contrast, indicated that the tendency for corporate personnel departments to be downgraded was far from universal and demonstrated considerable variation in the size and roles of such departments (Sisson and Scullion, 1985). Purcell and Ahlstrand (1994) argued that corporate HR managers were playing more of a monitoring and control function as a result of the shift to a decentralized approach. Paauwe's (1996) more recent case-study research on Dutch multinational companies highlighted that the corporate HR function was itself being downsized and some HR functions such as recruitment were increasingly being outsourced. However, those remaining in charge were considered to be of a high professional level and with ample financial means at their disposal to buy in specialist expertise when needed. Studies generally failed to consider the impact of the internationalization of business on corporate HR roles. Scullion and Starkey (2000), however, conducted an empirical study of 30 UK MNCs which examined the role of the corporate HR function specifically in the context of the international firm and identified three distinct groups of companies: centralized HR companies; decentralized HR companies; and transition HR companies, which are discussed below.

## Centralized HR companies

The first group comprised 10 companies which all operated in a large number of countries and were characterized by a high degree of coordination and integration of their foreign operations. All had large corporate HR staffs which exercised centralized control over the careers and mobility of senior management positions worldwide. Scullion and Starkey (2000) argued that in global firms the greater degree of central support for international management development reflects an increasingly strategic role for the corporate HR function. Reward systems for senior managers which aligned rewards with longer-term global business strategy (Bradley et al., 1998; Reynolds, 2000) further reinforced centralized control in the global firms studied. International assignments were increasingly linked to the organizational and career development process, and the management development function became increasingly important for developing high-potential local managers and third-country national staff. In particular, the practice of developing the latter two groups through developmental transfers to the corporate HQ, that is inpatriation (Harvey et al., 1999a), was becoming increasingly important in global firms.

## Decentralized companies

This group operated with a decentralized or highly decentralized approach and comprised 16 companies including five service MNCs and 11 manufacturing MNCs.

The trend towards decentralization had resulted in an overall reduction in the size of corporate offices in many UK organizations (Goold and Campbell, 1987; Scullion, 2002), and these companies tended to have a small number of corporate HR managers who undertook a more limited range of activities than their counterparts in the first group. However, a key finding of the research was that two-thirds of the decentralized companies reported an *increased* influence of corporate HR over the management of top management and senior expatriates in the previous five years. The need for greater coordination and integration associated with globalization had led to a shift away from the highly decentralized approach of the early 1990s (Storey *et al.*, 1997) and this was reflected in significant moves to establish central control over the careers and mobility of expatriates.

However, the coordination of international transfers of managers in the highly decentralized businesses was more problematic due to greater tensions between the short-term needs of the operating companies and the long-term strategic management development needs of the business. Scullion and Starkey (2000) highlight the increasing use of informal and subtle management processes by corporate HR to introduce a degree of corporate integration into the decentralized firm. In this context Bartlett and Ghoshal (1989) refer to the necessity of creating a matrix in the mindset of managers in order to deal effectively with all the diversity and complexity involved in managing a transnational organization. Paauwe and Deuwe (1995: 68–9) address the question of how this can be achieved, and argue that the socialization of managers in key positions (at headquarters and subsidiaries) is crucial. They argue that cultural transformation is needed in order to achieve socialization and normative integration and suggest a number of methods to help achieve this, including job-rotation, developing informal networks, forums to encourage cross-border transfer of knowledge and learning and, finally, encouraging other informal communication channels.

## Transition HR companies

The final group comprised four highly internationalized companies who had grown mainly through acquisitions. They were transition HR companies in the sense that they were in the process of shifting away from the decentralized approach adopted in the first half of the 1990s. There was a greater degree of central control over management development and the management of expatriates than in the decentralized companies, and strategic staffing had emerged as an important issue due to the growing importance of international acquisitions. A key challenge for the corporate HR function in these firms was to achieve a degree of central control using subtle and informal methods without compromising the internal consistency of the decentralized control system (Evans *et al.*, 2002). This supports findings of recent research which suggests that re-centralization may be a new trend (Arkin, 1999), and calls into question the view that central control over management of managers in the international firm has been abandoned.

In the first part of this section we examined the role of the corporate HR function in the international firm and suggested an emerging agenda for corporate HR which focuses on senior management development and developing a cadre of international managers. It was also argued that the more rapid pace of globalization has led to a more strategic role for HRM and that the role of the corporate HR function varies in different types of international firm. We now consider the related issue of the key competencies for the HR function.

## The competencies required for the HR function

The topic of the competencies required of the HR function has been under investigation by the IHRM research team at Michigan Business School for many years. Major blocks of data were gathered and analysed in 1988, 1992 and 1997 in the USA (Brockbank and Ulrich, 2002), and in the 1988 and 1992 rounds three competency categories were uncovered: business knowledge, HR functional capability and change management. In 1997, two additional categories were added: culture management and personal credibility. With every new round of the survey they were able to include more countries and continents in their Human Resource Competency Study (HRCS). The most recent one took place in 2002.

In that year the HRCS Michigan research team and its associated partners around the globe performed research in four continents: North America, Latin America, Asia and Europe, encompassing almost 250 companies and more than 7,000 respondents. Out of a range of 78 items and 15 distilled competencies, the following five domain factors emerged as making a positive difference for both the performance of the firm and the personal performance of the HR manager: *strategic contribution; personal credibility; HR delivery; business knowledge; and HR technology* (Brockbank *et al.*, 2002, internet). Below we highlight these five domains in more detail.

- Strategic contribution. High-performing companies have HR professionals involved in the business at a strategic level. These professionals manage culture, facilitate fast change, are involved in strategic decision-making and create market-driven connectivity. These four factors – culture management, strategic decision-making, fast change, and market-driven connectivity – together comprise the HR competency domain of Strategic Contribution.
- Personal credibility. HR professionals must be credible to both their HR counterparts and the business line managers whom they serve. They need to have effective relationships with key people both inside and outside their business. They need to promise and deliver results and establish a reliable track record. In addition, they must have effective written and verbal communication skills. The three factors – effective relationships, getting results, and personal communication, determine the domain of Personal Credibility.

- HR delivery. HR professionals deliver both traditional and operational HR activities to their business in four major categories:
  - *Development*: designing developmental programmes and challenging work experiences; offering career planning services; facilitating internal communication processes. These efforts include both individual development as well as organization-wide development.
  - *Structure and HR measurement*: restructuring the organization; measuring the impact of HR practices; managing the global implications of HR practices.
  - *Staffing*: attracting, promoting, retaining and outplacing appropriate people.
  - *Performance management*: designing performance-based measurements and reward systems and providing competitive benefit packages.
- Business knowledge. To become key players in the organization, HR professionals must understand the business and industry of the company they serve. Key areas of knowledge include applied understanding of the integrated value chain (how the firm integrates horizontally) and the firm's value proposition (how the firm creates wealth). The factor labour, representing institutional constraints such as labour legislation, is the third factor that constitutes the domain of Business Knowledge.
- HR technology. Technology is increasingly becoming a part of the workplace and is a delivery vehicle for HR services. HR professionals need to be able to leverage technology for HR practices and use e-HR/web-based channels to deliver value to their customers.

Following our review of the competencies required for the effective functioning of the HR function, we now turn our attention to broader issues of developing managers in the global firm.

# Management development in the global firm

This section will discuss some of the major challenges and constraints faced by international firms who seek to develop an adequate pool of global managers. We highlight the strategic importance of these constraints in relation to the implementation of global strategies. In this context, we consider issues regarding the international development of local managers, the low participation of women in international management, and constraints on the supply of international managers due to repatriation problems and barriers to international mobility. These issues are becoming more significant as shortages of 'international managers' are becoming an increasing problem for many international firms and often constrain the implementation of global strategies (Scullion, 1994; Gregerson *et al.*, 1998).

Many MNCs have focused most of their management development efforts on their parent-country national managers and have continued to neglect the development of their host-country managers (Dowling et al., 1999). More recently researchers have suggested a number of important strategies for MNCs who are seeking to develop host-country national managers (Scullion and Brewster, 2001), the most important of which is the need to utilize much further the practice of inpatriation (see previous section). It has been argued that this type of international transfer exposes host-country nationals to the headquarters' corporate culture and facilitates both the development of a corporate perspective and global teams (Harvey et al., 1999b).

## Constraints on the supply of international managers

Despite the growing shortages of international managers (Scullion, 2001), the evidence suggests that the participation of women in international management remains relatively low (Adler, 2002). While there has been significant growth in female expatriates since the 1980s, women still remain significantly under-represented in international management (Taylor et al., 2002). Empirical studies have shown that while organizations may be prepared to promote women through their domestic management hierarchy, far fewer women are given opportunities to expand their career horizons through access to international careers (Linehan, 2002). The lack of willingness to recruit and develop women as international managers is of some concern as recent research conducted on the outcome of women's global assignments has indicated that female expatriates are generally successful in those assignments (Caligiuri and Tung, 1999; Napier and Taylor, 2002). As global competition intensifies, competition for global leaders to manage overseas operations will steadily intensify, and MNCs must develop new ways to identify, attract and retain new pools of international executive talent (Black et al., 2000; Mayrhofer and Scullion, 2002), yet recent studies suggest that important formal and informal barriers remain to increasing women's participation in international management (Linehan and Scullion, 2002a).

The repatriation of managers has been identified as a major IHRM problem for multinational companies in Europe and North America (Dowling et al., 1999). Further, it has been argued that the failure by many companies to address this issue impacts adversely on the supply of international managers. There is growing awareness that potential expatriates will be more reluctant to accept the offer of international assignments in companies which fail to handle repatriation issues effectively (Scullion, 1994). Black et al. (1999) show that while retention of expatriate managers was a growing problem for many US MNCs, few firms have developed formal repatriation policies. In recent years the repatriation problem has become more acute for many European MNCs because internationalization has often taken place at the same time as downsizing of the domestic business, reducing opportunities for expatriate managers on re-entry. (Forster, 2000; Scullion, 1992). Recent studies confirm that many firms continue to adopt an *ad hoc* approach to repatriation and that many expatriate managers continue to experience the repatriation process as falling far short of expectations, and suggest the need for MNCs to develop a more strategic approach to repatriation and international career management (Stroh *et al.*, 1998; Linehan and Scullion, 2002b).

The growing *barriers to international mobility* present a further constraint on the ability of MNCs to implement their internationalization strategies. The demand for expatriates is increasing steadily, while the availability of people who are willing to accept global assignments is not increasing at the same rate (Caligiuri and Cascio, 1998; Adler, 2002). For many MNCs finding the required numbers of people with the desired competencies for international assignments is a major IHRM challenge (Gupta and Govindarajan, 2002; Schuler *et al.*, 2002; Schneider and Barsoux, 2003). A recent review indicates that international mobility is becoming more problematic in many firms due to several factors including uncertainties associated with re-entry; the growing unwillingness to disrupt the education of children; the growing importance of quality-of-life considerations; and, finally, continued uncertainty regarding international terrorism and political unrest (Scullion, 2001). There is some evidence to suggest that families are less willing to disrupt personal and social lives than was the case in the past (Forster, 2000). In addition, dual-career problems and disruption to children's education are seen as major barriers to future international mobility in many different countries and pose considerable restrictions on the career-development plans of multinationals (Harvey, 1998; Mayrhofer and Scullion, 2002).

## The main challenge: developing truly transnational managers

So far we have discussed how the changing international environment has forced most companies to develop multidimensional and heterogeneous strategies and structures. Bartlett and Ghoshal (1989, 1998) refer to the transnational as the ultimate organizational form for operating successfully in an international context. This development poses considerable challenges for the managers who have to carry out these strategies and construct these structures, and in this section we discuss the roles and responsibilities of transnational managers. Given the heterogeneity and multidimensionality of the transnational organization, it is virtually impossible for one person to possess all the skills necessary to be an effective transnational manager in each and every part of the company. According to Bartlett and Ghoshal, the answer to the question 'what is a transnational manager?' is 'a network of specialists, not a single individual' (Bartlett and Ghoshal, 1992: 124). The roles and responsibilities of transnational managers will be different for different parts of the organization. We will therefore distinguish three different management forms: global business management; worldwide functional management; and geographic subsidiary management (based on Bartlett and Ghoshal, 1992). In a final subsection we will also discuss the necessary capabilities for top management.

## Global business management

Effective global business management complies with the demands of global efficiency and competitiveness. Capturing scale and scope economies and coordinating and integrating activities across national and functional barriers are the fundamental tasks of the global business manager. In order to perform these tasks such a manager has three core roles and responsibilities: as a worldwide business strategist, an architect of a worldwide asset and resource configuration, and as a cross-border coordinator and controller.

In his role as worldwide business strategist the global business manager tries to reconcile the different perspectives of geographic, functional and business management in order to provide an integrated competitive strategy for his particular business. As architect of an asset and resource configuration he subsequently coordinates the distribution of key assets and resources to support the competitive strategy chosen. In this role, however, he also has to take other perspectives into account and will furthermore be guided by the company's administrative heritage of existing assets and resources. This distribution of assets and resources leads to a flow of materials, components and finished products that has to be coordinated by the global business manager in his role as cross-border coordinator. As transnational companies mostly rely on distributed sourcing this is a very complex task.

## Worldwide functional management

Effective worldwide functional management responds to the challenge of developing and diffusing innovations on a worldwide basis. Knowledge is transferred by links between functional experts around the world, and most worldwide functional managers play three basic roles: worldwide scanner of specialized information and knowledge; cross-pollinator of 'best practices'; and champion of transnational innovation.

As a worldwide intelligence scanner the worldwide functional manager scans the whole world for opportunities and threats, which may be in the form of a technological breakthrough or an emerging consumer trend. Functional managers are linked through informal networks, so that information is transmitted rapidly. In a transnational company subsidiaries can be an important source of capabilities, expertise and innovations, which can be transferred to other parts of the organization. It is the worldwide functional manager in his role as cross-pollinator of 'best practices' who spots these opportunities and transfers them in a way that breaks down the 'not invented here' syndrome. Transnational innovations are the focus of this role of champion of transnational innovation. The first form of transnational innovation, is called 'locally leveraged' (discussed in Chapter 1), and follows from the 'best-practices' approach – local innovations that have applications everywhere. A more sophisticated form of transnational innovation is termed 'globally linked', and 'This type of innovation fully exploits the company's access to worldwide information and expertise by linking and leveraging intelligence sources with internal centres of excellence wherever they may be located' (Bartlett and Ghoshal, 1992: 785).

## Geographic subsidiary management

Effective geographic subsidiary management involves first and foremost multinational responsiveness, responding to the needs of national customers and satisfying the demands of host-country governments. However, it also demands defending a company's position against global competitors and leveraging local resources and capabilities. The geographic subsidiary manager's very complex task can be divided into three main roles: bicultural interpreter, national defender and advocate, and frontline implementer of corporate strategy.

In the first role, bicultural interpreter, the geographic subsidiary (or country) manager must not only understand the demands of local customers, competitors and government, but also interpret this information and communicate it effectively to managers at headquarters who might not understand its importance. The country manager must also act in the opposite direction, interpreting the company's overall goals, strategies and values in such a way that they become meaningful to local employees and do not compromise local cultural norms. As a national defender and advocate, the country manager should try to counterbalance excessive centralizing pressures from global business managers and make sure that the interests of the local subsidiary are taken into consideration. The country manager's role as a frontline implementer of corporate strategy is an especially difficult one. He or she is pressured by local governments, unions and customers on the one hand, and constrained by a global strategy that often leaves little room for manoeuvring on the other. This manager's actions 'must be sensitive enough to respect the limits of the diverse local constituencies, pragmatic enough to achieve the expected corporate outcome, and creative enough to balance the diverse internal and external demands and constraints' (Bartlett and Ghoshal, 1992: 788).

## Top-level corporate management

Top-level corporate management has to take all the transnational challenges (efficiency, learning and responsiveness) into account. This means not only creating different management groups and giving them specific roles and responsibilities, but also continuously striving to maintain the 'organizational legitimacy' of each group. Balancing and integrating diverse and often conflicting interests is the key challenge for top-level corporate management, and in doing so there are three basic roles to fulfil: providing direction and purpose; leveraging corporate performance; and ensuring continual renewal.

A multidimensional and heterogeneous company runs the risk of falling apart if there is no common vision and a shared set of values to lead it towards common goals. It is the task of top-level corporate management in its role as provider of direction and purpose to create this common vision. This is, however, a rather long-term strategy. Top management's role of leveraging corporate performance makes sure that the company survives in the short run. To do so, top management balances the different coordination devices (formalization, centralization and socialization) to achieve the mix that maximizes corporate performance. Both a focus on the long-term mission and on short-term performance, however, can lead to a loss of flexibility if put to the extreme. Therefore, the third role of top management is to ensure continual renewal. Goals and values have to be adaptive; they are continually questioned and challenged to achieve the flexibility that is vital in a transnational environment.

# Conclusion

This chapter has attempted to assess critically some important theoretical developments in the area of strategic HRM in multinational companies (strategic IHRM). In the first section we explained that growth of research in this field was linked to two parallel developments, (a) the growth of research on strategic HRM issues which focuses on the links between strategy, HRM and organizational performance, and (b) the growth of interest in the strategic nature of IHRM. In the second section we reviewed three important models of strategic IHRM (Adler and Ghadar; Evans and Lorange; and De Cieri and Dowling) which integrate the strategic and international dimensions of HRM and show the need for strategic HRM systems to address the tension between the dual imperative of global integration and local responsiveness. We argue that these models have advanced our theoretical knowledge of strategic HRM in MNCs by enhancing our understanding of the links between strategy and IHRM and by identifying the key variables which are important in determining strategic IHRM approaches. The theoretical models suggest that MNCs will gain competitive advantage by using strategic HRM practices to support business objectives, but the lack of sound empirical work in this area was noted (Harzing, 1999).

In the third section we examined the role of the corporate HR function in the international firm and suggested that the more rapid pace of globalization led to a more strategic role for HRM. We highlighted that some MNCs operate with a global and centralized HRM strategy for top managers and high-potential host-country national managers and at the same time with a polycentric/decentralized approach for other staff. In this dual system, corporate HR manages a core of senior staff and key personnel while the rest of lower-level management and staff are managed at the subsidiary level (Scullion and Starkey, 2000). We also suggest that the role of the corporate HR function varies considerably in different types of international firms and that the range of activities undertaken by corporate HR can vary significantly between global and multidomestic multinationals. We also addressed the related question – what are the key competencies required of the HR specialist? Recent research has identified five key factors which make a positive difference for both the performance of the firm and the personal performance of the HR manager: strategic contribution; personal credibility; HR delivery; business knowledge; and HR technology (Brockbank and Ulrich, 2002).

In the fourth section we discussed some of the key management development challenges facing global firms. The development of high-potential host-country national managers was identified as a critical HR issue for many MNCs and the growing importance of inpatriation as a development strategy was outlined. We also examined some major constraints on the supply of international managers which are contributing to shortages of international managers and constraining the internationalization strategies of firms. Finally, in the fifth section we considered what we term the main challenge for international HRM – developing truly transnational managers. The emerging integrated transnational model of organization is redefining roles and responsibilities of managers from the top levels to the bottom of the organization (Bartlett and Ghoshal, 2003), and by examining global business management, worldwide functional management and geographic subsidiary management we showed how the roles and responsibilities of transnational managers vary for different parts of the organization.

## Discussion questions

1  Discuss the meaning of strategic IHRM.
2  What are the key roles for the corporate HRM function in multinational companies?
3  Identify some key management development challenges facing global companies.
4  To what extent do the models covered earlier in this chapter contribute to our theoretical understanding of strategic HRM in multinational companies.

## Further reading

Bartlett, C.A. and Ghoshal, S. (2003) 'Managing in a Transnational Network: New Management Roles, New Personal Competencies', in B. McKern (ed.), *Managing the Global Network Corporation*. London and New York: Routledge.

De Cieri, H. and Dowling, P.J. (1999) 'Strategic Human Resource Management in Multinational Enterprises: Theoretical and Empirical Developments', in P.M. Wright *et al.* (eds), *Research in Personnel and Human Resources Management*. Stamford, Conn.: JAI Press, 305–27.

Paauwe, J. and Boselie, P. (2003) 'Challenging "Strategic HRM" and the Influence of the Institutional Setting', *Human Resource Management Journal*, 13(3): 56–70.
Schuler, R., Budhwar, P.S. and Florkowski, G.W. (2002) 'International Human Resource Management', *International Journal of Management Reviews*, 4(1): 41–70.
Scullion, H. and Starkey, K. (2000) 'The Changing Role of the Corporate Human Resource Function in the International Firm', *International Journal of Human Resource Management*, 11(6): 1061–81.

# References

Adler, N.J. (2002) 'Global Managers: No Longer Men Alone', *International Journal of Human Resource Management*, 13(5): 743–60.
Adler, N.J. and Ghadar, F. (1990) 'Strategic Human Resource Management: A Global Perspective', in R. Pieper (ed.), *Human Resource Management: An International Comparison*. Berlin: De Gruyter, 235–60.
Arkin, A. (1999) 'Return to Centre', *People Management*, 8 May. 34–41.
Bartlett, C. and Ghoshal, S. (1989) *Managing Across Borders: The Transnational Solution*. London: Hutchinson.
Bartlett, C.A. and Ghoshal, S. (1990) 'The Multinational Organization as an Interorganizational Network', *Academy of Management Review*, 16(2): 262–90.
Bartlett, C.A. and Ghoshal, S. (1992) *Transnational Management*. Homewood, IL, Irwin.
Bartlett, C. and Ghoshal, S. (1998) *Managing Across Borders: The Transnational Solution*, 2nd edn. London: Random House.
Bartlett, C.A. and Ghoshal, S. (2003) 'Managing in a Transnational Network: New Management Roles, New Personal Competencies', in B. McKern (ed.), *Managing the Global Network*. London and New York: Routledge.
Becker, B. and Gerhart, B. (1996) 'The Impact of Human Resource Management on Organizational Performance: Progress and Prospects', *Academy of Management Journal*, 39(4): 779–801.
Black, J.S. and Gregerson, H.B. (1999). 'The Right Way to Manage Expats', *Harvard Business Review*, March/April, 52–63.
Black, J.S., Gregerson, H.B., Mendenhall, M.E. and Stroh, L.K. (1999) *Globalizing People through International Assignments*. Reading, MA: Addison-Wesley.
Black, J.S., Morrison, A.J. and Gregerson, H.B. (2000) *Global Explorers: The Next Generation of Leaders*. New York: Routledge.
Bradley, P., Hendry, C. and Perkins, S. (1998) 'Global or Multi-Local?: The Significance of International Values in Reward Strategy', in C. Brewster and H. Harris (eds), *International HRM: Contemporary Issues in Europe*. London: Routledge.
Brewster, C. (1994). 'The Integration of Human Resource Management and Corporate Strategy', in C. Brewster and A. Hegewisch (eds), *Policy and Practice in European Human Resource Management: The Evidence and Analysis from the Price*, Waterhouse Cranfield Survey. London: Routledge.
Brewster, C. and Scullion, H. (1997) 'A Review and an Agenda for Expatriate HRM', *Human Resource Management Journal*, 7(3): 32–41.
Brockbank, W., Sioli, A. and Ulrich, D (2002) 'So We are At the Table! Now What?' Working Paper, University of Michigan. (http: //webuser.umich.edu/Programshrcs/res_NowWhat.htm)
Brockbank, W. and Ulrich, D. (2002) *The New HR Agenda: 2002 HRCS Executive Summary*. University of Michigan Business School.
Caligiuri, P.M. and Cascio, W. (1998) 'Can We Send Her There? Maximising the Success of Western Women on Global Assignments', *Journal of World Business*, 33(4): 394–416.
Caligiuri, P.M. and Tung, R. (1999) 'Comparing the Success of Male and Female Expatriates from a US based Company', *International Journal of Human Resource Management*, 10(5): 763–82.
DeCieri, H. and Dowling, P.J. (1999) 'Strategic Human Resource Management in Multinational Enterprises: Theoretical and Empirical Developments', in P.M. Wright, L.D. Dyer, J.W. Boudreau and G.T. Milkovich (eds), *Research in Personnel and Human Resources Management: Strategic Human Resources Management in the Twenty-First Century*, Supplement 4. Stamford, CT: JAI Press.
Dowling, P. J., Welch, D.E. and Schuler, R.S. (1999) *International Human Resource Management: Managing People in an International Context*, 3rd edn. Cincinatti, OH: South Western College Publishing, ITP.
Doz, Y. and Prahalad, C.K. (1986) 'Controlled Variety: A Challenge for Human Resource Management in the MNC', *Human Resource Management*, 25(1): 55–71.

Edstrom, A. and Galbraith, J.C. (1977) 'Transfer of Managers as a Co-ordination and Control Strategy in Multinational Organizations', *Administrative Science Quarterly*, 22(2): 248–63.

Evans, P. and Lorange, P. (1989) 'The Two Logics Behind Human Resource Management' in P. Evans, Y. Doz, and A. Laurent (eds), *Human Resource Management in International Firms: Change, Globalization, Innovation*. London: Macmillan.

Evans, P., Pucik, V. and Barsoux, J.L. (2002) *The Global Challenge: Frameworks For International Human Resource Management*. New York: McGraw-Hill/Irwin.

Ferris, G., Russ, G., Albanese, R. and Martocchio, J. (1991) 'Personnel/Human Resources Management, Unionization, and Strategy Determinants of Organizational Performance', *Human Resource Planning*, 32(2): 215–17.

Forster, N. (2000) 'The Myth of the "International Manager"', *International Journal of Human Resource Management*, 11(1): 126–42.

Goold, M.C. and Campbell, A. (1987) *Strategies and Styles: The Role of the Centre in Managing Diversified Corporations*. Oxford: Basil Blackwell.

Gregersen, H., Morrison, A. and Black, J.S. (1998) 'Developing Leaders for the Global Frontiers', *Sloan Management Review*, Fall: 21–32.

Gupta, A.K. and Govindarajan, V. (2002) 'Cultivating a Global Mindset', *Academy of Management Executive*, 16(1): 116–26.

Harvey, M. (1998) 'Dual-Career Couples During International Relocation: The Trailing Spouse', *International Journal of Human Resource Management*, 9(2): 309–31.

Harvey, M., Novicevic, M. and Speier, C. (1999a) 'Inpatriate Managers: How to Increase the Probability of Success', *Human Resource Management Review*, 9(1): 51–82.

Harvey, M., Speier, C. and Novicevic, M. (1999b) 'The Impact of the Emerging Markets on Staffing the Global Organization', *Journal of International Management*, Fall, 5(3): 167–86.

Harzing, A.W.K. (1999) *Managing the Multinationals: An International Study of Control Mechanisms*. Cheltenham: Edward Elgar.

Hendry, C. (1994) *Human Resource Strategies for International Growth*. London: Routledge.

Hofstede, G. (1980) *Culture's Consequences: International Differences in Work Related Values*. Beverly Hills, CA: Sage.

Hunt, J. and Boxall, P. (1998) 'Are Top Human Resource Specialists Strategic Partners? Self Perceptions of a Corporate Elite', *International Journal of Human Resource Management*, 9(5): 767–81.

Kobrin, S.J. (1992) *Multinational Strategy and International Human Resource Management Policy*. Wharton School, University of Pennsylvania.

Kobrin, S.J. (1994) 'Is there a Relationship between a Geocentric Mindset and Multinational Strategy ?', *Journal of International Business Studies*, 25(3): 493–511.

Kochan, T., Batt, R. and Dyer, L. (1992) 'International Human Resource Studies: A Framework for Future Research', in D. Lewin *et al.* (eds), *Research Frontiers in Industrial Relations and Human Resources*. Madison, WI: Industrial Relations Research Association.

Lado, A. and Wilson, M. (1994) 'Human Resource Systems and Sustained Competitive Advantage: A Competency-based Perspective', *Academy of Management Review*, 19: 699–727.

Linehan, M. (2002) 'Senior Female International Managers: Empirical Evidence from Western Europe', *International Journal of Human Resource Management*, 13(5): 802–14.

Linehan, M. and Scullion, H. (2001) 'Factors Influencing the Participation of Female Executives in International Assignments', *Comportamento Organizacional e Gestao*, 6(2): 213–26.

Linehan, M. and Scullion, H. (2002a) 'Repatriation of European Female Corporate Executives: An Empirical Study', *International Journal of Human Resource Management*, 13(2): 254–67.

Linehan, M. and Scullion, H. (2002b) 'Repatriation of Female Executives: Empirical Evidence from Europe', *Women in International Management Review*, 17(2): 80–8.

Mayrhofer, W. and Scullion, H. (2002) 'Female Expatriates in International Business: Empirical Evidence from the German Clothing Industry', *International Journal of Human Resource Management*, 3(5): 815–36.

McKern, B. and Naman, J. (2003) 'The Role of the Corporate Center in Diversified International Corporations', in B. McKern (ed.), *Managing the Global Network Corporation*. London and New York: Routledge.

Milliman, J., Von Glinow, M. and Nathan, B. (1991) 'Organizational Life Cycles and Strategic International Human Resource Management in Multinational Companies: Implications for Congruence Theory', *Academy of Management Review*, (16): 318–39.

Napier, N.K. and Taylor, S. (2002) 'Experiences of Women Professionals Abroad: Comparisons Across Japan, China and Turkey', *International Journal of Human Resource Management*, 13(5): 837–51.

O'Donnell, S.W. (2000) 'Managing Foreign Subsidiaries: Agents of Headquarters or an Independent Network?', *Strategic Management Journal*, 21: 525–48.

Paauwe, J. (1996) 'Key Issues in Strategic Human Resource Management: Lessons from the Netherlands', *Human Resource Management Journal*, 6(3): 76–93.

Paauwe, J. and Boselie, J.P. (2002) *Challenging (Strategic) Human Resource Management: Integration of Resource-Based Approaches and New Institutionalism*. ERIM Report Series Research in Management, no. ERS-2002-40-ORG, 29.

Paauwe, J. and Boselie, P. (2003) 'Challenging "Strategic HRM" and the Influence of the Institutional Setting', *Human Resource Management Journal*, 13(3): 56–70.

Paauwe, J. and Dewe, P. (1995) 'Organizational Structure of Multinational Corporations: Theories and Models', in A.W. Harzing, and J. van Ruysseveldt (eds) *International Human Resource Management*. Thousands Oaks: Sage.

Paauwe, J. and Richardson, R. (guest editors) (1997) 'Introduction to Special Issue on HRM and Performance', *The International Journal of Human Resource Management*, 3(8): 257–62.

Perlmutter, H.V. (1969) 'The Tortuous Evolution of the Multinational Corporation', *Columbia Journal of World Business*, Jan/Feb, 9–18.

Prahalad, C.K. and Doz, Y.L. (1987) *The Multinational Mission*. New York: Free Press.

Pucik, V. (1992) 'Globalization and Human Resource Management', in V. Pucik, N. Tichy and C.K. Barnett (eds), *Globalizing Management*. New York: John Wiley.

Purcell, J.(1985) 'Is Anybody Listening to the Corporate Personnel Department?', *Personnel Management*, September.

Purcell, J. and Ahlstrand, B. (1994) *Human Resource Management in the Multi-Divisional Company*, Oxford: Oxford University Press.

Reynolds, C. (2000) 'Global Compensation and Benefits in Transition', *Compensation and Benefits Review*, 32(1): 28–39.

Schneider, S. and Barsoux, J.L. (2003) *Managing Across Cultures*, 2nd edn. London: Financial Times/Prentice Hall.

Schuler, R.S. (2000) 'The Internationalization of Human Resource Management', *Journal of International Management*, 6: 239–60.

Schuler, R.S., Budhwar, P.S. and Florkowski, G.W. (2002) 'International Human Resource Management: Review and Critique', *International Journal of Management Reviews*, 4(1): 41–70.

Schuler, R.S., Dowling, P.J. and De Cieri, H. (1993) 'An Integrative Framework of Strategic International Human Resource Management', *International Journal of Human Resource Management*, 4(4): 717–64.

Schuler, R.S. and Jackson, S.E. (eds) (1999) *Strategic Human Resource Management: A Reader*. Oxford: Blackwell.

Scullion, H. (1992) 'Strategic Recruitment and Development of the International Manager: Some European Considerations', *Human Resource Management Journal*, 3(1): 57–69.

Scullion, H. (1994) 'Staffing Policies and Strategic Control in British Multinationals', *International Studies of Management and Organization*, 4(3): 18–35.

Scullion, H. (1996) 'Staffing Policy and Practice in an International Food and Drink Company', in J. Storey (ed.), *Blackwell Case Studies in Human Resource and Change Management*. London: Blackwell.

Scullion, H. (2001) 'International Human Resource Management', in J. Storey, (ed.), *Human Resource Management*. London: International Thompson.

Scullion, H. (2002) 'The Management of Managers in International Firms: Strategic HR Issues for the Corporate HR Function', in M. Linehan, M. Morley and J. Walsh (eds), *International Human Resource Management and Expatriate Transfers: Irish Experiences*. Dublin: Blackhall Publishing.

Scullion, H. and Brewster, C. (2001) 'Managing Expatriates: Messages from Europe', *Journal of World Business*, 36(4): 346–65.

Scullion, H. and Starkey, K. (2000) 'The Changing Role of the Corporate Human Resource Function in the International firm', *International Journal of Human Resource Management*, 11(6): 1061–81.

Sisson, K. and Scullion, H. (1985) 'Putting the Corporate Personnel Department in its Place', *Personnel Management*, December, 36–9.

Storey, J., Edwards, P. and Sisson, K. (1997) *Managers in the Making: Careers, Development and Control in Corporate Britain and Japan*. London: Sage Publications.

Stroh, L. and Caligiuri, P.M. (1998) 'Strategic Human Resources: A New Source for Competitive Advantage in the Global Arena', *International Journal of Human Resource Management*, (9): 1–17.

Stroh, L., Gregerson, H.B. and Black, J.S. (1998) 'Closing the Gap: Expectations Versus Reality Among Repatriates', *Journal of World Business*, 33(2): 111–24.

Taylor, S., Beechler, S. and Napier, N. (1996) 'Towards an Integrative Model of Strategic International Human Resource Management', *Academy of Management Review*, 21(4): 959–85.

Taylor, S., Napier, N.K. and Mayrhofer, W. (2002) 'Women in Global Business: An Introduction', *International Journal of Human Resource Management*, 13(5): 739–42.

Vernon, R.G. (1966) 'International Investment and International Trade in the Product Cycle', *Quarterly Journal of Economics*, May: 190–207.

Welch, D. (1994) 'Determinants of International Human Resource Management Approaches and Activities: a Suggested Framework', *Journal of Management Studies*, 31(2): 139–64.

# 3

# Staffing policies and practices in European MNCs: strategic sophistication, culture-bound policies or *ad hoc* reactivity?

*Ingemar Torbiörn*

Human resource management (HRM) may generally be taken to deal with a strategic and coordinated use of four categories of managerial parameters: staffing; appraisal; rewards; and development (Fombrun, Tichy and Devanna, 1984). The ultimate goal of firms in handling these parameters may be the procurement of competence needed for successful company performance. As this goal may be divided into the subgoals of finding, keeping, developing, allocating or moving, and finally using competence, it is easy to see the complexity of the task of HRM in general and that of international human resource management (IHRM) in particular (Torbiörn, 1997). Thus, as parameters of HRM are applied across cultural contexts complexity increases mainly due to the *intercultural aspect*, that is how HRM measures figured out in one culture may work out as applied in one or several other cultures. This aspect reflects the central dilemma of international management (Doz, Bartlett and Prahalad, 1981) and certainly implies delicate decisions on the part of firms as regards all four parameters of IHRM.

This chapter deals with only one of these parameters, namely the staffing of international operations. Here IHRM will not, as is sometimes seen, be taken to mean staffing, but staffing will be used, and discussed, as a criterion indicative of IHRM strategies, as well as of company concern about cultural contexts, organizational needs or situational options. Thus the object of this chapter is not the staff as such, but what company use of staff may tell about strategies, policies or practices. Starting out by establishing the particular relevance of the staffing parameter for firm performance, the chapter proceeds by first discussing staffing practices as indicative of types of strategy used by MNCs, then factors that are demonstrated, or commonly held, to be determinants of international staffing. Finally we try to interpret staffing patterns in terms of strategies and determinants attempting to find out what may be distinctive of European MNCs. Here the ambition is not to find 'the' valid picture, but at least some picture. Therefore, the reasoning throughout the chapter will be of a pragmatic kind, interpreting research at face level without much concern about methodology or established validity. In a concluding section, however, we discuss validity and relevance across time of the criterion, that is categories of staff, used to identify a European picture.

## Staffing and firm performance: the intercultural side

Generally seen, staffing could not be held more important than the other aspects of IHRM. The act of staffing, that is the selection of individuals for certain roles or positions, and the use of this selected staff may be seen as one among other parameters, or as a tool intended for company success or competitiveness. However, particularly in international contexts as we shall argue in this section, staffing may take on dimensions of importance beyond a matter of just providing or allocating competence. Such a statement rests on the fact that culture and the mastery of cultural differences may be crucial for successful firm performance. This may require differentiation of measures within the setup of HRM parameters, and within each parameter across cultural scenes of operations. As concerns staffing of key positions, it also means that the issue of what category of staff is used may be relevant. Thus any individual, beyond professional skills, is a representative of his or her own culture; that is, he or she holds culturally determined norms (besides personal and group norms) for understanding and evaluating situations. As this staff also acts on behalf of their organizations, there should be, based on pragmatic reasoning, a link between staffing decisions and firm performance in local scenes. Such a link should manifest itself first through the functioning of the selected staff in the local setting. Beyond professional qualifications such functioning may be due to complexities of cross-cultural role relations (Torbiörn, 1985; Dowling et al., 1999). Second, such a link is mediated through the appropriateness of the decision to staff a position by a certain category of personnel, whether this decision is taken at HQ or elsewhere in a firm. Although this argument refers to intercultural phenomena, that is to effects from contacts between different cultures directly or indirectly, problems in intercultural contact may indeed be attributed to cultural factors, when in fact they may result from other, less apparent facets of situations such as clashes of individual or company norms not contingent on cultures.

Still, of the four branches of HRM, international staffing may offer the most apparent link to the essence of what is traditionally denoted transaction costs (Williamson, 1975) and to what may be denoted 'firm performance'. Thus internal as well as external transaction costs or cultural frictions may follow from inadequate communication, standards or trust between involved actors and from their behaviours, as this involves cultural norms (Erdener and Torbiörn, 2001). Decisions or acts by staff in the field, or by those selecting this staff, are on behalf of their organizations with subsequent effects upon the attainment of organizational goals. Thus, staffing of key positions holds a direct and particular relevance among IHRM parameters as regards company performance. As such it also bears upon the central versus local dilemma of international management (Doz et al., 1981). This dilemma entails restrictions or possibilities regarding the success or failure in balancing corporate versus subsidiary concerns, HQ versus field, strategic versus operative concerns, foreign versus host culture norms, integration versus differentiation, and so on. The handling of this balance invokes consideration of 'managerial empathy' as well as of potential 'ethnocentric traps' at HQ or home sites of MNCs and at operative host-culture levels of performance.

## The relation of staffing to IHRM

Much of the literature on IHRM, seen as a management tool, has focused on the parameter of staffing, and in particular on two alternative categories of staff, parent-country nationals (PCNs) and home-country nationals (HCNs). These categories form the most logical options in international staffing as they reflect the general dilemma of central versus local in the sense that the choice is about what norms should be used, those of the domestic culture of MNCs or those of the local cultural scene. The selection of one or the other category of staff may possibly be taken to indicate strategic orientations. Such a relation has been established as regards HR strategies or policies and the incidence of HR-related problems (Kopp, 1994). Unfortunately however, this focus of IHRM writings might have diverted the perspective from more general strategic business concerns in that they often deal with expatriation, in particular of PCNs, and here with more operative HR aspects of, for example, issues of adjustment, repatriation and so on. In addition, company use of two other categories of transfers implying expatriation is less well-studied.

For the purpose of this chapter they may not be as easy to interpret in terms of norms or company intentions. This holds for third-country nationals (TCNs), although most MNCs use them on grounds of personal professional qualifications. This also holds for transfers of HCNs from various cultures to HQs or domiciles of MNCs for learning corporate culture or for training before being relocated to their local contexts. (May the labelling of this category of expatriate staff as 'inpatriates' which is found in some writings possibly reflect ethnocentrism among scholars?

Indeed, Clark, Grant and Heijltjes (2000) claimed much IHRM research to be ethno-centric.) Although HR matters of expatriation are important in their own right, IHRM writings might more fully handle the issue of staffing by applying a broader managerial perspective. This might mean thinking in more general terms as, for example, which type of norms are needed for operations, what competence is needed on site and how may it be allocated or transferred there. In doing so IHRM writings may relate more logically to business strategy by taking into consideration non-personal options besides persons or staff, and as concerns international transfers of staff, by including more categories or directions of transfer than that represented by assigning PCNs from HQs to local sites.

## Interpreting patterns of staff

Holding on to such perspectives, this chapter will still understand the use of PCNs or HCNs in terms of patterns of staffing taken to reflect adopted strategies or policies or cultural and contextual conditions of MNCs' domicile or host cultures. Here the object of study is not staff itself but the composition or distribution of staff in terms of the two mentioned categories, that is the staffing behaviour of firms as regards key international positions. Thus, the patterns that emerge at the aggregate company level may mirror preferences or adopted policies or systematic effects on staffing decisions from other factors. Throughout this chapter the criterion or basis for interpretation of such patterns will be the proportions of either category, that is of PCNs or HCNs. As the chapter is based on inspection of results from a few reported studies and as these results do not present staff compositions at firm level, interpretation of patterns will be based on proportions at higher levels of aggregation. Still, for the purpose of this chapter to see what may be typical of European MNCs, proportions at regional and national levels may be informative, at least in two crude ways. First, for comparisons across regions or nations differences or similarities in staff composition may indicate differences or similarities in cultural, contextual, structural or strategic respects as they similarly may affect several firms *within* regions or nations. Second, the size of percentages or proportions may be taken to reflect variation *across* MNCs within regions or nations. Thus high or low proportions will be taken to allow for less variability whereas intermediate proportions allow more.

For high or low proportions of either PCNs or HCNs this means that policies or practices are more similar or uniform across MNCs within a region or nation, and that they are more uniformly applied across scenes of international operations. Such an interpretation, however, does not tell whether this uniformity comes from cultural, contextual or organizational causes. In-between or moderate proportions, on the other hand, are not so easy to interpret at levels of aggregation above single firms. Thus, understood at a regional level an in-between proportion might mean that nationality or domicile conditions of MNCs promote uniform but *between nations* differing staffing policies. At national level, an in-between proportion might mean variation in staffing across firms *within a nation* or variation across staffing decisions *within firms*. (It may be assumed here that the possibility of a great number of firms *uniformly* using an in-between proportion of PCNs and HCNs is a less likely explanation. It may also be assumed that an in-between proportion is unlikely to reflect for example a 50/50 split across firms using either 100 per cent PCNs or 100 per cent HCNs.) For this chapter the first interpretation at a national level of an in-between or moderate proportion is seen as the one most likely. Thus, although a crude criterion like the size of proportions might be treacherous, it is here taken to be sufficient for understanding a reality that is partly known beforehand.

## Strategies or policies?

In this section we shall discuss whether anything might be inferred about IHRM strategies by interpreting in isolation practices or patterns of staffing by PCNs or HCNs. Such an approach might be seen as justified or not by relating a theoretical description of HRM to a pragmatic interpretation. Storey (1995) gives a general definition of HRM as:

> a distinctive approach to employment management which seeks to achieve competitive advantage through the strategic deployment of a highly committed workforce using an integrated array of cultural, structural and personnel techniques. (Storey, 1995: 5)

Whereas Hendry (1994) holds that: 'international HRM appears as a series of fragmented responses to distinct and separable problems' (Hendry, 1994: 1).

A question then is what aspects of IHRM strategies do lend themselves to interpretation. Looking at the theoretical definition of HRM three assumptions are identified. First it assumes a relation between HRM and competitiveness, that is firm performance. Second it assumes that HRM measures are derived from overriding business goals, so-called 'external fit'. Third it assumes integration across HRM measures, that is that they are coordinated in support of each other, so called 'internal fit' (Wright and Snell, 1998). As regards the first assumption it is much debated at a general level whether there is such an effect from HRM and how it may be established (Huselid and Becker, 1996; Guest, 1997; Ehrnrooth, 2002). An assumption about a potential impact from international staffing upon firm performance is here taken to be sufficiently well-underbuilt based on the pragmatic argumentation above. However, this may not be verified through inspection of staffing patterns. The second assumption implies that the mode of staffing may be an answer to organizational needs as perceived by firms in view of cultural, structural and contextual conditions in interaction with company goals. Although studies seeking to integrate staffing with corporate strategy are rare (Brewster and Scullion, 1997), external fit may here be judged by taking staffing policies to be derived from organizational needs. As regards the third assumption of internal fit it relates to a contingency aspect of HRM and possibly to a resource-based view (RBV). Here, according to some theoretical formulations, the coordination of HR resources is taken to produce firm-specific 'sustained advantages' in favour of competitive strength (Barney, 1991; Lado and Wilson, 1994; Boxall, 1996). Regardless of whether such 'sustained advantages' may be conceptually or empirically identified, however, 'bundles or systems of HRM practices can stand on it's own feet' (Ehrnrooth, 2002: 99). The mere fact that, in international contexts, cultural factors may complicate coordination across HR-measures should emphasize the relevance of such coordination for example in terms of transaction costs faced by firms (Leepak and Snell, 1999; Erdener and Torbiörn, 2001). Thus, aspects of internal fit and resource-based HRM models seem particularly relevant in international HRM (Taylor et al., 1996; Bonache and Fernandez, 2000). Still they may not be judged by interpretation of staffing patterns alone.

Taken together it appears that international staffing practices as seen in isolation may not tell much about IHRM strategies according to a general theoretical definition of HRM. Rather, an interpretation at face value might support the 'fragmented responses' description. Such a guess might be justified on grounds that much writing on HRM is normative rather than explanatory, and that 'the terrain may not be adapted to the map'. A fragmented pattern is still a pattern and it may, using Mintzberg's (1987) terms, reflect 'deliberate' as well as 'emergent' strategies. Lacking other data than staffing patterns as they appear, the interpretation of what may systematically explain 'fragmentation' might provide clues about IHRM strategies or, at least, about 'policies' as this construct may be applied to the systematic use of single parameters regardless of whether it is coordinated with an 'array' of other measures. Such a limited approach might at least shed some light upon two other aspects of HRM strategies, that is whether they appear as universalistic or configurative. A universalist approach to HRM would imply that one best strategy is used uniformly across contexts (Guest, 1997). As regards international staffing this should mean a small variation in the use of PCNs or of HCNs. A configurative approach, rather than a 'contingent', is more about what mix of HR measures, for example of staff, may meet contextual demands. From an organizational perspective a universalist approach may represent concern about integrated management whether it aims at centralized or decentralized handling of matters. A configurative view may represent concerns about differentiation or adaptation (Taylor et al., 1996). This approach, as being more reactive or responsive to contexts should mean a more varied use of HR parameters and a selective use of PCNs and HCNs. Thus, in judging strategies from staffing patterns as they appear at some above-firm level of aggregation, small variation across firms should correspond to a very high or very low percentage of one or the other staff category. This might indicate universalist strategies. Percentages in between such extreme values might more likely be indicative of a configurative approach. Still the ultimate criterion of such a strategy would be variation across contexts within MNCs.

# Determinants of international staffing

What manifests as a pattern of staffing of a firm might have a varied setup of antecedents internal or external to MNCs. As it is beyond the scope of this chapter to elaborate in detail on the determinants of staffing, Figure 3.1 presents a schematic model of what may influence decisions regarding management of international operations as they ultimately emerge as staffing patterns at aggregate company levels. Basic to the model is the concept of norms, that is ways to handle things for the sake of company goals. Here Figure 3.1 displays possible concerns at several organizational levels pertaining to options regarding choice of norms and means to effectuate them. Important choices regard what norms to apply and how they may be modified and also whether the chosen norms may be uniformly applied across international operations or not. Finally at operative levels, the choice is between options to effectuate selected norms, for example by personal representation or by non-personal means. Choices at every level will ultimately affect staffing patterns, and choices may be influenced by intra-firm preferences and contextual factors at each level.

The model does not demonstrate the process of decision-making. Rather it tells that for every single decision, where several decisions sum up to a staffing pattern, a variety of concerns may be relevant whatever the outcome or final choice is. Thus no single number-one determinant of the choice between PCNs and HCNs may theoretically be nominated, nor of a resulting pattern of staff. Still, in practice, single determinants may be decisive in specific instances. Further, the model does not mean that decisions take into account all these concerns but it points to some aspects that should be relevant or rational from a perspective of attaining company goals. In reality, decisions of intercultural reach may often be affected by irrational elements like ethnocentrism, stereotyping, ignorance and misattribution. As the locus of decision-making is often embedded in the environmental context of the HQ and the domicile culture of MNCs (while consequences of decisions manifest elsewhere), this may tend to bias decisions towards isomorphic use of company norms. Regardless of whether deliberate or unintended, effects of country of origin (Ferner, 1997) may influence decisions and staffing patterns.

Theoretically, strategies and policies may be taken to emanate from goals and needs of the particular organizations. As regards international staffing such needs have been empirically identified as filling positions and developing organizations (Edström and Galbraith, 1977), or as operational needs dealing with the *managerial functions* of control and coordination or the use of competence besides strategic needs of career development (Torbiörn, 1982; Scullion, 1994; Harzing, 2001). Perception of such needs at organizational levels should then determine staffing. This implies that needs may also be derived from structural or contextual factors. Such

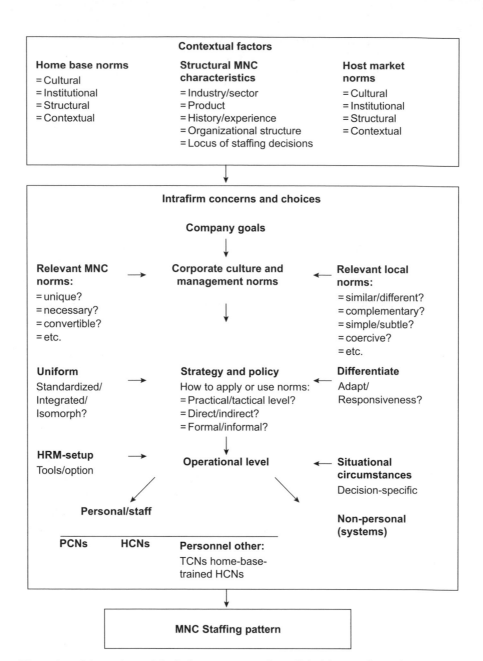

*Figure 3.1* Schematic model of relevant concerns in staff decisions as determinants of firm level staffing pattern

factors may be type of industry, history or experience of international operations or of specific host markets, organizational locus of decision-making regarding international staffing, the organization of home and host-market operations, for example the use of international divisions at HQs, of IJVs in certain markets, and so on. Organizational needs may also stem from corporate culture and adopted management principles.

However, as decisions on staffing international operations are basically about what norms to use, policies and practices may be influenced by home cultures of MNCs. *Corporate cultures* regarded as sets of norms must always to some extent reflect norms from the domicile *national culture* of organizations (Torbiörn, 1982), which means that organizational needs relating to one or the other category of staff, as they are perceived at the locus of decision-making, may themselves be culture-bound and thus influence company strategies (Hennart, 1998; Schneider, 1989). Thus, from a cross-cultural, comparative perspective, the interpretation of staffing patterns at regional or national levels may possibly tell us about cultural influences. Here regional or national staffing patterns appear as similarities or differences which may indicate culture-bound managerial values or IHRM strategies. The influence of culture upon IHRM and international staffing does not, however, prescribe one or the other of the strategies discussed above. Both types of policies may reflect the impact of cultural or institutional factors. Thus, as diverse host-culture conditions are seen as more relevant this might favour a configurative strategy. As the home culture of MNCs may uniformly affect IHRM, it might favour a universalist approach to be applied across culturally different local markets. Ideally, in trying to understand staffing patterns of MNCs regarding the impact of cultural factors, both home and host cultures need to be considered. Still, the issue of whether any value-based concern or strategy is functional rests upon its intercultural effectiveness as judged in combination with other measures taken.

However, what appear as cultural influences may rather reflect *institutional and structural conditions* of home or host markets that may systematically affect staffing. Structural characteristics may be the size and relative importance of the home market versus international activities, or of certain host markets *vis-à-vis* the home market. They may stem from history of international exposure of MNCs domicile cultures. They may also stem from a factual uniqueness of own management norms or principles *vis-à-vis* those of host cultures, or of perceived or factual cultural differences or 'distance' (Boyacigiller, 1990). Structural factors may also be the supply of labour at home or host markets, for example availability of candidates for expatriate assignments as well as various facets of host markets, for example complexity of institutional arrangements, labour-market regulations, and so on. Such factors may systematically affect staffing. However, the influence on decisions from *situation-specific circumstances* may not appear as a systematic determinant of staffing patterns interpreted at aggregate levels. Still it may not be uncommon that companies face situations in which planned or preferred intentions may not be realized, for example due to lack of candidates or of sufficient time to staff positions, extraordinary tasks to handle like trouble-shooting, and so on.

Insofar as preferences of home culture norms are based on *ethnocentrism*, this does not reflect any particular culture. As ethnocentric decisions at firm level systematically affect staffing this may be generally questioned (Hailey, 2000), for example, as causing cultural frictions. A staffing policy may not, however, be deemed ethnocentric based solely on evidence about proportions of PCNs and HCNs. Further, the efficiency of ethnocentric strategies may not be generally assumed (Mayrhofer and Brewster, 1996). The same holds for stereotyping, that is insufficient differentiation between host cultures. As stereotyping and ethnocentrism are general social psychological phenomena of particular relevance in intercultural contexts, they may not in themselves be interpreted beyond the level of individual firms. Thus, although the grounds for staffing may be termed ethnocentric, this may not be taken as a national or cultural characteristic.

# Regional comparisons

In judging cultural influences from staffing patterns as they appear at regional or national levels, similarity across MNCs within levels of comparison may be taken to indicate influences of cultural or structural characteristics of home markets as well as contextual factors, for example a similar appearance in host markets. Besides, a high or a low percentage of one or the other staff category might indicate universalist strategies as typical of some culture. Percentages in between such extreme values might indicate variation across MNCs within a certain level of aggregation. This may reflect variation in cultural, structural or contextual conditions, but also in types of strategies. Such variation should be explained at some lower or more precise level of aggregation.

Comparisons among US, Japanese and European firms have long shown typical differences in staffing international operations as regards the use of PCNs and HCNs. Thus US firms show a high proportion of HCNs and Japanese firms a high proportion of PCNs. Europe shows an intermediate proportion, using more PCNs than the USA, but fewer than do Japanese firms (Tung, 1988; Kopp, 1994; Harzing, 2000). This may reflect cultural differences as they manifest in principles of management (Bartlett and Goshal, 1992). Thus Japanese firms are often held to manage through centralization (many PCNs) whereas US firms use more formalized, indirect or non-personal parameters (few PCNs). US and Japanese firms as compared to European, may use strategies of more universalist types. Here explanations may primarily be sought among characteristics of domestic conditions, be they cultural, structural or institutional as such conditions, for example size of home markets, relate to international activities in general. On the other hand, a European approach of 'socialization' like that of the Japanese:

is also people-based, but does not depend to anything like the same degree on the transfer of acolytes from head office. Instead, it uses careful recruitment, development and acculturation of key decision makers to establish shared values and objectives across diverse nationalities. (Hendry, 1994: 89–90)

Judged at a regional level, however, a more varied use of PCNs and HCNs may not in itself be taken to indicate a socialization approach or configurative strategies as 'a' European characteristic. Such a conclusion would further require intermediate proportions of PCNs and HCNs at national levels for MNCs of several European cultures and ultimately intermediate proportions for several firms within such cultures. Neither may a varied pattern be taken to reflect cultural differences between Europe, the USA and Japan. The impact of MNCs' home cultures may not be evident until the concentration or dispersion of international activities across host markets is considered. As compared to the USA and Japan, a more varied European staffing pattern may indicate cultural, contextual or structural differences between European nations. Then, insofar as European staffing policies are culture-bound a varied pattern would emerge across several European cultures or home markets. Still, several structural or contextual factors that are typical of the European scene and that may favour variation in staffing patterns are presented by various authors (for example Hendry, 1994; Brewster and Harris, 2000; Scullion and Brewster, 2001; Jackson, 2002). Some of these factors may be typically in common for nations in Europe, some may be distinct from US or Japanese conditions, for example:

- MNCs located in many domiciles in Europe
- MNCs operating in many host markets within or outside Europe
- Relatively small domestic markets (central role of international operations)
- A long history of international dependency of nations
- Small distances within Europe may offer more options in staffing
- A process of cross-national integration of markets within the EU
- A high rate of restructuring and change of markets and firms within the EU
- A rapid process of internationalization of firms
- A large proportion of firms operate internationally
- Many small or medium-sized firms operate internationally
- International careers more valued by firms and staff
- Availability or lack of candidates (HCNs, PCNs) for international posts.

As seen, there may be many reasons why Europe as an aggregate shows a varied staffing pattern, or an in-between proportion as regards the use of PCNs and HCNs. So far, however, this pattern may not be taken to reflect common European cultural norms. Rather, cultural, structural or contextual factors of the European scene may explain this pattern as they variedly affect firms. In fact, the most decisive factor may be *variety itself* included in Europe as an aggregate. Such a characteristic as a varied setting or environment of firms may not equally pertain to firms in other regions. Thus national differences within Europe regarding institutional arrangements, labour-market regulations, languages, leadership styles, managerial and work values make decisions on staffing key positions multifaceted and somewhat delicate in terms of who may best perform in managerial roles. Several multinational studies including European countries tell about considerable differences between nations in Europe (Hofstede, 1980; Ronen and Schenkar, 1985; England and Harpaz, 1990; Kanter, 1991; Smith *et al.*, 2002). In view of this a characteristic of European management may well be a capacity to handle variety in terms of a varied setup of constraints and options and varying ways to act. As regards HRM practices, Bournois and Brewster (1993: 25) claim as a European regional characteristic 'to take more factors into account'.

## Europe, national level

At an aggregate national level, large variations in the proportions of PCNs and HCNs across domicile nations of MNCs may indicate cultural, structural or contextual determinants of national impact as such patterns may range from in-between proportions to high or low. An interpretation in terms of configurative strategies would be supported as long as in-between proportions may appear across several European countries. This may reflect small variation across domicile countries but large variation across firms within domiciles. Interpretations made with the frame of reference adopted for this chapter will be based on the excellent desk research by Anne-Wil Harzing. She classified, by interpretation of names, managing directors as HCNs (Harzing, 2000) or PCNs (Harzing, 2001). Through the wide coverage of regions, nations and firms and through the careful handling of data her studies present important input for understanding international staffing. This research used two sets of data.

One is a *small-scale mail survey* sample of 104 MNCs selected from the Fortune Global 500 list representing nine domicile countries and 239 subsidiaries in 22 host countries. This study includes several MNCs from each of the USA, Japan and seven European countries representing eight types of industry. These data to some extent also map categories of staff at other top-level functions than managing director (Harzing, 2000, 2001). As this small-scale survey sample is taken to illustrate staffing patterns at national levels in Europe, it shows, besides confirming the empirical pattern described at a regional level, large variation across countries in proportions of HCNs and PCNs. Thus proportions of PCNs are relatively low for British and French and high for German MNCs. This indicates an impact on staffing policies from cultural, structural or contextual differences within Europe. Interpreted in terms of strategy types it might indicate more universalist, but between them different, policies among on the one hand British and French, and on the other German firms. A three-cluster solution including all nations of the study grouped Germany with Japan, and UK/France with the USA. This difference is interpreted in terms of traditionally more formalized and impersonal control functions among Anglo-Saxon and French firms as compared to more informal but personal supervision among German and Japanese firms (Harzing, 2000).

Contrasting these countries where MNCs use high or low proportions of HCNs or PCNs, Harzing's small-scale sample identifies a group of countries with intermediate proportions (Finland, Netherlands, Sweden and Switzerland) which represents small domicile nations. According to the criterion adopted in this chapter, staffing policies may here be more varied across firms which may indicate configurative and possibly less culture-bound staffing policies. This might correspond to a responsiveness of firms from small domicile nations operating in large host markets and to traditions of great international dependence. So far, based on Harzing's (2000, 2001) small-scale sample results, it may be concluded that cultural differences within Europe and contextual factors as they are manifest at national levels may affect staffing policies of European firms. Further, analysis shows a strong association between staffing proportions and host nations of subsidiaries. Harzing (2000) concludes that Europe may not be considered homogeneous as regards staffing policies, neither with respect to origins of MNCs nor to host markets of their subsidiaries.

Harzing's (2000, 2001) second set of data are from an *archival sample study* based on secondary information on more than 200 MNCs representing 11 domicile countries and 2,689 subsidiaries in 48 host countries and representing 23 types of industry. The study includes a more limited set of variables than the small-scale survey, but the criterion of PCNs and HCNs is still based on names interpretation (Harzing, 2001). Here, results also show large variation across countries regarding the proportions of PCNs among European MNCs, although in comparison with the small-scale sample, proportions of PCNs vary less. Also as compared with the small-scale sample, proportions of PCNs are lower for some countries (Germany, Netherlands and Switzerland) and higher for France. Although MNCs from the UK still use relatively few PCNs and German MNCs relatively many, the ranking by proportions of comparable domicile countries is different. As the large sample used in the archival study includes more industries and more 'less global' firms, it might be more representative of the European scene.

The varied pattern displayed by the archival sample is less clearly understood in terms of cultural impact on management principles as referred to above. To this author, it suggests a more evident in-between proportion European pattern implying large variation across firms within domicile nations due to contextual factors at a national level, or to structural factors at organizational levels, for example industry and size of firms. Besides, this pattern may reflect a more or less systematic situational impact on staffing. Insofar as it reflects systematic effects it might be termed configurative. Insofar as it reflects unsystematic effects at company level it might be termed *ad hoc* or reactive. Harzing (2001) performed logistic regression analyses of both sets of data using information on home nationality of MNCs, host nationality of subsidiaries, cultural distance between home and host nations, as well as structural characteristics of home companies and subsidiaries, for example size, age, industry type. Although these analyses included data on firms other than European, results show that the selected sets of variables have high explanatory power for both sets of data in predicting the likelihood of a PCN as managing director of subsidiaries. Results thus support the model of factors influencing MNCs' staffing policies suggested by Harzing (2000, 2001).

In terms of the frame of reference adopted for this chapter, Harzing's model mainly predicts configurative staffing policies, that is variation across firms within domicile nations besides variation across nations. Particularly as regards the archival sample, an inspection of national-level proportions of PCNs indicates that configurative staffing policies may be characteristic of Europe. (The crude criterion of interpreting national-level proportions in terms of possible variation across firms within nations may, however, be less valid here in separating universalist from configurative policies.) A configurative pattern may be generally predicted from traditionally suggested firm-specific needs of filling positions and organizational development (Edström and Galbraith, 1977) or by operational needs of control, coordination and competence (Torbiörn, 1982) as such needs are perceived and handled according to contextual or situational factors. Insofar as these needs systematically affect staffing they may account for part of the unexplained variation in Harzings analyses. This variation may, however, also reflect situational reactivity or *ad hoc* decisions. Thus, taken together, if anything may be concluded as characteristic of staffing patterns among European MNCs, it is the mix itself.

## A changing pattern?

Although the character and determinants of European MNCs' staffing policies may have been basically the same for some time (Franko, 1976; Tung, 1988), the present pattern may reflect recent changes of global or European conditions or it may change due to ongoing processes. This section will discuss various developments at global, regional and firm levels which may potentially affect options and preferences in international staffing. As the volume of international operations increases, the number of international assignments grows naturally. However, some net effect on staffing practices from *globalization* of business may not be easily identified. Increasing competition may favour integrationist strategies as well as local responsiveness (Buckley and Casson, 1998). Insofar as the process of internationalization itself may change from gradual expansion (Porter, 1990) into direct from local to global (Doz *et al.*, 2001), staffing practices may change according to needs of local learning favouring the use of PCNs or HCNs.

Generally seen, *globalization* emphasizes the importance of international management competence and international careers. This creates a stronger need to assign PCNs for strategic reasons of competence development. Global talent tracking and recruitment mean that lateral assignments across international operations increase, that is of TCNs, and so may transfers of HCNs from various cultures to domiciles for learning or training. This will make interpretation of staffing patterns in bipolar terms a less clear criterion of intentions behind MNCs' policies.

One Scandinavian MNC, for example, using an internal job-seeking system globally for recruitment of key position staff does not make a distinction of categories of expatriate personnel in terms of PCNs, TCNs and HCNs brought home for training. Instead, those assigned to international jobs may, after a few assignment periods, choose between being 'home-based' or 'international'. Home-based persons are expected to sometime return to their domicile countries, whichever these may be. While serving abroad they benefit from the social security package, e.g. retirement conditions of their home countries. Internationals, on the other hand, are not expected to return to their home countries as employees of their company. Their social and economic conditions while serving abroad relate to what holds on a market for international management expertise, e.g. with pension plans located in some international trust fund. Although the system implies wage differences locally between staff doing the same type of job, HR officials report the system to work well in terms of more lateral mobility of staff and more internationalisation of HQ and local subsidiaries.

At a *regional* level, determinants of staffing may change according to the degree of openness between regions and the degree of within-region integration. In the case of protectionist or fortress-type regions, relatively more PCNs should be used insofar as more pronounced motives of control and know-how transfer follow from acquisitions or greenfield investments to establish presence inside regional barriers. Within the context of the EU, determinants of staffing may favour the use of both PCNs and HCNs. The restructuring of firms into larger, more competitive and integrated units requires cross-border coordination as well as more strategic concerns about staffing (Scullion and Brewster, 2001) which may favour the use of PCNs in strategic positions but of HCNs for local scenes. On the other hand, as small or medium-sized firms go international, and as firms enter new markets in Central and Eastern Europe, this may initially favour operative and pragmatic motives for PCN assignments.

Considering the impact of MNCs' *domicile cultures* on staffing patterns and assuming that cultural norms are resistant to change, national staffing patterns may not alter. For operations at *host markets* within the EU, however, the harmonization of some structural conditions and highly tangible norms emphasizes the need of smooth handling of unchanged, more subtle cultural differences. This may favour concern about what is culturally embedded and local responsiveness, that is more use of HCNs. Also, insofar as the traditional assumption remains relevant, that staffing as seen from a HQ perspective may reflect *organizational needs* of control, coordination and use (or development) of competence, staffing patterns may generally change insofar as such needs are related to changing structural features of firms. These may concern degrees of centralization, hierarchial structure, the ownership constellation and forms of international operations such as joint ventures, franchising, outsourcing of functions, and so on. Here no net effects on staffing may be concluded. However, as new means to fill traditional managerial functions come up, or as some needs appear more relevant, this may affect staffing. Thus, technical means of communication have drastically changed possibilities of system-based control, coordination, transfer and application of competence. Insofar as non-personal techniques may fulfil traditional tasks of PCNs this may increase the use of HCNs. Also increased strategic concern about building competence may favour assignments of PCNs for career development (Scullion and Brewster, 2001), but also expatriation the other way, that is of HCNs transferred from local scenes for learning.

As it might be concluded here that MNCs' needs for international transfers of staff may increase, scarcity of candidates for expatriate assignments in one or the other form may also affect staffing policies. Thus dual-career families may be unwilling to move, although shorter assignments, more home-leaves or commuting within Europe (Scullion and Brewster, 2001) may marginally affect willingness. Insufficient integration on the part of MNCs of careers abroad, and back home upon repatriation, may also reduce the will to sign for international transfers. Scarcity of PCN candidates may favour the use of other arrangements or staff categories like TCNs or HCNs. In view of a high tempo and short notice before positions are filled, such situations are not uncommon for firms. This is in support of a hypothesis of *ad hoc* staffing rather than of policy fulfilment.

# Discussion

In this section we shall take a critical view of three main themes of this chapter. First, we ask whether it is meaningful to interpret patterns of staffing at a regional, here European, level. Here, based on comparisons with other regions as well as on commonalities and differences among European nations we discuss what may typically lie behind a European staffing pattern as found in research. Second, we discuss whether this pattern may be taken as systematically applied strategic orientations or policies, or as a result of unsystematic *ad hoc* reactivity. Third, we question the validity and relevance of using a dichotomous criterion to conclude regarding some complex third phenomenon underlying staffing decisions.

## A European mix?

So far, the difficulty in reaching an overview sufficient to state something like a European IHRM strategy (Richey and Wally, 1998), or in particular a European style of staffing, is apparent. Despite the obvious relevance of the issue for under-standing behaviours of MNCs, one may generally ask at what level of aggregation it is meaningful or possible to interpret empirically stated staffing patterns. This holds in particular for a varied mix as being in itself characteristic of Europe. Insofar as such a mix is functional for firm performance, it emphasizes the relevance of a dif-ferentiated view among those in European MNCs in charge of staffing decisions. Also, a general message is that staffing based on stereotype or undifferentiated judge-ments may not be functional for European firms. As staffing decisions regarding PCNs or HCNs are often handled by line management supported by HR staff, a dif-ferentiated view may also be a characteristic of 'euromanagers' as described by Goffee and Jones (1995) to be oriented towards pragmatism and action based on a genuine understanding of cultural differences.

Further, insofar as it may be typical for European firms that HR functions are vested in line management (Brewster and Hegewish, 1994; Hiltrop *et al.*, 1995; Torbiörn, 1997), a mixed (or in-between) staffing pattern may even result from staffing decisions taken by different heads and at different occasions without strate-gic coordination. Insofar as this mix typically applies at company level beyond cul-tural impact from domicile nations, it should reflect that varied conditions of oper-ations promote variations in staffing as well as a varied use of other parameters. As many European MNCs, may not be as 'global' as US or Japanese MNCs, and as many of them operate mainly within Europe, their host environment or home base (Porter, 1990) is itself culturally diverse requiring local responsiveness and contextual fit based on well-informed decisions. Yet Harzing's (2000, 2001) studies demonstrate a strong impact from MNCs' domicile cultures. This may be logical as corporate cul-tures always, to some extent, reflect norms of home cultures of firms.

As discussed above, some principles of management are often seen as typically European in comparison with the USA and Japan; these refer to more socialization, personalization and less formalization. Still, although such an explanation may hold for a regional comparison, it may not be seen as typical in terms of being common across European nations. As culturally determined managerial values and behaviours differ between European nations (Burns *et al.*, 1995; Smith *et al.*, 2002) this might affect staffing. However, the interpretation at the country level of differences in staffing as cultural differences regarding some third phenomenon, for example man-agerial values, may mean attributing too much to culture as a determinant as well as stereotyping regarding firm-level behaviours.

## Strategy, policies or *ad-hoc* reactivity?

Taking the staffing mix as typical of European MNCs it may possibly be seen as a configurative approach as well as that US and Japanese firms may be more univer-salistic, but in different ways. Staffing patterns alone, however, do not tell about strategies in a 'coordinated' academic sense as we do not know about MNCs' use of other HR parameters. Rather, so far, they tell about policies. As such they are well-explained by Harzing's (2000, 2001) analyses. Both the small-scale sample and archival data fit well with her model, and the variables, taken together, displayed great explanatory power. Here, this was taken to reflect configurative policies as typical of European MNCs. Such policies should mean a systematically applied priority for *concerns about contexts* in line with what works best in the situations at hand. As part of a deliberate IHRM strategy this should mean a selective use of PCNs and HCNs. Thus, a more precise test of a 'configurative hypothesis' needs to focus on those MNCs showing in-between proportions of PCNs and HCNs and on the motives given by such firms.

Still, an estimation based on Harzing's (2001) results shows that a proportion of at least 25 per cent of the variation in staffing, taken at firm level, remains unexplained. Although some of this variation may be systematic as explained by variables not included in the analyses, it leaves room for a complementary *ad hoc* reactivity hypothesis. *Ad hoc* reactivity taken as a determinant of staffing should reflect occasional or unsystematic outcomes of staffing decisions where priorities are governed by *available options* in specific situations (rather than by planned concerns about what may work best). This is not to say that such reactivity should necessary mean second-best solutions. Also, considering the importance of decisions about key positions in subsidiaries, *ad hoc* reactivity should not mean staffing at random, although it might appear so in statistical terms. A recurring dependency on *ad hoc* solutions in staffing would likely result in mixed patterns similar to those reflecting configurative policies. However, whereas a configurative policy may be taken as an attribute of firms, *ad hoc* reactivity may not. Rather, it may be seen as a phenomenon reflecting volatile conditions that do not always allow situations to be handled in planned or intended ways. Thus, although MNCs may use deliberate strategies or policies of one or the other kind, the outcome of some staffing decisions, as influencing firm-level staffing patterns, may well be ascribed to *ad hoc* reactivity. A European pattern of mixed staffing might possibly 'converge' as more firms gain international experience within EU, as firms benchmark, etc., policies of MNCs may take on more configurative traits. On the other hand, insofar as a volatile reality may increasingly call for *ad hoc* staffing, this may possibly hold in particular for European MNCs in view of a growing competition, rapid restructuring and inclusion of new members in the EU.

## Staff categories – a criterion of what?

Considering the use of 'manager counts' as a face-level criterion of IHRM or of some assumed policy, one may generally ask what staffing really signifies. Although the use of staff proportions as a dependent variable reflecting the impact of various determinants may be interesting in itself, conclusions regarding some third or underlying phenomenon are always indirect and to some extent speculative, which should be exemplified by the approach adopted for this chapter. As said above, decisions on staffing should be too important to be left at random and choices should always reflect some managerial intention on the part of MNCs, be it strategic or meant only for particular occasions. Although managerial intentions of control, coordination and competence allocation have long since been demonstrated as relevant for the choice between PCNs and HCNs, one may ask whether such a dichotomous classification will remain relevant, in particular as restricted to the classification of managing directors or a few key positions. The argument here is not to present a critique of research done so far; yet one may raise the general question of whether categorization in bipolar terms of holders of one or a few positions may not be a skewed or too narrow criterion. As such it may reflect overattribution of HQs' managerial intentions as vested in, for example, managing directors. Or, it may reflect underattribution (or neglect) of managerial intentions associated with an increasing use of TCNs and of HCNs trained in domiciles of firms. Thus, part of reality, or of options regarding IHRM or staffing, is omitted when a bipolar criterion is used. Insofar as some coordinated IHRM strategy is used by firms, it may also disregard potential effectiveness in interaction (for example substitution or complementation) across other managerial parameters. Regardless of whether such options may affect what today appears as typical European staffing patterns, it questions the validity of a dichotomous criterion as a base for inferences about some third management characteristic. This limitation may even today hold in particular for European MNCs.

As regards research on IHRM in general, and what may affect staffing of international operations in particular, the meaning of a mixed and varied pattern taken as typical of Europe is not clearly demonstrated. In view of the pragmatic and crude frame of interpretation adopted for this chapter, this may not be surprising. Still a few tentative conclusions may be drawn:

- Variation in staffing is itself a characteristic of European MNCs, reflecting a culturally and structurally varied context of MNCs' domiciles and host markets.
- A varied context calls for a selective use of PCNs and HCNs across staffing decisions, as well as a general orientation towards handling variety. Insofar as selective staffing is systematically used, this represents configurative policies. Such policies may be typical of staffing in European MNCs, although *ad hoc* staffing may be a frequent phenomenon.
- Although staffing of international operations is important in itself, IHRM research needs wider criteria than dichotomous interpretation of staffing patterns. A complex and changing reality calls for wider criteria that include more *company* options in order to better understand firm behaviour.

## Further reading

Brewster, C. and Harris, H. (eds) (2000) *International HRM: Contemporary Issues in Europe*. London: Routledge.
Dowling, P., Welch, D. and Schuler, R. (1999) *International Human Resource Management*. Cincinnati, OH: South Western College Publishing.

## References

Barney, J. (1991) 'Firm Resources and Sustained Competitive Advantage', *Journal of Management*, 17(1): 99–120.
Bartlett, C. and Goshal, S. (1992) *Managing Across National Borders: The Transnational Solution*. London: Random House.
Bonache, J. and Fernandez, Z. (2000) 'Strategic Staffing in Multinational Companies: A Resource-Based Approach', in C. Brewster and H. Harris (eds), *International HRM: Contemporary Issues in Europe*. London: Routledge, 163–82.
Bournois, F. and Brewster, C. (1993) 'The Need for International Comparisons', *P+ European Participation Monitor*, issue no. 7: 19–26.
Boxall, P. (1996) 'The Strategic HRM Debate and the Resource-Based View of the Firm', *Human Resource Management Journal*, 6(3): 59–75.
Boyacigiller, N. (1990) 'The Role of Expatriates in the Management of Independence, Complexity and Risk in Multinational Corporations', *Journal of International Business Studies*, 21(3): 357–81.
Brewster, C. and Harris, H. (eds) (2000) *International HRM: Contemporary Issues in Europe*. London: Routledge.
Brewster, C. and Hegewish, A. (eds) (1994) *Policy and Practice in European Human Resource Management*. London: Routledge.
Brewster, C. and Scullion, H. (1997). 'A Review and Agenda for Expatriate HRM', *Human Resource Management Journal*, 7(3): 32–41.
Buckley, P. and Casson, M. (1998) 'Models of the Multinational Enterprise', *Journal of International Business Studies*, 29(1): 21–44.
Burns, P., Myers, A. and Kakabadse, A. (1995) 'Are National Stereotypes Discriminating?', *European Management Journal*, 13(2): 212–17.
Clark, T., Grant, D. and Heijltjes, M. (2000) 'Researching Comparative and International Human Resource Management: Key Challenges and Contributions', *International Studies of Management and Organization*, 29(4): 6–23.
Dowling, P., Welch, D. and Schuler, R. (1999) *International Human Resource Management*. Cincinnati, OH: South Western College Publishing.
Doz, Y., Bartlett, C. and Prahalad, C. (1981) 'Global Competitive Pressures and Host Country Demands', *California Management Review*, 23(3): 63–74.
Doz, Y., Santos, J. and Williamson, P. (2001) *From Global to Metanational: How Companies Win in the Knowledge Economy*. Boston: Harvard Business School Press.
Edström, A. and Galbraith, J. (1977) 'Transfer of Managers as a Coordination and Control Strategy in Multinational Organizations', *Administrative Science Quarterly*, 22(June): 248–63.

Ehrnrooth, M. (2002) 'Strategic Soft Human Resource Management – The Very Idea', PhD. Dissertation, Swedish School of Economics and Business Administration, Helsinki.

England, G. and Harpaz, I. (1990) 'How Working is Defined: National Contexts and Demographic and Organizational Role Influences', *Journal of Organizational Behavior*, (11): 253–66.

Erdener, C. and Torbiörn, I. (2001) 'International Staffing Patterns and Transaction Costs: Implications for Alliance Readiness and Firm Performance', in J. Genefke and F. McDonald (eds), *Effective Collaboration*. Chippenham, UK: Palgrave, 132–51.

Ferner, A. (1997) 'Country of Origin Effects and HRM in Multinational Companies', *Human Resource Management Journal*, 7(1): 19–37.

Fombrun, C., Tichy, N.M. and Devanna, M.A. (eds) (1984) *Strategic Human Resource Management*. New York: Wiley.

Franko, L. (1976) *The European Multinationals*. London: Harper and Row.

Goffee, R. and Jones, G. (1995) 'Developing Managers for Europe: A Reexamination of Cross-Cultural Differences', *European Management Journal*, 13(3): 245–50.

Guest, D. (1997) 'Human Resource Management and Performance: A Review and Research Agenda', *International Journal of Human Resource Management*, 8(3): 5–25

Hailey, J. (2000) 'Localization as an Ethical Response to Internationalization', in C. Brewster and H. Harris (eds), *International HRM: Contemporary Issues in Europe*. London: Routledge, 89–101.

Harzing, A. (2000) 'MNE Staffing Policies for the Managing Director Position in Foreign Subsidiaries: The Results of an Innovative Research Method', in C. Brewster and H. Harris (eds), *International HRM: Contemporary Issues in Europe*. London: Routledge, 67–88.

Harzing, A. (2001) 'Who's in Charge? An Empirical Study of Executive Staffing Practices in Foreign Subsidiaries', *Human Resource Management*, 40(2): 139–58.

Hendry, C. (1994) *Human Resource Strategies for International Growth*. London: Routledge.

Hennart, J. (1998) 'The Comparative Institutional Theory of the Firm: Some Implications for Corporate Strategy', *Journal of Management Studies*, 31(2): 193–207.

Hiltrop, J.-M., Despres, C. and Sparrow, P. (1995) 'The Changing Role of HR Managers in Europe', *European Management Journal*, 13(1): 91–8.

Hofstede, G. (1980) *Cultures Consequences*. Beverly Hills: Sage.

Hui, H. (1990) 'Work Attitudes, Leadership Styles and Managerial Behaviors in Different Cultures', in R. Brislin (ed.), *Applied Cross-Cultural Psychology*. London: Sage.

Huselid, M. and Becker, B. (1996) 'Methodological Issues in Cross-Sectional and Panel Estimates of the Human Resource-Firm Performance Link', *Industrial Relations*, 35(3): 400–22.

Jackson, T. (ed.) (2002) *International HRM: A Cross-Cultural Approach*. London: Sage.

Kanter, R. (1991) 'Transcending Business Boundaries: 1200 World Managers View Change', *Harvard Business Review*, May–June, 151–164.

Kopp, R. (1994) 'International Human Resource Policies and Practices in Japanese, European and United States Multinationals', *Human Resource Management*, 33(4): 581–99.

Lado, A. and Wilson, M. (1994) 'Human Resource Systems and Sustained Competitive Advantage: A Competency-Based Perspective', *Academy of Management Review*, 19(4): 699–727.

Leepak, D. and Snell, S. (1999) 'The Human Resource Architecture: Toward a Theory of Human Capital Allocation and Development', *Academy of Management Review*, January: 31–48.

Mayrhofer, W. and Brewster, C. (1996) 'In Praise of Ethnocentricity: Expatriate Policies in European Multinationals', *International Executive* 38(6): 749–78.

Mintzberg, H. (1987) 'The Strategy Concept: Five P's for Strategy', *California Management Review* 30(1): 11–24.

Porter, M. (1990) *Competitive Advantage*. New York: Macmillan.

Richey, B. and Wally, S. (1998) 'Strategic Human Resource Strategies for Transnationals in Europe', *Human Resource Management Review*, 8(1): 79–98.

Ronen, S. and Schenkar, O. (1985) 'Clustering Countries on Attitudinal Dimensions: A Review and Synthesis', *Academy of Management Review*, 10(3): 435–54.

Schneider, S. (1989) 'Strategy Formulation: The Impact of National Culture', *Organization Studies*, 10(2): 149–68.

Scullion, H. (1994) 'Staffing Policies and Strategic Control in British Multinationals', *International Studies of Management and Organization*, 24(3): 86–114.

Scullion, H. and Brewster, C. (2001) 'The Management of Expatriates: Messages From Europe', *Journal of World Business*, 36(4): 346–65.

Smith, P., Peterson, M. and Schwartz, S. (2002) 'Cultural Values, Sources of Guidance, and Their Relevance to Managerial Behavior', *Journal of Cross-Cultural Psychology*, 33(2): 188–208.

Storey, J. (ed.) (1995) *Human Resource Management: A Critical Text*. London: Routledge.

Taylor, S., Beechler, S. and Napier, N. (1996) 'Toward an Integrative Model of Strategic International Human Resource Management', *Academy of Management Review*, 21(4): 959–85.

Torbiörn, I. (1982) *Living Abroad: Personal Adjustment and Personnel Policy in the Overseas Setting*. Chichester: Wiley.

Torbiörn, I. (1985) 'The Structure of Managerial Roles in Cross-Cultural Settings', *International Studies of Management and Organization*, 15(1): 52–74.

Torbiörn, I. (1997) 'Staffing for International Operations', *Human Resource Management Journal*, 7(3): 42–51.

Tung, R. (1988) *The New Expatriates: Managing Human Resources Abroad*. Cambridge, MA: Ballinger.

Tung, R. (1998) 'A Contingency Framework of Selection and Training of Expatriates Revisited', *Human Resource Management Review*, 98(8): 23–38.

Williamson, O.E. (1975) *Markets and Hierarchies*. New York: Free Press.

Wright, P. and Snell, S. (1998) 'Toward a Unifying Framework for Exploring Fit and Flexibility in Strategic Human Resource Management', *Academy of Management Review*, 23(4): 756–72.

part *2*

# Managing the
# international HR cycle

# 4

# Training, learning and development in multinational organizations

*Paula Caligiuri, Mila Lazarova and Ibraiz Tarique*

In today's highly competitive global business environment, multinational companies (MNCs) recognize that human resources play a necessary role in developing and sustaining a competitive advantage. This competitive necessity has increased attention to human talent issues on a global scale. These include fostering a global corporate culture through a network of global leaders, and supplying resources to both enhance employees' cross-cultural competence and to increase employees' contributions to the organization's global business objectives (Evans *et al.*, 2002).

Using this global human talent approach requires an organization to have human resource (HR) systems which promote cross-cultural competence and international business acumen. While there are many components in the global HR system that contribute to its success, including selection, performance management, rewards and the like, this chapter will focus on the contribution of the training and development function. In particular, within the context of an entire HR system, this chapter will focus on ways in which training and development increase employees' global competence which enables individuals to work effectively across borders and work with those from diverse cultures.

We begin by discussing the differences between training and development initiatives and how they have evolved into strategic HR functions. We then discuss the issue of fit between a firm's business strategy and the organization of a firm's training and development function. We use the established conceptualization of transnational business strategy, the global integration versus local responsiveness framework (Prahalad and Doz, 1987; Bartlett and Ghoshal, 1989), to propose three approaches to organizing the training and development function: centralized, synergistic, or localized. Next, we discuss the major challenge across all three approaches to training and development. That is, to train and develop a variety of employees from different countries, from diverse cultural backgrounds, and with unique performance goals. We discuss the widely accepted training and development initiatives that multinational firms use to provide the various employee groups with cross-cultural competencies needed to perform effectively in a multicultural environment. Finally, we discuss, in detail, two popular initiatives: global leadership programmes and cross-cultural training programmes, illustrating their importance to building cross-cultural competence.

## The training and development function

The terms *training* and *development* tend to be combined to signify the set of activities used by firms to develop the competency base of their employees. Both have the same objective – to foster learning among the organizational members and to develop enriched and more capable workers who, in turn, can enhance organizational competitiveness and effectiveness. While similar in objective, the specific goals of training and development are, in fact, different.

In general terms, *development* has a broader organizational focus with a future-oriented time-frame, compared to *training*. Training tends to be individually-focused with a present (or near-future) time-frame. Training also addresses particular deficiencies in individuals, develops specific competencies, focuses on more tangible aspects of improving performance, and tends to be oriented towards solving short-term performance concerns. Development, on the other hand, is a broader effort which is linked to improving the organizational competence to fulfil a strategic need in the future. In the case of global competence, for example, development would be oriented towards broadening leaders' competencies for future global responsibilities. Training, in this same example, may include a one-day pre-departure cross-cultural awareness programme offered to an employee prior to his or her global assignment.

In the aggregate, some training programmes, when applied to a group of employees in a strategic and systematic way, are considered a subset of organizational development programmes (Hall, 1976; Conference Board, 1991; Gutteridge *et al.*, 1993; Hall, 1996). An example of this would be if an information technology (IT) organization (with a growing global presence) predicted that most of its programmers would be working in worldwide geographically-distributed teams in the next few years – and, in an effort to be proactive, sent all programmers to the following half-day training sessions:

- Multicultural team-building
- Effective remote communication
- How to run a tele-meeting
- Cross-cultural differences in e-mail and phone communication.

As the former example suggests, training and development are complementary functions, especially within a firm's *strategic* human resource system. Contrast this with a similarly placed IT firm that sends programmers to the same training classes when (and if) individual deficiencies are detected (for example, a poor performance appraisal suggests that given programmers need to work on their global team skills). This is an example of a training function that is not well-integrated with the development function – and not very strategic in nature. Multinational firms will vary on the extent to which they integrate training and development – and whether they integrate the training and development across their subsidiaries around the world. The next section will discuss the contingencies for the strategic alignment of the training and development function and the extent to which global integration is accomplished across various business strategies.

## Aligning training and development with business strategies

Within a multinational organization, managing a strategic training and development function can be especially challenging. In particular, multinational firms differ in their operations from those of domestic firms in terms of two complex dimensions: *geographic dispersion* and *multiculturalism* (Adler, 2002).

Geographic dispersion is the extent to which a firm is operating across borders and must coordinate operations across borders in order to be effective, whilst multiculturalism is the extent to which the workers, customers, suppliers and so on are from diverse cultural backgrounds and must coordinate the activities of people from diverse cultures in order to be effective. In leveraging both geographic dispersion and multiculturalism, transnational organizations must achieve a dynamic balance between the needs to be *centralized*, or tightly controlled by headquarters, and the need to be *decentralized*, to operate differently across diverse locations (Bartlett and Ghoshal, 1989). The achievement of this balance between centralization and decentralization can happen in a variety of ways.

As a strategy, extreme centralization can provide an organization with a variety of competitive benefits such as economies of scale, improved value-chain linkages, product/service standardization, and global branding. Extreme decentralization, however, can also be highly strategic enabling a firm to modify products or services to fully meet local customer needs, respond to local competition, remain compliant with various governments' regulations in different countries of operation, readily attract local employees, and penetrate local business networks. These two countervailing forces, centralization and decentralization, have also been labelled *global integration* and *local responsiveness* (Prahalad and Doz, 1987).

In order to be successful, every multinational firm should adopt a strategy that 'fits' the complexity of its environment (Ghoshal and Nohria, 1993), and research by Caligiuri and Stroh (1995) found that each diverse business strategy implies a different approach to managing human resources. Three general multinational strategies

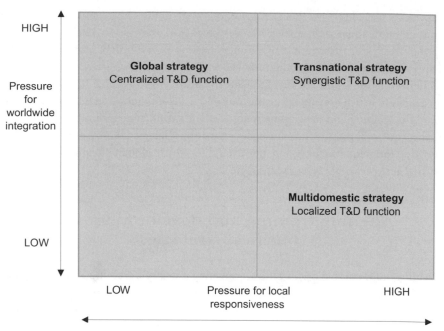

**Figure 4.1** Global strategy and the training and development (T&D) function

will be discussed with respect to the organization of the training and development function (Figure 4.1):

- Global
- Multidomestic
- Transnational

## Training and development aligned with a global strategy

Organizations pursuing a *global strategy* face strong pressures for worldwide integration but face weak pressures for local responsiveness (Ghoshal and Nohria, 1993). Such firms organize their operations into worldwide lines of business that are managed and controlled by headquarters. This central control is often critical because, in part, their basis for competition is a systematic delivery of products and services around the world (Bartlett and Ghoshal, 1989). Headquarters-controlled HR practices often follow in these international organizations where subsidiaries are required to comply with decisions from headquarters.

Worldwide, these organizations place a greater emphasis on training, rather than development, especially at the lower levels within the organization. Training tends to be geared towards functional competencies and maintaining consistency in given employee tasks. At higher levels in the organization additional attention is paid to training managers on how to transfer 'the corporate way of doing things' to host national subsidiaries. These transferring activities may be in the form of business trips, short-term assignments, or even long-term expatriate assignments. Thus, the overall objective of the training initiatives is to provide managers with the competencies needed for the successful transfer of technology, organizational culture and organizational philosophy from the headquarters to the subsidiaries, to work effectively with and manage subsidiary staff, and (in the case of expatriates) to comfortably live in the new culture (Adler and Bartholomew, 1992).

## Training and development aligned with a multidomestic strategy

Organizations pursuing a *multidomestic strategy* face strong pressures for local responsiveness and weak pressures for worldwide integration. Their structure resembles a decentralized group of local firms and their policies differ across countries, conforming to local market demands. Multidomestic organizations transfer almost all human resource practices, including the training and development function, to the host national subsidiaries. Decisions are made at the subsidiary level regarding the competencies needed by the local staff (at all levels), and the type of training and development initiatives required.

In cases where the headquarters of a multidomestic organization initiates a given training and development practice, they will put considerable emphasis on adapting the given practice to fit with the local culture (Thornhill, 1993; Francis, 1995). Human resource professionals who design, deliver and evaluate training programmes for local nationals recognize that cultural differences have significant implications for developing these programmes (Thornhill, 1993; Francis, 1995; Tarique, 2002). For example, the case-study method of content delivery is very popular among US trainees (especially when training on business skills), but this method may not be the most appropriate method of content delivery for Chinese trainees. Chinese participants are more likely to not express their opinions openly, as compared to US trainees, thus making the training method inappropriate and ineffective in this cultural context (Aguinis, 2002). Thus, human resource professionals working for multidomestic organizations need to take into consideration participants' cultural background and values when initiating any training programme.

## Training and development aligned with a transnational strategy

Organizations pursuing a *transnational strategy* face strong pressures for worldwide integration and for local responsiveness. These organizations attempt to develop an integrative and interdependent global network of subsidiaries that combines the benefits of worldwide integration with the benefits of local responsiveness. Subsidiaries are neither satellites of nor independent from headquarters, but rather are integral parts of a whole system with both global and local objectives. Each subsidiary is believed to make a unique contribution to this synergistic system. Decisions are a result of a collaborative process between headquarters and subsidiaries. As such, across all levels of the organization, the training and development function in transnational organizations integrates delivery worldwide from a unified strategic plan. Clearly, this is the most complex strategy to implement.

The HR cornerstone of organizations following a transnational strategy is that they tend to fill managerial positions at all levels, both at headquarters and in subsidiaries, from a worldwide pool of employees – regardless of nationality. Thus, one important goal of the training and development function is to help managers gain an *integrator* perspective (Kedia and Mukherji, 1999), enabling them to work, think and behave synergistically across borders and with people from diverse cultural backgrounds. According to Kedia and Mukherji (1999: 245) some of the qualities of an *integrator manager* include heightened awareness of diverse cultures (for example cultural knowledge) and enhanced global abilities and skills (for example the ability to speak multiple languages). They can bridge differences among people, values and cultures and manage these differences in meaningful and productive ways. They can immerse themselves in the dynamics of the complex global environment and seamlessly integrate complex networks of partnerships, alliances and relationships that shift and reconfigure over time. In order to encourage managers to think as *global integrators*, training and development departments in transnational organizations have engaged employees in a variety of initiatives, including international job rotations, global leadership development programmes, participation in geographically distributed global teams, cultural coaching, cross-national mentoring, structured business trips, languages classes, and the like.

# Training and developing for global work

We have seen how there are a variety of ways to organize training and development initiatives in a multinational firm to be consistent with a transnational business strategy. Irrespective of strategy, a major challenge that cuts across all three approaches is how to train and develop individuals optimally to possess the skills and competencies needed to cross cultures. In this section we describe various training and development initiatives to better prepare employees for global work (Table 4.1 summarizes these training and development initiatives and their respective goals).

## Training initiatives for global work

Cross-cultural training, diversity training and language training make up the three broad groups of training initiatives commonly used by multinational organizations. Depending on the needed cross-cultural competencies, each component may be used as a standalone initiative or used in conjunction with other components.

*Table 4.1*  Examples of training and development initiatives in global firms

| Training and development initiatives | Goals |
|---|---|
| Cross-cultural orientation (predeparture) | Comfortably live and work in host country |
| Cross-cultural training (in-country) | Increase cross-cultural adjustment |
| Diversity training | Increase ability to understand and appreciate multiple cultural perspectives |
| Language training | Fluency in another language |
| Traditional education in international management | Increase international business acumen and knowledge |
| Individualized coaching or mentoring on cultural experiences | Build cultural awareness; work on cultural 'blind-spots'; develop competencies for becoming an effective global leader |
| Immersion cultural experiences | Build extensive understanding of the local culture and increase ability to understand and appreciate multiple cultural perspectives |
| Cross-border global teams with debriefing | Learn skills to be a better leader (or team member) with multiple cultures involved in the team |
| Global meetings with debriefing or coaching | Learn skills to conduct a better meeting when multiple cultures are involved in the meeting |
| International assignment rotations with debriefing or coaching | Develop a deep appreciation for the challenges of working in another culture; increase global leadership competence |

Cross-cultural training helps employees who are working across cultures for business meetings, short-term assignments, long-term assignments, or on global teams. Cross-cultural training (CCT) helps individuals to:

- learn appropriate cultural behaviours and suitable ways of performing necessary job tasks in another country (Black and Mendenhall, 1990; Kealey and Protheroe, 1996);
- develop coping methods to manage unforeseen events in the new culture, and to reduce conflict due to unexpected situations (Earley, 1987); and
- form realistic expectations with respect to living and working in the new country (Black and Mendenhall, 1990; Black *et al.*, 1991).

Whereas cross-cultural training is designed to help individuals adjust to living and working conditions in the new culture, diversity training has a more general applicability. Diversity training can be offered to all employees in the organization. Diversity training is designed to help employees work effectively with a diverse workforce (for example co-workers, subordinates and supervisors who have different gender, age, ethnic, cultural and religious backgrounds) (Noe, 2001), to become aware of group-based differences among employees, and to decrease negative stereotyping and prejudice (Cox, 1993; Ferdman and Brody, 1996).

Foreign-language training complements both cross-cultural training and diversity training in that it provides employees with language skills that are needed to communicate with co-workers and individuals in other countries. As in the case of cross-cultural training, foreign-language training is also most often associated with global assignees. Individuals who must work in another country can be trained in the host-country language to improve their ability to communicate with local nationals. On the other hand, multinational companies can take the extra step to train key employees in all host countries in the common company language (Marchan-Piekkari *et al.*, 1999). This serves to improve both horizontal (among subsidiaries) and vertical (between subsidiary and headquarters) communication within the firm (Charles and Marschan-Piekkari, 2002).

## Developmental initiatives for global work

Cross-cultural competencies for future job responsibilities can be developed thorough formal education, individualized coaching/mentoring, and immersion programmes. *Formal educational programmes* aim to provide employees with foundational cultural knowledge in areas such as global strategic planning, cross-border leadership and cross-cultural negotiation. Such programmes include self-study courses offered electronically or in the traditional paper and pencil distance education format, off-site courses offered by academic institutions, in-house or on-site company seminars offered by subject-matter experts, and company-sponsored management development programmes (Noe 2001; Gupta and Govindarajan, 2002). Foundational cultural knowledge can also be acquired through *individualized coaching/ mentoring programmes*. These programmes, too, are normally associated with current or future global assignees and are used to provide them with a tailored programme that addresses the specific competency need of the expatriate; the programme is delivered by an experienced senior employee who works one-on-one with the expatriate. Employees can also acquire culture-specific competencies through *immersion programmes* in foreign cultures (Gupta and Govindarajan, 2002). Employees live in communities in foreign countries and develop an extensive understanding of the local culture by interacting with local nationals and participating in local traditions and customs (Noe, 2001).

Cross-border teams, global meetings and international job rotations can be used to help employees work effectively in teams composed of people from geographically dispersed units (Dowling *et al.*, 1999). Participation in *cross-border teams* allows for the development of cross-cultural competencies that can include in-depth knowledge about different cultures, cross-cultural communication skills, and interpersonal relationships (Gupta and Govindarajan, 2002). *International job rotations* and *cross-border meetings* can also provide employees with similar cross-cultural competencies. International job rotations involve sending employees on a series of short-term assignments to different countries, whereas cross-border meetings involve sending employees to meetings that take place in different geographic locations.

These training and development initiatives can be made available to all employees, but should be driven by the organization's business strategy (as discussed in the previous section). While it is highly unrealistic to assume that such initiatives will be (or indeed, *should be*) the norm for *all* employees in a multinational firm, increasing appreciation of cross-cultural competencies is likely to increase the breadth and depth of these initiatives in many companies (especially in transnational organizations). The trend is that these training initiatives described are, in fact, becoming increasingly popular and available to larger groups of employees doing international work, regardless of whether they perform their jobs as an assignee in a host country, as a global team member or in the headquarters' office.

## Training and development for global assignees

In a transnational organization, *global* leaders – who were once defined as 'those who accept global assignments' – are now defined as managers in a multinational organization with some level of global responsibilities, regardless of location. While it is true that training and development for global competencies should be present throughout many levels in transnational organizations, special consideration should still be given to global assignees living and working outside their own national borders. Thus, this section focuses on the unique training and development needs of global assignees.

Global assignees may be trained and developed in a variety of ways – however, selecting the most appropriate training and development initiative to match the type of global assignment can be a challenge for global human resource professionals. There is an increasing agreement among management researchers that not all expatriate assignments are the same. Individuals are sent abroad for a variety of reasons, for different durations of time, they are expected to complete different tasks, to interact with different employee groups, and so on. Holding the position of General Manager in the Cairo, Egypt subsidiary, is different from being a Systems Administrator in a team based in Sofia, Bulgaria. In considering the extent to which cultural interaction is needed and developed global competence is expected, Caligiuri (2005) has suggested a classification of global assignments into four categories: (1) technical, (2) developmental/high potential, (3) strategic/executive, and (4) functional/tactical. These types of assignments are described in detail in Box 4.1.

This four-type categorization has implications for training and development initiatives in that the cross-cultural competencies required for the successful completion of each assignment will vary depending on the type of assignment. Training

## Box 4.1    Types of global assignments

*Technical assignments.* This type of assignment is becoming increasingly more common as organizations are expanding their technical expertise worldwide. When technical skills do not exist in one geographic region, a global assignment may be necessary to fill a technical need. The typical technical assignment is similar in content to the assignee's domestic position. Specifically, these technical assignees are in an organizational setting fairly typical to the setting of the home country. Many of the global assignees on technical assignments will describe their work experience as 'quite similar' to what they were doing back home. It is not expected that these global assignees will have significant interactions with the host nationals working at the subsidiary location – and those interactions that inevitably will occur, will not greatly affect the outcome of the assignment. In other words, the person is being sent for his or her technical skills.

*Developmental/high potential assignments.* For some global organizations, sending expatriates abroad for two or more years to develop global competencies is consistent with their overall strategic human resource plan. Most organizations that utilize this type of global assignments do so within the context of their managerial development programme. These programmes are often rotational – with one of the rotations being in another country. While on this type of assignment, the goal is individual development. The central dimension of performance in this situation might be comparable to outcomes in any training or development programme: the acquisition of individual skills (negotiation, strategic decision-making, operations knowledge, and the like).

*Strategic/executive assignments.* Strategic assignments are usually filled by individuals who are being developed for high-level management positions in the future. These assignments tend to be high profile (e.g., general managers, vice-presidents) and the experience is viewed as both developmental and strategic. Thus, these individuals are not sent solely for developmental purposes, rather they are there to fill a specific need in the organization. These global assignees are the core 'critical' group of assignees. They may have the task of entering a new market, developing a country base in a new area, being the general manager of a joint venture, and the like. An inpatriate assignment, where high-profile managers from other countries take a global assignment in the headquarters country, is an example of a strategic assignment (Kobrin, 1988; Black *et al.*, 1992).

*Functional/tactical assignments.* The functional/tactical assignment is similar to the technical assignment with one distinct difference – significant interactions with host nationals are necessary in order for the assignment to be deemed successful. As with the technical assignment, a person will be sent to another country to fill a technical or managerial gap for the organization in that host country. While they are there, they will need to have positive interactions with host nationals for the assignment to be deemed successful; this social dimension of performance will have considerable weight in defining success, balanced by the technical/task dimension. This type of global assignment is the most common global assignment (Windham International and NFTC, 1998). These assignees are sent to fill a technical need. However, unlike technical assignees, cross-cultural skills are essential in order to be successful.

*Source*:    Caligiuri (1995).

programmes for individuals sent on technical assignments that do not require significant interactions with host nationals need to provide a cultural orientation or a 'how-to live in' approach. This cultural orientation would cover the basics of living in the given host country (for example information on the shopping and the transportation system in the host country). Functional or tactical assignees (the largest group of assignees in most countries) who are sent to fill in a technical position, yet interact with host nationals on a daily basis, will need training initiatives that go beyond a basic cultural orientation. Functional assignees would need some deeper training on how to work effectively with host nationals, and language training. The time-frame of training for both technical and functional assignees often occurs prior to the assignment or predeparture.

In contrast to technical or functional assignees, people sent on developmental (or high-potential) assignments and strategic (or executive) assignments require significant interactions with host nationals in order to be successful. This suggests a greater focus on intercultural communications and language fluency. Also, given that these positions are development-focused, training and development must be designed to develop greater cross-cultural competencies, international business acumen, intercultural negotiations, and the like. The time-frame for these training and development activities is often in-country (during the assignment) for strategic and developmental assignees. Table 4.2 summarizes the type of initiative that may be used for each type of foreign assignee.

*Table 4.2*  Expatriate assignment and training and development initiatives

| Training and development initiatives | Technical | Functional | Developmental | Strategic |
|---|---|---|---|---|
| Cross-cultural orientation (predeparture) | ✓ | ✓ | ✓ | ✓ |
| Cross-cultural training (in-country) | | ✓ | ✓ | ✓ |
| Diversity training | | ✓ | ✓ | ✓ |
| Language training | | ✓ | ✓ | ✓ |
| Traditional education in international management | | | ✓ | ✓ |
| Individualized coaching or mentoring on cultural experiences | | | ✓ | ✓ |
| Immersion in cultural experiences | | | ✓ | ✓ |
| Cross-border global teams with debriefing | | | ✓ | ✓ |
| Global meetings with debriefing or coaching | | | ✓ | ✓ |
| International assignment rotations with debriefing or coaching | | | ✓ | ✓ |

# Cross-cultural training for global assignees

As the previous section has suggested, across all types of global assignments, cross-cultural training (ranging from cultural orientation to intercultural competence-building) is a widely utilized training initiative. In this section we discuss some salient issues related to designing effective cross-cultural training initiatives. Traditionally, multinational firms have used cross-cultural training to increase the knowledge and skills of expatriates to help them operate effectively in the unfamiliar host culture (Kealey and Protheroe, 1996), and for more than 20 years cross-cultural training has been advocated as a means of facilitating effective cross-cultural inter-actions and cross-cultural adjustment (Brewster, 1995; Katz and Seifer, 1996; Kealey and Protheroe, 1996) and there has been a positive trajectory of growth with respect to the number of firms offering such training. For instance, in the early 1980s, Tung (1981, 1982) found that only 32 per cent of firms offered cross-cultural training, whilst almost 20 years later the 1998 Global Relocation Trends Survey Report indicated that 70 per cent of the 177 MNCs surveyed provided cross-cultural training of at least one-day's duration (Windham International and NFTC, 1998).

## Designing effective cross-cultural training (CCT) programmes

An important aspect of any cross-cultural training initiative involves determining how cross-cultural training effectively enhances expatriates' cross-cultural competencies and facilitates their adjustment to the new environment. In order to improve the effectiveness of cross-cultural training initiatives, it is important to follow a systematic approach to designing such initiatives (Tarique and Caligiuri, 2004). A well-designed cross-cultural training initiative can enhance the learning process of the expatriate and thus facilitate effective cross-cultural interactions and adjustment (Black and Gregersen, 1991; Caligiuri et al., 2001). To understand the systematic approach to designing training initiatives, Tarique and Caligiuri propose a five-phase process (see Figure 4.2)

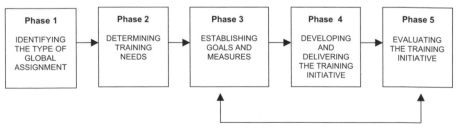

*Source*:   Adapted from Tarique and Caligiuri (2004).

*Figure 4.2*   Systematic process of designing effective CCT programmes

as a general strategy to follow in designing effective cross-cultural training programmes. The five phases are:

1 Identify the type of global assignment for which CCT is needed;
2 Determine the specific cross-cultural training needs (from the organization-
  level, assignment-level, and the individual-level);
3 Establish the goals and measures for determining training effectiveness;
4 Develop and deliver the CCT programme;
5 Evaluate whether the CCT programme was effective.

The *first phase* includes identifying the type of global assignment for which cross-
cultural training is needed. As discussed earlier, there are different types of global
assignments and cross-cultural training will differ based on the goals required for the
successful completion of each assignment. The *second phase* determines the specific
cross-cultural training needs. This involves conducting a cross-cultural training
needs analysis across three levels: the organizational level, the individual (or expatriate) level, and the assignment level. The organizational-level analysis determines the
organizational context for cross-cultural training. This analysis considers how cross-
cultural training can assist both headquarters and subsidiaries in supporting the
firm's strategy. The individual (or expatriate) level analysis identifies any special
needs that have to be addressed in cross-cultural training for the individuals who are
on the receiving end of the cross-cultural training, the expatriates themselves. This
analysis includes examining the expatriates' prior international experience, his/her
existing levels of cross-cultural competencies, how he/she perceives the issues the
cross-cultural training initiative is designed to address, and the needs of the expatriate's entire family. The assignment-level analysis determines the cross-cultural
competencies required for effective completion of the given assignment. This
includes identifying the important tasks required on the global assignment and the
type of cross-cultural competencies needed to perform those tasks effectively.

*Phase three* involves establishing short-term and long-term goals for determining
cross-cultural training effectiveness. Cross-cultural training goals should be stated in
detailed and measurable terms (Noe, 2001). Short-term goals can bring about cognitive, affective and behavioural changes (Gudykunst *et al.*, 1996). Cognitive goals
focus on helping expatriates understand the role of cultural values on behaviour in
the destination country, in both social and business contexts. Affective goals aim at
helping expatriates effectively manage their attitudes towards the new culture and
successfully handle negative emotions. Behavioural goals help expatriates form adaptive behaviours by emphasizing the cross-cultural skills they require in order to interact successfully with individuals from other cultures. While the short-term goals of
cross-cultural training will vary from assignment to assignment, the long-term
goal of many such training initiatives is to improve the rate of cross-cultural adjustment. This adjustment is important for all expatriates and would generalize across
assignments.

The *fourth phase* develops and delivers the cross-cultural training initiative. This involves determining the specific instructional content needed in order to achieve the stated goal, and the methods to deliver the instructional content and the sequencing of the training sessions. Based on the cross-cultural and intercultural communication research (for example Copeland and Griggs, 1985; Brislin *et al.*, 1986; Harris and Moran, 1991), Harrison suggests that content structure should follow an integrated approach consisting of both general cultural orientation (to understand factors that may influence one's receptiveness to effective cross-cultural interactions and to understand how cultures differ and the impact of these differences on expatriates) and specific cultural orientation (to help expatriates understand more about the specific culture to which they are being assigned).

Gudykunst *et al.* (1996) suggest that the methods to deliver the instructional content can be categorized as:

(1) Didactic culture general;
(2) Didactic culture specific;
(3) Experiential culture general;
(4) Experiential culture specific.

Didactic culture-general methods provide cultural general information to expatriates and include lectures, seminars, reading material, discussions, videotapes and culture-general assimilators. Didactic culture-specific methods, in contrast, present information on a particular culture. Methods used in this category include area studies, videotapes, orientation briefings, case studies, and the like. Experiential culture-general methods help expatriates experience the impact of cultural differences on their behaviours. Methods in this category include immersion programmes or intensive workshops. Experiential culture-specific methods, in contrast, help expatriates experience and learn from interactions with individuals from the host culture. This approach generally includes methods like role-playing, look-see trips, in-country cultural coaching, and language training (Gudykunst *et al.* (1996)).

Lastly, *phase five* evaluates whether the cross-cultural training initiative was effective. Evaluation refers to the systematic process of gathering information necessary to determine the effectiveness of cross-cultural training, generally defined in terms of the benefits expatriates receive from such training and the extent to which they have changed as a result of it. The evaluation process involves establishing measures of effectiveness, and developing research designs to determine what changes (for example cognitive, affective and behavioural) have occurred during the training. Results from the cross-cultural training evaluation should help the organization decide whether such training should be continued in its current form or modified.

# Recent trends in training and development for the global workforce

The expansion of globalization and ever-increasing sophistication in technology have given rise to two recent trends in global training and development: electronic cross-cultural training and global leadership development programmes. Both of these have seen a dramatic increase in usage over the past few years and are discussed in greater detail below.

## Electronic cross-cultural training

Recent advances in technology-based training, particularly CD-ROM, DVD, internet-based training, multimedia and distance learning, have resulted in a vast array of new cross-cultural training methodologies (Greengard, 1999; Mendenhall and Stahl, 2000). One interesting technology-based training innovation is the development of electronic cross-cultural training (e-CCT), that delivers training content via the internet/intranet in a variety of forms such as motion pictures, stills, text and sounds, and allows trainees to interact with the training content.

Compared to traditional cross-cultural training methodologies (for example lecture-based), e-CCT has several advantages: it enables firms to lower costs associated with delivering training content; it allows trainees to individualize and self-manage their learning experience; and it is easier to administer. For these reasons e-CCT is rapidly growing as an effective way of preparing expatriates to live and work in a new culture. Given that e-CCT contains highly specialized training content, many organizations depend on external training vendors to design, develop and deliver the e-CCT programme. Electronic cross-cultural training programmes come in a variety of packages, each with its own benefits and drawbacks, therefore selecting the right e-CCT vendor is very important to the success of the of the CCT programme. Figure 4.3 provides an example of e-CCT, and Box 4.2 a method for evaluating an e-CCT programme.

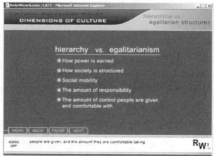

These examples are taken from an e-CCT programme offered by RW3©

*Figure 4.3*  Example e-CCT screenshots

# Box 4.2    Evaluation of e-CCT

With the inception of e-learning many organizations, cross-cultural training programmes are also beginning to be delivered via the internet or through organizations' intranet systems. To evaluate these electronic delivery CCT programmes, one should determine to what extent this system provides a complete programme of CCT, covering everything that would normally be covered in a comprehensive cross-cultural training programme. The content of e-CCT can be evaluated by asking these questions:

- Does the programme have a section explaining what culture is and how it affects daily life? Evaluate how well these are explained.
- Does the programme provide a framework (or model) for understanding culture – including several dimensions of culture? Are they easy to understand and apply to real life?
- Does the programme allow the participant an opportunity to evaluate his or her own cultural values? Is the cultural value assessment a reliable instrument? Ask to see the reliability evidence for the scales measuring the various dimensions (for example alpha coefficients).
- Can the participant's cultural values be evaluated against the host country's cultural values? How were the values applied to the host countries validated (be careful that they were not created by the author's perceptions)? Ask to see a report on the development process and the validation studies.
- Does the programme effectively explain the challenges of culture shock? Evaluate how well this concept is described.
- Does the programme include a self-assessment to help the expatriate consider the challenges for his or her family, career, and personality? As before, check carefully the reliability of the scales used to assess these concepts and validity reports which document the linkage between the dimensions assessed and criteria of expatriate success. (Be careful because there are tools that have been written to 'look' relevant – which have no practical or substantiated worth.)

In addition to the content of the system, several other factors should be considered when evaluating an electronic-delivery cross-cultural training programme. Some other factors to evaluate include:

- Is the programme self-directed? Is the participant able to move in and out of the programme easily? Are the basic materials presented before the more challenging information is offered? Would they need to start over if they exit the programme?
- Can expatriates access this information in real time, while they are on assignment? Are they allowed free access to the site – or do they have limited time or a limited number of accesses to the site?
- Is the system designed to tailor the information for the expatriates as they work through the training programme? For example, does the system remember the country in which the expatriate is living, that she has two children, etc.? The more

*Continued*

tailoring provided by the system, the more receptive the expatriate will be to interacting with the e-CCT system.

- Is the system relatively easy to use? Does it load quickly? Is the system easy to navigate?
- Is the information current? Check the country information – especially with those also offering broader relocation provisions (home searches, schools, etc.).

While e-CCT may be a cost-effective way to deliver training to many expatriates, international HR professionals are advised to select their vendors carefully – not solely on low cost or flashy graphics.

## Global leadership development programmes

Given the need to prepare future global leaders, many transnational organizations have instituted global leadership development programmes. The typical global leadership development programme is designed to give individuals exposure to working in (at least) one host national subsidiary. These programmes typically have a rotational component, where, for the duration of the assignment, the individual will spend between 12 and 24+ months in any given location, before moving to the next location.

The goal of these programmes is to give future leaders international assignments early in their career and expose them to the diversified businesses of the organization. Through them, it is believed that the participants will gain the skills necessary to manage successfully and lead anywhere in the world. The programme spans across a diversified organization's key businesses and participants are moved out of their comfort zones into increasingly challenging assignments. Ultimately, participants are assessed on their ability to achieve results and thus advance to the next level. The typical global leadership development programme is organized into at least three assignments, which range in length from 12 to 24 months and cover on average a 3–6-year time-frame. The assignments enable participants to gain cross-functional, international and cross-sector experience. Senior management closely monitors the performance of the selected participants in the programmes. Based on their evaluation, these participants tend to be highly coached, monitored and mentored for their future roles in the organization. Clearly, this is a tremendous investment of an organization's resources.

Initial research suggests that these programmes are successful, for the most part, in developing global competence in transnational organizations' future global leaders (Caligiuri and DiSanto, 2001). The greatest criticism of such programmes is that they are sometimes utilized in isolation from the greater human resource system. For example, it has been widely established that there are certain relatively immutable characteristics that are found in global leaders (such as openness, cognitive ability, emotional strength). These attributes should certainly be part of the recruitment and selection phase of the overall human resource system. Once properly selected, these characteristics create the *potential* for developing global leadership competencies – or, in other words, affect the ultimate success of a leadership development programme. Global leadership development programmes are clearly an example of how training and development must work within the framework of the broader, more strategic, human resource architecture.

# Conclusion

For many years, international work has been associated with traditional global assignees, relocating from one country to another, with the primary purpose of supervising the operations of a foreign subsidiary, serving as a liaison with headquarters, or providing some special expertise unavailable in the local labour market. Today, however, the landscape for international work is changing. Many people are involved with cross-border work – some without ever leaving their offices. Technological telecommunications improvements have led to a surge in communication across a variety of inter- and intraorganizational units with relative ease (time zones notwithstanding). Many employees work with customers and suppliers on a regular basis who are located in other countries, others are members of international teams and are required to maintain contact with colleagues and collaborators around the world. Frequent-flyers, who regularly travel from one country to another, have been taking the place of many long-term and short-term assignments. Even the nature of the expatriate assignment itself is changing – arrangements such as short-term assignments or commuter assignments are becoming increasingly common across organizations.

As this chapter has hoped to illustrate, vast and exciting changes within today's global business landscape have far-reaching implications for the training and development function. As more and more people at all levels of the organization communicate cross-culturally, the relevance (and, indeed, the necessity) of strategic, and truly global, training and development continues to grow. This function cannot act in isolation; rather, it must be well-integrated into an overall human resource strategy for the organization. Balancing the multiple demands of culture, business strategy, technology – and people – will keep global training and development professionals challenged for many years to come.

Discussion questions

1  Compare and contrast the four types of training and development strategies. Explain why an MNC's training and development strategy will differ depending on the type of global strategy?
2  Describe the 'five-phase' systematic approach to designing cross-cultural training programmes.
3  What are some of the advantages of using e-CCT?

# Further reading

Fowler, S.M. and Mumford, M.G. (1999) *Intercultural Sourcebook: Cross-Cultural Training Methods*, vol. 2. Yarmouth, ME: Intercultural Press.

Landis, D. and Bhagat, R.S. (eds) (1996) *Handbook of Intercultural Training*, 2nd edn. Thousand Oaks, CA: Sage.

Mendenhall, M., Kuhlmann, T. and Stahl, G. (2001) *Developing Global Business Leaders: Policies, Processes, and Innovations*. Westport, CT: Quorum Books.

Mendenhall, M. and Stahl, G. (2000) 'Expatriate Training and Development: Where Do We Go from Here?', *Human Resource Management*, 39: 251–65.

Noble, C. (1997) 'The Management of Training in Multinational Corporations: Comparative Case Studies', *Journal of European Industrial Training*, 21: 102–9.

# References

Adler, N. and Bartholomew, S. (1992) 'Managing Globally Competent People', *Academy of Management Executive*, 6: 52–65.

Adler, N.J. (2002) *International Dimensions of Organisational Behavior*, 4th edn. Cincinnati, OH: South-Western.

Adrian, R.T. (1993) 'Management Training across Cultures: The Challenge for Trainers', *Journal of European Industrial Training*, 17(10).

Aguinis, H. (2002) 'Cross-Cultural Implications for Instructional Design, Delivery, and Evaluation', Paper presented at the Annual Conference of the Society of Industrial and Organisational Psychology, Toronto, Canada.

Baird, L., Briscoe, J.P., Tuden, L.S. and Rosansky, L.M.H. (1994) 'World Class Executive Development', *Human Resource Planning*, 17(1): 1–16.

Bartlett, C.A. and Ghoshal, S. (1989) *Managing Across Borders: The Transnational Solution*. Boston, MA: Harvard Business School Press.

Black, J.S. and Gregersen, H.B. (1991) 'Antecedents to Cross-Cultural Adjustment for Expatriates in Pacific Rim Assignments', *Human Relations*, 44: 497–516.

Black, J.S., Gregersen, H.B. and Mendenhall, M.E. (1992) *Global Assignments: Successfully Expatriating and Repatriating International Managers*, 1st edn. San Francisco: Jossey-Bass.

Black, J.S. and Mendenhall, M. (1990) 'Cross-Cultural Training Effectiveness: A Review and a Theoretical Framework for Future Research', *Academy of Management Review*, 15: 113–36.

Black, J.S., Mendenhall, M. and Oddou, G. (1991) 'Toward a Comprehensive Model of International Adjustment: An Integration of Multiple Theoretical Perspectives', *Academy of Management Review*, 16: 291–317.

Brewster, C. (1995) 'Effective Expatriate Training', in J. Selmer (ed.), *Expatriate Management: New Ideas for International Business*. Westport, CT: Quorum Books.

Brislin, R.W., Cushner, K., Cherrie, C. and Yong, M. (1986) *Intercultural Interaction: A Practical Guide*. Beverly Hills, CA: Sage Publications.

Caligiuri, P.M. (2005) 'Performance Measurement in a Cross-national Context: Evaluating the Success of Global Assignments', invited book chapter for W. Bennett, D. Woehr and C. Lance (eds), *Performance Measurement: Current Perspectives and Future Challenges*. Mahwah, NJ: Lawrence Erlbaum Associates, Inc.

Caligiuri, P. and Di Santo, V. (2001) 'Global Competence: What Is It, and Can It Be Developed through Global Assignments?', *Human Resource Planning*, 24(3): 27–35.

Caligiuri, P., Phillips, J., Lazarova, M., Tarique, I. and Burgi, P. (2001) 'The Theory of Met Expectations Applied to Expatriate Adjustment: The Role of Cross-cultural Training', *International Journal of Human Resource Management*, 12: 357–72.

Caligiuri, P.M. and Stroh, L.K. (1995) 'Multinational Corporation Management Strategies and International Human Resource Practices: Bringing IHRM to the Bottom Line', *International Journal of Human Resource Management*, 6: 495–507.

Charles, M. and Marschan-Piekkari, R. (2002) 'Language Training for Enhanced Horizontal Communication: A Challenge for MNCs', *Business Communication Quarterly*, 65(2): 9–29.

Conference Board (H. Dennis and H. Axel) (1991) *Encouraging Employee Self-Management in Financial and Career Planning*. New York, NY: Conference Board.

Copeland, L. and Griggs, L. (1985) *Going International: How to Make Friends and Deal Effectively in the Global Marketplace*, 1st edn. New York: Random House.

Cox, T.H., Jr (1993) *Cultural Diversity in Organisations: Theory, Research and Practice*. San Francisco: Berrett-Koehler Publishers.

Dowling, P., Welch, D.E. and Schuler, R.S. (1999) *International Human Resource Management: Managing People in a Multinational Context*, 3rd edn. Cincinnati, OH: South-Western College Publishing.

Earley, P.C. (1987) 'Intercultural Training for Managers: A Comparison of Documentary and Interpersonal Methods', *Academy of Management Journal*, 30: 685–98.

Evans, P., Pucik, V. and Barsoux, J.-L. (2002) *The Global Challenge: Frameworks for International Human Resource Management* Boston, MA: McGraw-Hill.

Ferdman, B.M. and Brody, S.E. (1996) 'Models of Diversity Training', in D. Landis and R. S. Bhagat (eds), *Handbook of Intercultural Training*, 2nd edn. Thousand Oaks, CA: Sage Publications, 282–303.

Francis, J.L. (1995) 'Training across Cultures', *Human Resource Development Quarterly* 6(1): 101–8.

Ghoshal, S. and Nohria, N. (1993) 'Horses for Courses: Organisational Forms for Multinational Corporations', *Sloan Management Review*, 34(2): 23–36.

Greengard, S. (1999) 'Technology Is Changing Expatriate Training', *Workforce*, 78(12): 106–8.

Gudykunst, W.B., Guzley, R.M. and Hammer, M.R. (1996) 'Designing Intercultural Training', in D. Landis and R.S. Bhagat (eds), *Handbook of Intercultural Training*, 2nd edn. Thousand Oaks, CA: Sage Publications, 61–80.

Gupta, A.K. and Govindarajan, V. (2002) 'Cultivating a Global Mindset', *Academy of Management Executive*, 16: 116–26.

Gutteridge, T.G., Leibowitz, Z.B. and Shore, J.E. (1993) *Organisational Career Development: Benchmarks for Building a World-Class Workforce*, 1st edn. San Francisco: Jossey-Bass.

Hall, D.T. (1976) *Careers in Organisations*. Pacific Palisades, CA.: Goodyear Pub. Co.

Hall, D.T. (ed.) (1996) *The Career Is Dead—Long Live the Career: A Relational Approach to Careers*, 1st edn. San Francisco: Jossey-Bass Publishers.

Harris, P.R. and Moran, R.T. (1991) *Managing Cultural Differences*, 3rd edn. Houston, TX: Gulf Pub. Co.

Katz, J.P. and Seifer, D.M. (1996) 'It's a Different World Out There: Planning for Expatriate Success Through Selection, Pre-Departure Training and On-Site Socialization', *Human Resource Planning*, 19(2): 32–45.

Kealey, D.J. and Protheroe, D.R. (1996) 'The Effectiveness of Cross-Cultural Training for Expatriates: An Assessment of the Literature on the Issue', *International Journal of Intercultural Relations*, 20: 141–65.

Kedia, B.L. and Mukherji, A. (1999) 'Global Managers: Developing a Mindset for Global Competitiveness', *Journal of World Business*, 34: 230–51.

Kobrin, S.J. (1988) 'Expatriate Reduction and Strategic Control in American Multinational Corporations', *Human Resource Management*, 27: 63–75.

Marschan-Piekkari, R., Welch, D. and Welch, L. (1999) 'Adopting a Common Corporate Language: IHRM Implications', *International Journal of Human Resource Management*, 10: 377–90.

Mendenhall, M.E. and Stahl, G.K. (2000) 'Expatriate Training and Development: Where Do We Go from Here?', *Human Resource Management*, 39(2): 251–65.

Noe, R.A. (2001) *Employee Training and Development*, 2nd edn. Boston: McGraw-Hill/Irwin.

Prahalad, C.K. and Doz, Y.L. (1987) *The Multinational Mission: Balancing Local Demands and Global Vision*. New York: Free Press.

Tarique, I. (2002) 'Cross-Cultural Implications for Instructional Design, Delivery, and Evaluation'. Panel discussion at the Annual Conference of the Society of Industrial and Organisational Psychology. Canada: Toronto.

Tarique, I. and Caligiuri, P. (2004) 'Training and Development of International Staff', in A.W. Harzing (ed.) *International Human Resource Management*. Thousand Oaks, CA: Sage.

Thornhill, A.R. (1993) 'Management Training Across Cultures: The Challenge for Trainers', *Journal of European Industrial Training*, 17: 43–52.

Tung, R. (1981) 'Selecting and Training of Personnel for Overseas Assignments', *Columbia Journal of World Business*, 16: 68–78.

Tung, R. (1982) 'Selection and Training Procedures of US, European, and Japanese Multinationals', *California International Review*, 25: 57–71.

Windham International, and NFTC (1998) *Global Relocation Trends 1998 Survey Report*. New York: Windham International.

# 5

# Expatriate performance management in MNCs

*Marja Tahvanainen and Vesa Suutari*

## Introduction

### Strategic importance of performance management

To perform successfully in today's business environment, companies need to have a well-formulated company strategy directed towards creating and sustaining competitive advantage. Even more importantly, they need to have employees possessing the potential, the capabilities and the motivation to execute organizational strategies efficiently and effectively – and they need to be able to manage the employees effectively. Very often the major focus in the strategy process has been on strategy formulation, with less thought given to the implementation phase. This has resulted in the failure of strategic planning at the operational level, where personnel policies and practices play a central role in ensuring that the employees' work makes strategies materialize (Torraco and Swanson, 1995).

A firm should consider the human resource (HR) implications of its international strategies and recognize that people are a critical component of the implementation of such strategies (Dowling *et al.,* 1999). The situation has been stated to be very challenging for international HR specialists since the process of increasing commitment with international activities brings the HR function closer to the strategic core of the business and also changes the scope and content of human resource management (HRM) (Pucik, 1992). For example, in the globalization phase, a global human resource strategy that will put the right, competent people in the right place at the right time doing the right things needs to be developed in line with the global business strategy (Brake, 1997). According to Black and Ulrich (1999), the role of the HR professional in delivering global strategy is to (1) raise, define and clarify the capabilities required to win globally; and (2) invest, design and deliver HR practices that ensure these capabilities. Given the critical role of a company's global talent asset base, the role of HR must become more proactive and strategic – HR must become a fully integrated global business partner (Brake, 1999).

In this context, performance management (PM) is one of key HR processes. PM is a strategic HRM process which can help companies to bring strategy to individual employees, and turn employees' potential into the desired results (Delery and Doty, 1996). This process is becoming more central due to the increasing global integration needs in MNCs; that is, global integration is becoming a competitive necessity in a number of markets in which decentralized strategies were dominant in the past (Evans *et al.*, 2002). In order to succeed in such global integration, supporting global HR systems such as PM systems needs to be developed.

Although there are many variations of PM processes, they usually highlight the importance of strong goal-setting and appraisal as part of the overall system. Other elements of, or processes closely related to, a PM process can be for example training and development, and performance-related pay (Williams, 1991; Sparrow and Hiltrop, 1994). Thus, performance management can be viewed as an umbrella term that includes various elements.

In well-functioning PM processes, the elements are ultimately derived from the organizational goals and strategies. When operated successfully, PM will give the means for evaluating and continuously improving both individual and company performance against predefined business goals. It can also assist in other organizational processes which are important for a company's long-term success, such as organizational learning, change management, competence development and succession management. Thus, good performance management provides a company with a basis for managing the business of today and for developing it into the future – through the performance of its people (Williams, 1991). This productivity through people can, in fact, be one of a company's core competitive advantages, as the success that comes from managing people effectively is often not visible or is transparent as regards its source (Pucik, 1992; Pfeffer, 1995; Gratton, 1997). It has even been stated that if implemented appropriately, performance management is an area of HRM which has the potential to make the most significant contribution to organizational effectiveness and growth (Redman and Snape, 1992; Sparrow and Hiltrop, 1994).

## The scope of performance management in MNCs

The scope of performance management in MNCs is much broader and more complicated than PM in domestic companies, where primarily local employees are managed within the local political, legal and cultural environment. By definition, MNCs operate in many nations and face several different environments. Also, various types of employee groups are involved: locally operating local employees (for example Germans in a company unit in Germany), locally operating foreign employees (for example French who live and work permanently in Germany), expatriate employees (for example those who have been sent from a company's French unit to work in a German unit), and also those employees who are on some form of non-standard international assignment (for example virtual or short-term assignees, rotators, contractors).

In MNCs, decisions have to be made as to how to implement PM in different company units. For example, should all the units follow the same PM system or can the decision about the system be made locally? This question is connected to the strategic HRM approach which the company decides to follow; that is, single HR systems such as PM should be looked at from the strategic HRM perspective. Here the company has two basic approaches: standardization (that is standardization of all the major HRM practices internationally) and localization (the use of locally developed HRM practices). This decision is in turn connected to the total business strategy; that is, HR activities must support the business aims.

For example, the global strategy approach implies a focus on similarities, standardization, homogenization, concentration and coordination on a worldwide basis (Svensson, 2001). This kind of global strategy approach and globalization of business activities may lead to a substantial competitive advantage in the marketplace (Keegan and Green, 2000). According to Segal-Horn (1996), few companies still lend themselves to 'naive' global strategies, since all strategies require some degree of adaptation to regional and national conditions. Thus there has to be a balance and harmony between standardization versus adaptation, and homogenization versus tailoring, of business activities (Svensson, 2001). In line with this, Black and Ulrich (1999) state that the first critical capability that enables firms to integrate global activities appropriately and also to separate and adapt local activities effectively, is being able to determine what belongs to the core of the organization and what does not. Issues that belong to the core of a business generally relate to principles that give the firm its identity and issues which are important to customers. This core should be integrated and standardized throughout worldwide operations. In this kind of framework, the HR specialists must frame their HR strategies; here concerning the extent to which it is necessary and useful to standardize the PM practices internationally, and the ways of making it happen internationally. The global strategies will not become reality without supporting global HRM strategies and practices.

As stated at the beginning of this chapter, there are various kinds of focus groups when discussing performance management in an international context. In the following sections, the focus will be on one of these groups: on performance management of expatriates (that is on people who are on international assignment in foreign affiliates). This focus has been taken since expatriates are critical to MNCs' strategy formulation and implementation (see for example Evans et al., 2002), and thus it is particularly relevant to be able to manage their performance effectively. However, determining what represents effective performance management in the case of expatriates is not necessarily simple. In the case of expatriates, the context becomes more complicated in ways which can affect PM practices. For example, as expatriates' supervisors may be located in different countries than expatriates, the following types of questions arise: From what source(s) does the expatriate get to know what is expected of him or her? What types of performance goals are appropriate to his or her situation? How is the evaluation done? How to provide sufficient and appropriate training and development for expatriates – especially for those working in project-type assignments? How to meet the request for fairness in performance-related pay?

In the following sections, the different elements of expatriate PM are discussed. At the same time some empirical evidence on expatriate PM practices is presented on the basis of existing studies (Gregersen *et al.*, 1996; Tahvanainen, 1998; Suutari and Tahvanainen, 2002). The study by Gregersen *et al.* (1996) was carried out among 58 US multinationals, a study by Suutari and Tahvanainen (2002) among 301 Finnish expatriates, while the research by Tahvanainen (1998) consisted of a survey of 99 Finnish companies and an in-depth case study of one large Finnish MNC. The chapter will thus draw heavily on our own empirical work done in Finland. Further, we will discuss factors influencing the existence and the form of performance management practices; that is, the contextual factors of expatriate performance management. Lastly, a list of key criteria for effective PM is presented.

## Expatriate performance management practices

### Goal-setting

There are various routes through which performance expectations can be communicated to employees. One traditional route is a job description; another important channel is daily management. In addition, the employees themselves can set goals for their performance. A further route is goal-setting that takes place as part of a performance management process, and that is the primary focus here.

Many companies use the acronym SMART to help set good, effective goals (see for example Armstrong and Baron, 1998). The acronym SMART indicates that goals should be Specific, Measurable, Agreed, Realistic, and Time-related. Both laboratory and field research have repeatedly shown that the setting of specific goals dramatically improves employee performance. Specific performance goals are typically 'hard', that is objective, quantitative and directly measurable. They are, for example, profits, market share, return on investment, units produced, and turnover. Data on the achievement of hard goals are the easiest to collect and seemingly the easiest to interpret. Also, increasing goal specificity results in clear expectations and reduces the probability of misunderstandings between managers and subordinates (Locke and Latham, 1984). However, hard performance goals do have their drawbacks. They tend, for example, to be available for only a limited number of jobs (Ghorpade and Chen, 1995); and they are obtainable only when the employee produces a distinguishable output (Latham and Wexley, 1982). Furthermore, traditional quantitative goal-setting for managerial jobs has been said to be counterproductive because it focuses on short-term, seemingly effective outcomes.

Given the difficulties connected with the use of hard goals, they must be tempered with 'soft', or alternatively 'qualitative' goals for a more accurate evaluation of employee performance (Gregersen *et al.*, 1996). Soft performance goals consist of behaviours including character traits such as initiative, cooperation, loyalty and attitude; specific abilities and skills, degree of effort (Locke and Latham, 1984; Tziner, 1990); and impression-based ratings by supervisors and others (Jacobs, 1986). Using soft goals also has its disadvantages. They are subject to potential biases and inaccuracies, and data on soft goals are also much more difficult to collect and interpret than data on hard goals (Gregersen *et al.*, 1996).

With both types of goal there is also a question of whether such goals should be at the individual level or the team level. Prior literature on goal-setting (for example Locke and Latham, 1984; O'Leary-Kelly *et al.*, 1994) suggests that when a company is group-based, and employees' tasks are interdependent, the use of team-level performance goals would be appropriate.

With regard to empirical findings on goal-setting among expatriates it has been reported that among US MNCs various types of goals are typically (69% of companies) used, including hard criteria (35%), soft criteria (44%) and contextual criteria (11%) (Gregersen *et al.*, 1996). This practice is also commonly recommended (Gregersen *et al.*, 1996). In a survey among Finnish expatriates it appeared that the quantitative goals were most common (57%), but qualitative goals were also quite frequent (46%). Personal goals were slightly more common (46%) than team goals (40%) (Suutari and Tahvanainen, 2002).

*Who sets the goals?*
Literature on domestic performance management typically assumes that, in most cases, agreeing about performance goals is a joint effort between individuals and their physically close first-level manager. When talking about goal-setting in the case of expatriates, the situation is more complicated. Expatriates perform their job in a foreign location, and as a result of this, in terms of performance management they can be closely related to the home unit, and/or to the host unit, and/or even to some other, third-country company unit. The primary manager with whom they agree on their goals can consequently be located in any of these countries.

In a survey among Finnish expatriates it appeared that the most typical participant in the goal-setting process was the supervisor in the host country (66%). In slightly less than half of the cases, the expatriate himself/herself (49%) and the supervisor in the home country (41%) also participated in the official goal-setting. Other participants were not common (5%) (Suutari and Tahvanainen, 2002).

*Frequency of goal-setting*

Regarding the frequency of goal-setting, domestic literature reports that goals are typically set in supervisor–subordinate discussions. These discussions are held either (1) in connection with standard review cycles, for example every 12 months, or (2) at 'natural' (and often more frequent) points, such as the beginning of a project.

Research on Finnish expatriates showed that in over half of the cases (56%) the goals were set once a year (Suutari and Tahvanainen, 2002). In every fifth case (20%) the frequency was twice a year. Sometimes the goal-setting took place once at the beginning of the assignment (13%) and also other points of time were almost as common (11%). Further specifications of this 'other, what' item included comments such as monthly, once for every project, and irregularly.

## Performance evaluation

No matter how effectively goals are set for employee performance, goal-setting alone is not enough to ensure successful performance management systems. In addition, the employee's performance has to be evaluated against the goals set and the feedback given to him or her. This is the purpose of another core element of performance management processes: performance evaluation.

*Performance evaluators*

Research on domestic performance management shows that the most popular practice is for employees to be appraised solely by their immediate supervisor. There are, however, alternatives. Employees can evaluate themselves, which is referred to as self-evaluation (Armstrong and Baron, 1998). Also, the employee's peers are potential evaluators. The theoretical argument in favour of peer evaluation is that because peers often work in close proximity, they have ample opportunity to observe each other's behaviour. This is particularly useful when teamwork and participation are key aspects of the employee's performance (Sparrow and Hiltrop, 1994). Furthermore, outside evaluators, such as those representing upper management, internal customers or external customers, can act as evaluators. However, in order for them to be able to make appropriate evaluations, it is required that outside evaluators base their evaluations on direct observations of the employee in the work situation.

Lastly, a 360-degree feedback system can be used, whereby feedback about a target individual is typically solicited from the multiple sources reviewed above. According to Tornow (1993), the increasing popularity of 360-degree feedback stems from a belief in its having in-built characteristics for avoiding rater bias by providing more than one perspective. Furthermore, that many employees favour more than one rater. In the cross-cultural environment, in particular, the use of a team of performance raters is essential (Gregersen *et al.* 1996). However, broadening the base of evaluations does not automatically bring about better evaluations (Ghorpade and Chen, 1995). For example, using multiple raters raises the issue of disagreement: raters will have different perspectives when observing the performance of the individual, as they see different aspects of an employee's performance (Latham and Wexley, 1982). Or, peers may want to make themselves look good at their colleague's expense; a subordinate may hold a grudge for failing to get a disputed pay raise; or other managers may not like this employee's manager (Locke and Latham, 1984).

Research highlights that those selected to provide the evaluation information must be properly qualified to do so. The key criteria for qualifying as an evaluator include the following: (1) he or she has to be aware of the goals of the employee's job (Latham and Wexley, 1982); (2) he or she must have 'task acquaintance'; the amount and type of work contact of the evaluator with the person being evaluated is important (Murphy and Cleveland, 1991); (3) they must be capable of determining whether the observed performance is satisfactory (Latham and Wexley, 1982); (4) they should be persons whose opinions are valued by the individual and the organization (Tornow, 1993); and (5) anyone who conducts evaluations should be thoroughly trained with regard to recording accurately what is seen, and reporting what is seen to the target employee's manager who conducts the evaluation discussion with the employee, or to the employee him- or herself (Latham and Wexley, 1982).

With regard to empirical evidence on existing goal-setting practices among expatriates, Gregersen et al. (1996) have reported that the expatriate's immediate supervisor is the most common expatriate rater (either from the host country, 74%, or the home country, 39%); the expatriate as self-rater is the next most common rater. The companies studied rarely reported using peers, sponsors, subordinates or customers, but they did use either home or host-country HR professionals (12% and 17% respectively). Suutari and Tahvanainen (2002) have reported that in the clear majority of expatriate cases (69%) the performance of expatriates was officially evaluated. Typically (81%), the evaluation was made by comparing the performance of the expatriate with the previously set goals. The most typical performance evaluator was a supervisor in the host country (54%), and in about every third case the supervisor in the home country (35%) and/or the expatriate himself/herself (33%) participated in the performance evaluation. Less frequent were cases in which a supervisor from another country participated (11%), and/or in which there were other participants such as the board of the company, colleagues or customers (7%).

*Frequency of formal evaluation*
It is generally accepted that doing appraisals (evaluations) frequently and giving frequent feedback on performance are essential if improvement in performance is to be hoped for, or if the aim is to sustain a high level of performance. Also, empirical evidence shows that employees prefer frequent appraisals to those that take place seldom and at standard points (Bernandin, 1986). Currently, however, companies commonly appraise their employees once a year (Mathis and Jackson, 1988; Meyer, 1991). Similar findings were reported in the international literature reviewed.

The findings of the survey by Gregersen *et al.* (1996) showed that the majority of the expatriate performance appraisals (82%) are conducted annually, while 9 per cent are conducted at three- or six-month intervals. In line with the goal-setting frequencies among Finnish expatriates reported earlier, the most common (53%) frequency of performance evaluation was once a year. In about every fifth case (21%) the evaluation took place twice a year. Evaluation at the end of the assignment was less common (8%), but on the other hand about every fifth expatriate (18%) reported that the frequency deviated from the specified options. In such cases the evaluations were made, for example, monthly, four times a year or after every project.

## Training and development

The connection between goal-setting, performance evaluation and development needs of individuals is an additional important feature of a full PM system. Typically, goal-setting and PM literature assign three important reasons for employee training and development (T&D). Training and development are necessary when: (1) it is recognized in connection with goal-setting that an employee needs additional capabilities, achievable by training, in order to achieve the goals; (2) it is noticed in the performance evaluation that an employee did not meet the performance goals because of insufficient capability; (3) there are possibilities for improving the employee for future opportunities and challenges. Ideally, on the basis of the recognized lack of skills and abilities, as well as future plans, individual T&D goals are agreed on and documented in the superior–subordinate discussion. Given this, it is easy to understand why T&D has been said to be the primary process through which individual and organizational growth over time can achieve its full potential (Sparrow and Hiltrop, 1994), especially if employees' T&D needs are identified systematically, against present and future challenges, as they are in effective PM systems.

*Training and development for expatriate employees*
The attention given to training and preparation of expatriates is often linked to research into international adjustment (Harris and Brewster, 1999), and on that basis different types of predeparture preparation and training activities are suggested in the literature. Among the most-used training practices are language training, predeparture visits to the host country, informal briefings, job-related training and cross-cultural training (Björkman and Gertsen, 1993; Marx, 1996; Suutari and Brewster, 2001). Several models have been developed to aid in selecting appropriate training methods for expatriates in different situations (Mendenhall *et al.*, 1987; Black and Mendenhall, 1990; Baumgarten, 1995; Harris and Brewster, 1999).

It has also been pointed out that while T&D usually takes place before the assignment begins, it should also continue during the stay abroad (Björkman and Gertsen, 1993; Schell and Solomon, 1997; Mendenhall and Stahl, 2000; Suutari and Burch, 2001). It can be argued that the home units or headquarters cannot have as good understanding of the local environment, culture and organization as the locals have (Suutari and Burch, 2001), and thus a close involvement of the host unit in expatriate training and support is necessary. Similarly, the home unit should provide adequate support for expatriates while they are abroad and stay in contact with them.

More recently, the importance of training and support during the repatriation process has been stressed. Typically repatriation expectations have been found to be too optimistic and repatriates face more problems than they expect (Forster, 1994; Stroh *et al.*, 1998). According to the literature, for example, many expatriates experience a lack of clarity about their job situation after repatriation: they find themselves in a 'holding pattern' with no serious job to do, or in a new position with clearly less authority than they had whilst abroad (for a more detailed discussion, see for example Suutari and Brewster, 2003). Thus, it has been suggested that companies should develop better repatriation support practices which include predeparture career discussions, and repatriation job-planning, including longer-term career planning support. In addition, the literature is full of advice about the value of certain practices in the repatriation phase: a named contact person in the home country, re-entry counselling and family repatriation programmes, employee debriefings and succession planning (Gregersen and Black, 1995; Gregersen *et al.*, 1998; Handler and Lane, 1997; Harvey, 1989; Napier and Peterson, 1991; Reynolds and Bennett, 1991; Riusala and Suutari, 2000). Such practices could support the expatriates and their families in the repatriation process and help them to develop a more realistic picture of their repatriation (Stroh *et al.*, 1998; Suutari and Brewster, 2003). Such practices are seen as necessary by the expatriates themselves (Riusala and Suutari, 2000), as well as by company HRM representatives (Handler and Lane, 1997).

All in all, the PM process can provide frequent information about the T&D needs of expatriates – over and above needs related to cultural training – and help the organization to support and train the expatriates adequately. There is fairly little evidence, however, on how well the existing PM systems succeed in this task. It seems that depending on the type of expatriate – whether a middle manager or top manager, for example – T&D is involved in PM somewhat differently, and expatriates' satisfaction with it varies.

## Performance-related pay

Performance-related pay (PRP) is a term used to cover a variety of reward arrangements, for example a bonus or an incentive system. It has been said that unless the achievement of performance goals is linked to significant outcomes for both the manager and the employee, there is no guarantee of performance improvement. On the other hand, if it is linked, the linkage can motivate the employee to work hard to achieve the goals, and the manager to facilitate the employee in his or her attempts (Saul, 1992; Dowling and Richardson, 1997). Along with intrinsic rewards (that is rewards that the individual receives from doing the job: achievement, pride, autonomy, personal growth and development, and so on), extrinsic rewards, especially performance-related pay, can play an important role in this respect. Performance-related pay has been said to be one of an organization's most powerful reward components (Szilagyi, 1998). Thus it is not surprising that in much of the prior PM literature it is regarded as one of the key elements in effective processes.

The literature identifies several conditions for PRP effectiveness. First, as applies to all reward systems, employees need to value the extra money they will make under the plan in order for any positive efforts to result. Connected with this, the amount of money must be seen by the workers as worthy of their efforts. Further, for a PRP scheme to be effective it must be possible to measure goal achievement accurately. If employees see that a PM system does not do so, pay arrangements that depend on the system will probably not be regarded as fair (McKenna and Beech, 1995; Dowling and Richardson, 1997). Next, for the employee to perform optimally, a PRP scheme needs to be planned so that it rewards an individual on all critical functions of the job, not only on some easily measurable functions. A further condition for PRP effectiveness is that the employee must perceive that money is tied to performance; that is, the PRP scheme must be easy to understand. Also, to motivate employees to improve their performance continuously or to keep it at a high level, employees must be able to control their performance. Another aspect of this issue is employee ability: employees cannot increase their performance if they do not have the requisite aptitude or knowledge. Lastly, a requirement presented for PRP effectiveness is that the money must be given soon after the desired behaviour and/or outcome has taken place (Latham and Wexley, 1982; Cascio, 2003).

## Expatriates' performance and PRP

Expatriate compensation (salary, benefits, allowances) is a topic about which much has been written in the expatriation literature. Many of the writings deal with designing effective compensation packages for expatriates, and as part of that discussion it is often mentioned that incentive bonuses can be part of an expatriate's salary (Reynolds, 1988; Harvey, 1996). There is often much discussion in the literature as to what currency it is beneficial to pay bonuses to expatriates in, so that in terms of tax efficiency the outcome is as good for the expatriate, and the company, as possible (Dowling et al., 1999). On the other hand, the literature describing how, at the practical level, bonuses or any other type of PRP are determined on the basis of performance, is very scarce.

The use of performance-based bonuses appears to be a fairly common practice, at least in a Finnish context; in a survey among Finnish expatriates it appeared that 37 per cent of them received performance-based bonuses (Suutari and Tornikoski, 2001). When the levels of satisfaction with compensation practices were analysed, it appeared that there were many expatriates who felt that their salary should depend more on the results which they achieve and thus called for performance-related bonuses. In a case study by Tahvanainen (1998) it appeared that except for project expatriates, almost all the other type of expatriates' performance was linked to performance-related pay (PRP) through incentive objectives.

The results indicated that only very few expatriates were fully satisfied with their incentive or bonus system (Tahvanainen, 1998), and perhaps that was the reason why most of those interviewed did not perceive PRP as a great performance motivator. Similar findings have been reported in the prior literature on PRP (Saul, 1992; Marsden and Richardson, 1994; Dowling and Richardson, 1997). Several of the PRP pitfalls suggested in the prior literature (Locke and Latham, 1984; McKenna and Beech, 1995; Dowling and Richardson, 1997) came up as reasons for PRP's inadequacy: not everyone valued the extra money that it was possible to make through the system; a few interviewees complained that the way of measuring achievement of the incentive objectives was invalid; some brought up their concern that incentive objectives were not set for the right job functions; the relationship between the PM goals and the incentive objectives was not always clear; and further, a typical reason for customer project expatriates' dissatisfaction was that, often, the incentive or bonus was paid to the employee months after the foreign assignment had ended.

## Contextual factors of expatriate PM

Like management processes in general, performance management is also likely to get its specific form depending on the context where it is used. Therefore, in addition to knowing what practices companies use in managing expatriate performance, it is necessary to know what factors influence the existence and the form of such practices; that is, what are the contextual factors of expatriate performance management and how do they influence the PM process. Our studies (Tahvanainen, 1998; Suutari and Tahvanainen, 2002) have identified the following contextual factors: (1) company size, (2) a company's level of internationalization, (3) the position of the expatriate in the organizational hierarchy, (4) task type, (5) organizational structure, and (6) host unit location.

### Company size

In line with general management literature (for example Mintzberg, 1989) which suggests that there is a linkage between the *size of a company* and the adoption of formal management processes, there is a linkage between the size of a company and expatriate PM (Tahvanainen, 1998; Suutari and Tahvanainen, 2002). Bigger companies typically have more formal PM practices. In line with this, the findings among Finnish expatriates indicated that PM practices in bigger companies had several characteristics in comparison with smaller companies: performance goals were more typically in a written form, the level of performance was more commonly officially evaluated, and official evaluation frequencies (yearly and half-yearly evaluations) were more frequently used. In addition, in bigger companies supervisors in the host company participated more commonly in the PM process and team-level goals were more typical. Box 5.1 illustrates the development of PM practices along with increasing company size through a company example.

## A company's level of internationalization

The level of internationalization of a company has a significant influence on expatriate performance management practices, as can be seen from the following examples. When the expatriate has 'other supervisors' in addition to the first-hand supervisor directing their work, such supervisors of less international companies are more commonly in the home country, while highly international companies have such supervisors more often located in some other country than the home or the host country. Also, in highly international companies it is common for expatriates to have performance goals in a written form and their evaluation is made in comparison with previously set performance goals. Furthermore, it is more usual in such companies that a supervisor from the host country participates in PM.

---

### Box 5.1    Effects of company size on PM

Company size has several effects on PM, as has been explained in the text. The following transcript from an interviewee with a Sales Director summarizes many of them. It illustrates the evolution of PM in line with the increasing company size:

> In the beginning, when there were not even a handful of employees in this company unit, no formal PM was carried out. Not even then, when we [the employees] were about ten in total. We still worked as if we had been a big team and actually, there was not really a need for any official performance management. We talked through all issues until they were clear to everyone. Gradually, we started to follow the company's global PM system but to be honest, for years we did so just to make the HR happy. Once the number of employees had grown to be substantially larger – we are already 150 or so – and we had learnt how to make good use of PM, our attitude towards [formal] PM changed. Now it's seen by most of the staff as serving important purposes such as communicating and aligning performance goals, motivating employees, and, in a way, improving the working climate. The whole process is implemented much more properly than earlier. Performance goals are set, and performance during the past performance period is evaluated regularly. Performance-related training and development, as well as payment, are considered as well.

---

## Position of the expatriate in the organizational hierarchy and task type

In the case of employees working nationally, the literature reports an established linkage between the nature of the job (referring to the type of job and its organizational level) and employee performance management (Hendry et al., 1997; Dowling et al., 1999). The consequences of the linkage have been found to be reflected in all elements of performance management, also in the case of expatriates. The *position of the expatriate in the organizational hierarchy* is a significant contextual variable. For example, written performance management goals are more common in all management positions, and in particular at top management and management levels, than in other positions. Host-country supervisors naturally participate less typically in the PM process at the top management level (and at management level) than in lower level positions. Quantitative goals are most frequent in top management positions and least common in expert and clerk positions, while no differences have been identified with regard to qualitative and team goals.

Effects that the *task type* can have on expatriate PM can be seen in several areas. For example, among those in general management positions there were several typical PM process characteristics which differentiated them from others: supervisors were more often in some other country than in the home or host country, host-country managers were not so typically involved in PM processes, and both quantitative and qualitative goals were more typically used in the process. To take another example: in technical functions supervisors were typically located in the host and home countries, official goals were not so commonly defined, and thus neither qualitative nor quantitative goals existed so commonly. Table 5.1 shows the key characteristics of PM in the case of different types of expatriates. In the table, expatriates are divided into five categories: (1) top managers, (2) middle managers, (3) business establishers, (4) project employees, and (5) R&D project personnel. It was common to PM in all the groups that employees needed to know what was expected of them, they needed to know how well they were performing; and they needed to have the opportunity to develop their competencies, to meet the requirements of present and future job assignments. Some differences in PM among the groups were clear, however, in terms of whether, and how generally, performance goals were set formally, who sets them, and of what type the goals are; how generally expatriates' performance is evaluated formally; who conducts the evaluation; whether training and development plans are agreed on with expatriates, and whether they have a possibility of attending training while on the assignment; and, lastly, how clear a linkage there is, and of what type, between personal performance and pay.

## Organizational structure

In the vast bulk of the literature it has been implicitly assumed that performance management occurs in a line organization where every employee has one definite

**Table 5.1** Summary of the key performance management characteristics in five types of expatriate groups

| | Top manager | Middle manager | Business establisher | Customer project | R&D project |
|---|---|---|---|---|---|
| Goal setting | • to a great extent self-developed goals that are agreed with manager(s) located in another country (at the HQ or area HQ) <br>• emphasis on clear, financial goals | • the manager in a host location sets the goals, yet many expatriates also have a manager at HQ <br>• goals vary from fairly specific to very specific | • goals are agreed with the primary manager, located either in the host or the home 'country <br>• relatively few, broad goals | • no formal, work-related goal setting | • the manager in the host location sets the goals <br>• goals vary from vague to specific |
| Performance evaluation | • by the manager(s) located in another country | • when actually done, performed by a manager in the host location <br>• satisfactory amount of ongoing performance feedback for most | • by the primary manager(s) <br>• satisfactory amount of ongoing performance feedback for some | • formal evaluation rather nonexistent; if it happens, it is done by a host country manager <br>• insufficient amount of ongoing feedback | • by a manager in the host location <br>• satisfactory amount of ongoing performance feedback |
| Training and development | • expectation that the expatriate raises the issue | • discussed and agreed with the host location manager <br>• expatriates engaged in training while on assignment | • discussed and agreed with the primary manager <br>• expatriates had no time to engage in training while on assignment | • discussed and agreed with an administrative manager in the home country <br>• expatriates had no time to engage in training while on assignment | • discussed and agreed with a host country manager <br>• expatriates had no time to engage in training while on assignment |
| Performance-related-pay | • clear linkage between performance and incentives | • all worked under an incentive scheme, yet the linkage between performance and pay was often unclear | • most worked under an incentive scheme, yet the linkage between performance and pay was often unclear | • entitled to yearly bonuses that were not linked strictly to individual performance | • some expatriates entitled to bonuses that were often only partly linked only in part to individual performance |

manager (see for example Locke and Latham, 1984; Murphy and Cleveland, 1991; Williams, 1991; Sparrow and Hiltrop, 1994). In the IHRM literature it is recognized that expatriate employees can have two supervisors, one in the host country and another in the home country, and these supervisors often expect partly different outcomes and/or behaviours from the expatriate (Mendenhall and Oddou, 1991; Black *et al.*, 1992; Gregersen *et al.*, 1996). However, this again implies a more traditional line relationship.

Our studies (Tahvanainen, 1998; Suutari and Tahvanainen, 2002) have identified and supported the linkage between organizational structure, whether matrix, line or project organization, and expatriate performance management. In fact, the influence of the organizational structure can be seen in several aspects of performance management. For example, in organizations with a matrix structure written goals exist more often, the local supervisor participates more commonly in the PM process, official evaluations are more typical, and qualitative goals are more often in use than in other structure types. On the other hand, in project organizations the following characteristics are more typical than in other organizational types: local supervisors are not so typically involved in the process (or do not exist at all), written goals are less common, and evaluations appear to take place more often only after the repatriation.

## The host unit location

National culture, and thus the location of the host unit, is one significant contextual factor of expatriate performance management. Depending on the culture where the expatriate is performing, his or her performance is managed somewhat differently according to the cultural context, especially if his or her performance is managed by a local manager. Naturally, local managers tend to manage their subordinates, whether local or representatives of another culture, in ways they themselves consider to be effective (De Cieri and Dowling, 1995; Dowling *et al.*, 1999). If a company is applying a global, standardized performance management system, the differences in performance management implementation between cultures may be smaller but, as recent research shows, differences still exist (Lindholm, 2000).

Among the Finnish expatriates, several influences of the host unit location on the PM system were identified when the analysis was performed across three cultural areas: Europe, North America and Asia. For example, among those expatriates in North America there were several PM characteristics that differentiated them from expatriates in the other areas: the first-hand supervisor was more typically a local person, local managers participated more commonly in the PM process, official goal-setting appeared to be a more common practice, goal-setting twice a year was more common, and quantitative goals less common.

As a last point regarding the contextual factors of PM we want to emphasize how critical they are when managing expatriate performance. Depending on the mix of contextual factors and their interaction, expatriate PM can vary significantly, as

Box 5.1 and Table 5.1 illustrate. The case study of one large multinational underlined this point: despite the company's standard performance management system intended for global use, expatriate performance was managed differently in at least five categories of expatriate assignments (Tahvanainen, 1998).

## Conclusions: key criteria for effective PM

As has become evident, numerous different situations can be faced in expatriate PM as a consequence of contextual factors and their interaction. Therefore, as tempting as it may be, it is not possible to present a best-practice model for expatriate PM. However, it is possible to determine a set of key criteria for effective performance management:

1  The expatriate should know the expected level of performance;
2  The expatriate should know on what basis performance will be evaluated, also by whom and when;
3  Evaluation is reliable and it focuses on issues which are critical in one's job: the expatriate receives feedback and thus knows how he or she is performing;
4  The expatriate receives constant training and development;
5  The expatriate knows whether and how his or her performance is linked to pay;
6  Ideally, the expatriate knows how his or her performance during the assignment is linked to the next career step.

The first criterion is that all employees should have a right to know what is expected of their performance. Some situations are, however, more prone to uncertainty about performance expectations than others. For example, when the employee has several managers, they all might want somewhat differing and sometimes contradictory outcomes from the employee's performance. Or, when an organization's structure has been changed, it is typically unclear for quite some time who is responsible for what matters, who has the power to decide about the future performance directions, and so on. When we combine this with existing cross-cultural differences in PM practices and communication in general, the situation becomes more complex.

Regarding the second criterion, it should be the right of all employees to know on what grounds their performance will be evaluated, by whom and at what point in time. On the other hand, this requires that clear and systematic PM systems are created. Systematic performance management also requires a lot of time from supervisors. For example, having face-to-face discussions with often quite an extensive number of individuals requires a lot of time and also communication skills. If the supervisors do not see that the benefits of the systems are clearly more extensive than the problems they cause or the resources they require, they can easily stop having such discussions. A similar outcome may appear if the process does not provide enough accurate and relevant material for the evaluation purposes; as a consequence, the process may become a 'paperfilling exercise', which has no real influence at the workplace. Or, even worse, as a result of unmet employee expectations, the consequences are negative.

The aspect of getting feedback on one's performance, taken up in criterion three, is sometimes hard to meet if the manager is geographically distant from the employee. Positive recognition and giving feedback is part of every managers' job, but in reality employees are often not very satisfied with the amount and type of feedback they receive. In addition, cross-cultural differences in appropriate forms of providing feedback are extensive and it might thus be difficult for expatriates to correctly interpret the feedback they receive from foreign colleagues and supervisors. The situation is similar when home-country supervisors try to interpret the messages sent from the host countries to the evaluation process, that is, cross-cultural misunderstandings might take place.

The fourth criterion for effective performance management requires that the expatriate should receive constant training and development, but empirical data shows that in practice this criterion is not always met (Tahvanainen, 1998). Especially expatriates who have been sent abroad primarily for transferring knowledge and know-how for local employees find this rather uncomfortable. As one expatriate in China put it:

> Expatriates are here to train the locals, and they should have better knowledge than the locals have. But what happens after a certain time is, the expatriates are training the Chinese with their knowledge, and at the same time the Chinese get additional training. Nothing wrong with that, we end up with Chinese who have better knowledge than the expatriates, but expatriates who are on long term assignments end up returning home with outdated knowledge.

Furthermore, effective PM requires that expatriates should know whether and how their performance is linked to pay. Given that one of the key purposes of performance-related pay systems is to motivate employees to perform at their best in supporting fulfilment of the company's strategic performance goals, the criteria might seem rather peculiar. However, research has indicated that sometimes these criteria are in danger of not being met. For example, and as pointed out earlier, research has reported unclarity about the incentive measures and justification for paying bonuses (Tahvanainen, 1998).

Ideally, and as taken up in the sixth criterion, the expatriate would know how his or her performance during the assignment is linked to their next career step. In practice, meeting this criterion is even more challenging than in a national setting since those involved in deciding about the expatriate's next job position are often geographically distant and thus typically do not know much about his or her present abilities and interests. In addition, existing research on the effects of international assignments of future careers indicate that in reality the repatriation process is often far from being well-planned, as can be seen in the example of Box 5.2.

## Box 5.2    Challenging career planning for expatriates

Mike Hamilton left the UK where he was the head of the account team to go to Hong Kong for two years. He was replaced in the UK. He is now managing director in Hong Kong, and his assignment is due to end in three months. Mike has informed his old HR manager that he does not want to stay in Hong Kong any longer, and asked what else is there. His old line manager does not exist any more – he has long since moved elsewhere.

The company unit in the UK does not necessarily have a role for him at that senior level. Furthermore, there is not enough information in the UK about what Mike has actually done as managing director in Hong Kong to use that experience. To complicate things, when Mike went to Hong Kong, he was (sort of) promised that after the assignment, there would be something for him in America. But who is responsible then to find that? It's certainly not the HR manager in America, because he does not know a thing about Mike Hamilton. Presumably it could be the line manager who was involved in sending Mike to Hong Kong and who made the promise, but that person has moved jobs, is doing something quite different now. The HR manager in the UK is not particularly interested in replacing him, or in where he goes, because he is not needed in the UK. However, looking at the situation from the company perspective, Mike is a very talented person that the company should keep. Now, who should look after Mike Hamilton's, and the company's, interests? The HR person in the UK has his blinkers on in looking at the UK, and nobody actually worries about Mike. The danger is that if Mike does not see some kind of commitment from the company's side, he will start to get his CV together. He is very marketable, and he will get another job very easily. He is already getting the headhunters calling him.

Remembering the effect that contextual factors have on expatriate PM, it is clear that, depending on the situation, the means to meet the criteria vary. For example, those expatriates whose task is to establish a foreign unit are the very first, or at least amongst the very first, employees the company has in the foreign location in question. Thus, goal-setting for those employees has to take place by a manager in the home office, and, likewise, the expatriate's performance must be evaluated by someone at the home unit.

It is important to note that the listed criteria for effective PM apply to all types of employees, not only to expatriates. Of course, all types of employees should know what is expected of them, how their performance will be evaluated, and so on. Still, however, there are situations when expatriate PM should be different from local employees' PM. In those situations, if treated alike, the criteria for effective PM are not met in the case of expatriates. These situations are faced more typically in less-international than in highly international companies. Typically, the less-international company is smaller in size, it has not standardized its management systems to the extent its more internationalized compatriot has, and it is typically structured as a line organization. In less-international firms it is also typical that company units drive towards their own business goals. As a consequence of these factors the expatriate can face the typical challenges attached to expatriate PM, for example it is not clear who should set performance goals for the person and who should evaluate his or her performance; how often discrepant goals should be handled; and, furthermore, if a manager located in the home country evaluates the expatriate's performance how can a fair evaluation be guaranteed? In contrast, highly international companies are often structured as global matrix organizations, they apply a standardized PM system in all their operations, and company units aim at global company goals. As a consequence, differences between expatriates' and other types of employees' PM can be practically non-existent.

Before closing this chapter, we would like to point out its key limitations. First, the chapter has leaned heavily on our own empirical studies of the topic – primarily, because studies by other researchers have not been available. Second, we have limited our examination to a set of key contextual factors although there are other contextual factors of PM which prior research has identified (Tahvanainen, 1998). These factors include the existence of a standard, globally utilized performance management system in a company, the style and skills of the employee and the manager concerning job and performance management, and top management support. The effects of these factors are yet to be confirmed by a large-scale survey.

Lastly, the focus of this chapter has been on those international employees' PM who are on traditional, long-term foreign assignments. Recent surveys (PricewaterhouseCoopers, 2000, 2002; ECA, 2001) show that during the past few years there has been a strong tendency for companies to increase the use of other than traditional, long-term foreign assignments in managing their global operations. These alternative ways are being termed non-standard international assignments, and they include short-term, commuter, virtual, contractual and rotational assignments. Further research is needed to find out how the performance of employees on non-standard assignments is managed, and how it should be managed (Welch and Fenwick, 2003; Welch, Worm and Fenwick, 2003).

# Summary

This chapter has examined some key performance management issues faced in the case of expatriate employees. First, the strategic importance of PM was discussed in general, pointing out that when implemented effectively, PM has the potential to be a strategic HRM process which can help companies to bring strategy to individual employees, and turn employees' potential into the desired results (Delery and Doty, 1996). Then, we outlined the scope of performance management in MNCs by covering the central questions of standardization versus localization, and the various employee groups working for multinationals. The main part of the chapter focused on expatriate employees' PM. We described how goals are set for expatriate performance, how expatriates' performance is evaluated, and how training and development as well as performance-related pay issues are dealt with. Further effort was put into discussing the factors influencing the existence and the form of performance management practices, that is, the contextual factors of expatriate performance management: (1) company and host unit size, (2) a company's level of internationalization, (3) the position of the expatriate in the organizational hierarchy, (4) task type, (5) host unit location, and (6) organizational structure. Throughout the review of the factors, examples were given as to how they affect expatriate PM. Finally, we introduced a set of key criteria for effective performance management, and pointed out that the criteria apply to all the various employee groups within MNCs, not only expatriates.

---

### Discussion questions

1  What are the potential consequences for a company of not managing expatriates' performance successfully?
2  How would you feel about being evaluated by someone who is located in a different country than the one where you perform your job? Why so?
3  If you were a line manager to an expatriate, responsible for setting performance goals for him or her, what kind of goals would you suggest for the person? Why?
4  What challenges are involved in a situation where a local manager is responsible for discussing with the expatriate his or her T&D needs, especially those related to long-term career plans?

---

## Further reading

Lindholm, N., Tahvanainen, M. and Björkman, I. (1998) 'Performance Appraisal of Host Country Employees: Western MNCs in China', in C. Brewster and H. Harris (eds), *IHRM: Contemporary Issues In Europe*. London: Routledge.
Suutari, V. and Tahvanainen, M. (2002) 'The Antecedents of Performance Management amongst Finnish Expatriates', *International Journal of Human Resource Management*, 13(1): 55–75.
Tahvanainen, M. (2000) 'Expatriate Performance Management: The Case of Nokia Telecommunications', *Human Resource Management*, 39(2, 3): 267–76.

## References

Armstrong, M. and Baron, A. (1998) *Performance Management: The New Realities*. Wiltshire: Cromwell Press.
Baumgarten, K. (1995) 'Training and Development of International Staff', in A.-W. Harzing and J. Van Ruysseveldt (eds), *International Human Resource Management*. London: Sage, 205–28.
Björkman, I. and Gertsen, M. (1993) 'Selecting and Training Scandinavian Expatriates: Determinants of Corporate Practice', *Scandinavian Journal of Management*, 9(2): 145–64.

Black, J.S., Gregersen, H.B. and Mendenhall, M. (1992) *Global Assignments: Successfully Expatriating and Repatriating International Managers*. San Francisco: Jossey-Bass.

Black, J.S. and Mendenhall, M. (1990) 'Cross-Cultural Training Effectiveness: A Review and Theoretical Framework for Future Research', *Academy of Management Review*, 15: 113–36.

Black, J.S. and Ulrich, D. (1999) 'The New Frontier of Global HR', in P. Joynt and P. Morton (eds), *The Global HR Manager*. London: Institute of Personnel and Development.

Brake, T. (1997) *The Global Leader. Critical Factors for Creating the World Class Organization*. Chicago: Irwin Professional Publishing.

Brake, T. (1999) 'The HR Manager as Global Business Partner', in P. Joynt and P. Morton (eds), *The Global HR Manager*. London: Institute of Personnel and Development.

Cascio, W.F. (2003) *Managing Human Resources: Productivity, Quality of Work Life, Profits*. New York: McGraw-Hill/Irwin.

De Cieri, H. and Dowling, P.J. (1995) 'Cross-Cultural Issues in Organizational Behaviour', in C.L. Cooper and D.M. Rousseau (eds), *Trends in Organizational Behaviour*, 2: 127–45.

Delery, J.E. and Doty, D.H. (1996) 'Modes of Theorizing in Strategic Human Resource Management: Tests of Universalistic, Contingency, and Configurational Performance Predictions', *Academy of Management Journal*, 39(4): 802–35.

Dowling, B. and Richardson, R. (1997) 'Evaluating Performance-Related Pay for Managers in the National Health Service', *International Journal of Human Resource Management*, 8(3): 348–66.

Dowling, P.J., Welch, D.E. and Schuler, R.S. (1999) *International Human Resource Management. Managing People in a Multinational Context*, 3rd edn. Cincinnati, OH: South-Western College Publishing.

ECA (2000/2001) *Latest Trends in Pay and Benefits for International Assignments* (ECA).

Evans, P., Pucik, V. and Barsoux, J. L. (2002) *The Global Challenge: Frameworks for International Human Resource Management*. New York: McGraw-Hill/Irwin.

Forster, N. (1994) 'The forgotten employees? The experiences of expatriate staff returning to the UK', *International Journal of Human Resource Management*, 5(2): 405–25.

Ghorpade, J. and Chen, M.M. (1995) 'Creating Quality-Driven Performance Appraisal Systems', *Academy of Management Executive*, 9(1): 32–41.

Gratton, L. (1997) 'Tomorrow People', *People Management*, July 22–7.

Gregersen, H. and Black, J. (1995) 'Keeping High Performers after International Assignments: A Key to Global Executive Development', *Journal of International Management*, 1(1): 3–21.

Gregersen, H.B., Hite, J.M. and Black, J.S. (1996) 'Expatriate Performance Appraisal in U.S. Multinational Firms', *Journal of International Business Studies*, Fall, 711–38.

Gregersen, H.B., Morrison, A.J. and Black, J.S. (1998) 'Developing Leaders for the Global Frontier', *Sloan Management Review*, Fall, 21–32.

Handler, C.A. and Lane, I.M. (1997) 'Career Planning and Expatriate Couples', *Human Resource Management Journal*, 7(3): 67–78.

Harris, H. and Brewster, C. (1999) 'An Integrative Framework for Pre-Departure Preparation', in C. Brewster and H. Harris (eds), *International HRM. Contemporary Issues in Europe*. London: Routledge.

Harvey, M. (1989) 'Repatriation of Corporate Executives: An Empirical Study', *Journal of International Business Studies*, 20(1): 131–44.

Harvey, M. (1996) 'Planning Perspective', *Columbia Journal of World Business*, 102–118.

Hendry, C., Bradley, P. and Perkins, S. (1997) 'Missed a Motivator?', *People Management*, 5: 20–5.

Jacobs, R.R. (1986) 'Numerical Rating Scales', in R.A. Berk (ed.), *Performance Assessment: Methods and Applications*. Baltimore, MD: John Hopkins University Press.

Keegan, W.J. and Green, M.S. (2000) *Global Marketing*. Upper Saddle River, NJ: Prentice Hall.

Latham, G.P. and Wexley, K.N. (1982) *Increasing Productivity through Performance Appraisal*. Reading, MA: Addison-Wesley.

Lindholm, N. (2000) *Globally Standardized Performance Management Policies in Multinational Companies' Subsidiaries in China*, Swedish School of Economics and Business Administration, Finland. Helsinki: University Press.

Locke, E.A. and Latham, G.P. (1984) *Goal Setting: A Motivational Technique that Works!* Englewood Cliffs, NJ: Prentice-Hall.

Marsden, D. and Richardson, R. (1994) 'Performing for Pay? The Effects of 'Merit Pay' on Motivation in a Public Service', *British Journal of Industrial Relations*, 32(2): 243–62.

Marx, E. (1996) *International Human Resource Management in Britain and Germany*. London: Chameleon Press.

Mathis, R.L. and Jackson, J.H. (1988) *Personnel/Human Resource Management*. St Paul, MN: West Publishing.

McKenna, E. and Beech, N. (1995) *The Essence of Human Resource Management*. Cornwall: TJ Press.

Mendenhall, M., Dunbar, E. and Oddou, G. (1987) 'Expatriate Selection, Training, and Career-Pathing', *Human Resource Management*, 26(3): 331–45.

Mendenhall, M. and Oddou, G. (1991) *Readings and Cases in International Human Resource Management* (Boston: PWS-Kent).

Mendenhall, M. and Stahl, G. (2000) 'Expatriate Training and Development: Where Do We Go from Here?', *Human Resource Management*, 39(2, 3): 251–65.

Meyer, H.H. (1991) 'A Solution to the Performance Appraisal Feedback Enigma', *Academy of Management Executive*, 5(1): 68–76.

Mintzberg, H. (1989) *Mintzberg on Management: Inside our Strange World of Organizations*. New York: Free Press.

Murphy, K.R. and Cleveland, J.N. (1991) *Performance Appraisal: An Organizational Perspective*. Needham Heights, MA: Allyn & Bacon.

Napier, N. and Peterson, R. (1991) 'Expatriate Re-Entry: What Expatriates Have to Say', *Human Resource Planning*, 14(1): 19–28.

O'Leary-Kelly, A.M., Martoccio, J.J. and Frink, D.D. (1994) 'A Review of the Influence of Team Goals on Group Performance', *Academy of Management Journal*, 7(5): 1285–301.

Pfeffer, J. (1995) 'Producing Sustainable Competitive Advantage Through the Effective Management of People', *Academy of Management Executive*, 9(1): 55–72.

PricewaterhouseCoopers (2000) *Managing a Virtual World: Key Trends 2000/2001*.

PricewaterhouseCoopers (2002) *Managing Mobility Matters – a European Perspective*.

Pucik, V. (1992) 'Globalization and Human Resource Management', in V. Pucik, N.M. Tichy and C.K. Barnett (eds), *Globalizing Management. Creating and Leading the Competitive Organization*. New York: John Wiley.

Redman, T. and Snape, E. (1992) 'Upward and Onward: Can Staff Appraise their Managers?', *Personnel Review*, 1(7): 32–46.

Reynolds, C. (1988) 'Cost-Effective Compensation of Expatriates', *Topics in Total Compensation*, 2(4): 319–26.

Reynolds, C. and Bennett, R. (1991) 'The Career Couple Challenge', *Personnel Journal*, 48: 42–51.

Riusala, K. and Suutari, V. (2000) 'Expatriation and Careers: Perspectives of Expatriates and Spouses', *Career Development International*, 5(2): 81–90.

Saul, P. (1992) 'Rethinking Performance Appraisal', *Asia Pacific Journal of Human Resources*, 30(3): 25–39.

Schell, M.S. and Solomon, C.M. (1997) *Capitalizing on the Global Workforce: A Strategic Guide to Expatriate Management*. New York: McGraw-Hill.

Segal-Horn, S. (1996) 'The Limits of Global Strategy', *Strategy and Leadership*, November, 12–17.

Sparrow, P. and Hiltrop, J.-M. (1994) *European Human Resource Management in Transition*. Hertfordshire: Prentice Hall.

Stroh, L.K., Gregersen, H.B. and Black, J.S. (1998) 'Closing the Cap: Expectations versus Reality among Expatriates', *Journal of World Business*, 33(2): 110–24.

Suutari, V. and Brewster, C. (2001) 'Expatriate Management Practices and Perceived Relevance: Evidence from Finnish Expatriates', *Personnel Review*, 30(5): 554–577.

Suutari, V. and Brewster, C. (2003) 'Repatriation: Empirical Evidence from a Longitudinal Study of Careers and Expectations among Finnish Expatriates', *International Journal of Human Resource Management*, 14(7): 1132–51.

Suutari, V. and Burch, D. (2001) 'The Role of On-site Training and Support in Expatriation: Existing and Necessary Host-Company Practices', *Career Development International*, 6(6): 298–311.

Suutari, V. and Tahvanainen, M. (2002) 'The Antecedents of Performance Management amongst Finnish Expatriates', *International Journal of Human Resource Management*, 13(1): 55–75.

Suutari, V. and Tornikoski, C. (2001) 'The Challenge of Expatriate Compensation: The Sources of Satisfaction and Dissatisfaction among Expatriates', *International Journal of Human Resource Management*, 12(3): 1–16.

Svensson, G. (2001) 'Glocalization' of Business Activities: A 'Glocal Strategy' Approach, *Management Decision*, 39(1): 6–18.

Szilagyi, A.D. (1998) *Management and Performance*, 4th edn. Santa Monica: Goodyear.

Tahvanainen, M. (1998) *Expatriate Performance Management: The Case of Nokia Telecommunications*. Helsinki School of Economics and Business Administration, series A-134. Helsinki: Helsinki School of Economics Press.

Tornow, W.W. (1993) 'Introduction to Special Issue on 360-degree Feedback', *Human Resource Management*, 32(2–3): 211–219.

Torraco, R.J. and Swanson, R.A. (1995) 'The Strategic Role of Human Resource Development', *Human Resource Planning*, 18(4).

Tziner, A. (1990) *Organization Staffing and Work Adjustment.* New York: Praeger.

Welch, D.E. and Fenwick, M. (2003) 'Virtual Assignments: A New Possibility for IHRM?', *Management International Review*, 2.

Welch, D.E., Worm, V. and Fenwick, M. (2003) 'Are Virtual Assignments Feasible?', *Management International Review*, 1: 95–114.

Williams, S. (1991) 'Strategy and Objectives', in F. Neale (ed.) *The Handbook of Performance Management.* Exeter, UK: Short Run Press.

# 6

# International compensation: costs and benefits of international assignments

*Jaime Bonache and Zulima Fernández*

## Introduction

The traditional approach to international compensation focuses on the design details of the salary packages of expatriates. The issues usually considered refer to what components are to be included in their wages (base pay, variable pay, perquisites, benefits, incentives), where to establish the compensation basis (should their compensation be based on their home country, the host country, or some other variation), tax protection (how to protect expatriates' compensation packages against the effects of additional foreign taxation), or who should be paying (does it make sense to split payments between home, host and parent companies)?

These operative questions capture the attention of those in charge of managing these systems who, given the existing difficulties in the design and access to the required information (cost of living, taxation, purchasing powers and salary levels in the countries where the MNE operates), tend to resort to external advisors (Reynolds, 2000). In short, the problem of compensation seems to have an essentially technical nature which can be solved with the assistance of an expert.

International compensation, however, could have a greater relevance from a theoretical and strategic point of view. Like any other investment, compensations are fixed according to the costs and benefits expected. Bearing these two items in mind, this chapter has two main aims: (1) to examine the costs involved in international assignments as well as the situations in which using expatriates is a cost-effective solution, and (2) to discuss the benefits the company obtains by using expatriates.

Our aim is to show that, contrary to what is generally assumed, expatriates are not necessarily a costly option for a company and that even when design of the compensation package is, perhaps, the most urgent task, it is by no means the most important factor when analysing the problem of international compensation.

A more theory-based approach, focused on global costs and benefits is, in our opinion, a more sensible way to address the problem.

# Costs of international assignments

The use of expatriates to fill managerial positions in an MNE's subsidiaries is a widespread practice (Mayrhofer and Brewster, 1966). In fact, in the case of Japanese companies, 75 per cent of their subsidiaries' managers are expatriates, according to a Kopp survey (1994). European and American MNEs follow a very similar pattern, with 54 per cent and 51 per cent respectively. International destinations involve, however, high salary costs. As shown in a survey carried out by Management Europe Centre, the salary cost of an expatriate is approximately three times as high as a local employee's. In some countries, such as China, expatriates have been estimated to earn between 20 and 50 times as much as local employees (Chen et al., 2002). What is the reason for such high costs?

Most companies use the so-called 'balance-sheet' approach when fixing expatriate wages. The objective of this approach is to maintain the expatriate's purchasing power and to make assignments financially attractive. The former implies calculating different categories of expenses involved when an employee has to live abroad (goods and services, housing, taxes and savings), providing differentials so that wages are adapted to local standards. The latter implies offering the employee monetary incentives. There are further benefits such as housing and transfer facilities, company car, language training and so on, which may also be offered. This explains the high salary costs mentioned above.

What is certainly surprising is why, within a business context under unremitting pressure to keep costs down, MNEs should continue to implement such an apparently costly solution. In other words, why do MNEs prefer to recruit internally instead of the local market when seeking to hire managerial personnel for subsidiaries?

Thus presented, the question is similar to the one raised by Coase (1937), which laid the foundations of the theory of transaction costs (TTC): if markets are so efficient when conducting transactions, why do organizations exist? The parallelism between both questions is not purely accidental. Following Williamson (1990), the TTC can be applied to any situation in which a transaction or an exchange is being conducted. In fact, this theory has been applied to analyse a large number of exchange phenomena, such as vertical integration (Klein et al., 1978), corporate strategy (Teece, 1982, 1986), joint ventures (Hennart, 1991) relationship with clients (Jones, 1987) or the decision to subcontract certain positions or tasks (Masters and Miles, 2002). Our interest is to apply the TTC to the transaction made between the company and the employee when occupying a managerial position in a subsidiary.

In this transaction, the employee contributes human capital and behaviour (Wright et al., 1994) in exchange for a series of rewards. By human capital, we understand the knowledge, experience, skills and abilities inherent in the employee. We also include behaviour because, as Wright *et al.* (1994) assert, the employee's human capital does not provide any value to the firm unless it is utilized through the employee's behaviour. The TTC states that transaction features determine the governance structure to be used in each case: local market, internal organization or hybrid forms. In our case, we will analyse the features of this employment relationship in order to know whether it is more convenient to resort to the market – in this case, of local managers – when the need to fill a vacancy arises or, on the contrary, to internalize the transaction and resort to the company's personnel, which would lead to the expatriation of managers.

Following Williamson (1975), transactions can differ according to three dimensions: (a) frequency and expected duration of the exchange; (b) the degree of uncertainty to which it is subject; and (c) the specificity of the assets associated with the exchange. How do these dimensions operate in the employment relationship we are interested in?

Regarding the first dimension, international assignments vary in duration and frequency. Staff members may sometimes be sent abroad in order to carry out a very specific and technical task, and, once it is finished, there is no need for them to stay any longer (for example, the setting up of a certain IT system in a subsidiary). In other cases, such as the one we wish to refer to here, the assignment takes longer because it involves taking over the subsidiary's management (or any of its functional areas) for a lengthy period of time, usually a two to four-year stay on average (Bonache *et al.*, 2001).

As regards the second dimension, the decision to appoint managers is a rather complex one, and the conditions under which this decision is taken have a high degree of uncertainty. Many contingencies may arise during the relationship. The company needs to know whether or not the candidate will be able to overcome any setback which might come up; but a selection mistake is always possible. Such a possibility is due to the confluence of two factors regarding human behaviour: bounded rationality and opportunism (Williamson, 1981, 1993). As regards the first factor, human agents are assumed to be 'intendedly rational, but only limited' (Simon, 1961). In the case we are analysing here, this means that the company's decision-making body has access to limited information and also limited ability to process that information. In addition to this, candidates have the potential to behave opportunistically. By this term, Williamson (1985) refers to a type of behaviour such as lying, stealing, cheating and making calculated efforts to mislead, distort, disagree, obfuscate or otherwise confuse. This behaviour, which results from the combination of limited rationality and self-interest (Alchian and Woodward, 1988), occurs when people are driven by self-interest, no matter how detrimental their attitude can be to others, and whenever such a behaviour is not easy to detect by the other party. According to Williamson and Ouchi (1981), not all candidates will necessarily have opportunistic behaviours, but some will. The problem stems from the great difficulty in separating *ex ante* those who are opportunist from those who are not.

In our context, these two factors create a framework leading to two potential problems (Williamson, Wachter and Harris, 1994): *adverse selection*, when prospective employees conceal some revealing information which would otherwise evidence their lack of knowledge, experience and abilities required for the position; and *moral hazard*, which occurs once the successful candidate has been appointed and is driven by self-interest, regardless of the level of congruence with the objectives of the organization. This kind of behaviour arises when the company cannot easily detect it in advance. This is the situation that MNCs have to face. In the international scene there exists a large number of circumstances (distance, cultural changes, different market structures, and so on) that may impair the HQ's ability to gauge the potential (when appointing the candidate) or the competence (once appointed) of the manager's working performance.

Finally, specific assets are those whose value in their present use is higher than the value they would have in any alternative use (Klein *et al.*, 1978). Let us think, for example, of company-specific knowledge, such as knowledge of the company procedures, policies and culture. In the event of leaving the company, such assets will not be as productive since they require the confluence of the other company resources.

Once specific assets are locked into a relationship, there is a situation of dependency which could favour opportunistic behaviours, called 'hold-up' in the literature, both on the company's side and on the employee's. Opportunism on the employee's side is that which we wish to focus on. How does it operate? In the hypothetical case of selecting a local manager and training him or her in the values and procedures of the company (acquiring, thus, the human capital specific to the company), the employee could become highly productive in knowing not only the business idiosyncrasy of the host country, but also the operating ways of the company. Without this manager, the organization could not achieve the same results. This might be a potential incentive for him to exploit the situation and, under the threat of leaving or changing companies, renegotiate his terms and conditions in order to secure the rents. How this situation is to be tackled will depend on the degree of mutual dependency (see Alchian and Woodward, 1988). What we would like to stress here is that if specific assets exist, then this type of opportunism, leading to renegotiation of the original terms and conditions of the agreement, is a possibility which should not be overlooked. Table 6.1. presents the possible opportunistic behaviours resulting from the employment characteristics already analysed, together with the problem which the organization might have to confront.

To increase the efficiency of the exchange, and/or to prevent opportunistic behaviours, the organization will have to incur transaction costs. By this term, we refer to the costs of planning, adapting and monitoring task completion (Williamson, 1981). Following Jones and Wright (1992), we can distinguish four main types of transaction costs:

1   *Selection and recruitment costs.* The costs incurred in overcoming adverse selection. This item also includes the costs of gathering information about the

*Table 6.1*  Problems in a manager's appointment for a subsidiary

| Characteristics of the employment relationship | Possible opportunistic behaviour of the candidate | Problem the organization must confront |
| --- | --- | --- |
| Uncertainty | The candidate may conceal some revealing information which would evidence his lack of the human capital required | Adverse selection |
| | The candidate may be driven by self-interest, at the expense of the organization | Moral hazard |
| Specific assets | The candidate could exploit his acquired knowledge in order to renegotiate the original terms and conditions of the agreement | Hold-up |

candidate as well as costs associated with negotiation and final drawing-up of the contract with the appointed candidate.

2   *Training and socialization costs.* These are costs associated with the development of the subsidiary manager's skills and abilities, together with their acquisition of the company policies and cultural standards.

3   *Monitoring and evaluating the subsidiary's managers.* The costs incurred in safeguarding the organization against moral hazard. These will include costs of HQ's managers and managerial time spent on supervising, as well as costs associated with the implementation of appraisal and feedback systems.

4   *Enforcement.* The organization will have to take action in the event of a breach of contract on the part of the subsidiary's manager. This will obviously originate new costs for the company.

The basic premise of transaction cost economics is that transactions will tend to take place in a form that minimizes the combined costs of the transaction. Applying this argument to our reasoning, we can state that, when deciding whether to recruit a local manager or an expatriate, the organization will have to consider the total transaction costs associated with each alternative and opt for the most efficient one, that is the one which minimizes such costs. The question can therefore be formulated in the following terms: when are the transaction costs of using expatriates lower than those of using local nationals?

As we have seen, the supposition that people may behave opportunistically is at the root of transaction costs. Therefore, if this prejudice could be replaced for a higher degree of trust in the parties' integrity to fulfil their obligations, costs would certainly be reduced. This provides us with an important clue as to what kind of situations we wish to highlight. Several authors (Boyacilliger, 1990; Nohria and Ghoshal, 1994; Yan *et al.*, 2002) have stated that expatriates are very frequently regarded as 'trustworthy' employees sent abroad to represent the interests of the company. Hence, we should have to specify the situations in which this 'trust' factor plays a decisive role and the extent to which it can be undertaken by expatriates.

To determine the situations in which trust is a crucial factor, and consequently the use of expatriates a more efficient option, we will have to distinguish between those situations emerging from organizational factors (such as international expansion of the company, knowledge required, strategy of the company and the type of position to be filled in the subsidiary), and those situations emerging from institutional factors, such as culture and regulations of the host country. If we analyse these situations, we will find that trust is a key factor in all of them, although not the only one; the level of training required also plays a key role.

## Level of international expansion

Several advantages have been highlighted in the literature about the use of local managers, among which we wish to emphasize the following: (1) they can speak the language, they are familiar with the culture and the local political system and they usually belong to the social elite of the host country, which enables the subsidiary to obtain a better market share and to eliminate problems of adaptation of expatriates and their families (Hamill, 1989); (2) they ensure continuity in the subsidiary's management, avoiding in this way the frequent substitutions of expatriates often accompanied by unjustified managerial changes in the subsidiary; (3) they represent significant savings on salary costs, yet allow for a margin to offer monetary incentives to attract the best local candidates; (4) motivation and career opportunities of local staff are enhanced in this way, since managerial positions are not kept for HQ's employees; and (5) local acceptance of the MNE is also favoured (Grosse and Kijawa, 1988).

Let us imagine a company which, persuaded by such advantages, wishes to recruit a local manager. How does it go about it? If the company's entry into the international market is only recent, the task might turn risky and uncertain due to the company's ignorance of the local labour market and the fact that it lacks a pool of local candidates already working for them. To overcome adverse selection and prevent potential opportunism, the company will have to spend a longer period of time as well as more resources in the selection process. Simultaneously, as we shall see in our next section, local candidates might have to familiarize themselves with the company products and procedures, which will force the company to invest in training and socialization, incurring corresponding costs. Finally, to prevent moral hazard from people whom the company 'does not know', it will also have to incur higher control and assessment costs.

However, this set of costs can be totally reduced by recruiting 'trustworthy' employees, or else as the company acquires a higher level of international expansion.

Consequently, it is unsurprising that in the early stages of internationalization, there is a stronger tendency to use expatriates.

## Type of knowledge required

Not all managerial work requires the same knowledge and abilities; for certain positions, for example, the knowledge required is country-specific. Let us think, for example, of a local marketing director with remarkable business skills and a wide contact network within the local market. If a good work performance in this case does not necessarily mean having company-specific knowledge, then he might prove to be a more efficient option than an expatriate.

For other positions, on the contrary, a good work performance can only occur when the employee has company-specific knowledge. In fact, the presence of an MNE in foreign markets is frequently justified by its set of company-specific knowledge which gives it a competitive advantage over local companies (Dunning, 1988; Teece, 1986) and this compensates for the disadvantage of being foreign (MNEs are comparatively less-familiar with the national culture, the structure of the local industry, and other aspects of doing business in a given country).

Where company-specific knowledge is required, expatriates can be a more efficient recruitment option:

- If the company competes on a company-specific knowledge basis, the HQ employees' abilities are assumed to be also applicable in the subsidiary. Otherwise, the company would not have opted to establish itself in that country.
- Such knowledge and skills are often only obtainable after a long time in the company. If a local manager is recruited, the company will have to incur a number of training costs which could otherwise have been saved if an internal employee had been chosen.
- Such training costs are high. In fact, the level of knowledge about the firm, its operations, its personnel, its traditions, and so forth required for the higher-level positions considered in our case, is likely to be much higher and therefore more costly to acquire (Baron and Kreps, 1999). Consequently, the company will obviously try to recover the training costs incurred in training its national employees instead of training new local managers in those skills.
- A local manager might not be motivated to be trained since the position might be regarded as a mere transitional step to another organization (what is the use of investing time and energy in acquiring certain knowledge whose productive value is mostly lost in other companies?), or else because he/she fears becoming increasingly dependent on the company, which would enable it to exploit the situation and renegotiate his terms and conditions (Alchian and Woodward, 1988).
- The company is prepared to protect that knowledge more effectively. A trained local manager might threaten to transfer this knowledge to the company's rival,

or renegotiate his terms and conditions and appropriate the rents that are generated from this knowledge, evidencing thus the type of opportunism already defined as *hold-up*. On the other hand, expatriates, as long as they are 'trustworthy employees', are less likely to show this type of opportunistic behaviour, which will save the company monitoring and enforcement costs.

## Strategy

MNEs have two main ways of competing in the market: on a country-to-country basis, or on a global basis. Some of the early classic studies of expatriation showed how the number of expatriates tends to be larger in global companies (Edstrom and Galbraith, 1977). The higher use of expatriates in such firms is usually explained in terms of process information requirements (Boyacilliger, 1990). Global companies usually have a high degree of interdependence among their units so that the activities of one of the units has an effect on the others. Integration and coordination among units does not occur spontaneously. Each unit tends to deal with its own tasks, to pursue its own functional objectives and to confront its own environmental pressure. Furthermore, managers of interdependent units may lack information regarding the global impact their decisions might have. Consequently, their decisions are not likely to be the most efficient ones for the entire organization. Under these circumstances, the HQ might find it necessary to make use of assignments among subsidiaries and between subsidiaries and the HQ. With this measure, such managers improve their network knowledge, are well-aware of the impact of their decisions and develop multiple contacts, which allows them to act as links between interdependent units.

However, the higher use of expatriates in global companies can also be explained in terms of transaction costs. Managerial positions in the interdependent units usually require making decisions that span other units of the corporation. Therefore, the costs of error of those higher up in the hierarchy are very high. This implies both a higher reluctance to recruit staff they are not well-acquainted with, and an increase of uncertainty due to potential opportunistic behaviour. Under these circumstances, the higher costs associated with expatriates may also compensate for the lower selection, training and assessment costs.

## Type of position

Baron and Kreps (1999) make a distinction between *star jobs* and *guardian jobs*. The former are those in which a bad performance is not too bad, but a good performance is very good for the company. An example of this type of position could be that of a manager running a fairly independent subsidiary as regards products, brand image and HQ's procedures, whose main function is to develop new products or managerial processes adapted to the local market.

A guardian job is one in which a good performance is only slightly better for the firm than an average performance, but a bad performance is a disaster. A guardian job could be that of a subsidiary's manager whose main role is to represent the organization when faced with a group of global clients, where the organization's reputation is a valuable asset. Most of the subsidiary managers in the financial sector belong to this category.

The type of position to be occupied affects the time and resources invested in the selection and assessment process of candidates. For a star job, the costs of a hiring error are small relative to the upside potential from finding an exceptional individual. Therefore, the organization will be less-concerned about the problems which information asymmetries and opportunism may cause in the recruitment phase and will thus be prepared to assume higher risks in the decision-making process. On the other hand, for guardian jobs it is essential for candidates to have the required qualifications in order to make sure that their performance will not be detrimental to the company's image or global reputation in any way. The higher salary costs incurred by the company in recruiting 'trustworthy' employees might compensate for the costs which a selection error may cause in these cases.

## Cultural distance

Multinational companies make use of two main mechanisms, different but complementary to each other, to control their subsidiaries' performance: *centralization* and *formalization*. Centralization refers to the degree that decisions (that is, the introduction of new products or changes in the managerial processes) are taken in the HQ. Formalization depends on the existence of a well-defined set of rules and procedures regulating the tasks and the ways to proceed in different situations. Although this mechanism limits the subsidiary's autonomy, it also reduces HQ's direct involvement since direct control is replaced by rules and procedures.

However, when a great cultural distance separates the HQ from the subsidiary, none of these mechanisms have proved to be efficient enough, since they represent some sort of straitjacket acting as a deterrent for the subsidiary to confront political, legal, economic or cultural complexities specific to its environment (Nohria and Ghoshal, 1994).

Within the problem of control mechanisms in units with great cultural distance, we can discuss recruitment options. Cultural differences between HQ and subsidiaries increase information asymmetries and opportunist potential, so in the case of recruiting local managers the company will have to incur higher selection, training and control costs. These costs aiming to prevent adverse selection and moral hazard could otherwise be reduced by sending a 'trustworthy' manager to the subsidiary. The function of these employees is to act as interpreters and to represent the interest of the HQ in the subsidiary. As the company acquires experience in the host country and considering that trust is the result of repeated relationships (Williamson, 1975), distrust and uncertainty are reduced, and local managers can eventually be trusted.

**Table 6.2**  Situations in which expatriates may be a cost-effective solution

| Factor | Situation |
|--------|-----------|
| Level of international expansion | The company has no international experience |
| Knowledge required | Firm-specific knowledge needs to be transferred |
| Company strategy | Transnational or global |
| Type of position | Guardian |
| Culture of the host country | Differs significantly from the parent country |
| Regulations in the host country | It casts doubts on the fulfilment of contracts |

## Regulation

Legal safety and defence of the contracting parties' interests have proved to be of paramount importance in financial markets when opting for a control mechanism (LaPorta *et al.*, 1997). The primacy of markets over other types of financing solutions responding to a more internal type, such as bank financing or controlling shareholders, depends on the legal code and law courts of the different countries (*Ibid.*). Countries under the Common Law tend to resort to markets more frequently than those countries under the Civil Law, based on Roman Law.

Hence, it is not surprising that the acquisition of another essential resource for the company, its managers, should follow the same pattern. As long as MNEs do not trust the host-country's legislation and law courts, they will be likely to make use of expatriates since they are subject to the norms and law courts of the parent country. Otherwise they would incur high transaction costs in the event of a breach of contract. Table 6.2 shows a summary of cases in which expatriation is comparatively a more economical solution than the use of local managers.

## Investment recovery: benefits of assignments

In the last section we have detected some of the situations in which making use of expatriates to occupy certain positions abroad is a cost-effective solution. This can be so whenever, in addition to salary costs, we also consider other additional costs (selection, training and control costs, among others) which are generally omitted in the expatriate literature. In other words, the higher salary costs incurred in using expatriates could be compensated for by a reduction in other transaction costs.

So far, we have only considered the item 'costs', with no direct assessment of the possible benefits associated with expatriation. The truth is that, as shown in a recent review of the literature on expatriation (Bonache *et al.*, 2001), international assignments enable multinational companies to achieve important strategic objectives. Recognizing the strategic objectives of multinational companies is equivalent to identifying the sources of their success, and along these lines Bartlett and Ghoshal (1989) have argued that international companies have to pursue three different but complementary objectives:

- *Local responsiveness.* MNEs should carry out an exhaustive analysis and investigation of markets and differentiate their products to fit the preferences of their clients, the characteristics of the sector, and the cultural and legal environment of each of the national markets in which they operate.
- *Global integration.* MNEs should coordinate operations of their geographically dispersed units so as to take advantage of different national factors of production, to leverage economies of scale in all activities, and to share costs and investments across different markets and international subsidiaries.
- *Developing innovation and organizational learning.* This requires that the different units (HQ and subsidiaries) should learn from each other and exchange innovations in management systems.

The achievement of these objectives might create the need to assign or move personnel among different units, thus creating expatriates, in order to transfer knowledge and experience, to coordinate globally integrated interdependent units, or to make sure that local adaptation is not achieved at the expense of the HQ. Therefore, the benefits of international assignments, with the corresponding investment recovery, will have to be assessed:

1  *During expatriation.* Benefits will be obtained as long as expatriates fulfil their assignments effectively – knowledge transfer, control and coordination of local operations, knowledge acquisition which can be useful in future. In this way, the MNE will achieve the three strategic objectives mentioned above.
2  *In repatriation.* During this phase, benefits will be obtained as long as the company manages to keep the employee, to make use of his or her expertise on their return, to encourage them to apply the acquired knowledge in future assignments or to transfer it to other employees. Only if the company succeeds in carrying out these tasks will the organizational learning objective be achieved.

Research has shown that such benefits are not obtained automatically. On the contrary, there is a high ratio of failure in international assignments. Following Black and Gregersen (1999), 10–20 per cent of American managers sent abroad return before scheduled due to adaptation problems; around 30 per cent of those who stayed in the host country as planned failed to meet their supervisors' expectations regarding working performance; in addition, 25 per cent of the expatriates leave the company within a year after repatriation to work for a rival company. The high failure rate means that high financial costs are incurred with no recovery. The main question that should be posed is the following: On what does international assignment success depend?

The traditional literature states that success depends, to a large extent, on cross-cultural adaptation, as well as selection and training practices (Black and Gregersen, 1999). More recently, Yan *et al.* (2002) have shown that assignment success in both the expatriation and repatriation phases depends on the alignment of expectations of the employee and the organization. Consistent with the approach we have adopted here, Yan *et al.* (2002) also analyses international assignments as an employment relationship which pursues efficiency, but they add two elements:

1 They consider both the organization's and the employee's points of view, since both have multiple motives: they are driven by self-interest (opportunism), but they also fight to meet their commitments.

2 They complement the economic approach with a psychological perspective. While the former is focused on efficiency in the employment relationship, the possibility of opportunism and how to eliminate it, the latter is focused on the tacit expectations involved in the relationship.

In the case of an international assignment, there is an explicit contract regarding tasks and responsibilities in exchange for certain rewards. However, there is also an implicit contract regarding the expectations of mutual obligations, as well as norms and desirable or acceptable behaviours on both sides. Expectations of the impact of the assignment regarding career opportunities are the employee's deepest concern when formulating his psychological contract in an international assignment.

Each party can regard the contract as being either relational or transactional. While the former is based on loyalty and willingness to establish a long-term relationship, the latter is concerned with learning and establishing a relationship to accomplish a short-term project. Both organization and employee may be motivated to establish a relational agreement. The employee's motivation might respond to the fact that he believes the organization offers high development potential and career opportunities, or simply because he enjoys his commitment to this particular company. The company, on the other hand, has several reasons to establish a long-term relationship (Lepak and Snell, 1999):

1 Expatriates with a long-term approach towards the company seem to be better prepared to adapt to the different contingencies which may arise during the assignment, even when they might be detrimental to themselves in the short run. They might, for example, agree to take on unexpected or unattractive tasks if they find they can reap the benefits in the future, through promotions, assignments abroad, and so on. In this sense, a relational agreement provides the company with greater functional flexibility (Baron and Kreps, 1999).

2 Results of the expatriate's work are only produced on a long-term basis. Market penetration or the building up of a solid client portfolio are generally

long-term objectives and need the same time framework to train and motivate employees.

3 Expatriates' functions might also demand a firm commitment to the company. When tasks are straightforward and the output easy to measure (for example, the establishment of a new system of information in a subsidiary) it is possible to design a working system with little margin for employees to stray from specific tasks. In this case, a transactional agreement will be enough. However, when tasks are complex and the output difficult to specify and measure (cultural transfer to the subsidiary, for example), it is essential to rely on commitment and motivation since external controls (very effective for non-complex tasks) cannot be effectively implemented. To carry out these tasks, expatriates under a transactional agreement are less-devoted and concerned with the company's welfare.

4 For a good work performance, expatriates need to have a high level of specific human capital. As we have seen, many of the tasks involved in their jobs require a good knowledge of the company and its members, its products and decision-making procedures, among other factors. These abilities and relationships take time to be acquired and only those who aim to stay in the company long enough are interested in learning them, since their productive value is much lower in other companies.

The psychological contract could be violated by both parties, which means that obligations are not met. This implies that opportunism not only occurs on the part of the agent, as we have already mentioned in the first part of this chapter. For example, the company might persuade the employee into believing that a certain assignment is important for his career, when in fact it is not. Considering both perspectives and both types of contract (relational versus transactional), Yan *et al.* (2002) distinguish four scenarios, each of which gives rise to different possibilities of expatriation success, as shown in Table 6.3.

As regard *Mutual loyalty*, both parties regard the contract as relational. Each of them expects to give and receive loyalty, and they are committed to a long-term relationship.

*Table 6.3*  Possibilities of success in international assignments

| Type of scenario | Results for the organization | |
|---|---|---|
| | In expatriation | In repatriation |
| 1  Mutual loyalty | High success | High success |
| 2  Agent opportunism | Moderate success | Failure |
| 3  Principal opportunism | Moderate success | Low success |
| 4  Mutual transaction | Moderate to high success | Stronger possibilities of success than in scenarios 2 and 3 |

*Source*:   Based on Yan *et al.* (2002).

In this scenario the organization is likely to have planned the assignment as part of a business strategic plan and their employees' development, and therefore wishes to see the results of the acquired experience in the long run. The employee will also see the assignment as a development opportunity and believes that a successful expatriation will promote him within the organization. A high level of success is then likely to happen.

*Agent opportunism* implies to a disparity in perceptions. The organization regards the contract as relational, whereas the employee believes it is a transactional contract. During the expatriation phase, the employee is not likely to be heavily involved in his functions since he does not share the long-term expectations of the assignment. On the contrary, the employee might get involved in social networks and activities tending to increase his marketability, might also contact other companies in search of better offers, or try to increase his negotiation power. As a result, his working performance could be badly affected, and he could also decide to leave the assignment or yet the organization, depending on his level of self-interest. During the repatriation phase, the company might regard any attempt to leave the organization as an act of betrayal, for this would certainly not meet the company's expectations.

With *principal opportunism*, a disparity in perceptions is also present. The organization regards the contract as transactional, whereas the employee believes it is a relational contract. For example, the company may provide misleading information and create false expectations of the impact of the assignment. This might lead to a short-term success, since the employee is bound to complete his assignment successfully. However, he will feel betrayed on his repatriation phase when he realizes that his psychological contract has been violated and, consequently, might feel impelled to leave the organization. For the organization, on the other hand, this would not be read as failure but as low success, since it did not have great retention expectations anyway. In both scenarios, a weaker commitment of the organization towards the employee results in a lesser degree of support: less resources (budgets, advice, support, etc.) leading to moderate success in the expatriation.

In the mutual transaction scenario, both parties regard the contract as transactional. The relationship is based on the project, with no further commitment. From the organization's point of view, the task may be self-contained and independent, or else a routine task, with none of the above-mentioned features which characterize a long-term relationship. The employee is motivated by the prospect of acquiring international experience and thus improving his career opportunities. During the expatriation phase, success may be moderate since there could be a lack of total commitment and involvement on both sides. The employee might be already thinking of a future opportunity and the organization may not be prepared to invest all its resources in it. Nevertheless, success could also be high since expectations are shared, and this might lead to a strong willingness to complete the task successfully, with no energy devoted to keeping up appearances. During the repatriation phase, it is difficult to speak of failure since no expectations were ever cherished. However, if the expatriation has been successful, there is a good chance for the relationship to carry on.

The model presented here is static despite the fact that psychological contracts are subject to changes (Yan *et al.*, 2002). There are environmental, organizational and individual factors which might alter the expectations. Let's imagine, for example, an initial relationship of mutual loyalty. Once the employee is in the host country, he could well receive job offers from different companies as a result of his higher visibility and the contacts he might build up once there, or simply because of his talent. This will motivate the employee to behave opportunistically (the scenario would then change into one of agent opportunism) by changing companies or renegotiating his terms and conditions. Since these alternative job opportunities increase his negotiation power within the company, the company will probably have to incur a higher salary cost in order to keep his services and its compensation would thus be affected.

# Conclusion

In the decision-making process involving the use of either expatriates or local managers for the MNE's subsidiaries, salary and non-salary costs (that is, selection, training, monitoring and enforcement costs) should be considered. Taking these non-salary costs into account, we have argued that under certain circumstances (a company with a low international expansion, the need to cover a guardian job, the need to exploit specific knowledge, adoption of a global strategy, great cultural distance of the host country, or distrust of the host-country's legal system), expatriates can be a cost-effective solution. This explains the apparent contradiction formulated at the beginning of our work: why, within a business context under unremitting pressure to keep costs down, multinational companies keep making use of such a costly solution.

On the other hand, to analyse the extent to which expatriates are expensive, we should take into account not only the costs but also the benefits. Investments made in expatriates, through their compensation packages, will be recovered as long as the assignment is successful, but success does not come spontaneously. On the contrary, research has shown that failure in both the expatriation and repatriation phase is common in a large number of MNEs. A key factor in the success or failure of international assignments is the initial alignment of expectations between the organization and the employee (the psychological contract between both parties) and how it evolves over time, which could eventually affect the compensation package. Establishing and maintaining a relationship of mutual loyalty is the best way to ensure that expatriates' high costs are beneficial to the company, since these are the grounds on which the company can greatly benefit from international assignments.

To sum up, we can state that although looking into the design details of compensation packages may be the most urgent task, it is not the most important need in this area. Building trust, insofar as costs are affected by it, is perhaps a more relevant factor from a purely economic perspective.

> ## Discussion questions
>
> 1 Why are expatriates so expensive? Is there any way to reduce this cost?
> 2 What are the costs incurred in recruiting candidates from the local labour market instead of expatriates?
> 3 Is there any situation in which the costs of using expatriates may be lower than those of using local nationals?

## Further reading

Chen, C.C., Choi, J. and Chi, S.C. (2002) 'Making Justice Sense of Local–Expatriate Compensation Disparity: Mitigation by Local Referents, Ideological Explanations, and Interpersonal Sensitivity in China–Foreign Joint Ventures', *Academy of Management Journal*, 45(4): 807–26.

Jones, G. and Wright, P. (1992) 'An Economic Approach to Conceptualizing the Utility of Human Resource Management Practices', *Research in Personnel and Human Resource Management*, 10: 271–99.

Reynolds, C. (2000) 'Global Compensation and Benefits in Transition', *Compensation and Benefits Review*, 32(1): 28–39.

Yan, A., Zhu, G. and May, D. (2002) 'International Asignments for Career Building: A Model of Agency Relationships and Psychological Contracts', *Academy of Management Review*, 7(3): 373–86.

## References

Alchian, A.A. and Woodward, S. (1988) 'The Firm is Dead; Long Live the Firm: A Review of Oliver E. Williamson's', *The Economic Institutions of Capitalism, Journal of Economic Literature*, 26: 65–79.

Baron, J. and Kreps, D. (1999) *Strategic Human Resources: Frameworks for General Managers.* New York: Wiley.

Bartlett, C.A. and Ghoshal, S. (1989) *Managing Across Borders: The Transnational Solution.* Boston: Harvard Business School Press.

Black, J.S. and Gregersen, H.B. (1999) 'The Right Way to Manage Expats', *Harvard Business Review*, 77(2): 52–60.

Bonache, J., Suutari, V. and Brewster, C. (2001) 'Expatriation: A Developing Research Agenda', *Thunderbird International Management Review*, 43(1): 3–20.

Boyacigiller, N. (1990) 'The Role of Expatriates in the Management of Interdependence, Complexity and Risk in Multinational Corporation', *Journal of International Business Studies*, 21(3): 357–81.

Chen, C.C., Choi, J. and Chi, S.C. (2002) 'Making Justice Sense of Local–Expatriate Compensation Disparity: Mitigation by Local Referents, Ideological Explanations, and Interpersonal Sensitivity in China–Foreign Joint Ventures', *Academy of Management Journal*, 45(4): 807–26.

Coase, R.H. (1937) 'The Nature of the Firm', *Economica*, 4 (new series): 386–405.

Dunning, J.H. (1988) 'The Eclectic Paradigm of International Production. A Restatement and Some Possible Extensions', *Journal of International Business Studies*, 19(1): 1–31.

Edstrom, A. and Galbraith, J. (1977) 'Transfer of Managers as a Coordination and Control Strategy in Multinational Organizations', *Administrative Science Quarterly*, 22: 248–63.

Ghoshal, S. and Moran, P. (1996) 'Bad for Practice: A Critique of the Transaction Cost Theory', *Academy of Management Review*, 21(1):13–47.

Grosse, R. and Kijawa, D. (1988) *International Business: Theory and Managerial Applications.* Homewood, IL: Irwin.

Hamill, J. (1989) 'Expatriate Policies in British Multinationals', *Journal of General Management*, 14(4): 19–26.

Hennart, J.F. (1991) 'The Transaction Costs Theory of Joint Ventures: An Empirical Study of Japanese Subsidiaries in the United States', *Management Science*, 37: 483–97.

Jones, G.R. (1987) 'Organization–Client Transactions and Organizational Governance Structures', *Academy of Management Journal*, 30: 197–218.

Jones, G. and Wright, P. (1992) 'An Economic Approach to Conceptualizing the Utility of Human Resource Management Practices', *Research in Personnel and Human Resource Management*, 10: 271–99.

Klein, B., Crawford, R.A. and Alchian, A.A. (1978) 'Vertical Integration, Appropriable Rents, and the Competitive Contracting Process', *Journal of Law and Economics*, 21: 297–326.

Kopp, R. (1994) 'International Human Resource Policies and Practices in Japanese, European and United States Multinationals', *Human Resource Management*, 33(4): 581–99.

La Porta, R., López de Silanes, F. and Schleifer, A. (1997) 'Legal Determinants of External Finance', *Journal of Finance*, 52(3): 1131–50.

Lepak, D.Y. and Snell, S. (1999) 'The Human Resource Architecture: Toward a Theory of Human Capital Allocation and Development', *Academy of Management Review*, 24(1): 31–48.

Masters, J.K. and Miles, G. (2002) 'Predicting the Use of External Labor Arrangements: A Test of the Transaction Costs Perspective', *Academy of Management Journal*, 45(2): 431–42.

Mayrhofer W. and Brewster C. (1996) 'In Praise of Ethnocentricity: Expatriate Policies in European Multinationals', *International Executive*, 38(6), Nov/Dec: 749–78.

Nohria N. and Ghoshal, S. (1994) 'Differentiated Fit and Shared Values: Alternatives for Managing Headquarters–Subsidiary Relations', *Strategic Management Journal*, 15: 491–502.

Reynolds, C. (2000) 'Global Compensation and Benefits in Transition', *Compensation and Benefits Review*, 32(1): 28–39.

Rugman, A. (1981) *Inside the Multinationals: The Economics of Internal Markets*. London: Croom Helm.

Shane, S. (1994) 'The Effect of National Culture on the Choice between Licensing and Direct Foreign Investment', *Strategic Management Journal*, 15(8): 627–42.

Simon, H. (1961) *Administrative Behavior*. New York: Macmillan.

Teece, D. J. (1982) 'Towards an Economic Theory of the Multiproduct Firm', *Journal of Economic Behavior and Organization*, 3: 39–64.

Teece, D. (1986) 'Transaction Cost Economics and the Multinational Enterprise. An Assessment', *Journal of Economic Behavior and Organization*, 7: 21–45.

Williamson, O. (1975) *Markets and Hierarchies: Analysis and Antitrust Implications*. New York: Free Press.

Williamson, O. (1981) 'The Modern Corporation: Origins, Evolution, Attributes', *Journal of Economic Literature*, 19: 1537–68.

Williamson, O. (1985) *The Economic Institutions of Capitalism: Firms; Markets, Relational Contracting*. New York: Free Press.

Williamson, O. (1990) 'Chester Barnard and the Incipient Science of Organization', in O.E. Williamson (ed.), *Organization Theory: From Chester Barnard to the Present and Beyond*. New York: Oxford University Press, 172–206.

Williamson, O. (1993) 'Transaction Cost Economics and Organization Theory', *Industrial and Corporate Change*, no. 2: 107–56.

Williamson, O.E. and Ouchi, W.C. (1981) 'The Markets and Hierarchies Perspective: Origins, Implications, Prospects', in A.H. Van de Ven and W.F. Joyce (eds), *Perspectives on Organization Design and Behaviour*. New York: Wiley, 347–70.

Williamson, O.E., Wachter, M.L. and Harris, J.E. (1994 [1975]) 'Understanding the Employment Relation: The Analysis of Idiosyncratic Exchange', *Bell Journal of Economics*, 6(1): 250–78.

Wright, P.M., McMaham G.C. and McWilliams, A. (1994) 'Human Resources and Sustained Competitive Advantage: A Resource-Based Perspective', *International Journal of Human Resource Manangement*, 5(2): 301–26.

Yan, A., Zhu, G. and May, D. (2002) 'International Assignments for Career Builing: A Model of Agency Relationships and Psychological Contracts', *Academy of Management Review*, 7(3): 373–86.

# 7

# International careers and repatriation

*Margaret Linehan and Wolfgang Mayrhofer*

## Introduction

Today's global business environment presents strategic challenges for organizations as they rapidly internationalize through strategic alliances, joint ventures, international subsidiaries, and so on. As a result, firms are increasingly sending their employees on international assignments both to implement current global strategies and to enhance the organization's capabilities for the future. These assignments usually last from two to five years (depending on the country of origin), and often expatriates are 'out of sight, out of mind' of the parent company during that time (Allen and Alvarez, 1998; Hammer *et al.*, 1998). The company does not worry about this employee until the foreign assignment is over. In other words, little or no planning is done for the repatriation of the executive or for how the foreign arrangements fit into the career path of the individual. It has been stated that career mobility is the major factor, apart from pay, that appears to lead individuals to accept work overseas. Interestingly, data on the degree to which international assignments actually enhance one's chances for success seem to be mixed. Many companies say that they seek to develop internally sophisticated executives and consider the employee's future in making assignments. There are many cases, however, in which such assignments are undertaken with little thought to future career paths or the company's long-range plans. This leads to the phenomenon of the overseas manager who returns home to find that his or her company is ill-prepared to utilize his or her special expertise.

Both practitioners and academics tend to assume that repatriation should be easy – after all, the person is 'coming home'. Research suggests, however, that managers may find that adjusting to being home is more difficult than adjusting to being overseas (Forster, 1994; Stroh, 1995; Adler, 1996). For some managers, the process of adjustment may be so difficult that the only solution they see is to seek employment elsewhere. Research indicates that between 20 per cent and 50 per cent of all expatriates resign – a significantly higher percentage than among non-repatriate executives (Stroh, 1995; Black and Gregersen, 1998).

The problems associated with repatriation are essentially twofold: career advancement opportunities, and relocation on return. Although companies make an effort to facilitate adaptation to the foreign environment – such as providing predeparture training and other types of relocation assistance, including finding accommodation – most do little for the individual on repatriation because they assume that the problems of re-entry to the home country and home operation are minimal. Tung (1988a) suggested that the re-entry process can be particularly painful when expectations of upward career advancement are not realized. Frustration sets in when the repatriate finds he or she is not able immediately to use the skills and experience required abroad. Tung's research further illustrated that in many United States' multinationals, some repatriates found that their career progression had stagnated. In fact, some high achievers refuse an overseas assignment for fear that it may result in a negative career move. In a survey conducted by Moran, Stahl and Boyer, Inc. (1988), a consulting firm in Colorado, only 4 per cent of the United States' companies surveyed considered overseas assignments as having 'a positive effect on career advancement'.

Preparing managers for foreign assignments has been the focus for many academic researchers in the past decade. An often neglected area of research in international human resource management is what happens to the subsequent career path of the individual on return. In other words, did the international assignment have a positive impact on the person's overall career development and subsequent advancement in the organization? Clague and Krupp (1978) suggested that international assignments should be perceived not just as a means to solve specific job crises overseas, but as an integrated part of the employees' careers. Whether or not the move is intended to be career development for the individual, the assignment out and reassignment back should be considered as part of an integrated whole, preferably prior to the initial move. Both the expatriation assignment and the repatriation move should be examined as parts of an integrated whole, not as two discrete – much less unrelated – events in the individual's career path.

## Dimensions of repatriation

The complexity of the repatriation problem varies from company to company and from person to person. The situation is also affected by such factors as the number of years spent abroad, the purpose of the overseas assignment, the foreign location and the executive's age. Clague and Krupp (1978) reported that studies on corporate approaches to repatriation show that repatriates generally face three principal problems: readjustment to the organization, reacclimation to the broader environment, that is the home country's way of life, and personal finances or, to broaden the focus, the psychological reactions to repatriation. These are separate, although obviously connected elements.

# Readjustment to the organization

Reintegration into the corporate hierarchy is unquestionably the most critical worry confronting returning executives, because it has, or can have, a major impact on the individual's career. It is the area in which a lack of awareness or responsiveness by the company leads to the most bitter frustration on the part of an employee. Often a repatriate believes that the level of responsibility given to him or her at headquarters is not comparable to that which he or she enjoyed overseas. The repatriated executive would have been accustomed to an amount of independence and initiative not as common in domestic assignments, so he or she may feel powerless when placed at the same level as people with similar seniority and skills levels who have not worked abroad. Foreign positions tend to be professionally challenging, with the foreign manager acting almost as an entrepreneur. The more outstanding the performer, the more difficult it will be to adjust to the domestic organizational climate. Many repatriated managers report that if they had been given a choice between coming home to a lateral position or transferring to another overseas location in a lateral job, they would have picked the latter. But, they are usually not given the choice.

# Reacclimation to the 'old new environment'

This concern is often more serious for the family than for the repatriating executive. Because family members have become used to foreign ways, customs at home frequently seem strange or even annoying. Clague and Krupp (1978) noted that the general feeling may perhaps best be expressed by the comment that when they went abroad they knew they were foreigners. On returning from abroad, people find themselves under great pressure to become completely settled right away, since, after all, they are now 'home'. There is a general feeling among returning expatriates that other people – both in the company and outside it – should be sympathetic to the fact that coming home necessitates pulling up roots just as going abroad does, and that another adjustment period is required.

# Psychological aspects of repatriation

In any organization, employees have a psychological or unwritten contract with managers and other members of the organization. Included in this contract is the set of expectations the employees have concerning how they will be treated by management and employees. If individuals believe that the rewards they are receiving equal or exceed their contributions, they will likely remain committed to the organization. If their expectations are not met, however, lower levels of commitment will likely result.

According to Rousseau (1989), two general types of psychological contracts tend to be evident in organizations: transactional contracts and relational contracts. Transactional contracts focus primarily on economic issues within a specific time frame, for example money or labour hours. In contrast, relational contracts encompass not only economic exchanges but also socio-emotional. The substance of a relational exchange is generally less-measurable, more varied and more subjectively defined than a transactional exchange. Stroh *et al.* (1998) suggest that relational contracts are relevant to the study of employees in general but especially to the study of managers returning from international assignments. Most expatriates have more than 10 years of employment with the parent company that sends them overseas, so the international assignment is but one segment in an extended period of transactions between the individual and the organization. Although international assignments are single episodes in themselves, expectations about what will occur after the experience are closely intertwined with broader, dynamic expectations the individual has about his or her career within the organization. Additionally, the individual's expectations on repatriation generally encompass a wide spectrum of the individual's work and non-work life.

Recent theoretical and empirical work shows that there are a whole variety of possible psychological outcomes to job relocations, including repatriation. For some employees and their families these are extremely rewarding and beneficial experiences. For others they can be highly stressful, disruptive and problematic life-events (Munton and Forster, 1993). Most research, however, suggests that steps can be taken by companies to ease this process. For example, the length of notice given to employees prior to a job move is a crucial factor in facilitating adaptation. The more accurate the expectations which employees have about the new job the better will be the chances of successful adjustment. According to Forster (1994), however, an important overlooked element is the objectivity of the information which is provided by the home company prior to the return home (for example, about job opportunities in the home company).

Research with employees in a domestic context has illustrated that employees and their families who are relocating want regular communication between themselves and their employers during the course of the move, and a direct and accessible source of information about relocation-related issues within the company. Munton's (1991) research showed that the period of notice given to families can also have a critical bearing on the adjustment process. The longer employees have to prepare for moves the easier it is for them to plan effectively for, and to maintain a sense of control over, the move. Stress research has consistently demonstrated that feelings of control are an important safeguard against potentially stressful life events like repatriation.

Research by Nicholson and West (1988) found that once an employee has actually started a new job, the degree of freedom they have to do their job (role discretion), a lack of uncertainty (role conflict), and a lack of ambiguity about what they should actually be doing in their job (role clarity), are all positively correlated with successful adjustment to a new work role. This adjustment is also mediated by the social support available to employees in new work situations – particularly if the job move has involved marked changes to the content of their jobs. West and Nicholson (1989) pointed out that downward mobility can be, psychologically, a very damaging experience. It often reduces both motivation to work and actual performance and increases the likelihood of inter-organizational job moves.

Another important variable in adaptation to repatriation is the degree of adaptability, cohesion and communication in families. Families who are unable to adapt or communicate their problems and anxieties to each other often have greater adjustment problems during repatriation. Forster (1994) pointed out that if the partners and families of relocating employees are experiencing difficulties and stress, this can have a knock-on effect on the work performance of those employees. Similarly, Munton (1991) found that if partners and families can adapt quickly to the return home the principal breadwinner should adjust better, both at work and at home. Munton concludes that, in addition, these employees are less likely to take work-related problems home.

The major financial problems for a returning expatriate are the loss of special allowances and premiums and the effect of inflation on housing prices at home. Even though most companies urge their executives to think of the overseas premium as a separate part of their compensation, most companies pay the premium on an ongoing basis as part of an employee's regular pay cheque. Consequently, a family often tends to gradually absorb the extra money into its normal day-to-day spending pattern, becoming accustomed to a higher standard of living than it can have when it is repatriated and no longer receives the premium. The problem of rising home prices is also a concern as many expatriates may have sold their houses when they went abroad and simply cannot afford to buy comparable homes on their return.

## Process of repatriation

Given the growing proportion of business transactions that involve crossing national, cultural, linguistic, sectoral and other borders (see for example Bartlett and Goshal, 1991; Czinkota et al., 1994), it is no surprise that the number of people working internationally is growing: they take on foreign assignments through classic expatriation, join the group of internationals constantly moving from country to country, work in new forms of international assignments like frequent commuter assignments, continuous short-term visits to company locations abroad, and so on (see for example Brewster, 1991; Tung, 1988b; Thomas, 1998). But it is not only people moving around internationally; from a more comprehensive perspective, international careers evolve.

Careers are a central phenomenon of individual, organizational and societal reality. Far from being restrained to individual phenomena like rapid promotion, careers are located at the 'intersection of societal history and individual biography' (Grandjean, 1981: 1057) and thus link micro- and macro-frames of reference (Schein, 1978) which have traditionally been regarded as indissoluble (Hughes, 1937; Barley, 1989; Gunz, 1989). They can be regarded as a specific sequence of positions within a social space (Mayrhofer, 1996). Within the world of work, these positions are often jobs within the social space of an organization (Dyer, 1976) or a specific career field (Iellatchitch *et al.*, 2001). Within such a framework, international careers consist of a sequence of jobs in different organizations, countries and cultures (see for example Tung, 1988a). In this way, a process perspective is introduced (see also Peltonen, 1998, who explicitly uses a tournament perspective for repatriate career mobility).

Each career move – be it domestic or international – can be interpreted as a transition. Transitions can be conceptualized as phases of change that bridge two more stable zones. They emerge if events do or fail to occur, which in turn change conceptions about one's self and the world and which require changes in the behavioural, motivational and cognitive area (Schlossberg, 1981). Conceptually, transitions are often interpreted in the light of role theory (see Allen and Van de Vliert, 1984). Various authors offer frameworks describing core dimensions of transitions in general (Glaser and Strauss, 1971), work-related transitions (Nicholson, 1990) and international career transitions (Mayrhofer, 1996). Consequently, transitions play a major role in domestic as well as international careers. One of the major problems in (career) transitions is the uncertainty linked to them and the need for collective actors like the society, countries or organizations as well as individual actors like expatriates or their spouses to structure and influence the transitions (for specific problems for females see, for example Caligiuri and Lazarova, 2002).

One way of conceptualizing and potentially influencing transitional processes and their inherent uncertainties are *rites de passage*. Using secular-ceremonial elements, the transition between the old and the new position is structured via different kinds of rites that offer interpretation and meaning to the passagee as well as the social environment. The concept of *rites de passage* can also be used to understand and manage repatriation as a specific type of international career move: the transition to one's country and organization of origin after an international assignment.

## Conceptual framework: *rites de passage*

The concept of *rites de passage* is developed in the major work of the French ethnographer Arnold van Gennep (1986). He is, among others, interested in the analysis of various types of transitions and develops a structural scheme for such transitions that is – so he claims – suitable as a universal pattern for different kind of transitions. In terms of explanatory power, the structural scheme is limited. However, it allows a reduction of the complexity of ritual behaviour linked with transitions, provides a systematic view on various ritual expressions and relates them to each other.

Van Gennep claims that in all societies various social groups exist with different degrees of autonomy that are separated from each other to a greater or lesser extent. Beside their differences, these groups also have some joint characteristics, at least as common categories for description. Examples are: social origin, religion, profession, generational status or age group. The life course of human beings – in other words, the career of an individual – is essentially characterized by two phenomena. First, the individual simultaneously belongs to various social categories. For example, he or she is a member of a certain age group, has a specific social origin putting him or her into a certain strata or segment of society, has a certain position in social life because of the emerging relation to the economic system and the position within or outside this system, and so on. Second, belonging to these social categories is not static. The individual constantly has a career, that is she or he is on the move, thus changing social categories. Inevitably, this involves constantly moving across boundaries, either through deliberate choice or without any intention. People get older, change profession or leave the employment system, they marry and get divorced again, they leave headquarters for a work assignment abroad, they join a cadre of globally mobile professionals, and so on – and all these moves include moving across one or several boundaries (for the importance of organizational boundaries see van Maanen and Barley, 1984; for boundary spanning see Aldrich and Herker, 1977; for crossing intra-organizational boundaries see Schein, 1971; for viewing foreign assignments as organizational boundary management see Mayrhofer, 1997).

However, moving across boundaries is dangerous; for the individual as well as for the social context. For example, the society or the organization crossing boundaries is linked with a number of uncertainties. Changing social categories puts the individual into a situation where new social demands occur, where established patterns of behaviour and interpretation are challenged and do not necessarily provide an adequate response to the demands, where the transition from the old to the new context can fail because the individual is not prepared for letting the old go, accepting a transitory phase of 'being in-between' where one belongs neither to the old nor to the new situation, or where integration into the new situation becomes too difficult because neither the individual nor the social context is ready for or aware of the transition.

For the social context, boundary crossing of individuals is linked with uncertainty, too. The dynamic element of transition challenges the more static constitution of a social structure. A new configuration of individuals in a specific social category might produce a new dynamic, which, in turn, influences the social system. For example, a new cohort entering the university system can challenge established processes because of the number of new students, because of their differing norms, values and expectations, and so on.

Rites have a double function. On the one hand, from a systems perspective, they replace uncertainty, that is an external attribution pattern for success and failure, by risk, that is an internal attribution pattern. Thus, they allow a social system to conceptualize individual moves as part of its own functioning and not as something external (for the case of organizations preferring risk over uncertainty, see for example Luhmann, 1988). On the other hand, rites try to ease the transition for the individual as well as the social context through creating expectancy. They cope with the spatial, social and temporal aspects of transitions that are loaded with uncertainty. Through different types of rites this uncertainty is – at least partly – transformed into expectable steps. Social relationships and social antagonism is expressed, social conflicts are either avoided or channelled, and support for orientation as well as integration is provided through adequate rites.

Beyond the 'direct' functional dimension rites also have a symbolic aspect. In other words: they 'do' as well as 'say' something (Trice and Morand, 1989: 399). Award ceremonies demonstrate this quite clearly. When the best salespersons of a company are honoured by giving them a special prize, the mere functional dimension of providing a temporal and spatial framework for awarding the prize is clearly of minor importance. The symbolic aspects dominate: who is present, where does the ceremony take place, who speaks, how and to whom is this announced, and so forth.

The van Gennep framework proposes three different types of rites accompanying role transitions:

- *Rites de séparation* characterize the transition away from the old position, the process of 'letting go' and separation
- *Rites de marge* are linked to an intermediate state, a 'neither–nor' where the individual is in an ambiguous state in which he or she is no longer in the previous position but has not yet reached the next position
- *Rites d'agrégation* support the integration into the new position.

Many aspects of modern organizational life can be interpreted as transitional moves across boundaries, for example the integration of new organizational members, promotions, joining high seniority groups because of a long history with the organization, and so on. In these instances, secular instead of religious–spiritual rituals play the more important role. Secular rituals do not explicitly rely on a religious or spiritual framework – although some may argue that much of what happens in strong-culture organizations is very closely related to that – but try to order and regulate parts of the organizational life. They create the impression of legitimacy and authority for persons, organizations, events, values, views of the world and so on, and evoke harmony and order instead of conflict and disorder (Trice and Morand, 1989: 398).

The framework of *rites de passage* can be used to structure some of the individual experience and social, especially organizational efforts to deal with the various processes linked with transitions in such an international environment. For example, the various steps during the selection and preparation of people going on a foreign assignment include elements of *rites de séparation*. Selecting people into a group of a 'chosen few', assigning to them a specific status, separating them from their normal work during preparation, and symbolically honouring them as giving them an important task far from home can be interpreted as segregating them from the mainstream. Planned buffer stripping, that is the lack of support of organizations during the local adaptation process can be seen as an example for *rites de marge*. Individuals abroad are deliberately brought into a situation where their transitory status is emphasized and where there is a 'controlled' risk possibly paying off in terms of a more rapid adaptation to the local situation. Assigning a local mentor or an invitation to informal socializing after work can be regarded as *rites d'agrégation* that signal to the individual as well as to the social context that the person has made a further step in the process of finding a place in the new social categories after the international job move.

The framework can, however, also be used to discuss the process of repatriation. In the prototypical case, this transition involves expatriates returning home at the end of their foreign assignment to their country and organization of origin.

## *Rites de séparation*: letting go

As indicated above, rites de séparation are linked with loosening the ties to the 'old' position. They signal to the expatriate as well as to the social environment that the time of the foreign assignment is running out and that it is legitimate and necessary for the individual as well as the social context – in the case of repatriation often: the expatriate and the home as well as the host country organization – to loosen the connection with the current task, work and social environment, to look for new opportunities within the organization, and so on. More precisely, a number of well-known instruments and mechanisms within the expatriation and repatriation process can signal to the expatriate the beginning of the transition back home, thus taking over the function of *rites de séparation*. Specifically, mentoring relationships and negotiations about the future job after returning home can be mentioned.

Mentoring is usually conceptualized as 'the developmental assistance provided by a more senior individual within a protégé's organization – that is, a single dyadic relationship' (Higgins, 2001: 264). For more than two decades, researchers have studied a great variety of different aspects of the mentor–protégé relationship and its various consequences, especially in terms of career advancement (see for example Clawson, 1980; Kram, 1985; Dreher and Ash, 1990; Scandura, 1992; Ragins, 2000). Also in the international field, mentoring is often mentioned as an important way of keeping contact between the expatriate and headquarters.

The mentor is not only responsible for the constant contact, but becomes especially important during repatriation. The future perspectives within or outside the company after returning home are constantly an issue at least at a latent level. However, as the endpoint of the foreign assignment comes closer, it becomes more urgent and 'hot'. At the same time, the new prominence of this issue and the various

*Table 7.1* Typical tensions and areas of conflict between repatriate and organization of origin

| Repatriate | Misfit | Organization of origin |
|---|---|---|
| • Available | ⚡ | • Preferred/necessary |
| • Increased social competence | ⚡ | • Less leadership responsibility abroad |
| • Experience with a broad spectrum of decisions | ⚡ | • Narrow task spectrum |
| • Partly outdated technical know-how | ⚡ | • Immediate performance in new position preferred available/necessary |
| • Promotion | ⚡ | • Lack of career opportunities |
| • Use of acquired know-how | ⚡ | • Little use for new competencies |
| • Integration into social networks within organization | ⚡ | • Colleagues show lack of interest or envy |
| • Maintenance of foreign standard of living | ⚡ | • Financial downgrading due to hardship bonus etc. |

*Sources*:   Kühlmann and Stahl (1995: 182); Erten-Buch and Mattl (1999: 354).

ways in which it is addressed, including in a mentoring relationship, also serve as rites. They signal both to the expatriate and the social environment – family, home and host-country organization – that the end of the assignment comes closer and that change is ahead. Thus, the change of content in the mentoring relationship is a visible signal for the start of an uprooting process.

In addition to changes in the mentoring relationship, formal negotiations between the expatriate and the responsible persons at headquarters are a regular part of this phase. Again, these negotiations can be interpreted as rites that indicate the closing of the foreign assignment and the first steps of entering a transition phase. In these negotiations, there are some typical sources for tensions due to different expectations, positions of interest and practical considerations. Table 7.1 shows some of the most frequent areas of tensions between the expatriate and the organization of origin.

As can be seen, these conflicts are neither easy to avoid nor easy to solve and can lead to tough decisions on the side of the repatriate as well as the organization. In any case, these conflicts clearly signal to all involved that things become more fluid – which leads to the next stage of the transition, with rites linked with it.

## *Rites de marge*: being in-between

Rites de marge have the function of signalling and structuring a stage of 'neither–nor'. The passagee is no longer tied to the old position, but nevertheless, integration into the new position/role is not yet done. This intermediary status serves as a time where changes can occur and where the individual as well as the social environment have to be aware that little routine and standards exist regardless of 'officially' being in the old or the new position. This stage can broadly be compared to the middle stage of the well-known 'unfreeze–change–refreeze' steps in organizational development. Within the repatriation process, this stage involves readjustment processes and often a culture shock in reverse. Both experiences indicate that the individual is in search of new meaning and has no secure roots neither in the old nor the new position.

Cross-cultural readjustment is the transition from a foreign culture back into one's home culture. It is the experience of facing previously familiar surroundings after living in a different environment for a significant period of time. The repatriation of a corporate executive into the domestic organization and social environment simultaneously has a sudden and profound impact on the individual as well as family members. There is an unanticipated re-entry culture shock or sense of loss and isolation resulting from a lack of current behavioural understanding of the repatriates' home country (Harvey, 1982). The executive and family members have missed out on many events, fads and trends and experienced social isolation that was not expected, making the problem that much more difficult to deal with by each individual (Kendall, 1981). According to Tung (1988a), European organizations have reported that repatriation may be an equally traumatic experience as expatriation because of problems of reabsorption, both professional and personally.

The impact of repatriation on the expatriate and family members may become a significant issue among employees who are considering a foreign assignment if their company does not have a programme for dealing with the complex repatriation dilemma. Forster (2000) found that the biggest single problem encountered by British companies over the last 10 years has been with the repatriation of employees, rather than with the management of expatriation. Previous research also identified re-entry as a major personnel issue for international companies: Repatriating executives from overseas assignments is a top management challenge that goes far beyond the superficial problems and costs of physical relocation. The assumption is often that since individuals are returning home they should have no trouble adapting; however, experience has shown that repatriation is anything but simple (Corporation, 1978).

Studies have found that returning staff can face 'reverse culture shock' and other problems of adaptation (Johnston, 1991; Black, 1992). This often occurs when there is a significant mismatch between people's expectations prior to their repatriation and what they actually encounter after they return home. There are a number of well-documented reasons as to why this happens in companies: if the home organization has undergone restructuring or other forms of organizational change; if streamlining or decentralization has made some jobs redundant; if take-overs or mergers have resulted in a 'clear-out' of senior and middle-management positions; if the repatriates' original job roles have changed radically or been removed altogether while they have been abroad; if they have not been kept up-to-date about these changes or received adequate retraining or information prior to their return; if expatriates have unrealistic expectations about their career prospects and quality of life outside work after their return; if the organization has been experiencing problems of rationalization or 'downsizing' and is looking to 'off-load' more mature employees; or if the organization did not engage in any strategic forward planning and forecasting into the likely effects of their overseas plans on the management of both expatriation and repatriation (Forster, 1994). Another study has also indicated that many British companies appear to adopt an *ad hoc* 'sink or swim' attitude towards both employees and their families returning home (Johnston, 1991). This pattern is repeated in American companies where many do not make any explicit provision for the return of expatriates (Black, 1992).

Research conducted by Black *et al.* (1992a) in the United States found that 60 per cent to 70 per cent of repatriating employees did not know what their positions would be before they returned home. Sixty per cent said their organizations were vague about repatriation, about their new roles within the company and about their career progression. Moreover, they felt the companies disregarded their difficulties in adjusting back to life in the United States. When American expatriates found jobs within their companies, 46 per cent had reduced autonomy and authority. Black *et al.* further found that contrary to the belief that many Americans take international assignments for advancement, only 11 per cent were promoted, and 77 per cent of Americans actually took jobs at lower levels on repatriation than their international assignments.

## *Rites d'agrégation*: keeping high performers after international assignments

*Rites d'agrégation* characterize the final phase of a role transition. They are closely related to the new position within the social system and structure the process of role acquisition. They guide the individual as well the social environment during the fuzzy process of 'learning the ropes' of the new position. Within repatriation, this stage and the respective activities are closely linked with all the individual and organizational efforts of finding adequate tasks and perspectives for the repatriate. Specifically, the explicit and/or implicit signals about the use of the skills acquired abroad, the assignment of challenging and attractive new jobs and the decision processes about staying or leaving can be interpreted as rites that structure this phase.

During an international assignment, expatriates usually invest a significant amount of time and energy into developing international perspectives and skills (Tung, 1988b; Black *et al.*, 1992a). Managers are often sent overseas explicitly to gain global perspectives that will facilitate future strategy formulation and implementation responsibilities, and after returning home expatriates generally expect that their international skills will be utilized to enhance a firm's competitive position (Black et al., 1992b; Harvey, 1982). Unfortunately, the repatriation reality seems to be that repatriates are more often than not placed in 'holding patterns' without any real job assignment for several months, and relatively few receive promotions when returning home (Black and Gregersen, 1991a; Black et al., 1992a).

In contrast, if repatriates sense a genuine value of international experience and are promoted for having gained international experience, they are likely to view such corporate responses as positive reciprocation for investments they individually made to develop international skill-sets. Bagozzi (1978) and Homans (1974) suggested that valuing international experience and receiving a promotion on repatriation should relate positively to repatriates' intentions to stay in the parent company.

According to Gregersen and Black (1995), commitment to the parent company is a key factor in retaining high-performing executives after repatriation. Gregersen's (1992) research suggested that providing repatriates with a clear role or job when returning home can significantly enhance commitment to a parent company, and that the overall level of financial support expatriates receive after returning home is another important factor. Several respondents in both Gregersen's (1992) research and Gregersen and Black's (1995) study commented that when firms fail to provide adequate financial support on repatriation that commitment to the parent company decreases.

Gregersen and Black also suggested that in addition to engendering commitment to a parent company, facilitating repatriation work adjustment is another critical factor in retaining global executives. Similarly, earlier research by Black and Gregersen (1991b) pointed to role discretion as one of the most important means of facilitating work adjustment. Greater role discretion (that is over what, who and how work gets done) seems to facilitate repatriation work adjustment. Greater role discretion allows repatriates increased flexibility in utilizing methods for achieving tasks that they have mastered in the past and believe will be effective in the future, as well as providing greater freedom to experiment with new methods. Also, given the high levels of autonomy that most expatriates have while overseas, greater role discretion on repatriation seems to ease the psychological adjustment to work back home again. Black and Gregersen's research also suggested that another factor which affects repatriation work adjustment is role clarity. Many repatriates in their study indicated that they did not know what their job was or did not have a defined job for several months after returning home. Black and Gregersen suggested that firms can facilitate repatriation work adjustment (as well as commitment to a parent company) by planning further in advance for the return of executives and by making the jobs (the content, objectives and limitations) clearer to repatriates.

Gregersen and Black (1995) summarize that compared to leaving an overseas assignment, leaving a firm once one has returned to one's home country may be relatively easier. The geographical distance from one's home country and restricted employment alternatives in the overseas host country may make leaving an international assignment and moving to a new company difficult and enhance the relationship between expatriation adjustment and intentions to stay in the overseas assignment. In contrast, residing back in one's home country may make alternative employment opportunities relatively easier to explore and may weaken the relationship between repatriation adjustment and intention to stay with the parent firm. It is clear, therefore, that multinational companies can help develop global competence in executives by carefully crafting human resource policies to retain their best expatriates after they return home from international assignments. By so doing, multinationals can develop the strategic executive resources for effective formulation and implementation of successful international strategies (Barney, 1992; Morrison and Roth, 1992).

Stroh et al. (1998) stress the importance of closing the gap between expectations and reality for expatriates returning to their parent companies. By providing repatriates with accurate expectations about job demands, constraints and discretion in their new job, as well as in such nonwork-related parts of their lives as living standards and the overall financial situation, repatriates will not only more likely stay with their company on return, but also will be more committed to both their local work units and parent companies.

## New developments in the future

Much of the literature as well as this chapter implicitly or explicitly assumes a standard model of expatriation: an organization with operations abroad sends a male employee on a foreign assignment for a limited period of time. After the assignment expires, he returns home and reintegrates into the organization and country of origin. This standard model is still a very dominant form of working internationally. Nevertheless, this thinking needs expansion into at least three directions.

First, the number of female expatriates is slowly increasing. Although it still does not reflect the proportion of female managers in general, over the last decades one can see rising numbers of females working abroad (Taylor *et al.*, 2002). In turn, this has consequences for the repatriation debate since specific problems arise with female international managers repatriating. Second, focusing on 'expatriation' obfuscates that there are various types of expatriations. Although no expatriation is exactly the same, there are typical reasons why individuals accept foreign assignments and why organizations send individuals abroad. The resulting types of expatriation lead to different problems when it comes to repatriation. Third, new forms of international assignments are developing. Due to new organizational forms, better and faster commuting possibilities, new technologies and cost pressure, classic expatriation is partly replaced, but to a greater extent supplemented by new ways of working internationally. Such 'quasi-expatriations' again lead to different questions in the area of repatriation.

# Repatriation of female international managers

There is a dearth of empirical research which details the repatriation phase for female international managers, presumably because of their relative scarcity. Recent research on factors influencing the adjustment of women on global assignments virtually ignores the repatriation issue (Caligiuri and Cascio, 1998; Caligiuri et al., 1999; Caligiuri and Tung, 1999). Research conducted by Linehan and Scullion (2002) with female repatriated managers found that many of the difficulties experienced at the repatriation stage are similar for both males and females. The executives in their research, however, observed that, as females, they experienced greater uncertainty regarding re-entry because many female international managers are in a pioneering role. The managers also suggested that tokenism, isolation, lack of role models and being test cases for future international female managers were significant difficulties for them when they returned to their home organizations.

Female international managers are still in a pioneering role, and as they do not have female role models or female career paths to follow, this further increases the uncertainties regarding re-entry to their home organizations. The return of pioneering female executives with international experience can cause difficulties for home managers when allocating the returning female executives to suitable positions. Outgrowing home organizations is a risk shared by female and male managers after their international experiences, but missed promotional opportunities because of being overlooked is, however, a greater risk for female international managers due to the pioneering role the majority of females occupy. The repatriated females in Linehan and Scullion's research, however, now see themselves as role models, which they believe will positively influence the careers of future female international executives in their organizations.

The female managers believed that if they had the support of mentors or networks during their international assignment the re-entry process might have been easier, as they would have been informed of developments in their home organizations while abroad. Linehan and Scullion suggest that in an international management context, and particularly at the repatriation stage of the international career move, a mentoring relationship is even more important than in domestic management. Mentors provide the contact and support from the home organization which in turn facilitates re-entry, and reduces the 'out of sight, out of mind' syndrome. Linehan and Scullion also suggest that networking may be particularly important for the repatriation of female managers as a significant number of women may not have had mentors. The exclusion of female managers from business and social networks, however, compounds their isolation, which in turn may prevent female managers from building up useful networking relationships that would be advantageous for their repatriation. Given the absence of family and friends while abroad, the benefits provided by formal and informal networking in international management are of greater value when re-entering home-country organizations.

Linehan and Scullion conclude that many European-based multinationals have a low sense of awareness of the need for repatriation programmes in general and a lack of appreciation of the particular needs of female executives in relation to the repatriation process. Their research suggests that companies should develop integrated approaches to repatriation for female executives, which incorporate both organizational/career issues and individual issues, and that effective mentoring and networking strategies are key elements of successful repatriation management for female executives.

## Different types of repatriation

Generally speaking, organizations use expatriates for three major reasons: transfer of know-how and qualifications because of a temporary lack of local technical skills; improving managerial efficiency through enhanced opportunities of exerting influence; and investment into human capital, that is personal development of the assignees and the organizational workforce (Kammel and Teichelmann 1994). A recent study shows that the three main reasons for long-term assignments are skill-transfer (74 per cent), managerial control (62 per cent) and management development (60 per cent) (see CReME Executive Report 2000: 6). Whereas the former reason is mainly linked with sustaining the operating procedures, both the enhancement of managerial efficiency through controlling the foreign operations and the investment into human capital are closely tied to the issue of integration in MNCs, resulting from a permanent – and most likely insoluble – tension in MNCs between the tendency towards organizationwide 'global' standardization and the necessity of adapting to the 'local' environment (Czinkota et al., 1994; Phatak, 1995). Following this, two dimensions emerge as crucial: controlling foreign operations and developmental reasons.

MNCs try to influence their foreign operations via expatriates in a direct, immediate way and on a short-term basis. Expatriation following this line of reasoning mainly serves as a measure to unify the control of the governing units of the organization headquarters. Expatriates are put into a specific formal and informal position to exert influence on managerial and informal processes and structures as well as socialization processes (Edström and Galbraith, 1977; Kumar and Karlshaus, 1992).

A second major reason besides control is investment in human capital. Immediate effects on the technical qualification profile, growing intercultural competence and building a basis for future career development and promotion due to organizational policies requiring a foreign assignment for certain positions can be mentioned here. The stay abroad helps them build personal networks, gives them a new understanding of the international dimensions of business, and enables them to better consider regional, national and local peculiarities in their actions, for example. In other words, they are better prepared to handle the tensions between integration and differentiation (Pausenberger and Noelle, 1977; Tung, 1988a).

Based on these considerations, one can differentiate between four ideal types of expatriation patterns when dichotomizing the degree to which foreign assignments (a) are linked with immediate control considerations; and (b) are part of systematic investment into human capital through personnel development measures (see Figure 7.1). These four ideal types can be described as follows.

- Type 1 exists in MNCs that send expatriates abroad primarily for the reason of coordination and control, and where there is only a little emphasis on personnel development issues. Expatriation is an important means to control the foreign activities or to align them with the overall corporate strategy. Likewise, expatriates are used in transition or crisis periods where it is crucial to control the current and future course of a foreign business unit tightly. This pattern can be metaphorically termed 'watchdog' or 'trouble-shooting' logic.
- Type 2 is at work if foreign assignments are important for the overall immediate coordination and integration tasks as well as part of a personnel development concept. The jobs that are filled through expatriation are important in terms of management and control. At the same time, the careers of the expatriates are not limited to those kinds of task or the current job. Instead, these assignments are part of the process of acquiring different aspects of leadership competency that enable the expatriates to take over even more responsibility in the mid-range perspective. This pattern can be termed 'senior management' or 'high potential' logic.
- Type 3 emphasizes personnel development. Control and management issues do not play a central role during the foreign assignments. Under this logic, personal development and growth through getting international experience, getting to know people, widening one's horizon for the international dimension of business and so on are central. The actual kind of job done during the assignment is not the most important thing. This pattern can be called 'developmental' or 'junior' logic.

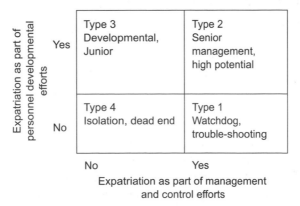

*Figure 7.1*  Typology of repatriation patterns

- Type 4 occurs when expatriation has neither much to do with coordination and control issues nor with investment into human capital or career development. An assignment under this logic is internally a very clear signal of punishment, being put aside or lack of potential. Metaphorically, one can call this pattern 'isolation' or 'dead-end' logic.

These logics can be characterized in more detail along various dimensions that describe the visible elements used to manage expatriates' careers; that is career paths and staffing strategies and the norms, rules and regulations that become evident in them (see Mayrhofer, 1996, 2001, for greater detail). Depending on the type of expatriation pattern, different consequences for repatriation arise.

Repatriation within a type 1 'watchdog, trouble-shooting' pattern is rather difficult. The position abroad was important, the expatriate was a 'headquarters ambassador', clearly important to the headquarters as well as the subsidiary. Because of the important decision and the inclusion into central interaction and decision-making networks the expatriate has often entered 'inner circles' not available until now. This often creates expectations about the future job after returning home that cannot be fulfilled. In turn, this might lead to disappointment and ultimately to leaving the organization. Likewise, the long-term consequences of taking over the role of watchdog/trouble-shooter are not entirely clear. Frequently this role is linked with tough decisions that create quite significant resistance and 'enemies', and consequently this might affect the future career within the organization because of micro-politics, for example through barriers that are built by those opposed to measures taken during the foreign assignment.

Within a type 2 'senior-management' pattern, a similar situation occurs. Occupying a prominent position during a foreign assignment, often in one of the foreign operations with high strategic importance, brings with it an increasing level of aspiration concerning material as well as non-material incentives. Specifically, career advancement is expected. After returning to the home organization, it is often difficult to fulfil these expectations.

A type 3 'developmental, junior' pattern leads to a different situation. Often the duration of the foreign assignment is not very long, which makes reintegration easier. Likewise, the expectations linked with the foreign assignment differ from those developed within a type 1 or 2 pattern. Within a type 3 pattern, expectations concerning career advancement are built, too. However, expatriates within this pattern are, currently, often not placed so high in the hierarchy and are much more open to different career routes. Thus, a greater number of alternatives are still available to them, all of which makes the repatriation process easier.

In its pure form, a type 4 'isolation, dead-end' pattern does not contain repatriation since its ultimate goal is to keep the expatriate away from core organizational units. If through a change in organizational politics the expatriate is transferred back to the organization of origin, repatriation is not easy. The expatriate is linked with a potential stigma, either that of failure or exile or that of 'triumphant return'. Both labels make a smooth repatriation process unlikely because of the high visibility of the returnee.

## Quasi-expatriation and repatriation

Changes in the international environment, in international organizations, and in the expatriates themselves are reflected in a growing debate about the significance of expatriation in its 'traditional' form (Mayrhofer and Brewster, 1996). Some argue that classic expatriation will lose its significance and will partly be replaced as well as supplemented by different forms of foreign assignments that can be termed 'quasi-expatriation'. There are a number of reasons for that:

- Technological developments such as the increasing use of e-mail, telephone and video conferencing, real-time computer information from around the world, as well as the improvement of travel possibilities increasingly offer alternatives to the traditional form of long-term expatriation (Scullion and Brewster, 2001).
- A growing number of small and medium-sized enterprises (SMEs) are on the threshold of internationalization, and their approach to market-entry strategies cannot be compared with and explained by theories of internationalization that have been developed from research in large multinational enterprises (Scullion, 1999). The traditional form of long-term expatriation is something they often cannot afford in terms of money or of personnel, respectively.
- In Europe, the geographical as well as the legal and administrative situation supports alternatives to long-term international assignments, such as Eurocommuting and frequent flying (Forster, 2000; Scullion and Brewster, 2001).
- A larger number of regional economic zones as well as the growing number of mergers between MNCs will also foster cross-border recruiting as well as a perception of expatriates who – travelling within the EU – are said to be not really abroad and therefore not to need special treatment, contracts and the like.
- Project-dominated organizational forms also affect the area of expatriation. Founding a subsidiary may be defined as a project run by specialists who are not part of the company itself; the parent company only supervises this process by frequent visits to the operation site (Harris, 2000).
- Merging companies of different countries may see no need to set up operations in the foreign countries. They are already well-established by one of the new partners (Scullion and Brewster, 2001).

Evidence from case studies conducted in the German clothing industry (Mayrhofer and Scullion, 2002) as well as in the Spanish clothing industry (Bonache and

Cervino, 1997) gives interesting examples of industries operating successfully with a large number of 'quasi-expatriates'. An ongoing study into new forms of international working, carried out among 65 MNEs by the Centre for Research into the Management of Expatriation (CReME) reveals supporting results. A higher increase can be observed in the proportion of short-term assignments (67 per cent), and international commuter assignments as well as frequent-flyer assignments (52 per cent) than in traditional long-term assignments (Harris, 2000).

In different forms of 'quasi-expatriation' a number of 'classic' problems well-known from the expatriate discussion occur. Selection and preparation problems, encountering different cultures, and the specific problems females face in such situations are just some of the issues that emerge. However, there are also some distinct differences if the classic expatriation–repatriation cycle is interrupted because expatriation no longer exists in its original form. The idea of a 'cycle' with distinctive stages becomes questionable, preparations for foreign assignments get new dimensions, for example how to prepare for a fluid situation with a constant mix between well-known and not so well-known situations, the issue of support during the assignment requires new solutions, and so forth.

Repatriation takes on new form and meaning, too. If the picture changes from a 'macro' cycle of selection, training, assignment and repatriation that spans over several years to a much more diverse situation containing, for example, a constant flow of micro-cycles lasting days or weeks as in the case of frequent traveller arrangements or the lack of a return in the case of becoming an international, this has consequences for repatriation. Either repatriation becomes completely obsolete or it has to be defined in a new way.

In the case of frequent-traveller arrangements, the continuously occurring return of the 'quasi-expatriate' has to be managed. For the individual, this situation can be compared with constantly being a boundary-spanner who is 'at home' in different worlds and, at the same time, building bridges and spanning boundaries. Repatriation in this sense does not mean helping people to reintegrate, but to cope with such a mixed situation and the specific situation of boundary-spanning.

Likewise, if the individual is involved in a series of international assignments with no, or only short, periods of working in the organization and country of origin, the issues involved in repatriation change. Again, reintegration into the familiar context of 'home' is not the primary issue or it may not be an issue at all. The emphasis lies in helping the individual to prepare for the next international move. That can involve coping with identity problems such as, 'Who am I? Where are my professional and cultural roots?' that can arise, and also the family dimensions of constantly being on the move such as, 'Which school system offers the best portability of qualifications and certification for the kids? How can we cope with dual-career problems when both spouses have a career of their own?' or that future career opportunities open as well as close because of such a pattern. Such a form of repatriation can use some of the know-how acquired in traditional research and practice, but this is still in its early stages.

# Conclusions

Multinationals have begun to experience difficulty in attracting executives to accept foreign assignments, and one of the contributing factors in this reluctance to go abroad is the ambiguity that surrounds the executive's career on repatriation. Just as multinationals have recognized the need to train executives for foreign assignments, they must also develop a plan or process for facilitating the re-entry of executives into domestic operations. Re-entry positions signal the importance given to international experience. If the repatriate is promoted or his/her international experience is valued by the home organization, then the international assignment is interpreted as a positive career move. If the repatriated manager, however, does not have a suitable position to return to, or expatriation is seen as 'out of sight, out of mind', other employees may decide that the acceptance of an international assignment is a high-risk decision in terms of future career progression within the organization.

The increasing empirical and anecdotal evidence illustrates that re-entry to the home country presents new challenges as the repatriate copes with what has been termed *re-entry shock*, or *reverse culture shock*. Dowling *et al.* (1999) proposed that given the more profound effect that job-related factors appear to have, *re-entry shock* is perhaps a more accurate term to describe the readjustment process experienced upon repatriation. Adler (1996) suggested that organizations fail to profit from the potential benefits of employees' overseas assignments. For the organization to benefit fully from its investment in overseas assignments, both the home organization and the repatriates need to understand the re-entry transition. Both management and repatriates must identify job skills acquired or enhanced overseas, and systematically find ways in which those skills can be integrated and productively used in the home organization. Management needs to understand the full importance of staying in contact with overseas staff members, of planning for their return, and of recognizing the value of their overseas experience. The attitudes of managers who stay at home must be changed, as well as the evaluation and reward schemes.

The multinational company must act to solve repatriation problems in order to retain valuable employees and to encourage the acceptance of international positions. Most of the solutions have relatively low costs, and involve better communication and organizational sensitivity to the stresses and pressures involved in the return of expatriates to an unfamiliar domestic environment. Most repatriation problems can be solved through planning and better communication. The problems and their solutions seem relatively simple, but many multinationals have not yet considered that the repatriate may have some adjustments to make. It is assumed that 'They're home, aren't they?'

> ## Discussion questions
>
> 1 To what extent do new forms of expatriation (quasi-expatriation) change the 'classic' problems and views on repatriation?
> 2 What are typical phases in work-related transitions?
> 3 How do rites help to manage work-related transitions?
> 4 How do different types of expatriation change the issues that expatriates and their organizations face during the repatriation process?

## Further reading

Feldman, D.C. and Tompson, H.B. (1993) 'Expatriation, Repatriation, and Domestic Geographical Relocation: An Empirical Investigation of Adjustment to New Job Assignments', *Journal of International Business Studies*, 24(3): 507–29.

Peltonen, T. (1997) 'Facing the Rankings from the Past: A Tournament Perspective on Repatriate Career Mobility', *International Journal of Human Resource Management*, 8(2): 6–23.

Stroh, L.K., Gregersen, H.B. and Black, J.S. (1998) 'Closing the Gap: Expectations Versus Reality Among Repatriates', *Journal of World Business*, 33(2): 111–24.

Trice, H.M. and Morand, D.A. (1989) 'Rites of Passage in Work Careers', in M.B. Arthur, D.T. Hall and B.S. Lawrence (eds), *Handbook of Career Theory*. Cambridge: Cambridge University Press, 397–416.

## References

Adler, N.J. (1996) *International Dimensions of Organizational Behavior*, 3rd edn. Boston, MA: Kent.

Aldrich, H. and Herker, D. (1977). 'Boundary Spanning Roles and Organization Structure', *Academy of Management Review*, 2 April: 217–30.

Allen, D. and Alvarez, S. (1998) 'Empowering Expatriates and Organizations to Improve Repatriation Effectiveness', *Human Resource Planning*, 21(4): 29–39.

Allen, V.L. and Van de Vliert, E. (eds) (1984) *Role Transitions*. New York: Plenum.

Bagozzi, R.P. (1978) 'Marketing as Exchange: A Theory of Transactions in the Market Place', *American Behavioral Scientist*, 21: 93–102.

Barley, S.R. (1989) 'Careers, Identities, and Institutions: The Legacy of the Chicago School of Sociology', in M.B. Arthur, D.T. Hall and B.S. Lawrence (eds), *Handbook of Career Theory*. Cambridge: Cambridge University Press, 41–65.

Barney, J. (1992) 'Integrating Organizational Behavior and Strategy Formulation Research: A Resource Based Analysis', *Advances in Strategic Management*, 8: 39–61.

Bartlett C. and Goshal, S. (1991) *Managing Across Borders: The Transnational Solution*. London: London Business School.

Black, J.S. (1992) 'Coming Home: The Relationship of Expatriate Expectations with Repatriation Adjustment and Job Performance', *Human Relations*, 45(2): 113–222.

Black, J.S. and Gregersen, H.B. (1991a) 'When Yankee Comes Home: Factors Related to Expatriate and Partner Repatriation Adjustment', *Journal of International Business Studies*, 22: 671–94.

Black, J.S. and Gregersen, H.B. (1991b) 'When Yankee Comes Home: Factors Related to Expatriate and Spouse Repatriation Adjustment', *Journal of International Business Studies*, 22: 671–694.

Black, J.S. and Gregersen, H.B. (1998) *So You're Going Overseas: A Handbook for Personal and Professional Success*. San Diego: Global Business Publishers.

Black, J.S., Gregersen H.B. and Mendenhall, M.E. (1992a) *Global Assignments: Successfully Expatriating and Repatriating International Managers*. San Francisco: Jossey-Bass.

Black, J.S., Gregersen H.B. and Mendenhall, M.E. (1992b) 'Toward a Theory of Repatriation Adjustment', *Journal of International Business Studies*, 4: 737–60.

Bonache, J. and Cervino, J. (1997) 'Global Integration Without Expatriates', *Human Resource Management Journal*, 7(3): 89–100.

Brewster, C. (1991) *The Management of Expatriates*. London: Kogan Page.

Caligiuri, P. and Cascio, W. (1998) 'Can We Send Her There? Maximising the Success of Western Women on Global Assignments', *Journal of World Business*, 33(4): 394–416.

Caligiuri, P., Joshi, A. and Lazarova, M. (1999) 'Factors Influencing the Adjustment of Women on Global Assignments', *International Journal of Human Resource Management*, 10(2): 163–179.

Caligiuri, P. and Lazarova, M. (2002) 'A Model for the Influence of Social Interaction and Social Support on Female Expatriates' Cross-Cultural Adjustment', *Journal of International Human Resource Management*, 13(4): 772–91.

Caligiuri, P. and Tung, R. (1999) 'Comparing the Success of Male and Female Expatriates from a US Based Multinational Company', *International Journal of Human Resource Management*, 10(5): 763–82.

Clague, L. and Krupp, N.B. (1978) 'International Personnel: The Repatriation Problem', *Personnel Administrator*, April: 29–33.

Clawson, J.G. (1980) 'Mentoring in Managerial Careers', in C.B. Derr (ed.), *Work, Family, and the Career*. New York: Praeger, 144–165.

Corporation, B.I. (1978) 'Successful Repatriation Demands Attention, Care and Dash of Ingenuity', *Business International*, 3: 65–7.

CReME (Centre for Research into the Management of Expatriation) (2000) *Executive Report 2000*. Cranfield: Cranfield School of Management.

Czinkota, M.R., Ronkainen, I.A. and Moffet, M.H. (1994) *International Business*, 3rd edn. Dryden: Fort Worth.

Dowling, P.J., Welch, D.E. and Schuler, R.S. (1999) *International Human Resource Management: Managing People in a Multinational Context*, 3rd edn. Cincinnati, OH: South-Western College Publishing.

Dreher, G.F. and Ash, R.A. (1990) 'A Comparative Study of Mentoring Among Men and Women in Managerial Positions', *Journal of Applied Psychology*, 75: 539–46.

Dyer, L. (ed.) (1976) *Careers in Organizations*. Ithaca, NY: Cornell University.

Edström, A. and Galbraith, J.R. (1977) 'Transfer of Managers as a Coordination and Control Strategy in Multinational Organizations', *Administrative Science Quarterly*, 22 June: 248–63.

Erten-Buch, C. and Mattl, C. (1999) 'Interkulturelle Aspekte von Auslandseinsätzen', in D.V. Eckardstein, H. Kasper, and W. Mayrhofer (eds), *Management: Theorien-Führung-Veränderung*. Stuttgart. 321–56.

Forster, N. (1994) 'The Forgotten Employees? The Experiences of Expatriate Staff Returning to the UK', *International Journal of Human Resource Management*, 5(4): 405–427.

Forster, N. (2000) 'The Myth of the 'International Manager' *The International Journal of Human Resource Management*, 11(1): 126–42.

Glaser, B.G. and Strauss, A.L. (1971) *Status Passage*. Chicago: Aldine.

Grandjean, B.D. (1981) 'History and Career in a Bureaucratic Labor Market', *American Journal of Sociology*, 86(5): 1057–92.

Gregersen, H.B. (1992) 'Commitments to a Parent Company and a Local Work Unit During Repatriation', *Personnel Psychology*, 45(1): 29–54.

Gregersen, H.B. and Black, J.S. (1995) 'Keeping High Performers After International Assignments: A Key to Global Executive Development', *Journal of International Management*, 1(1): 3–31.

Gunz, H. (1989). *Careers and Corporate Cultures. Managerial Mobility in Large Corporations*. New York: Basil Blackwell.

Hammer, M.R., Hart, W. and Rogan, R. (1998) 'Can You Go Home Again? An Analysis of the Repatriation of Corporate Managers and Spouses', *Management International Review*, 38(1): 67–79.

Harris, H. (2000) *New Forms of International Working*. Cranfield: Center for Research into the Management of Expatriation.

Harvey, M. (1982) 'The Other Side of Foreign Assignments: Dealing with the Repatriation Dilemma', *Columbia Journal of World Business*, Spring: 53–9.

Higgins, M. (2001) 'Reconceptualizing Mentoring at Work: A Developmental Network Perspective', *Academy of Management Review*, 26(2): 264–88.

Homans, G.C. (1974) *Social Behavior: Its Elementary Forms*. New York: Harcourt Brace Jovanovich.

Hughes, E.C. (1937) 'Institutional Office and the Person', *American Journal of Sociology*, 43: 404–13.

Iellatchitch, A., Mayrhofer, W. and Meyer, M. (2001) 'The Fields of Career. Towards a New Theoretical Perspective', Paper presented at the European Group of Organisation Studies, Lyon, France.

Johnston, J. (1991) 'An Empirical Study of the Repatriation of Managers in UK Multinationals', *Human Resource Management Journal*, 1(4): 102–9.

Kammel, A. and Teichelmann, D. (1994) *Internationaler Personaleinsatz*, München/Wien.

Kendall, D. (1981) 'Repatriation: An Ending and a Beginning', *Business Horizons*, November–December: 21–5.

Kram, K.E. (1985) *Mentoring at Work: Developmental Relationships in Organizational Life*, Glenview, IL: Scott, Foresman.

Kühlmann, T.M. and Stahl, G.K. (1995) 'Die Wiedereingliederung von Mitarbeitern nach einem Auslandseinsatz', in T.M. Kühlmann (ed.), *Mitarbeiterentsendung ins Ausland*. Göttingen: Hogrefe, 177–211.

Kumar, N.B. and Karlshaus, M. (1992) 'Auslandseinsatz und Personalentwicklung. Ergebnisse einer empirischen Studie über den Beitrag der Auslandsentsendung zur Karriereperspektive von Stammhausmitarbeitern', *Zeitschrift für Personalforschung*, 6(1): 59–74.

Linehan, M. and Scullion, H. (2002) 'Repatriation of European Female Corporate Executives: An Empirical Study', *International Journal of Human Resource Management*, 13(2): 254–67.

Luhmann, N. (1988) *Die Wirtschaft der Gesellschaft*. Frankfurt: Suhrkamp.

Mayrhofer, W. (1996) *Mobilität und Steuerung in International Tätigen Unternehmen*, Stuttgart: Schäffer-Poeschel.

Mayrhofer, W. (1997) 'Auslandseinsatz als Instrument des Informationellen Grenzmanagements International tätiger Unternehmen – eine systemtheoretisch orientierte Analyse', in G. Schreyögg and J. Sydow (eds), *Managementforschung 7 – Gestaltung von Organisationsgrenzen*. Berlin: De Gruyter, 111–57.

Mayrhofer, W. (2001) 'Organisational International Career Logics (OICLs). A Conceptual Tool for Analysing Organisational Expatriation Patterns and Their Consequences for the Management of Organisations', *Thunderbird International Business Review*, 43(1): 121–44.

Mayrhofer, W. and Brewster, C. (1996) 'Ethnocentric Staffing Policies in European Multinationals', *International Executive*, 38(6): 749–78.

Mayrhofer, W. and Scullion, H. (2002) 'All Equal? The Importance of Context – Empirical Evidence about Male and Female Expatriates from the German Clothing Industry', *International Journal of Human Resource Management*, 13(5): 815–36.

Moran, Stahl, & Boyer, Inc. (1988) *Status of American Female Expatriate Employees: Survey Results*. Boulder, CO: Moran, Stahl, & Boyer.

Morrison, A.J. and Roth, K. (1992) 'A Taxonomy of Business-Level Strategies in Global Industries', *Strategic Management Journal*, 13: 399–418.

Munton, A. (1991) *Managerial Job Relocation and Stress: A Two-Year Investigation*. Sheffield: University of Sheffield.

Munton, A. and Forster, N. (1993) *Job Relocation: Managing People on the Move*. London: Wiley.

Nicholson, N. (1990) 'The Transition Cycle: A Conceptual Framework for the Analysis of Change and Human Resource Management', in G.R. Ferris, and K.M. Rowland (eds), *Organizational Entry* Greenwich, Conn.: JAI, 209–64.

Nicholson, N. and West, M. (1988) *Managerial Job Change: Men and Women in Transition*. Cambridge: Cambridge University Press.

Pausenberger, E. and Noelle, G.F. (1977) 'Entsendung von Führungskräften in ausländische Niederlassungen', *Zeitschrift für betriebswirtschaftliche Forschung*, 29: 344–66.

Peltonen, T. (1998) 'Narrative Construction of Expatriate Experience and Career Cycle: Discursive Patterns in Finnish Stories of International Career', *International Journal of Human Resource Management*, 9(5): 875–92.

Phatak, A.V. (1995) *International Dimensions of Management*, 4th edn. Cincinnati: South-Western Publishing.

Ragins, B.R. (2000) 'Marginal Mentoring: The Effects of Type of Mentor, Quality of Relationship, and Program Design on Work and Career Attitudes', *Academy of Management Journal*, 1177–95.

Rousseau, D.M. (1989) 'Psychological and Implied Contracts in Organizations Employee', *Responsibilities and Rights Journal*, 2: 121–39.

Scandura, T.A. (1992) 'Mentorship and Career Mobility: An Empirical Investigation', *Journal of Organizational Behavior*, 13: 169–74.

Schein, E.H. (1971) 'The Individual, the Organization, and the Career: A Conceptual Scheme', *Journal of Applied Behavioral Science*, 7: 401–26.

Schein, E.H. (1978) *Career Dynamics*. Reading, MA: Addison-Wesley.

Schlossberg, N.K. (1981) 'A Model for Analyzing Human Adaptation to Transition', *The Counselling Psychologist*, 9: 2–18.

Scullion, H. (1999) 'International HRM in Medium-Sized MNEs: Evidence from Ireland', in H. Harris (ed.), *International HRM: Contemporary Issues in Europe*. London: Routledge, 48–63.

Scullion, H. and Brewster, C. (2001) 'The Management of Expatriates: Messages from Europe?', *Journal of World Business*, 36(4): 346–65.

Stroh, L.K., (1995) 'Predicting Turnover Among Repatriates: Can Organizations Affect Retention Rates?', *International Journal of Human Resource Management*, 6(2) 443–56.

Stroh, L.K., Gregersen, H.B. and Black, J.S. (1998) 'Closing the Gap: Expectations Versus Reality Among Repatriates', *Journal of World Business*, 33(2): 111–24.

Taylor, S. Napier, N.K. and Mayrhofer, W. (2002) 'Women in Global Business', *International Journal of Human Resource Management*, 13(4): 160–6.

Thomas, D. (1998) 'The Expatriate Experience. A Critical Review and Synthesis', in J. Cheng and R. Peterson (eds), *Advances in International Comparative Management*. Stanford, Conn.: JAI.

Trice, H.M. and Morand, D.A. (1989) 'Rites of Passage in Work Careers', in M.B. Arthur, D.T. Hall, and B.S. Lawrence (eds), *Handbook of Career Theory*. Cambridge: Cambridge University Press, 397–416.

Tung, R.L. (1988a) 'Career Issues in International Assignments', *Academy of Management Executive*, 2(3): 241–4.

Tung, R.L. (1988b) *The New Expatriates: Managing Human Resources Abroad*. Cambridge, MA: Ballinger.

Van Gennep, A. (1986) *Übergangsriten*. Frankfurt: Campus.

Van Maanen, J. and Barley, S.R. (1984) 'Occupational Communities: Culture and Control in Organizations', *Research in Organizational Behavior*, 6: 287–365.

West, M. and Nicholson, N. (1989) 'The Outcomes of Job Changes', *Journal of Vocational Behaviour*, 34: 335–49.

# 8

# Issues in the management of industrial relations in international firms

*Emer O'Hagan, Patrick Gunnigle and Michael J. Morley*

## Introduction: managing industrial relations in international firms – national or international?

Scholars became interested in the area of industrial relations (IR) in international firms as early as the 1960s. In a seminal study on four of the world's largest international firms, Perlmutter (1969) produced a typology outlining three different approaches to international human resource management (IHRM). The first category in his typology was the ethnocentric approach. This meant that the human resource management (HRM) traditions practiced in the home country and headquarter base were regarded as superior and implemented in all the subsidiaries worldwide. The second category Perlmutter located was the polycentric model in which corporate headquarters devolved autonomy over human resource matters to each subsidiary. The final category, entitled 'geocentrism', entailed the wholly international firm. The notion is that managers in both headquarters and within subsidiaries work for the interest of the company rather than their country. It involves host and home-country managers collaborating together on an equal platform for the benefit of the firm.

Perlmutter argued that the geocentric approach was becoming prevalent amongst international firms. He saw geocentrism as the end point in an inevitable process of evolution, and he assumed that most successful international corporations would eventually adopt the geocentric perspective.

These notions initiated a long-standing debate on whether multinational corporations (MNCs) tended to adopt local (host-country) HRM and IR practices when establishing subsidiaries, or whether they adopt the practices employed at headquarters (home country), thereby shaping the dominant IR and HRM norms throughout the host country. A subsequent literature emerged pivoted around the host country versus country-of-origin thesis.

In this literature, it is argued by some commentators that the organization of production, and the management of IR systems within MNCs' subsidiaries, remains distinctly national in character. Richard Hyman (1994), for example, claims that national practices and conditions are too deeply embedded for a homogeneous transnational style of industrial relations to take hold in subsidiaries throughout Europe. This approach, labelled the 'host-country' stance argues that multinational corporations come under immense pressure to adopt the IR practices of those regions in which they invest.

This stance was given some empirical basis from the findings of the Cranet project which entailed a broad quantitative survey of HR and IR practices in large firms throughout some 25 countries (Brewster et al., 2000). The scale of the study made it difficult to pinpoint distinct patterns, as strong national traits exist throughout the countries surveyed, but one major finding which emerged was that despite the growth of economies of scale, technological developments therein and growing competition, IR practices have stubbornly retained their national distinctions (Morley et al., 1996).

A counter-argument has emerged within the European context in particular, fuelled by the implementation of the Single European Act and the subsequent flourishing of 'Euro-companies' (Schulten, 1996: 304–9). Commentators have argued that the combination of a tariff-free Europe, economies of scale and new technology for monitoring production have made MNCs a 'new force' within the European economy (Marginson and Sisson, 1994: 16). Marginson and Sisson claim that with this spread in global corporate structures, the influence of the host country over IR practices is likely to diminish. They point to three means by which the 'host-country' practice will be replaced by the 'country-of-origin effect'. They refer to the routine monitoring which headquarters now conduct on subsidiaries, and also point to the growth of Euro-company IR whereby managerial organization is centralized so that headquarters decisions have precedence over nationally based subsidiaries.

Ferner and Edwards (1995) list more channels by which host-country IR practices may become subordinated by the country-of-origin effect. They explain that firms can develop a strong, 'clan-like' international corporate culture that helps firms diffuse IR practice from one plant within the corporation to another. A host of empirical case studies have analysed the mechanism through which MNCs superimpose novel IR techniques onto indigenous methods. The best-known example is Womack et al.'s (1990) study which claimed that lean production is the undisputed best practice in manufacturing management, providing 'an omnipotent system and unequivocal blessing' (Berggren, 1993: 163).

This chapter looks at a number of issues in the management of IR in international firms and asks whether industrial relations at the level of the firm context is practised according to national and local traditions, or, alternatively, whether IR practices are becoming internationalized through the influence of MNCs and international regulations of MNC activity, such as those developed by the European Union (EU). In a nutshell, the chapter seeks to explore some important contextual considerations which may be viewed as potential convergence influences in IR.

The chapter is organized into three main sections. The first section introduces trade unions' role at the international level and the national level. This is discussed in relation to the host-country and country-of-origin literature. The second section examines employers' associations. They are also looked at in terms of their international and national functions. A case study is used to analyse employers' associations and the host-country and country-of-origin debate. Section three introduces the subject of collective bargaining within international firms generally. The chapter concludes by analysing how three branches of collective bargaining operate within international firms; firstly employee involvement and participation, secondly grievance, discipline and termination, and finally industrial conflict.

## Trade unions and the international firm

### International trade unions

The history of trade unions reflects that of the private firm in the sense that they both emerged onto the international level at the early stages of industrial capitalism. These trade union internationals are known as International Trade Secretariats (ITSs). They began to flourish in the aftermath of the First World War and the International Labour Organization was launched in Geneva in 1919 as a wing of the League of Nations. At the outset, these institutions were established to exchange information and promote international labour solidarity in the face of growing international firms. However, they quickly became fragmented and embroiled in the cold war's icy battles, with the International Confederation of Free Trade Unions (ICFTU) opposing the communist-led World Federation of Trade Unions (WFTU) (Gallagher, 1995).

International trade unionism never managed to develop into dynamic representatives of employees on the international domain, and the cold war fracture is only one explanation for this. De Nijs (1995) produces a number of other explanations for this truncated development, arguing that trade unions failed to develop a tradition of international solidarity because they did not regard multinational corporations as their 'natural' opponents until late in the day; the mid-1960s. He noted that management at corporate headquarter level tended to make strategic decisions on information gleaned above and beyond the borders of national systems, thereby placing decision-making largely outside the reach of the national parties. Additionally, trade unions are often not provided with adequate information to foresee how decisions are likely to be made within MNCs. For example, information on key strategic issues such as investment and research and development are usually highly centralized.

---

## Box 8.1 Reasons for trade union fragmentation

- MNCs and international trade unions did not regard each other as 'natural' opponents until the 1960s
- Locus of decision-making is situated outside national boundaries
- Key information is rarely decentralized and transparent
- Inadequate knowledge of mechanisms in international strategies
- MNC's ability to relocate national investment
- National trade unions fail to delegate power up to international trade unions.

*Source:* De Nijs (1995).

---

A related factor is that trade unions may not be familiar with or adequately understand key mechanisms which shape international strategies, such as financial reporting. Finally, trade union mobilization has been weakened by the ability of international firms to withdraw from a country and reorganize production internationally.

De Nijs further notes that international trade unions' weakness over the years is not only a result of the manner in which MNCs organize, but is also a byproduct of international trade unions' internal structure. For example, national trade unions, like governments, are reluctant to delegate power and autonomy up to international representative organizations. To date, international trade unions have been confined to a representative role within international institutions such as the EU: they have never developed power-broker relations (see Box 8.1). Trade unions' history is embedded within the national state and each developed in response to the cultural and structural differences which pertain in national-level IR systems, legal systems and social traditions.

## Trade unions: the national level

An understanding of the diversity in national trade unions and national systems of IR is essential to obtain a grasp of how international firms handle their IR. A debate has emerged on national trade unions which is pivoted around an optimistic/pessimistic dichotomy. The optimistic account claims that, with a number of exceptions, the majority of national unions have shown resilient sticking power in the face of enormous challenges such as internationalization of production, decentralization of bargaining structures and radical demographic changes in labour markets (Crouch and Traxler, 1995). The pessimistic thesis holds that trade unions are experiencing a deep-seated crisis which undermines the leverage and positions which they held in the postwar period of industrial growth (Ross and Martin, 1999). As Table 8.1 indicates, the trends in trade union membership globally appear to span the whole continuum from South Africa, which has witnessed definitive growth in the post-apartheid period, to France which has experienced steep decline, and from

*Table 8.1*  Trade union density

| | Trade union density (1995, %) | Change in trade union density (1985–95, %) |
|---|---|---|
| South Africa | 40.9 | 130.8 |
| Canada | 37.4 | 1.8 |
| United States | 14.2 | −21.1 |
| Australia | 24.3 | −29.6 |
| Sweden | 91.1 | 8.7 |
| United Kingdom | 32.9 | −27.7 |
| France | 9.1 | −37.2 |
| Italy | 44.1 | −7.4 |
| Hungary | 60.0 | −25.3 |

*Source*:  ILO (1997).

Sweden where membership growth is steady, to Italy where decline in numbers is small but significant.

The dichotomy of approaches may be because trade union power is a difficult subject to assess. It is not always accurate to focus on the issue of organizational resiliency such as union membership, union centralization, levels of collective bargaining and wage-setting, because institutions can persist as hollow structures long after they have outlived their original purpose (Ross and Martin, 1999). One may obtain a greater insight into trade union power by looking at the different systems of industrial relations in which they operate.

Countries such as the USA, the UK and increasingly Australia, Canada and New Zealand operate a decentralized system of collective bargaining where negotiations take place at the enterprise level (Poole and Warner, 1998). The Japanese model is underpinned by the US-style of enterprise-level bargaining, however the state plays a larger role than in the US case. The Japanese state coordinates employment policies to support industries and to protect employees involved in restructuring. This model differs greatly from that found in developing countries, for example Africa and Latin America. Trade unions in these regions tend to be weakened by the precarious nature of employment there; the predominance of agricultural and informal sectors limits the development of systems of social dialogue. Additionally, trade unions in many of these countries channel a lot of their energies into political issues which have emerged in post-colonial contexts. 'The European Model', in contrast, traditionally involves national and industry-wide bargaining over areas such as wages and working-time arrangements. While this model is challenged by growing trends of decentralization, it is still the predominant picture (Poole and Warner, 1998).

But these are only broad regional trends. Within each region, and often within certain sectors, IR practices differ quite radically. Within Europe alone one can locate a broad range of systems (Van Ruysseveldt and Visser, 1996a). As we have seen, some commentators argue that MNCs adapt their IR and HR practices according to the regional traditions found in the host country, while others contend that MNCs tend to employ the strategies and practices which they use in the home country.

## Host country versus country of origin and trade unions

This debate is reflected in studies on MNCs' relations with trade unions. For example, Dowling *et al.* (1999) look at US MNCs and note that union avoidance is deeply rooted in American managers' value systems; they claim that ideology is an important factor in shaping the HR and IR practice in US-owned subsidiaries. This influence is stronger, they suggest, if the revenues from the home market are large relative to revenues from overseas operations, which is frequently the case in US firms. They conclude that ideology, lack of experience with unions and sheer economic dominance contributes to a tendency in US-owned firms to establish union-free zones in overseas subsidiaries regardless of the national labour practices. However, this perspective has not gone unchallenged. Gunnigle *et al.* (2002) tested whether US MNCs are less likely to adopt local HR practices than European firms, finding that the nature of HR practices adopted is not simply shaped by the origin of the firm. Rather, they argue that the host country's labour-policy traditions and IR is the significant variable. Therefore, in countries such as Ireland and the UK, where domestic HR and IR practices are less codified, US-owned plants are under less pressure to localize practices, and, for example, to recognize trade unions. In contrast, US firms are more likely to localize in countries with highly regulated employee practices such as Germany and Sweden (*ibid.*). Indeed research has shown that administrations within economies which are dependant on MNCs tend to recognize the significance of national policies for MNCs' strategies. Ireland's ability to attract American MNCs is certainly partly due to the weak trade union rights which prevail there (Gunnigle *et al.*, 1998; D'Art and Turner, 2002; O'Hagan, 2002: 143–52).

# Employers' associations and the international firm

## International employers' associations

International employers' organizations were established in response to the growth of supranational governmental organizations, rather than to the emergence of an international labour movement. Therefore, institutions such as the Union of Industrial and Employers' Confederation of Europe (UNICE) in Brussels, the International Organization of Employers (IOE) in Geneva, and the Business and Industry Advisory Committee to the OECD (BIAC) in Paris tend to be of more recent origin and concerned with a more limited domain than their trade union counterparts

(Bamber and Lansbury, 1993). National-level employers' associations were established for a host of reasons, including an effort to counter the growth of trade unionism, to develop employer alliances to regulate the market, and in response to growing state intervention in the employment relationship (Bean, 1985). However, employers began to organize at the international level for quite different reasons. From the perspective of the international firm, international employers' associations serve three main functions; they lobby on behalf of business and capital; they provide information to their members and they help develop and monitor international guidelines.

## Lobbying on behalf of business and capital

Large companies tend to establish strong links with their national government to encourage them to develop a pro-business environment conducive to industrial growth. Similarly, as MNCs flourished, international companies began to form associations with the aim of encouraging a business-friendly environment at the international level.

A glance at the EU provides an excellent example of the crucial role which international business associations play in regard to IR in international firms. The UNICE was established in 1958 as the official voice of industry in Europe; it is made up of 33 employers' federations from 25 European countries. The UNICE is systematically approached by the EU Commission for its opinion on proposals. Its former Secretary-General, Zygmunt Tyskiewicz, explained, 'We are in touch. It's a very open bureaucracy, the Commission, it is very approachable. And they feel that we can help them' (Balanyá et al., 2000: 38). The UNICE 'Mission' is:

> to influence decision-makers at the European level. Of course the word 'lobby' is not used, but that's what it's all about. (Interview with Christophe de Callatäy, UNICE Communications Director, Brussels, 18 November 1998, in Balanyá et al., 2000: 37)

## Providing information for members

The European Commission does not employ many officials, it depends on consultation with interest representatives amongst others for drafting directives and monitoring compliance with them (Streeck and Schmitter, 1992: 202). The UNICE represents employers' interests on every issue which the EU addresses, from taxes and training to energy and carbon dioxide emissions. The UNICE is the official voice of employers in the EU's Social Dialogue. The Treaty on European Union requires the European Commission to solicit opinions or recommendations from the social partners before it submits legislative proposals to the Council. Besides this *official* voice the UNICE represents employers on a European level by approaching EU ministers individually and through national-level media, such as the *Financial Times*. This approach has paid dividends, an example being the UNICE's opposition to a Europe-wide energy tax to reduce greenhouse gas emissions. Attempts to introduce such a tax were snuffed out in 1992, 1995, 1997 and, most recently, 1998 in the face of opposition of industry and a few member states (Balanyá *et al.*, 2000).

Similarly, the American Chamber of Commerce, or AmCham, is a lobby group representing 145 US-based corporations. AmCham is regarded as one of the most powerful lobby groups in Brussels, and has helped to shape key policy areas including the EU's stance on incineration and regulations on electronic commerce.

## Monitoring and developing international guidelines

Postwar growth resulted in the flourishing of MNCs so that, by 1980, of the 100 largest economic powers in the world, 53 were countries and 47 were MNCs (Regan, 1984). The OECD responded to this phenomenal growth of business by drafting guidelines for multinational enterprises. The guidelines were first introduced in 1976, and represented the first internationally agreed framework for cooperation in the field of international direct investment and multinational enterprises which was accepted and supported by business and labour (OECD, 1991). The guidelines are voluntary and there are no means by which transgressions can be judged or penalized. But consultation facilities are provided by the international organizations for unions and employers (Bamber and Lansbury, 1993).

## National employers' associations

Despite employers' three key international functions, it appears that business still prefers to act on a national level and the evidence suggests national employers' associations are the real players in establishing the type of IR which international firms must comply with. All the research concludes that employers, like their labour counterpart, tend to be reluctant to delegate power to supra-national associations (Lanzalaco, 1992; Greenwood, 1997). Streeck and Schmitter (1992: 206) explain, 'By not delegating authority upwards to the European level, employers were and still are able to confine institutions like the Social Dialogue to a strictly non-binding, consultative status'. While institutions such as the UNICE and AmCham wholly support the integration of regional trading zones such as the EU, they do not support the simultaneous growth of these zones' regulatory capacity. When it comes to governing IR, employers' associations, even those belonging to MNCs, prefer to operate within a national framework, (see also Box 8.2):

> The Commission does work at the behest of the Council of Ministers … [E]ffectively, it goes back to the national level and what national governments collectively decide to do, is what the Commission will progress. So, I think it shouldn't be forgotten that in order to influence anything that is going on in Europe, the national level can be just as effective as approaching bodies, be it the Commission or whoever. (Interview with O'Hagan conducted with Social Affairs Executive, Irish Business and Employers Confederation, September 1996)

## Box 8.2    Case study: McDonald's IR practices – the predominance of the national level

Managers at MNC headquarters do not tend to influence industrial relations throughout subsidiaries in a universal manner. Instead, despite their global presence, they usually operate nationally in an effort to shape employee relations in their favour. Research into McDonald's illustrates this approach.

McDonald's tops the German fast-food market with an annual turnover of DM 4,235 million per year. Germany, with its strong statutory forms of worker representation, presented the McDonald's corporation with an enormous challenge. Royle notes that management 'back home' tend to be opposed in principle to the notion of employee participation and involvement and indigenous managers reflect this stance. He found that management adopted a number of tactics over the years to avoid employee participation in any form. In the early 1970s after McDonald's first established itself in Germany, the company simply failed to fulfil national statutory obligations in industrial relations in a rather cavalier fashion. The company was able to ignore such legislation because it is registered as an American, rather than a German, limited liability company (*Gesellschaft mit beschrankte Haftung* – GmbH). However, this outright opposition to national IR practices created a hostile public reaction and management switched strategies. By the mid-1980s McDonald's aimed to discourage the establishment of Works Councils by using more subtle techniques. 'Flying squads' of trouble-shooters were deployed in those firms in which employees wished to establish works councils. More recently, a 1994 document distributed by the German head office indicated a further change in tactics. It urges store managers to handle the Works Council issue very carefully, leaving all major decision-making on the matter to the head office in Munich. It recommends that those stores which already operate a Works Council should occupy the works councillors with tasks, such as organizing Christmas celebrations, to distract them from more normal IR business. The German study clearly shows that it was necessary to address the issue of employee participation in a manner which was suitable for the German context, and very early on the US headquarters' approach was found to be wholly unsuitable.

*Source*:    Based on Royle (2002).

## Collective bargaining

Employers' and employees' representatives or trade unions engage in collective bargaining in both MNCs and indigenous companies alike. Collective bargaining lies at the heart of IR at the local, national and international level. The International Labour Organization (ILO, 1980, cited in Bean, 1985: 70) has defined collective bargaining as:

> An institutionalised procedure ... of joint determination of the rules to govern the terms and conditions of employment of the workers concerned and the labour-management relationship itself.

As discussed above, it is possible to locate a variety of collective bargaining systems according to the country and the sector, and we saw that while these patterns are by no means static, one can draw up a typology of such systems. Collective bargaining in America, for example, is comprised of a unionized sector which operates on the basis of traditionally adversarial relations between management and labour. But a large proportion of the US labour force is un-unionized and IR interactions in these circumstances are characterized by broad management discretion over the terms and conditions of employment (Poole and Warner, 1998). Canada, the UK, Australia and New Zealand share this category. In these countries management and labour negotiate with each other in an informal manner which rarely involves state intervention, so this bargaining tends to take place at the sectoral, plant or even individual level, rather than at the national level.

The second category in the typology is broadly corporatist in nature which means that centralized, or national-level trade unions and employers' organizations are integrated in economic planning of the national economy in a non-conflictual manner. Often, this planning includes the state in a tripartite model and focuses on incomes policy or wage restraint. Bean (1985: 123) looks at the postwar West German model and explains, '[i]n practice the emphasis was upon moderating wage settlements to pay guidelines and with cooperation rather than conflict in industrial relations'.

Other countries which adopted this strategy include the Netherlands, Austria, the Scandinavian countries and, in recent years, Ireland. This typology has been substantiated by research conducted by Gunnigle, Turner and Morley (1998) which found that management-driven forms of employment flexibility are less likely to occur in countries with more sophisticated traditions of employee involvement. For example, as Table 8.2 indicates, countries such as Spain, Ireland and the UK are more likely to utilize temporary and fixed-term contracts compared with more regulated countries such as Denmark and Germany.

Some commentators suggest that these typologies are not merely significant for academic analysis, but that the collective bargaining traditions which a country practices largely shape MNCs' international global strategies. Lipietz (1997) suggests that it is possible to divide the industrialized world into core and peripheral zones of industrial regimes, arguing that employers and national administrators hold that

*Table 8.2* European typology: use of fixed-term and temporary contracts (comparison of means, range of 0–5)

|         | Use of fixed term contracts | Use of temporary contracts |
|---------|------------------------------|------------------------------|
| Spain   | 3.3                          | 2.9                          |
| Ireland | 1.8                          | 2.4                          |
| UK      | 1.5                          | 2.2                          |
| Denmark | 1.0                          | 1.8                          |
| Germany | 1.9                          | 1.0                          |

*Source:* Gunnigle, Turner and Morley (1998: 438).

profitability can be achieved through one of two broad strategies, namely rigidity or flexibility. The latter obtains competitiveness through flexible, sub-standard employment contracts and the absence of robust systems of employee representation and participation. The former achieves competitiveness through quality production underpinned by strong structures of employee involvement, complemented by a strong labour law base. Lipietz points to the advantages that core economies hold by being privileged with institutions which nurture trust, security and productivity in the workplace. Similarly, he stresses that countries that obtain competitiveness through flexible working practices tend to consolidate this 'low-road' strategy by attracting foreign direct investment on the basis of these flexible features.

Research has shown that national administrations shape industrial policy with an eye to attracting FDI (O'Hagan, 2002), likewise, international firms appear to base location decisions on, among other things, national systems and institutions of industrial relations (Cooke and Noble 1998). Marginson *et al.* (1995) found that the majority of firms which they examined did continually compare and assess performance data across national subsidiaries. Similarly, Coriat's research (1995) and Windolf's study (1989) show that the combination of international production units and computers has fundamentally altered IR systems within subsidiaries. As we saw at the start of this chapter, a recurrent question in the extant literature is whether the presence of MNC units throughout the world is resulting in a convergence of IR practices or whether national practices pertain despite these exogenous pressures. The remainder of the chapter examines this question by focusing on three key components of collective bargaining; firstly, employee involvement and participation; secondly, grievance, discipline and terminations; and finally, industrial conflict.

## Employee involvement and participation

While different countries implement various types of employee involvement and systems of participation, it is possible to organize these systems into two broad categories. Geary (1996: 47) makes a distinction between consultative and delegative participation and team-working. The latter involves an environment in which employees are encouraged to make their views known but management retains the veto on decisions. Examples of participation of this nature can be found in countries such as Ireland, the UK and the USA which have voluntarist traditions and where shopfloor relations are often established according to managerial prerogative. In the former, however, employees are empowered to decide on the best course of action in work-related matters. This is referred to as 'direct participation' and examples of this can often be found in countries in which statutory systems of employee representation exist. The best example here may be the German Works Council system in which employees are entitled to rights of co-determination over key issues (Lane, 1989).

Another pattern which emerges when one examines the area of employee involvement is its tendency to be treated very differently in indigenous industries than in

MNCs. This is particularly the case in countries such as Ireland, Hungary and the Czech Republic which are deeply dependent on attracting foreign investment and which, therefore, tend to devise industrial policy which appeals to international capital (Pollert, 1999; O'Hagan, 2002). Research shows that MNCs utilize these flexible IR standards provided by states. For example, Ireland is one of the few countries in Europe in which employers are not legally obliged to recognize and negotiate with trade unions where they have been established in a firm (D'Art and Turner, 2002; Gunnigle, O'Sullivan and Kinsella, 2002; O'Hagan, 2002: 143–52). Since the 1980s non-recognition of trade unions is most likely to occur in US-owned plants which have established in Ireland (Gunnigle, 1995), and between 1985–97, 85.2 per cent of US-owned companies failed to recognize a trade union. This compares with 65.7 per cent of Irish-owned companies and 31 per cent of other foreign-owned companies (Roche, 2001). This trend is very significant for Ireland as US-owned firms tend to operate in some of the fastest growing sectors of the economy. By 1998, they were responsible for 70 per cent of Irish industrial exports (O'Hagan, 2002: 150). Similar trends can be recognized in Hungary, a country which competes with Ireland for FDI (Holohan, 2000; O'Hagan, 2002). While the 1992 Hungarian Labour Code introduced a system of works councils into Hungary's employee practices, it appears that the statutory innovation is ignored or undermined by many MNCs in Hungary (Tóth, 1997). Box 8.3 presents a case study of the European Works Council Directive.

*Chairing meetings*
Table 8.3 shows that management is less likely to chair EWC meetings in those countries with strong social partner traditions. This is the case in only 7 per cent of agreements established under German legislation and 36 per cent of those established under Swedish, while management chairs EWCs in 77 per cent of those established under Belgian legislation, 50 per cent of those established under Dutch and 73 per cent of those established under Irish legislation. Similarly, agreements concluded under German and Swedish legislation are most likely to have EWCs chaired by employees, with 48 per cent and 14 per cent respectively. This is least likely in the Irish case (5 per cent).

*Nature of select committees*
There is evidence that 'good practice' is spreading across MNCs' IR practices as Table 8.4 indicates. Here, the majority of select committees that are established tend to be employee-only institutions, rather than joint bodies. However, within this trend another pattern is discernible. Those EWCs established under German, Swedish and Dutch legislation are much more likely to have employee-only joint committees than EWCs established under Irish and Belgian legislation. The lower propensity for employee-only select committees in Belgium and Ireland may reflect their national IR traditions. Employers tend to be the stronger partners in the Belgian case (Van Ruysseveldt and Visser, 1996b), and the Irish voluntarist tradition means that

## Box 8.3    Case study: The European Works Council Directive

The European Works Council (EWC) establishes a European Works Council Directive or information and consultation framework in every multinational enterprise which has 1,000 employees or more within those states signed up to the Directive and with at least 150 in each of two or more of these countries. The Directive is only established within firms in which either management takes up the initiative or where employees request that an EWC should be established. After over 25 years of lobbying for such a development organized labour in Europe held that the EWC Directive would address fears of social dumping which had grown up in the wake of the Single European Act (Marginson and Sisson, 1998).

Carley and Marginson undertook a study on the operation of EWCs. The data they gathered provides interesting insights into how MNCs implemented the EWC Directive. It codes the contents of 386 agreements established under Article 13 of the Directive, and, from October 1999, 71 agreements which were established under Article 6 of the Directive. Carley and Marginson caution that it is not possible to detect 'national EWC patterns' from the data (Carley and Marginson, 2000: 10); however, the following figures suggest that distinct 'national EWC patterns' do emerge*.

Carley and Marginson explain that the research enabled them to distinguish between two types of agreements; those which were largely formal or symbolic in nature, and those EWCs which were established with the potential to develop a genuine active role. They suggest these EWCs can be recognized on the basis of the degree of management unilateralism involved in EWC activities (2000: 50). The following section looks at a few of these.

* The majority of the countries in the database only account for a small proportion of the total number of agreements. This raises methodological problems with trying to establish country patterns based on the results of only one or two MNCs. In the case of Article 6, in three cases the company is based in more than one country, which distorts the results slightly as the same company ethos is duplicated on these occasions (Carley and Marginson, 2000: 5). Additionally, the results do not always equal 100 per cent as the details of the agreements vary to some extent from country to country and not all agreements address the questions posed in detail which leaves a gap in the data.

*Source*:    Based largely on O'Hagan (2002), where a more extensive study may be found.

employees do not tend to be systematically involved in any information or consultation bodies (with the exception of semi-state companies).

*Committee accorded a continuing role in receiving information and consultation*
It is notable that of those agreements which do allow for select committees, only the minority accorded the committee a role in receiving information and consultation on an ongoing basis. This is a role which Carley and Marginson (2000) regard as underpinning genuine EWCs. The EWC concluded in the countries discussed here only attributed this role to works councils in the minority of cases, never in more than a quarter of the national cases (see Table 8.5).

*Table 8.3*  Who chairs EWC meetings?

| | Ireland | | | Germany | | | Sweden | | | Belgium | | | Netherlands | | |
|---|---|---|---|---|---|---|---|---|---|---|---|---|---|---|---|
| | Art. 13 | Art. 6 | Total | Art. 13 | Art. 5 | Total | Art. 13 | Art. 6 | Total | Art. 13 | Art. 5 | Total | Art. 13 | Art. 6 | Total |
| Total % total no. | 100% 12 | 100% 7 | 100% 19 | 100% 89 | 100% 6 | 100% 95 | 100% 22 | 100% 6 | 100% 28 | 100% 17 | 100% 9 | 100% 26 | 100% 18 | 100% 13 | 100% 31 |
| Management | 75% 9 | 71% 5 | 73% 14 | 8% 7 | – | 7% 7 | 41% 9 | 17% 1 | 36% 10 | 76% 13 | 78% 7 | 77% 20 | 44% 8 | 54% 7 | 50% 15 |
| Employee | 8% 1 | – | 5% 1 | 52% 46 | – | 48% 46 | 18% 4 | – | 14% 4 | 18% 3 | – | 11% 3 | 17% 3 | – 3 | 10% 3 |
| Joint/ rotatory | 8% 1 | 14% 1 | 10% 2 | 3% 3 | 17% 1 | 4% 4 | – | – | – | – | – | – | 33% 5 | 46% 6 | 37% 11 |
| Not specified | 8% 1 | 14% 1 | 10% 2 | 36% 32 | 83% 5 | 39% 37 | 36% 8 | 83% 5 | 46% 13 | 6% 1 | 22% 2 | 11% 3 | 6% 1 | – | 3% 1 |

Table 8.4 What is the nature of those select committees which do exist?

| | Ireland | | | Germany | | | Sweden | | | Belgium | | | Netherlands | | |
|---|---|---|---|---|---|---|---|---|---|---|---|---|---|---|---|
| | Art. 13 | Art. 6 | Total | Art. 13 | Art. 6 | Total | Art. 13 | Art. 6 | Total | Art. 13 | Art. 6 | Total | Art. 13 | Art. 6 | Total |
| Total % with SC | 67% 8 | 86% 6 | 74% 14 | 56% 50 | 33% 2 | 55% 52 | 91% 20 | 100% 6 | 93% 26 | 53% 9 | 89% 8 | 65% 17 | 67% 12 | 92% 12 | 77% 24 |
| Total no. of SC | | | | | | | | | | | | | | | |
| Joint Body | 25% 2 | 33% 2 | 29% 4 | 14% 7 | 50% 1 | 15% 8 | 20% 4 | – | 15% 4 | 56% 5 | 25% 2 | 41% 7 | 17% 2 | 17% 2 | 17% 4 |
| Employee only Body | 62% 5 | 67% 4 | 64% 9 | 84% 42 | 50% 1 | 83% 43 | 75% 15 | 83% 5 | 77% 20 | 44% 4 | 75% 6 | 59% 10 | 83% 10 | 83% 10 | 83% 20 |

Note that not all companies who have joint committees specified the nature of the committees.
SC = select committees.

Table 8.5 Is select committee accorded a continuing role in receiving information and consultation?

| | Ireland | | | Germany | | | Sweden | | | Belgium | | | Netherlands | | |
|---|---|---|---|---|---|---|---|---|---|---|---|---|---|---|---|
| | Art. 13 | Art. 6 | Total | Art. 13 | Art. 6 | Total | Art.13 | Art. 6 | Total | Art. 13 | Art. 6 | Total | Art. 13 | Art. 6 | Total |
| Total % and no. with Committee | 100% 8 | 100% 6 | 100% 14 | 100% 50 | 100% 2 | 100% 52 | 100% 20 | 100% 6 | 100% 26 | 100% 9 | 100% 8 | 100% 17 | 100% 12 | 100% 13 | 100% 25 |
| Yes | – | 50% 3 | 21% 3 | 16% 8 | 50% 1 | 17% 9 | 10% 2 | 67% 4 | 23% 6 | – | – | – | 8% 1 | 23% 3 | 16% 4 |

Overall, then, a picture of conflicting trends emerges. On the one hand the data show that 'good practice' is being spread and the EWC Directive has clearly acted as a catalyst for social learning between negotiators involved in drafting EWC constitutions within MNCs. However, another pattern is discernible, namely that the agreements tend to reflect the national IR practices within those jurisdictions in which they are established. The Irish and Belgian agreements tend to empower management more than the others, reflecting their voluntarist and promanagement traditions respectively. Similarly, German and Swedish-based agreements are more likely to empower the employee, a trait which reflects their national IR institutions.

## Grievance, discipline and terminations

Briscoe (1995: 180–4) explains that the basic dilemma which faces HR managers in international firms involves the ethics of decision-making in foreign operations. He explains that managers who comply with local codes and HR traditions could be criticized for implementing practices which would be wholly unacceptable in the firm's home country. He writes that while it may appear liberal and open-minded to avoid ethical imperialism and accept local practices, this may entail infringements of internationally agreed codes on, for example, child labour, and gender and ethnic diversity. On the other hand, Briscoe adds, one could be accused of cultural and ethical imperialism if one tries to adopt a single set of universal ethical principles while managing an international firm. Additionally, of course, employing internationally accepted ethical codes may run counter to the manager's commitment to gaining a profit.

One area in which practices differ fundamentally from country to country is that of grievances, discipline and terminations of contracts. Briscoe illustrates how radically different these systems can be by comparing different statutory requirements which arise in the case of redundancies:

[A] terminated forty-five-year-old employee with twenty years' service and a salary of US$50,000 in Belgium would be owed US$94,000 in severance pay. A similar employee terminated in Ireland would be owed US$13,000 and in Venezuela US$106,000. (Briscoe, 1995: 159)

A review of the supra-national, national and sub-national legislation in the area of equality indicates the complexity of the challenge which IHR managers face.

### Equality legislation in the European Union
Throughout the 1970s the European Community developed a number of Directives covering equality of gender in the workplace. Examples include the Equal Pay Directive (75/117/EEC) and a Directive on equal treatment regarding access to employment, vocational training, promotion and working conditions (76/207/EEC). Until recently the equality provisions under the founding Treaty of Rome had been restricted to sex

equality, but in 2000 the EU issued two Directives to be implemented by 2003 which broadened the notion of equality. The Race Directive (2000/43/EC) aims to ensure that racial discrimination be outlawed at the European level, specifically in regard to employment but also with respect to training and the provision of goods and services within the EU. The Employment Directive (2000/78/EC) requires member states to introduce measures on unfair discrimination on the grounds of sexual orientation, religion or belief; disability and age in the areas of employment and training (Larkin, 2002).

*Equality legislation in the UK*
The UK has already had fairly extensive provisions on equality within the workplace for many years. Great Britain has legislation in place to protect people from discrimination on grounds of sex, race and disability – the Sex Discrimination Act and Equal Pay Act; the Race Relations Act; and the Disability Discrimination Act – three organizations have been established to promote equality in those areas: the Equal Opportunities Commission, the Commission for Racial Equality and the Disability Rights Commission. However, some amendments will need to be made to these Acts to ensure consistency with European law. For example new legislation will be introduced to outlaw discrimination at work and in training on grounds of sexual orientation, religion and age.

*Equality legislation in Northern Ireland*
Due to the political situation in Northern Ireland the region has developed equality legislation which differs quite radically from that which pertains throughout the rest of the UK (the Equality Commission for Northern Ireland website is www.equalityni. org/yourrights/equalitylaw.htm). Northern Ireland did implement UK-wide equality legislation such as the Sex Discrimination (Northern Ireland) Order 1976 (amended 1988) and the Disability Discrimination Act 1995. Additional legislation, which applies solely to Northern Ireland, makes it unlawful to discriminate against someone on the grounds of religious belief or political opinion. The order places a number of significant duties on employers that are not found in other anti-discrimination legislation either in Northern Ireland or in Great Britain. For example all private-sector employers with more than 10 full-time employees working more than 16 hours per week are required to register with the Equality Commission and to submit an annual monitoring return to the Commission detailing the (religious) community background of their workforce. Box 8.4 presents a case study of termination procedures as they are affected by equality legislation.

## Industrial conflict

The nature of industrial conflict between management and employees within international firms is quite different to that found in indigenous firms. Bean (1985) argues that this difference is a result of the asymmetrical power relations between MNCs'

## Box 8.4　Case study: termination procedures in Renault

Despite these differences which exist in equality legislation within one state there is evidence that the growth of MNCs and the internationalization of production is creating a trend towards an international norm in procedures relating to grievance, discipline and terminations. A convergence of this nature is most clearly reflected in EU legislation. In February 1997 Renault unexpectedly announced the closure of its Belgian production plant in Vilvoorde by July of that year. As a result more than 3,000 Renault employees and an estimated 1,500 employees in direct supply companies were estimated to lose their jobs. There was a general consensus that the decision ignored national codes of conduct, ILO and OECD procedures and EU legislation on collective redundancies and works council rights which state that employees have to be notified before a decision about a factory closure is made and informed about the ways in which the company plans to deal with the consequences for the employees.

The closure procedure saw an unprecedented wave of reaction. The Belgian and Flemish governments strongly condemned the closure and the style of communication. Belgian employers and their organizations VBO (Federation of Belgian Enterprises) and VEV (Flemish Federation of Enterprises) also reacted with dismay against the closure. A rarely-witnessed international solidarity emerged following the factory closure. Work stoppages were organized not only in other Belgian car assembly plants, but also Renault plants in France and Spain. These reactions resulted in innovations at the national and European level in an effort to prevent future mass redundancies being announced at such short notice. At the EU-level, this resulted in a new directive on *national* systems of negotiations and consultation.

*Source*:　Information from the European industrial relations webpages. www.eiro.eurofound.ie/ 1997/03/feature/BE9703202f. html; www.eiro.eurofound.ie/2002/05/feature/BE0205304F.html; and www.eiro.eurofound.ie/ 2000/12/feature/EU0012285F.html.

management and national unions or even governments. He explains that the main consideration here is the firm's ability to relocate at will when the employment environment is no longer deemed desirable. Dowling *et al.* (1999) suggest that the sense of powerlessness which trade unions feel in relations with MNCs lies in a number of variables over and above their ability to mobilize. These include the following five factors:

- *Formidable financial resources*: trade unions are weakened by MNC's ability to absorb losses through industrial action in one subsidiary and still show an overall profit worldwide.
- *Alternative sources of supply*: MNCs can source goods and components from a number of plants worldwide to reduce dependency in the event of industrial action.
- *Remote locus of authority*: MNCs' structures for decision-making may be opaque due to the centralization of key decision-making to the distant and obscure company headquarters.

- *Numerous product lines*: most MNCs operate a number of production facilities which makes each subsidiary and potential conflict less significant for the firm.
- *Superior knowledge and expertise in labour relations*: MNCs hold all the information on companies' future strategies and they have the resources to address industrial conflict when it arises.

Clearly, international firms act as a destabilizing force for IR systems which were largely stable in the postwar period. However, despite the imbalance of power relations there is evidence that trade unions are rising to the challenges of globalization and, rather than being snuffed out, industrial conflict is, on occasions, shifting up the international level (ILO, 1997).

*Some examples of international industrial conflict*
Taylor (1999: 3) stresses that the notion that MNCs systematically adopt aggressive and exploitative policies towards employees and trade unions is largely exaggerated, explaining that:

> To a great extent, multinational enterprises believe in and practice the slogan – 'think globally, act locally'. As a result many of them operate within legal and social constraints imposed upon them by the countries in which they invest.

However, Taylor qualifies this approach, pointing out that the global trend is one of increasing repression of trade unions. He cites the ICFTU annual report on violations of trade unions which found that in 1998 nearly 300 trade unionists were killed standing up for their rights, a further 1,681 were tortured or ill-treated, and 2,329 detained without trial. Intimidation occurred in 33,369 specific cases. Repression occurred across 79 countries including Colombia, Indonesia, Burma, Algeria, Nigeria and China (ICFTU, 1998: 5–6, cited in Taylor, 1999: 10). While international firms are rarely *directly* involved in violations of this nature, the spread of export-processing zones and the enforcement of structural adjustment programmes is.

Taylor (1999: 5) highlights some cases where labour has organized and mobilized at an international level to address such injustices. His examples include the 1996 offensive which the Postal, Telegraph and Telephone International spearheaded against Sprint, the US company, after it dismissed Hispanic workers who tried to organize a union at its subsidiary in San Francisco. Subsequently, *Deutsche Postgewerkschaft*, a German telecommunications union, demanded that Deutsche Telekom should introduce a code of labour standards as part of its deal to launch a $2.7bn joint venture with Sprint. French telecommunication workers also managed to hold up a similar agreement between Sprint and France Telecom while STRM, the Mexican telecom company, drew up charges against Sprint for alleged breaches of the labour-side clauses in the North Atlantic Free Trade Agreement. Taylor gives other accounts of robust international labour mobilization including the sporadic action

## Box 8.5    The case of ABB Alstom Power

Erne (2002: 6) notes that ABB Alstom Power may be regarded as a rare example of a true multinational with 'genuinely global aspirations'. He traces developments when the company informed representatives that it planned a merger which would threaten 12,000 of the 58,000 in all the company's units. The study recounts how the employees initially organized dynamically on an international level using the European Works Council as a vehicle of organization, through a Euro demonstration, and the EU Parliament. However, Erne stresses that the international employees' reaction to the merger and subsequent restructuring ended when the merger resulted in the end of the original company's European Works Council and labour representatives became involved in national negotiations. The grievance procedures in this case, as in most others, were addressed at the national level by national level subsidiaries.

*Source:*    Erne (2002).

which dockers in the USA, Australia, Spain and Israel took in solidarity with the dismissed dockers in Liverpool in 1997–98; the international campaign organized against the anti-union behaviour of Bridgestone, the Japanese tyre manufacturer, at its US subsidiary of Firestone, where strikers were replaced by substitute workers; and the international campaign which employees of the corn-processing plant in Illinois, A E Stanley, organized in the early 1990s when a 10–12-hour four-day week was introduced. The campaign entailed a boycott of major A E Stanley customers such as Miller, Pepsi and Tate Lyle.

While these examples give the impression that an international labour movement is beginning to emerge in parallel with global corporations, a move which could suggest the convergence of IR towards a supranational code of norms, it appears that these cases may be the exception rather than the rule. On the whole, industrial conflict is rarely coordinated on the international arena as the case study shown in Box 8.5 indicates.

## Conclusions

This chapter has set out to examine whether industrial relations in international firms feature national and local practices, or, as some literature suggests, are industrial relations in MNCs converging towards an international model, shaped by the respective headquarters. The former thesis has been referred to in the literature as the 'host-country' debate and the latter as the 'country-of-origin effect'. In short, the chapter has assessed the notion that IR practices in international firms are converging as production is internationalized.

The overall picture which emerges from this review of the research is quite clear. It appears that despite the flourishing of international firms and the growth of supra-national regulations of industrial relations over the last century and more, IR practices in international firms are still rooted at the national level.

The chapter has shown that the social partners have made some efforts to operate at the international level, but despite the emergence of their respective institutions onto the international stage, both trade unions and employers are still most dynamic at the national level.

Although we have witnessed some very exciting international experiments in the area of employee involvement and participation, this aspect of IR is, as yet, most effectively regulated at the national, sectoral or firm level, as the case study on the European Works Council indicates. Likewise, the discussion on grievances, discipline and terminations stressed that there are some signs that international institutions are being developed to regulate this area, in particular in the wake of the Renault Vilvoorde case. However, these practices still differ radically from country to country and even within countries.

The final section, which focused on industrial conflict, indicates that some conflicts have been fought out on the international stage. However, as the ABB Alstom Power case study demonstrates, these battles and large-scale mobilizations of labour and management can all too easily fragment and usually retreat back to the national level.

On the whole, while MNCs operate effectively on the national level and there are embryonic institutions emerging to regulate them, industrial relations are still most frequently played out within national boundaries; the examples of industrial-relations practices converging to an international norm are still very much the exception. It appears therefore that the host-country thesis is currently the most convincing. However, it is notable that most of the developments in international industrial relations examined resulted from legal innovations unfolding within the EU. As institutions such as the EU expand in size and significance, they may provide models for employers and employees globally. Developments such as this married with technological breakthroughs in communications could eventually shift industrial relations onto the international stage leaving the host-country influences far behind.

Discussion questions

1 Explain why trade unions and employers' associations have failed to organize effectively at the international level.

2 List some examples of industrial practices which are converging towards an 'international norm'. Use the case studies outlined to explain why these tend to be the exception.

3 Why is it important for international firms to understand fully the grievance, discipline and terminations procedures of the host country. Discuss the ethical dilemma which international human resource managers face in this respect.

# Further reading

Bamber, G. and Lansbury, R. (1993) *International and Comparative Industrial Relations*. London: Routledge.
Gunnigle, P., Murphy, K.R., Cleveland, J.N., Heraty, N. and Morley, M. (2002) 'Localization in Human Resource Management: Comparing American and European Multinational Corporations', *Advances in International Management*, 14: 259–84.
Marginson, P. and Sisson, K. (1994) 'The Structure of Transnational Capital in Europe', in R. Hyman and A. Ferner (eds) *New Frontiers in European Industrial Relations*. Oxford: Blackwell Business.
O'Hagan, E. (2002) *Employee Relations on the Periphery of Europe*. Basingstoke: Palgrave Macmillan.

# References

Balanyá, B., Doherty, A., Hoedeman, A., Ma'anit, A. and Wesselius, E. (2000) *Europe Inc.: Regional and Global Restructuring and the Rise of Corporate Power*. London: Pluto Press.
Bamber, G. and Lansbury, R. (1993) *International and Comparative Industrial Relations*. London: Routledge.
Bean, R. (1985) *Comparative Industrial Relations*. London: Croom Helm.
Berggren, C. (1993) 'Lean Production – The End of History'?, *Work Employment and Society*, 7(2): 163–88.
Brewster, C., Mayrhofer, W. and Morley, M. (eds) (2000) *New Challenges for European Human Resource Management*. Basingstoke: Palgrave Macmillan.
Briscoe, D. (1995) *International Human Resource Management*. New Jersey: Prentice-Hall.
Carley, M. and Marginson, P. (2000) *Negotiating European Works Councils*. Dublin: European Foundation for the Improvement of Living and Working Conditions.
Cooke, W. and Noble, D. (1998) 'Industrial Relations Systems and US Foreign Direct Investment Abroad', *British Journal of Industrial Relations*, 36(4): 581–609.
Coriat, B. (1995) 'Variety, Routines and Networks: The Metamorphosis of Fordist Firms', *Industrial and Corporate Change*, 4(1): 205–27.
Crouch, C. and Traxler, F. (1995) *Organized Industrial Relations in Europe: What Future?* Aldershot. Avebury.
D'Art, D. and Turner, T. (2002) 'Union Growth and Recognition: The Irish Case in a Comparative Context', Department of Personnel and Employment Relations Working Paper no.1, Limerick: University of Limerick.
De Nijs, W. (1995) 'International Human Resource Management and Industrial Relations', in A. Harzing and J. Van Ruysseveldt (eds), *International Human Resource Management*. London: Sage.
Dowling, P., Welch, D. and Schuler, R. (1999) *International Human Resource Management*. Cincinatti, OH: South Case Western.
Erne, R. (2002) *Explaining Translational Collective Action*. Paper presented at the RLDWL Congress Labour, Globalisation and the New Economy. Osnabrück, Germany, 22–25 May.
Ferner, A. and Edwards, P. (1995) 'Power and the Diffusion of Organisational Change within Multinational Enterprises', *European Journal of Industrial Relations*, 1(2): 229–57.
Gallagher, J. (1995) 'Solidarity Forever', in *New Statesman and Society Guide to the Trade Union and Labour Movement*, New Statesman and Society (supplement) 2 September.
Geary, J. (1996) 'Working at Restructuring Work in Europe', *Irish Business and Administrative Research*, 17: 44–57.
Greenwood, J. (1997) *Representing Interests in the European Union*. London: Palgrave Macmillan.
Gunnigle, P. (1995) 'Collectivism and the Management of Industrial Relations in Greenfield Sites', *Human Resource Management Journal*, 5(3): 24–40.
Gunnigle, P., Murphy, K.R., Cleveland, J.N., Heraty, N. and Morley, M. (2002) 'Localization in Human Resource Management: Comparing American and European Multinational Corporations', *Advances in International Management*, 14: 259–84.
Gunnigle, P., O'Sullivan, M. and Kinsella, M. (2002) 'Organised Labour in the New Economy: Trade Unions and Public Policy in the Republic of Ireland', in D. D'Art and T. Turner (eds), *Irish Employment Relations in the New Economy*. Dublin: Blackhall Press.
Gunnigle, P., Turner, T. and Morley, M. (1998) 'Employment Flexibility and Industrial Relations at Organisation Level: A Comparison of Five European Countries', *Employee Relations*, 20(5): 430–42.
Hall, M. (1992) 'Behind the European Works Council Directive', *British Journal of Industrial Relations*, 30(4): 547–66.

Holohan, R. (2000) 'Hungary Told of Irish Commitment to Bigger EU', *Irish Times*, 5 April.

Hyman, R. (1994) 'Industrial Relations in Europe', *European Journal of Industrial Relations*, 1(1): 17–46.

ICFTU (1998) *Annual Survey of Violations of Trade Union Rights*. Brussels: ICFTU.

ILO (International Labour Office) (1997) *World Employment Report*, 1996–97. Geneva: ILO.

Lane, C. (1989) *Management and Labour in Europe*. Aldershot: Edward Elgar.

Lanzalaco, L. (1992) 'Coping with Heterogeneity', in J. Greenwood, J. Grote and K. Roint (eds), *Organised Interests and the European Community*. London: Sage.

Larkin, M. (2002) 'Next Year and Beyond – The Equality and Race Directives and Age Discrimination'. Paper presented at Legal-Island Conference, Discrimination, Equality Law and Flexible Working in Northern Ireland. Belfast, 24 October.

Lipietz, A. (1997) 'The Post-Fordist World: Labour Relations, International Hierarchy and Global Ecology', *Review of International Political Economy*, 4(1): 1–41.

Marginson, P., Armstrong, P., Edwards, P.K., Purcell, J. (1995) 'Extending beyond Borders', *International Journal of Human Resource Management*, 6(3): 702–19.

Marginson, P. and Sisson, K. (1994) 'The Structure of Transnational Capital in Europe', in R. Hyman and A. Ferner (eds), *New Frontiers in European Industrial Relations*. Oxford (UK): Blackwell Business.

Marginson, P. and Sisson, K. (1998) 'European Collective Bargaining', *Journal of Common Market Studies*, 36(4): 505–28.

Maurice, M., Seiller, F. and Silvestre, J-J. (1986) *The Social Foundations of Industrial Power*. London: MIT Press.

Morley, M., Brewster, C., Gunnigle, P. and Mayrhofer, W. (1996) 'Evaluating Change in European Industrial Relations', *International Journal of Human Resource Management*, 7(3): 640–56.

OECD (1991) 'The OECD Declaration and Decisions on International Investment and Multinational Enterprises'. Paris: OECD.

O'Hagan, E. (2002) *Employee Relations in the Periphery of Europe*. Basingstoke: Palgrave Macmillan.

Perlmutter, H. (1969) 'The Tortuous Evolution of the Multinational Corporation', *Columbia Journal of World Business*, 4: 9–18.

Pollert, A. (1999) *Transformation at Work*. London: Sage Publications.

Poole, M. and Warner, M. (1998) *The IEBM Handbook of Human Resource Management*. London: International Thomson Business Press.

Regan, C. (with Eccles P.) (1984) '*75:25 Ireland in an Unequal World*'. Dublin: Development Education Commission of CONGOOD.

Roche, W. (2001) 'Accounting for the Trend in Trade Union Recognition in Ireland', *Industrial Relations Journal*, 32(1): 37–54.

Ross, G. and Martin, A. (1999) 'European Unions Face the Millennium', in A. Martin and G. Ross (eds), *The Brave New World of European Labor*. Oxford: Berghahn Books.

Royle, T. (2002) 'Multinational Corporations, Employers' Associations and Trade Union Exclusion Strategies in the German Fast-food Industry', *Employee Relations*, 24(4): 437–60.

Schulten, T. (1996) 'European Works Council', *European Journal of Industrial Relations*, 2(3): 303–24.

Streeck, W. and Schmitter, P. (1992) 'From National Corporatism to Transnational Pluralism', in W. Streeck, *Social Institutions and Economic Performance*. London: Sage Publications.

Taylor, R. (1999) *Trade Unions and Transnational Industrial Relations*. ILO, Labour and Society Programme. Geneva: ILO.

Tóth, A. (1997) 'The Invention of Works Councils in Hungary', *European Journal of Industrial Relations*, 3(2): 161–81.

Van Ruysseveldt, J. and Visser, J. (1996a) *Industrial Relations in Europe*. London: Sage Publications.

Van Ruysseveldt, J. and Visser, J. (1996b) 'Weak Corporatism Going Different Ways?', in J. Van Ruysseveldt and J. Visser, *Industrial Relations in Europe*. London: Sage Publications.

Windolf, P. (1989) 'Productivity Coalitions and the Future of European Corporatism', *Industrial Relations*. 28(1): 1–20.

Womack, J. Jones, D. and Roos, D. (1990) *The Machine That Changed the World*, New York: Rawson Associates.

part **3**

# Contemporary issues
# in international HRM

# 9

# Women in international management

*Margaret Linehan*

The low number of women on global assignments is a matter of concern, notwithstanding the available research suggesting that female international managers are quite successful (Adler, 1994; Taylor and Napier, 1996; Caligiuri and Tung, 1999; Linehan, 2000). Recent years have seen rapid increases in global activity and global competition in all industrialized countries, resulting in more women entering lower-level managerial positions. Despite women's increased investment in higher education, their greater commitment to management as a career, the shortages of international managers, and equal opportunity legislation, female international managers in every country remain a small fraction of those in senior management positions. Given the historical scarcity of local women managers in most countries, firms still question if women can function successfully in cross-border managerial assignments. There is an assumption that the relative scarcity of local women managers forms a basis for accurately predicting the potential for success, or lack thereof, of expatriate women (Adler, 1994).

In recent years, research on women in global assignments has been increasing (see for example Adler, 1984a, 1984b, 1987, 1993, 1994; Westwood and Leung, 1994; Harris, 1995a, 1995b; Taylor and Napier, 1996; Caligiuri and Tung, 1999; Linehan, 2000). The first issue raised in the research on female global assignees addresses whether a gender bias exists against appointing women to global assignments. This issue is worthy of investigation given that the number of female global assignees is proportionally low in relation to the overall size of the qualified labour pool. Although women represent over 50 per cent of the world population, in no country do women represent half, or even close to half, of the corporate managers. According to Izraeli and Adler (1994), in all countries men control political and economic power and, subsequently, management as a profession is controlled primarily by men. Major barriers hinder women's progress in international management, including such obstacles as: stereotypical perceptions of women's abilities and qualifications; traditional attitudes towards women's family roles; women's minimal access to the social networks from which companies recruit managers and executives; and a broadly based discrimination against women. According to Kanter (1977), a 'masculine ethic' of rationality has given the managerial role in the West its defining image for most of the twentieth century:

> This 'masculine ethic' elevates the traits assumed to belong to some men to necessities for effective management: a tough-minded approach to problems; analytic ability to abstract and plan; a capacity to set aside personal emotional considerations in the interests of task accomplishment; and a cognitive superiority in problem-solving and decision making. (Hearn and Parkin, 1988: 20–1)

Systematic investigation of women's progress in management is relatively new. It began in North America in the early 1970s, in Western Europe in the early 1980s, in Asia towards the mid-1980s, and in the former Communist countries of Eastern Europe, as well as in the People's Republic of China towards the end of the 1980s. During the 1980s and early 1990s there was a great deal of speculation about whether women could be effective in international business, particularly as expatriates in environments which were typically hostile towards women. According to Dallafar and Movahedi (1996), research on women in international management was, up to the early 1980s, primarily restricted to the role of the expatriate wife – especially the wife of a Western manager – in facilitating or hindering her husband's performance overseas. Adler (1993) argues that, as a result of a historical scarcity of local female managers in most countries, organizations have often questioned whether women can function successfully in cross-border managerial assignments. According to Brewster (1991), another negative reason for not appointing women to international management positions may result from a tendency of organizations to confuse the role of female expatriate managers with that of the female expatriate partner, whose frequent failure to adapt has been one of the most commonly cited reasons for premature expatriate returns.

The 2–3 per cent of expatriates represented by women in the early 1980s has now increased to 12–15 per cent (Caligiuri et al., 1999). The number of female international managers, however, is still proportionally low in relation to the overall size of the qualified female labour pool. Research from Australia, Canada, Europe and the United States reports that the number of female managers in these countries range between 25 and 45 per cent (Hede and O'Brien, 1996; Tung, 1998; Florkowski and Fogel, 1999; Linehan, 2000). Several studies have found that, while organizations may be prepared to promote women through their domestic managerial hierarchy, few women are given opportunities to expand their career horizons through access to international careers (Adler and Izraeli, 1988; Linehan and Scullion, 2001). The substantial underrepresentation of women in expatriate assignments is significant from the perspective that, despite the increasing globalization of industries and business operations, international experience is increasingly considered as a requisite for promotion to the top of the organizational hierarchy (Black et al., 1992). Multinational organizations tend to send their 'fast-track' managerial employees on expatriate assignments to develop global competencies. Expatriates in these positions find these appointments to be developmental experiences and report the acquisition of tangible skills while on assignment, skills which are value-added for their organizations (Oddou and Mendenhall, 1991).

## Commonly held myths about women in international management

Adler's (1984a, 1984b, 1987) pioneering research has addressed the underrepresentation of women on global assignments, identifying some of the myths perpetuated by organizations that inhibit women from procuring global assignments. In brief, one myth is the assumption by decision-makers that women are not motivated to seek international assignments (Adler, 1984a). Another myth that inhibits women from procuring a global assignment is that host-national men will not transact business with women, and addressing this concern Adler (1987) obtained responses from expatriate women regarding their perceptions of host-nationals' attitudes towards them. The study found that only 20 per cent of the respondents perceived any negative attitudes from the host nationals. In addition, 42 per cent of the women reported that being female was an asset in the host-national environment.

A frequently cited reason for the limited use of women expatriates is the reluctance of host-country nationals in general to transact business with Western women (Adler, 1987), and has been suggested that female expatriates' acceptance by host nationals may, in part, be predicted by the values and beliefs of the host nationals towards women at work.

In Adler's (1987) study, American female expatriates were found to be just as successful as their male counterparts overseas – even in male-dominated cultures such as Japan and Korea. Taylor and Napier (1996) also found that there were no significant differences between American male and female expatriates in their adjustment to the work situation and overall living conditions in Japan. Asian businessmen tend to view a female expatriate first as a parent-company representative, second as a foreigner and third as a female. According to Adler (1987), female expatriates who were assigned to Asian countries perceived that they were treated as if they were very competent. Based on these observations, Adler deduced that the host nationals most probably assumed that 'if a *woman* was sent by a company, then she *must* be exceptionally competent'. Research conducted by Linehan (2000) with female international managers, based in Europe, found that when a woman is promoted to top management she has to be 'very, very, good' and, because of bias based on gender difference, she has to be better than men to get to the top. In a similar study with female expatriates in Hong Kong, the respondents believed that 'if you are perceived as a competent manager and could do the job', gender was incidental (Westwood and Leung, 1994).

# Do women international managers manage in similar ways to their male colleagues?

Cross-cultural studies and reviews undertaken to compare male and female managers, in terms of managerial efficiency and performance, have produced results which reveal that there are far more similarities than differences in terms of managerial efficiency and performance. Although unanimity on the existence and type of differences and their effects has yet to be reached, studies suggest, however, that male and female managers are perceived differently (Powell, 1999; Yeager, 1999). Where differences do occur, they tend to be found not so much in the way each gender 'manages', but stem from factors associated with the low proportion of female managers, attitudinal differences, prejudices, discrimination and different life circumstances and stressors of female managers in comparison to male managers. Many of these differences are regarded as negative and, therefore, hamper the career advancements of women in international management.

Research by Izraeli and Adler (1994) and Schein (1975) suggests that the specific image of an ideal manager varies across cultures, yet everywhere it privileges those characteristics that the culture associates primarily with men. They point out from their research that this belief is widely supported by male managers, and that successful management is associated with masculinity. The requirements for effective managerial performance are not 'culture-free' but are influenced by the national culture in which the behaviour is performed, and that effective performance requires managers to adapt their behaviours accordingly. According to Marshall (1984), sex-role stereotypes relating to management seem to have evolved in a way that males are typed as being more task-oriented, objective, independent, aggressive and generally more capable than females in handling managerial responsibilities. Female managers are generally stereotyped as being more passive, gentle, consideration-oriented, more sensitive and less suited than males for positions of senior responsibility in organizations.

Adler (2002) suggests that, depending on their respective company's perspective, people judge either men's or women's ways of managing internationally to be superior. Similarly, depending on one's perspective, a diversity of global management styles is judged either to benefit or to detract from companies' global effectiveness, competitiveness and ultimate success. Adler further suggests that given most companies' lack of experience in sending women abroad on global assignments, a disproportionate number of decisions are based on managers' perceptions – their best guesses – as to what the impact of being a woman and a global manager will be, rather than on observing the behaviour and impact of women who are working internationally.

Fisher (1999) concludes that women have many exceptional faculties for managing internationally, including:

> a broad contextual view of any issue, a penchant for long-term planning, a gift for networking and negotiating ... a preference for co-operating, reaching consensus, and leading via egalitarian terms ... an ability to do and think several things simultaneously ... emotional sensitivity ... and a talent with words. (Fisher, 1999: xvii)

## Are companies reluctant to send women on international assignments?

While organizations may be prepared to promote women through their domestic managerial hierarchy, few women are given opportunities to expand their career horizons through access to international careers. Mandelker's (1994) term, the 'glass border', describes stereotypical assumptions by home-country senior management about women as managers and about their availability, suitability and preferences for international appointments. According to Berthoin-Antal and Izraeli (1993), the structure of the international managerial role may allow senior home-country management to discriminate against women. The role of the international manager involves even more uncertainties than the role of the domestic manager, and as uncertainty increases the need for trust, uncertainty is perceived as having further implications for limiting women international managers. The need for certainty motivates managers to select others who are most similar to themselves, and presumably more likely to be trustworthy and predictable. Situations of uncertainty also increase the likely use of stereotypes, and in the absence of reliable knowledge about future performance or in situations where past experience is limited, stereotypical beliefs about the characteristics and abilities of men and women are employed by home-country senior managers. These stereotypical beliefs result in women's deselection for more senior managerial international positions (Izraeli and Izraeli, 1985). It is suggested that where uncertainty is greater, headquarters tend to select men as expatriates.

Chusmir and Frontczak (1990) have argued that qualified female employees may be overlooked because men make most of the decisions about whom to send, and many men hold traditional views and stereotypes about women in positions of international management. Not surprisingly, the result can be a self-fulfilling prophecy: qualified female candidates are likely to form negative attitudes about the likelihood of being selected and, consequently, do not actively pursue international positions.

According to Dallalfar and Movahedi (1996), much is assumed by home-country senior managers about the requirements of international managers and the abilities needed for fulfilling such roles. These assumptions typically cast women in a relatively disadvantaged position in the corporate structure. In particular, assumptions and perceptions by home-country managers are reinforced by the traditional profile of the typical male international executive, who is approximately 31 years old when he first goes abroad, is married with an accompanying spouse who is mobile and committed, spends at least three years on each foreign assignment, and has three such assignments during his career (Harris, 1995a). Harris further suggests that research shows that senior management chooses managers who have 'high potential' in their home organizations as future international managers. Potential international managers are often identified at early stages in their careers, where separation of work from family and chronological career timetables are seen as important for career development. White *et al.* (1992) noted that the concept of career has traditionally been reserved for men. For women, it was expected that working outside the home would be a secondary activity, as they were perceived to have a 'job' rather than a 'career'. Some women have difficulties adhering to progressive, linear career models, which are designed for traditional male career paths, due to their interrupted career patterns, for example for child-bearing and child-rearing. This may lead to occupational segregation in organizations which allow senior management to assume that women have difficulty in partaking in international management. The segregation of men and women into different categories of appointments is considered to be institutionalized discrimination (Izraeli and Adler, 1994). When this segregation pattern is established, senior managers use women's absence from certain managerial positions, including international assignments, to justify women's continued exclusion from such positions. Women may also experience further organizational discrimination as a result of the considerable uncertainty surrounding: (1) what an international manager should do; (2) the qualifications required for getting the job; and (3) the skills required for the job.

A number of attributes are considered to be universally desirable in an international manager, and these attributes are shown to privilege the lifestyle that societies most frequently reserve for men. Beliefs, such as that successful managers must prove their worth by their early thirties, that career breaks to care for family members indicate a lack of organizational commitment, and that being the last person to leave at night demonstrates organizational commitment, 'all advantage a lifestyle more easily pursued by men than women' (Izraeli and Adler, 1994: 12).

When women's suitability for international assignments is being discussed, marital status becomes an issue. Stereotypical thinking and the double standard towards married managers become evident because, whether single or married, the female manager's family status is presumed to be problematic. It has been suggested that male managers tend to believe that a single woman, away from the social influence of her home country, is more vulnerable to harassment and other dangers than a man would be. In the case of single women in international management, some human resource executives have expressed concerns about women's physical safety and the hazards involved in travelling in underdeveloped countries. Additionally, concerns have been expressed by senior home-country management regarding single women's loneliness, isolation and physical safety, which excludes them from working in remote underdeveloped countries. In contrast, if a married woman accepts an international assignment, home-country senior managers may be concerned with potential tensions in the family, and with the problems associated with dual-career issues. A further problem which female managers face is that senior management in home-country organizations believe that entry into a new job abroad requires total involvement and longer than usual hours of work. The international woman manager is, therefore, likely to be even less available to her family while abroad than during her home-country employment. Home-country senior managers may assume that, because of these difficulties, women may not want to partake in international assignments. Historically, therefore, it seems that one of the most difficult aspects of an international assignment for women, either married or single, is obtaining the assignment in the first place. The practice (intentional or incidental) of selecting only a small number of women for international assignments may be contributing to the already existing workplace phenomenon known as the 'glass ceiling', whereby one finds fewer and fewer women the higher one looks in the organizational hierarchy.

## Dual-career couples

A growing number of international transfers combined with an increasing percentage of dual-career couples in the workplace has made organizations realize that they must address dual-career issues in order to increase the success of their international assignments. One of the most important factors in determining the success of an overseas assignment is the willingness of a spouse or partner to leave home – and possibly a career   to live abroad. According to research findings, spouses' reluctance to give up their own career is a growing reason for rejecting foreign assignments (Punnett, 1997; Schell and Solomon, 1997; Harvey, 1998) and, also, the influence of the spouse or family is a primary reason for costly premature returns (Tung, 1987; Black and Stephens, 1989; Kamoche, 1997). Due to such difficulties, there is a critical need for corporate programmes for dual-career couples on international assignments. Currently, most issues concerning dual-career couples are left to the individual couple to resolve with no help from the company. Harvey (1996) suggested that no one factor could have as great an impact on multinational corporations than the dual-career phenomenon. Carmody (1989) and Shellenbarger (1992) noted that, despite profound changes in workforce composition, organizational policies and practices are still largely predicated on the outmoded assumption that employees are, predominantly, males from traditional families – the traditional family being one in which the husband is the sole breadwinner and the wife the home-maker and child-rearer.

Dual-career partners have special career needs, since they rarely have unfettered discretion over their own career development. For many, there exists a precarious balance between career and home due to the inextricable relationship between work and family, which is especially pronounced for women (Bielby and Bielby, 1992; Smith, 1997). Managing career moves for both partners simultaneously is usually a difficult process, and the conflicts associated with career transitions can be either eased or increased by organizational policies. Business uncertainty means that few employers can guarantee jobs on repatriation, thus compounding career uncertainty when two partners are repatriating (Feldman and Thompson, 1993).

An assumption, often made by senior home-country managers, that women in dual-career marriages do not want an international posting is a further problem for female international managers. As more women move into management positions, the 'accompanying spouse' is increasingly likely to be the male partner that has to put his own career on hold, and some organizations expect dual-career status to generate greater employee hostility to geographical relocation. As the majority of international managers is still male, the non-working expatriate spouse group is largely female, and the non-working husband may find himself the lone man in a group composed otherwise of wives. In addition to these concerns, work-permit restrictions by some host countries make it difficult for a spouse to work; for example the United States, Australia and Switzerland seldom grant work permits to both spouses. In other countries it may be socially unacceptable for the male partner to be the home-maker, and the traditional volunteer activities that wives have been encouraged to undertake may not be available or appropriate for males in some countries.

In addition, sex-role stereotypes suggest that male accompanying spouses will be less willing to relocate internationally than female spouses. It may be construed that a male accompanying spouse following his wife on an international assignment is a significant departure from social norms associated with the male role as primary provider for the family (Brett et al., 1992). The male accompanying spouse is, therefore, considered atypical, and they have been conditioned to feel less worthy if they are not contributing financially. In a dual-career couple, willingness to relocate internationally would be reduced if the accompanying spouse made a significant contribution to the financial well-being of the family unit. This suggests that male spouses may need the same understanding and support as their women counterparts, but they may need more emotional support, and this may be difficult to find. One such group are members of the Brussels-based STUDS (Spouses Trailing Under Duress Successfully) who form a group of approximately 80 male accompanying spouses providing support for their executive partners' careers, as well as holding golf outings, fund-raising events and social evenings. The STUDS group provides a social network for the accompanying spouses, which in turn helps them to settle into their new locations.

Punnett et al. (1992) also suggested that additional emotional stress is experienced when the accompanying spouse is male, and that this can lead to some dual-career couples preferring to avoid international transfers, thereby sacrificing the female partner's career advancement. One consultant depicts the problem thus: 'The employee moves into a career without skipping a beat, the trailing spouse is left to cope with the hassles of international transfer. The employee changes office while the trailing spouse changes lives' (Fawcett, 1994).

## Understanding the barriers to women in international management

Burke and Davidson (1994) caution that in attempting to identify specific reasons for women's lack of advancement to senior management positions, it is important to remember that managerial and professional women live and work in a larger society that is patriarchal, a society in which men have historically had greater access to power, privilege and wealth. Men have generally served as standards by which others, including women, are compared. Women are often studied to see how they depart from the male standard, both in choice of a career and in career development. In relation to women's career development, Perun and Bielby (1981) noted that research on adulthood in women has focused on the family cycle at the expense of the work cycle. In their view, the outcome was that no formal theory of women's occupational behaviour existed. According to White et al. (1992), theoretical advances have been made since 1982, although most have received some challenging criticism, as career-development theorists have generally based their models on studies of men.

Diamond (1989) points out that a variety of attitudes and behaviours still present barriers to women's optimal career development, and particularly to their participation in non-traditional occupations. Women are often discouraged from entry into non-traditional professions, and for those who do enter, they are subjected to harassment and hostile behaviour. An investigation beyond career-development theory reveals a combination of organizational and sociocultural factors which can play a large part in the underrepresentation of women in international management. These barriers can be largely divided into (1) the effect of an organization's formal policies on women's opportunities in international management; and (2) the influence of informal organizational processes in determining women's participation in international management.

## Formal policies

Among the most cited corporate barriers are recruitment and selection barriers, and organizational policies and structural barriers. According to Rothwell (1984), many jobs are still seen as 'men's' or 'women's' jobs and this influences the initial intake of a particular gender to organizations. Rothwell points out that if the initial intakes for particular career routes are unbalanced, it is unlikely that the pattern will improve later, particularly in organizations which have a policy of 'promotion from within' where possible.

Harris and Brewster (1999) noted that an examination of the international manager-selection literature reveals a mismatch between theory and practice, with extensive lists of theoretical criteria relating to effective international managers, most of which resemble a cross-cultural 'wish-list' in respect of the vast array of skills and abilities required. Selection processes are equally depicted as both formal and professional. How much the theory of international manager selection reflects actual practice has, however, been questioned (Brewster, 1991). Harris and Brewster's (1999) research on international selection revealed that the 'open/formal' system was heavily influenced by informal practices. This is seen to be particularly problematic for women, given the fact that between 85 and 95 per cent of international managers are currently men. Within a selection context where the nature of the vacancies reflect a male-type bias, there appears to be even more need for selection systems to ensure that potential 'prejudice' on the part of selectors is constrained by a process which forces them continually to question their assumptions about women's suitability and, critically, their acceptability in international management positions. Previous research by Brewster (1991) and Scullion (1994) on selection systems for international assignments also illustrated the informal system where primarily subjective knowledge of an individual determines who is seen to 'fit in' best with existing organizational norms.

Linehan's (2000) in-depth interviews with 50 senior female international managers confirmed the use of the informal international selection system in organizations based in Europe, since *none* of the managers was offered an international assignment. All 50 managers had to ask for their international career move and in many instances (particularly for married women) had to repeatedly stress that their personal circumstances would not interfere with their assignment abroad.

According to Storey (1989), much depends on the organization's view of women; whether they are viewed as a cost or investment, or as he expresses it, 'valued asset rather than variable cost'. Management's perception of women in an organization and the level of understanding of their specific problems will to a large extent determine the nature of the employers' 'women-friendly' policies and the employers' levels of commitment to them. Research by Dickens (1992), however, cautions that various 'flexibility' initiatives such as home-working or part-time working for women, which are often cited as evidence of an equal opportunities approach, may be double-edged in that they are seen as 'atypical' because they differ from the male norm. Further research by Dickens (1994) suggests that even if career breaks are open to, and taken by, both men and women, they are likely to be taken for different reasons and to be regarded differently by the organization. Time out taken to study is considered as career enhancing, but time out if used for childcare is considered career detracting, reflecting the low value placed on women's experience in household and family management despite the organizational, managerial and interpersonal skills involved.

Another serious corporate barrier that women in international management face is the attitude of senior male managers towards them. In addition to employer practices, deep-seated attitudes remain towards working women. Employers often see women as being less ambitious, not worth training or promoting (because they may leave to have children), less reliable (because of domestic responsibilities), and generally less committed to work than male counterparts. According to Davidson and Cooper (1992), the typical employer attitude that women are 'poor training and promotional investments' – who leave work on marrying and/or starting a family – is particularly detrimental to those who work continually after marriage and to single women who do not marry, a profile which fits the majority of women in international management.

Another attitude attributed to employers is that women are far less committed to work and far less able to undertake a full time career than men. When promotion arises and when an employer is given the choice between a man and a woman with equal qualifications, the woman is frequently viewed as the greater risk. Flanders (1994) articulates this typical employer attitude:

When it comes to promotion and career development, women are judged not so much on their abilities and achievements, but on assumptions about their family life, responsibilities, and future intentions. (1994: 5)

Schwartz (1989) similarly notes:

Men continue to perceive women as the rearers of their children so they find it understandable, indeed appropriate, that women should renounce their careers to raise families ... Not only do they see parenting as fundamentally female, they see a career as fundamentally male ... This attitude serves to legitimise a woman's choice to extend maternity leave and even, for those who can afford it, to leave employment altogether for several years. (1989: 67)

Schein *et al.* (1994) concluded that male attitudes to managerial women are strong, consistent and pervasive and appear to be a global phenomenon. While it seems relatively easy for women to gain employment at the lower levels of organizations in their home organizations, it is still proving very difficult for them to reach middle, upper and senior international management positions. There are major organizational barriers constituting the glass ceiling, including a lonely and non-supportive working environment; treating differences as weaknesses; excluding people from group activities because of their differences; and failure to help individuals to prepare to balance work and personal life issues. When women are selected for international assignments, however, they encounter further difficulties. Strategies used by home-country senior management to reduce risk under conditions of uncertainty include the limiting of the woman's international assignment to internal rather than to external client contacts, and to a short-term rather than to an extended stay, or even to define her assignment as temporary (Berthoin-Antal and Izraeli, 1983).

Previous research by Adler similarly noted that:

> Although this defining the job as temporary may appear to be a logically cautious strategy, in reality it tends to create an unfortunate self-fulfilling prophecy. As a number of women reported, if the company is not convinced that you will succeed it will communicate its lack of confidence to foreign colleagues and clients as a lack of commitment. The foreigners will then mirror the company's behaviour by also failing to take you seriously. (Adler, 1987: 169–92)

These strategies are designed by organizations to reduce uncertainty for the woman international manager, even though uncertainty may actually be increased by the adoption of these strategies thus increasing the likelihood of failure. In addition to encountering barriers to advancement towards senior-level positions and international management, women also face barriers associated with industry-sector and managerial functions. Fisher (1987) notes that opportunities for women in management may be greater in industries like computers and telecommunications, suggesting that these industries have not been in existence long enough to have established rules about who is or should be a manager, relying more on managerial ability than on gender to make employment decisions.

Izraeli and Adler (1994) suggest that global competition and the need for top-quality managers are making women's promotion into senior management a business issue, rather than strictly an issue of equity. For success, continued change is needed at the individual, organizational and societal levels. Schein (1994) suggests that while laws and corporate practices focusing on objective criteria and removing structural barriers are important, it seems that now is the 'time to address ways to change stereotypical attitudes as well'.

## Informal organizational processes: networking

Informal socialization processes for managers include informal networking and informal mentoring, which provide training in managerial career norms and help individual managers to gain membership of their career group. Peer relationships, developed through networks, are different from mentoring relationships in that they often last longer, are not hierarchical, and involve a two-way helping. Barham and Oates (1991) stress the importance of networking skills in particular for the international manager because he or she will need to be able to exploit information, expertise and other resources wherever they might be found in the organization worldwide. They suggest that the international manager must have an aptitude for developing a network of cooperative relationships and informal alliances across the organization. Barham and Oates further suggest that while a lot can be done at a corporate level to encourage the formation of networks, it is up to managers themselves to create informal networks. According to Harris (1995b), however, female international managers may be disadvantaged in accessing informal career networks – as an important aspect of the informal socialization process is sharing with members of a group who are similar to themselves and who have similar backgrounds. In this regard, women are seen as 'non-typical, and therefore risky' by men who comprise the majority of informal networks.

According to Smith and Hutchinson (1995), there is not much empirical research literature available on interpersonal organizational networks. Extant research studies, however, indicate that one of the most frequently reported problems experienced by both women and racial minorities is the limited access to or exclusion from informal interaction networks. Powell (1999) suggested that women's lack of advancement to high levels of management often results from their having less fully developed informal networks than men. Women, however, have been largely excluded from 'old-boy' networks traditionally composed of individuals who hold power in the organization (Fagenson, 1986; Linehan and Scullion, 2002). An earlier study by Edström and Galbraith (1997) also suggested that networks influence the distribution of power in organizations, and that some multinational organizations use international transfers of managers as a method of control based on socialization. In this process 'socialized' managers create international 'verbal' information networks which will influence the distribution of power in organizations. The process of socialization is achieved by frequent transfers which force the manager to sacrifice many of the advantages of a stable domestic life. According to Harris (1995b), however, female managers are 'doubly disadvantaged' under such circumstances as, first, women are often excluded from informal organization networks and as a result have less access to positions of power in organizations. Second, the requirement for frequent transfers may be more difficult for women because of their traditional family responsibilities of child-bearing and child-rearing.

Scase and Goffee's research (1989) established that attempts by male managers to exclude females from joining old-boy networks merely reinforce existing stereotypes of negative male attitudes towards female managers. Davidson and Cooper (1992) also suggested that certain established traditional male institutions have developed exclusively male customs and traditions, which perpetuate the old-boy network and safeguard it from female intrusion. Burke and McKeen (1994) observed that managerial women are still less-integrated with important organizational networks, and it is these internal networks that influence critical human resource decisions such as promotion and acceptance.

According to O'Leary and Ickovics (1992), networking is essential for success in any professional career. Networks usually involve contacts with a variety of colleagues for the purpose of mutual work benefits. Research by Henning and Jardim (1977) also supports the importance of networking, and they add that an important characteristic of networking and the old-boy system is that it is dependent on informal interactions involving favours, persuasion and connections to people who already have influence. Parker and Fagenson (1994) advised that it is important for women to penetrate male networks to a greater extent if they wish to become sufficiently visible to win organizational promotions.

Ibarra's (1992) research investigated differences in men's and women's access to informal networks at work. Some of the findings of the study were that men had greater centrality and better relationships with the same sex in their network relationships than women. Men were more likely than women with the same education and experience to gain access to networks of their mentors and to be drawn into key political groups. In contrast, women found themselves between two networks: a women's network which provided social support, and a male-dominated network which provided assistance in attainment of workplace effectiveness. Research by Linehan and Scullion (2002) and Davidson and Cooper (1992) indicated that, although it is beneficial for female managers to network with women, there are still more benefits to be gained from networking in established male-dominated groups, as power in organizations is still predominantly held by men. Ibarra suggested that these two groups often subject women to the stress of conflicting advice, forcing them to maintain a delicate balance between the women's and men's networks, because either network may reject them because of their commitment to the other.

Research by Adler (1987) and Harris (1995a) suggested that female managers can miss out on international appointments because they typically lack mentors, role models, sponsorship or access to appropriate networks – all of which are commonly available to their male counterparts. Their findings indicate that the exclusion of female managers from business and social networks compounds their isolation, which in turn prevents female managers from building up useful networking relationships which should be advantageous to their international careers. Similarly, Kram and Isabella (1985) found that peer relationships provided a range of developmental supports for personal and professional growth at all career stages. Burke and McKeen (1994) suggested that peer relationships provide several career and psychological functions; peer relationships, 'unlike mentoring relationships, were characterized by mutuality, with both individuals experienced at being the giver as well as the receiver of various functions'.

It is apparent, therefore, that the informal networking facilities which are available to male international managers are not equally available to female managers. If women are excluded from informal networks they may lack information, advice, influence and power which are important for international career success. Networking may be particularly important for career and personal development for female managers as a significant number of women may not have benefited from mentors. Although the impact of informal networking processes remains an underresearched area, it is clear that managerial women are still less-integrated in organizational networks, and it is these networks which can influence promotion and acceptance.

# Mentoring

According to Burke and McKeen (1994), studies on both networking and mentoring suggest some similarities. Both mentors and peer relationships can facilitate career and personal development; networking can be useful at all stages in career development, while mentors are particularly useful at the early stages of career development. According to Ragins (1989), one explanation for the disparity in advancement of women to senior management is the gender difference in the development of mentoring relationships. Research suggests that mentoring relationships, while important for men, may be *essential* for women, as female managers face greater organizational, interpersonal and individual barriers to advancement (Burke and McKeen, 1994; Collins, 1983; Kanter, 1982). Although mentoring relationships may be particularly important for the advancement of women in organizations, there is a smaller supply of mentors available to women than to men, and women may be less likely than men to develop these relationships (Burke, 1984; Brown, 1985; Burke and McKeen, 1994). There are many possible explanations for the infrequency of mentoring relationships among women in organizations. Generally, these explanations are that (1) women may not seek mentors; and (2) mentors may not select female protégées (Ragins, 1989).

According to Ragins, one reason why women may be less likely than men to seek mentors is that they may fail to recognize the importance of gaining a sponsor, and may 'naively assume that competence is the only requisite for advancement in the organization'. Other difficulties in approaching male mentors may be compounded by the female's fear that her attempts to initiate a relationship may be misconstrued as a sexual approach by either the mentor or others in the organization (Clawson and Kram, 1984; Reich, 1986). Women may also have trouble finding mentors because there may be potential discomfort in cross-gender relationships (Burke and McKeen, 1994).

The second explanation put forward for the underrepresentation of women in mentoring relationships is that mentors may be unwilling to select female protégées. The selection process may therefore be biased by the tendency of male mentors to choose male protégés. Even if women are considered as suitable candidates for the protégée role, male mentors may choose male protégés because they may be more comfortable developing a professional and personal relationship with another male (Ragins, 1989). Research studies have found that a key element in the selection process is the degree to which the mentor identifies with the protégé and perceives the protégé as a younger version of himself (Blackburn et al., 1981; Bowers, 1984). Ragins argues that male mentors may be reluctant to sponsor female protégées because they perceive them as being a greater professional risk than their male counterparts; the failure of a protégé could be a reflection on the competency and judgement of the mentor. Mentors of female protégées may therefore have more 'at stake' and may profit less from the relationship than mentors of male protégés (Ragins, 1989).

If women are not selected as protégées by male mentors, they may wish to seek female mentors, but then another difficulty may arise concerning the availability of a female mentor, as there are still very few senior female managers in comparison to males. As Vinnicombe and Colwill (1995) noted, 'there are few top-level executives whose mirror reflects a woman'. Research by Linehan and Walsh (1999) also established that females are more likely to be mentored by males, because of the lack of women in senior management positions. The few females in mentoring positions therefore receive an overload of requests from the relatively larger block of women in lower levels of the organization, which may result in a reduction of access to mentors. Female mentors reported that high organizational visibility was a problem, with the female mentor and female protégée combination being the most visible of all the mentor combinations and therefore entailing the greatest risk (Bowers, 1984; Ragins, 1989). Research by Cooper and Hingley (1983) suggested that women need female mentors who can act as role models, and believed that women may miss opportunities for career advancement because of a lack of such role models. This lack probably gives rise to responses which mirror the behaviour of successful male executives, which may further isolate women as women's lifestyle does not easily adapt to the male managerial model. Other previous research has shown that where a female mentor is available to act as a role model, it is likely that the aspiration levels of managerial women will be raised, even for work traditionally done by males (Hackett and Betz, 1981; Barclay, 1982).

Factors other than gender which play a more important role in the pairing of mentor and protégé include the similarity in the personal traits of mentors and protégés. Vinnicombe and Colwill's (1995) research revealed that when asked to describe the characteristics of their ideal mentors and protégés, both men and women choose people who are similar to themselves rather than people who are stereotypically masculine or feminine.

Research studies have identified the lack of mentoring and networking relationships as the most significant barrier facing women managers in their transition from middle to senior management (Noe, 1988; Dreher and Ash, 1990). Davidson and Cooper (1992) also found that successful female managers often report that at least one of their superiors has been instrumental in helping their careers. Linehan's (2000) research revealed that, in an international management context, a mentoring relationship is even more important than in domestic management. Mentors provide the contact and support from the home organization, which in turn facilitates re-entry – in addition to improving the self-confidence of protégées, increasing their visibility in organizations and increasing their promotional prospects. Additionally, the research revealed that 40 of the 50 managers interviewed had the benefit of mentoring relationships and believed that the opportunities for them to partake in international assignments would have been partly attributed to mentoring relationships. The research also suggested that, in the absence of family and friends, their mentors also provided many support benefits, and helped to keep them in touch with their home organizations, which in turn reduced the 'out of sight, out of mind' disadvantage.

Previous studies on mentoring in organizations reported that more women than men in senior management positions had mentors (Ragins, 1989; White *et al.*, 1992; Burke and McKeen, 1994). In summary, although mentors may be quite essential for advancement in organizations, female managers tend to be hindered in their attempts to obtain mentors because of interpersonal and organizational barriers.

## Conclusions

Despite the significant advances women have made in managerial careers, women are still left out and neglected in international assignments (Rowe and Snizek, 1995; Black and Gregersen, 1999). Adler (2002) notes that few global companies have reached the stage at which they consistently value diversity, and few women have, as yet, had the opportunity to use all their strengths in the service of senior-level global positions. Similarly, Linehan's (2002) research illustrated that female managers are offered international assignments 'only in rare circumstances'. This contrasts with the career experiences of their male counterparts to whom offers of international assignments are frequently made. Female managers have to strive harder than their male colleagues to prove their worth and they have the ongoing burden of managing their gender identity in the male-dominated environment of organizational management. One of the most significant barriers to women in management is the widespread and gratuitous distinction between managers based solely on gender. The perception of female international managers is that in most countries, and as Schein (1989) suggested, to think manager is to think male.

Research with female international managers concludes that women can be successful in foreign countries (Caligiuri and Tung, 1999; Linehan, 2000; Napier and Taylor, 2002). Thus, foreign women professionals may be more readily accepted abroad than was initially thought or expected. Unless human resource management policies and informal processes, however, are re-examined and reassessed, women will remain a small minority in international human resource management. According to Kanter (1994), senior management needs to recognize that in a global economy, 'Meritocracy – letting talent rise to the top regardless of where it is found whether it is male or female – is becoming essential to business success'.

---

### Discussion questions

1 If women and men manage differently, are the differences primarily an advantage or disadvantage to companies' global effectiveness, competitiveness and ultimate success?
2 Discuss the reasons why women are still 'left at home' when it comes to international assignments, and recommend action strategies for women in such organizations.
3 What role, if any, does the gender of a prospective international assignee play in how international assignments are perceived and in who is selected for that assignment?

# Further reading

Adler, N.J. and Izraeli, D.N. (eds) (1994) *Competitive Frontiers: Women Managers in a Global Economy.* Oxford: Basil Blackwell.
Davidson, M.J. and Cooper, C.L. (eds) (1993) *European Women in Business and Management.* London: Penguin.
Linehan, M. (2000) *Senior Female International Managers: Why So Few?* Aldershot: Ashgate.
Taylor, S., Napier, N.K. and Mayrhofer, W. (eds) (2002) 'Women in Global Business', Special Issue', *International Journal of Human Resource Management*, 13(5).

# References

Adler, N.J. (1984a) 'Women Do Not Want International Careers: And Other Myths about International Management', *Organizational Dynamics*, 13: 66–79.
Adler, N.J. (1984b) 'Expecting International Success: Female Managers Overseas', *Columbia Journal of World Business*, 19: 79–85.
Adler, N.J. (1987) 'Pacific Basin Managers: A Gaijin, Not a Woman', *Human Resource Management*, 26(2): 169–92.
Adler, N.J. (1993) 'Competitive Frontiers: Women Managers in the Triad', *International Studies of Management and Organization*, 23(2): 3–23.
Adler, N.J.(1994) 'Competitive Frontiers: Women Managing Across Borders', in N.J. Adler and D.N. Izraeli (eds), *Competitive Frontiers: Women Managers in a Global Economy.* Oxford: Basil Blackwell, 22–40.
Adler, N.J. (2002) 'Global Managers: No Longer Men Alone', *International Journal of Human Resource Management*, 13(5): 761–72.
Adler, N.J. and Izraeli, D.N. (eds) (1988) *Women in Management Worldwide.* New York: M.E. Sharpe.
Barclay, L. (1982) 'Social Learning Theory: A Framework for Discrimination Research', *Academy of Management Review*, 7: 587–94.
Barham, K. and Oates, D. (1991) *The International Manager.* London: Economist Books.
Berthoin-Antal, A. and Izraeli, D.N. (1983) 'A Global Comparison of Women in Management: Women Managers in their Homelands and as Expatriates', in E.A. Fagenson (ed.), *Women in Management: Trends, Issues and Challenges in Managerial Diversity.* London: Sage, 52–96.
Bielby, W. and Bielby, D. (1992) 'I Will Follow Him: Family Ties, Gender-role Beliefs, and Reluctance to Relocate for a Better Job', *American Journal of Sociology*, 97(5): 1241–67.
Black, J.S. and Gregersen, H.B. (1999) 'The Right Way to Manage Expatriates', *Harvard Business Review*, March–April: 52–62.
Black, J.S., Gregersen, H.B. and Mendenhall, M.E. (1992) *Global Assignments.* San Francisco: Jossey-Bass.
Black, J.S. and Stephens, G.K. (1989) 'The Influence of Spouse on American Expatriate Adjustment and Intent to Stay in Pacific Rim Overseas Assignments', *Journal of Management*, 15(4): 529–44.
Blackburn, R.T., Chapman, D.W. and Cameron, S.M. (1981) 'Cloning in Academe: Mentorship and Academic Careers', *Research in Higher Education*, 5(4): 315–27.
Bowers, A.G. (1984) 'Mentors and Protégés in Male-Dominated Cultures: The Experience of Top-level Women Executives', *Dissertation Abstracts International*, 45(9): 3103B.
Brett, J.M., Stroh L.K. and Reilly, A.H. (1992) 'What Is It Like Being a Dual-Career Manager in the 1990s?', in S. Zedeck (ed.), *Work and Family.* San Francisco: Jossey-Bass.
Brewster, C. (1991) *The Management of Expatriates.* London: Kogan Page.
Brown, D.A. (1985) 'The Role of Mentoring in the Professional Lives of University Faculty Women', *Dissertation Abstracts International*, 47(1): 160A.
Burke, R.J. (1984) 'Mentors in Organizations', *Group and Organization Studies*, 9(3): 353–72.
Burke, R.J. and Davidson, M.J. (1994) *Women in Management: Current Research Issues.* London: Paul Chapman.
Burke, R.J. and McKeen, C.A. (1994) 'Women in Management: Current Research Issues', in M.J. Davidson and R.J. Burke (eds), *Women in Management: Current Research Issues.* London: Paul Chapman, 1–8.
Caligiuri, P.M., Joshi, A. and Lazarova, M. (1999) 'Factors Influencing the Adjustment of Women on Global Assignments', *International Journal of Human Resource Management*, 10(2): 163–79.
Caligiuri, P.M. and Tung, R.L. (1999) 'Comparing the Success of Male and Female Expatriates from a US-based Multinational Company', *International Journal of Human Resource Management*, 10(5): 763–82.
Carmody, H. (1989) *Work and Family.* Paper presented to Australian Family Research Conference, 27 November, Ballart: Victoria.

Chusmir, L.H. and Frontczak, N.T. (1990) 'International Management Opportunities for Women and Men Paint Different Pictures', *International Journal of Management*, 7(3): 295–301.

Clawson, J.G. and Kram, K.E. (1984) 'Managing Cross-gender Mentoring', *Business Horizons*, 27(3): 22–32.

Collins, N.W. (1983) *Professional Women and Their Mentors*. Englewood Cliffs, NJ: Prentice Hall.

Cooper, C.L. and Hingley, P. (1983) *The Change Makers*. London: Harper & Row.

Dallalfar, A. and Movahedi, S. (1996) 'Women in Multinational Corporations: Old Myths, New Constructions and Some Deconstruction', *Organization*, 3(4): 546–59.

Davidson, M.J. and Cooper, C.L. (1992) *Shattering the Glass Ceiling: The Woman Manager*. London: Paul Chapman.

Diamond, E.E. (1989) 'Theories of Career Development and the Reality of Women at Work', in B.A. Gutek and L. Larwood (eds), *Women's Career Development*. Beverly Hills, CA: Sage, 15–27.

Dickens, L. (1992) *Whose Flexibility?: Discrimination and Equality Issues in Atypical Work*. London: Institute of Employment Rights.

Dickens, L. (1994) 'Wasted Resources?: Equal Opportunities in Employment', in K. Sisson (ed.), *Personnel Management: A Comprehensive Guide to Theory and Practice in Britain*. Oxford: Blackwell, 253–96.

Dreher, G. and Ash, R. (1990) 'A Comparative Study of Mentoring Among Men and Women in Managerial Professional and Technical Positions', *Journal of Applied Psychology*, 75(5): 539–46.

Edstrom, A. and Galbraith, J. (1977) 'Transfer of Managers as a Co-ordination and Control Strategy in Multinational Organizations', *Administrative Science Quarterly*, 22(2): 248–63.

Fagenson, E.A. (1986) 'Women's Work Orientation: Something Old, Something New', *Group and Organization Studies*, 11(1): 75–100.

Fawcett, K. (1994) 'Trailing Spouse Often Must Fend for Self', *USA Today, European International Edition*, 19 August: 02a.

Feldman, D. and Thompson, H.B. (1993) 'Expatriation, Repatriation and Domestic Relocation: An Empirical Investigation of Adjustment to New Job Assignments', *Journal of International Business Studies*, 24(4): 507–29.

Fisher, A.B. (1987) 'Where Women are Succeeding', *Fortune*, 3 August: 78–86.

Fisher, H. (1999) *The First Sex: The Natural Talents of Women and How They are Changing the World*. New York: Random House.

Flanders, M.L. (1994) *Breakthrough: The Career Woman's Guide to Shattering the Glass Ceiling*. London: Paul Chapman.

Florkowski, G.W. and Fogel, D.S. (1999) 'Expatriate Adjustment and Commitment: The Role of Host Unit Treatment', *International Journal of Human Resource Management*, 10: 783–807.

Hackett, G. and Betz, N.E. (1981) 'A Self Efficacy Approach to the Career Development of Women', *Journal of Vocational Behaviour*, 18: 326–39.

Harris, H. (1995a) 'Organizational Influences on Women's Career Opportunities in International Management', *Women in Management Review*, 10(3): 26–31.

Harris, H. (1995b) 'Women's Role in (International) Management', in A.W. Harzing and J. Van Ruysseveldt (eds), *International Human Resource Management*. London: Sage, 229–51.

Harris, H. and Brewster, C. (1999) 'The Coffee-Machine System: How International Selection Really Works', *International Journal of Human Resource Management*, 10(3): 488–500.

Harvey, M. (1996) 'Dual-career Couples: The Selection Dilemma in International Relocation', *International Journal of Selection and Assessment*, 4(4): 215–27.

Harvey, M. (1998) 'Dual-Career Couples During International Relocation: The Trailing Spouse', *International Journal of Human Resource Management*, 9(2): 309–31.

Hearn J. and Parkin, W.P. (1988) 'Women, Men, and Leadership: A Critical Review of Assumptions, Practices and Change in the Industrialized Nations', in N.J. Adler and D.N. Izraeli (eds), *Women in Management Worldwide*. Armonk, NY: M.E. Sharpe, 17–40.

Hede, A. and O'Brien, E. (1996) 'Affirmative Action in the Australian Private Sector: A Longitudinal Analysis', *International Review of Women and Leadership*, 2: 15–29.

Henning, M. and Jardim, A. (1997) *The Managerial Woman*. London: Pan Books.

Hoschild, A. (1989) *The Second Shift*. New York: Viking.

Ibarra, H. (1992) 'Homophily and Differential Returns: Sex Differences in Network Structure and Access in an Advertising Firm', *Administrative Sciences Quarterly*, 37: 422–47.

Izraeli, D.N. and Adler, N.J. (eds) (1994) *Competitive Frontiers: Women Managers in a Global Economy*. Oxford: Basil Blackwell.

Izraeli, D.N. and Izraeli, D. (1985) 'Sex Effects in Evaluating Leaders', *Journal of Applied Psychology*, 70(1): 148–56.

Kamoche, K. (1997) 'Knowledge Creation and Learning in International HRM', *International Journal of Human Resource Management*, 8(3): 213–25.

Kanter, R.M. (1977) *Men and Women of the Corporation*. New York: Basic Books.

Kanter, R.M. (1982) 'The Impact of Hierarchical Structures on the Work Behavior of Women and Men', in R. Kahn-Hut, A.K. Daniels and R. Colvard (eds), *Women and Work: Problems and Perspectives*. Oxford: Oxford University Press, 234–47.

Kanter, R.M. (1994) 'Comments on Nancy A. Nichols', *Reach for the Top: Women and the Changing Facts of Work Life*. Boston, MA: Harvard Business School Press, as cited in the book review by John R. Hook in *The Academy of Management Executive*, 8(2): 87–9.

Kram, K.E. and Isabella, L. (1985) 'Mentoring Alternatives: The Role of Peer Relationships in Career Development', *Academy of Management Journal*, 28: 110–32.

Linehan, M. (2000) *Senior Female International Managers: Why so Few?* Aldershot: Ashgate.

Linehan, M. (2002) 'Senior Female International Managers: Empirical Evidence from Western Europe', *International Journal of Human Resource Management*, 13(5): 802–14.

Linehan, M. and Scullion, H. (2001) 'European Female Expatriate Careers: Critical Success Factors', *Journal of European Industrial Training*, 25(8): 392–418.

Linehan, M. and Scullion, H. (2002) 'Breaking Through the Old Boy's Network in Europe — Still a Major Obstacle to the Career Development of Female International Managers', Paper presented at the British Academy of Management Annual Conference. London.

Linehan, M. and Walsh, J. (1999) 'Mentoring Relationships and the Female Managerial Career', *Career Development International*, 4(7): 348–52.

Mandelker, J. (1994) 'Breaking the Glass Border', *Working Woman*, 19(1): 16.

Marshall, J. (1984) *Women Managers: Travellers in a Male World*. Chichester: Wiley.

Napier, N.K. and Taylor, S. (2002) 'Experiences of Women Professionals Abroad: Comparisons Across Japan, China and Turkey', *International Journal of Human Resource Management*, 13(5): 837–51.

Noe, R. (1988) 'An Investigation of the Determinants of Successfully Assigned Mentoring Relationships', *Personnel Psychology*, 41: 457–79.

Oddou, G. and Mendenhall, M.E. (1991) 'Succession Planning for the 21st Century: How Well are We Grooming our Future Business Leaders?', *Business Horizons*, 34: 26–34.

O'Leary, V. and Ickovics, J.R. (1992) 'Cracking the Glass Ceiling: Overcoming Isolation and Alienation', in U. Sekaran and F.T. Leong (eds), *Womanpower: Managing in Times of Demographic Turbulence*. London: Sage, 7–30.

Parker, B. and Fagenson, E.A. (1994) 'An Introductory Overview of Women in Corporate Management', in M.J. Davidson and R.J. Burke (eds), *Women in Management: Current Research Issues*. London: Paul Chapman, 11–25.

Perun, P.J. and Bielby, D.D.V. (1981) 'Towards a Model of Female Occupational Behaviour: A Human Development Approach', *Psychology of Women Quarterly*, 6: 234–52.

Powell, G. (ed.) (1999) *Handbook of Gender in Organizations*. Thousand Oaks, CA: Sage.

Punnett, B.J. (1997) 'Towards Effective Management of Expatriate Spouses', *Journal of World Business*, 32(3): 243–57.

Punnett, B.J., Crocker, O.I. and Stevens, M.A. (1992) 'The Challenge for Women Expatriates and Spouses: Some Empirical Evidence', *International Journal of Human Resource Management* 3(3): 585–92.

Ragins, B.R. (1989) 'Barriers to Mentoring: The Female Manager's Dilemma', *Human Relations*, 42(1): 1–22.

Reich, M.H. (1986) 'The Mentor Connection', *Personnel* 63(2): 50–6.

Rothwell, S. (1984) 'Positive Action on Women's Career Development: An Overview of the Issues for Individuals and Organizations', in C.L. Cooper and M.J. Davidson (eds), *Women in Management: Career Development for Managerial Success*. London: Heinemann, 3–31.

Rowe, R. and Snizek, W.E. (1995) 'Gender Differences in Work Values: Perpetuating the Myth', *Work and Occupations*, May: 215–29.

Scase, R. and Goffee, R. (1989) *Reluctant Managers: Their Work and Lifestyles*. London: Unwin Hyman.

Schein, V.E. (1975) 'The Relationship Between Sex Role Stereotypes and Requisite Management Characteristics', *Journal of Applied Psychology*, 60(3): 340–4.

Schein, V.E. (1989) 'Sex Role Stereotyping and Requisite Management Characteristics, Past, Present and Future', Working Paper Series, no. WC 98–26. National Centre for Management Research and Development, University of Western Ontario.

Schein, V.E. (1994) 'Managerial Sex Typing: A Persistent and Pervasive Barrier to Women's Opportunities', in M.J. Davidson and R.J. Burke (eds), *Women in Management: Current Research Issues*. London: Paul Chapman, 41–52.

Schein, V.E., Mueller, R., Lituchy, T. and Liu, J. (1994) *Think Manager — Think Male: A Global Phenomenon?* Gettysburg, PA: Gettysburg College Management Department Working Papers.

Schell, M.S. and Solomon, C.M. (1997) *Capitalizing on the Global Workforce: A Strategic Guide to Expatriate Management*. New York: McGraw-Hill.

Schwartz, F.N. (1989) 'Management Women and The Facts of Life', *Harvard Business Review*, 67(1): 65–76.

Scullion, H. (1994) 'Staffing Policies and Strategic Control in British Multinationals', *International Studies of Management and Organization*, 24(3): 86–104.

Shellenbarger, S. (1992) 'Lessons From the Workplace: How Corporate Policies and Attitudes Lag Behind Workers' Changing Needs', *Human Resource Management*, 31(3): 157–69.

Smith, C.R. (1997) 'Career Transitions of Dual-Career Couples: An Empirical Study', *Career Development International*, 2(5): 229–37.

Smith, C.R. and Hutchinson, J. (1995) *Gender: A Strategic Management Issue*. Sydney: Business & Professional Publishing.

Storey, J. (ed.) (1989) *New Perspectives on Human Resource Management*. London: Routledge.

Taylor, S. and Napier, N. (1996) 'Working in Japan: Lessons from Women Expatriates', *Sloan Management Review*, 37: 125–44.

Tung, R. (1987) 'Expatriate Assignments: Enhancing Success and Minimising Failure', *Academy of Management Executive*, 1: 117–26.

Tung, R. (1998) 'American Expatriates Abroad: From Neophytes to Cosmopolitans', *Journal of World Business*, 33: 125–44.

Vinnicombe, S. and Colwill, N.L. (1995) *The Essence of Women in Management*. London: Prentice Hall.

Westwood, R.I. and Leung, S.M. (1994) 'The Female Expatriate Manager Experience: Coping with Gender and Culture', *International Studies of Management and Organization*, 24: 64–85.

White, B., Cox, C. and Cooper, C. (1992) *Women's Career Development: A Study of High Flyers*. Oxford: Blackwell.

Yeager, M. (ed.) (1999) *Women in Business*. Cheltenham: Elger Reference Collection.

# 10

# Managing human resources in cross-border alliances*

*Randall S. Schuler, Susan E. Jackson and Jacqueline Fendt*

Merging a U.S. and a European company, as we have done, is a particularly complicated process. The management styles are totally different. People have different views on how to manage a global organization. The British and American philosophies are so apart on those subjects they're almost impossible to reconcile.

Jan Leschly, former CEO GlaxoSmithKline

The media often portray business organizations as warring enemies who define their own success by the demise of their competitors. Executives sometimes use similar imagery to motivate their 'troops': What such images ignore are the strong interdependencies among business organizations and the degree to which cooperation results in mutual gains. Just as nations have discovered the benefits of economic cooperation, businesses have learned that success often depends on forming strategic alliances. Due to the formation of strategic alliances among companies often viewed as fierce competitors, industries are sometimes completely transformed (Freidheim, 1998).

Successfully managing strategic alliances is surprisingly difficult, however. The 1998 DaimlerChrysler cross-border merger illustrates some of the management challenges inherent in managing cross-border alliances. Competitive forces in the global auto industry initially led the two companies to merge, but while the combination looked good on paper, cultural differences interfered with management's ability to quickly reap the economic benefits they had anticipated. Clashes due to differences in country cultures and company cultures nearly doomed the new company's

* Adapted from our book, R. Schuler, S. Jackson and Y. Luo, *Managing Human Resources in Cross-border Alliances* (London: Routledge, 2004), based upon earlier works: R. Schuler, 'HR Issues in International Joint Ventures,' *Journal of International Human Resource Management* (February, 2001): 1–50; and R. Schuler and S. Jackson, 'HR Issues and Activities in Mergers and Acquisitions', *European Management Journal* (June 2001): 59–76.

success, and it seemed to take years for management to focus on a common vision and agree to the need for a single unifying culture. Although the alliance seems now to be succeeding, the initial years of difficulty might have been avoided if the managers had understood and appreciated the many HR issues that would require their attention (Apfelthaler, Muller and Rehder, 2002).

# Strategic alliances among firms

In general, *strategic alliances* involve two or more firms agreeing to cooperate as partners in an arrangement that's expected to benefit both firms. Sometimes strategic alliances involve one firm taking an equity position in another firm. In the most extreme case, one firm acquires the other firm, but less extreme equity positions also are common. Ford, for example, has equity in both foreign and US auto-parts producers, but it has not acquired these companies. Many strategic alliances do not affect legal ownership, however. In the airline industry, a common type of alliance is between an airline and an airframe manufacturer, and in high-tech industries strategic alliances allow older, established firms to gain access to the hot new discoveries being made by scientists in universities and in small, creative organizations. For example, the US biotechnology industry is characterized by networks of non-equity relationships between new biotechnology firms dedicated to research, and new product development and established firms in industries that can use these new products, such as pharmaceuticals. In return for sharing technical information with the larger firms, the smaller firms gain access to their partners' resources for product testing, marketing and distribution (Liebeskind *et al.*, 1996).

In this chapter, we focus on strategic alliances between firms that are headquartered in different countries. We refer to these as *cross-border alliances*, or CBAs. Cross-border alliances can be defined as partnerships that are formed between two or more firms from different countries for the purpose of pursuing mutual interests through sharing their resources and capabilities (Doz and Hamel, 1998; Yan and Luo, 2000). As is true for strategic alliances in general, there are many types of cross-border alliances, but two broadly categories are those that involve equity investments and those that involve no shared equity or joint capital investment.

A non-equity cross-border alliance is an investment vehicle in which profits and other responsibilities are assigned to each party according to a contract. Each party cooperates as a separate legal entity and bears its own liabilities. Non-equity alliances have great freedom to structure their assets, organize their production processes and manage their operations. This type of alliance can be developed quickly to take advantage of short-term business opportunities, then dissolved when their tasks are completed. Among the many types of non-equity alliances are joint exploration projects, research and development consortia, co-production agreements, co-marketing arrangements, and long-term supply agreements.

International joint ventures and international mergers and acquisitions are two major types of equity-based cross-border alliances. Such arrangements typically represent a long-term collaborative strategy. Furthermore, as we explain throughout this chapter, equity-based alliances require active day-to-day management of a wide variety of human resource (HR) issues. Some of the HR issues that are critical to the success of equity-based cross-border alliances may also arise in non-equity cross-border alliances, but they may be less central to the success of the alliance. In equity-based cross-border alliances, however, long-term success is impossible unless HR issues are managed effectively. While there are many lessons that can be transferred from our discussion of equity-based cross-border alliances to managing HR issues in non-equity alliances, most of our discussion focuses on describing the challenges of managing human resources in equity-based cross-border alliances. More specifically, we focus on international joint ventures and international mergers and acquisitions.

## International joint ventures

An international joint venture (IJV) is one type of equity-based cross-border alliance. Alliance partners form a joint venture when they create a separate legal organizational entity representing the partial holdings of two or more parent firms. In international joint ventures, the headquarters of at least one partner is located outside the country of the joint venture. Joint ventures are subject to the joint control of their parent firms. The parent firms, in turn, become economically and legally interdependent with each other.

Firms form IJVs for many reasons. In some countries the host government provides strong incentives to foreign firms to use joint ventures as a mode of entry into their markets (Geringer and Herbert, 1989). Another reason may be to gain rapid access to new markets. Learning is another objective behind many IJVs. By partnering with local companies instead of entering a market on their own, foreign firms can more quickly develop their ability to operate effectively in the host country. IJVs also provide a means for competitors within an industry to leverage new technology and reduce costs. In the auto industry, for example, Ford, General Motors, DaimlerChrysler, Nissan and Renault formed an IJVs Covisint, in order to manage their supply chains using business-to-business e-commerce (Greenlaugh, 2000). Ford's former CEO Jac Nasser explained the reasoning behind the formation of this IJV: 'We see this technology [e-business] as so powerful that, for it to be optimized, we need it to become an industry standard. So, rather than have 15 different standards out there ... we figured out that it would be more efficient if the basic architecture was common.' Assuming Covisint succeeds, it will fundamentally alter supply-chain relationships within the automobile industry.

For various reasons, managing IJVs successfully is difficult, and many ultimately fail, often through poor management of human resource issues. Prior to formation of an IJV, human resource management (HRM) professionals can help the potential partners assess their cultural compatibility. As the new entity is formed, recruiting and selecting of key executives to staff the IJV becomes critical. With the staff in place, HRM practices that align employees' skills and motivations with the business objectives of the IJV can determine whether it ultimately achieves the desired outcomes.

## International mergers and acquisitions (IM&As)

Companies today need to be fast, efficient, profitable, flexible, adaptable, future-ready and have a dominant market position. Without these qualities, it is virtually impossible to be competitive in today's global economy. In addition to participating in strategic alliances to develop the capabilities they need to compete, many firms evolve and grow through mergers or acquisitions. Among the most significant transnational merger and acquisition deals in recent years have been Daimler–Chrysler, Chase–J.P. Morgan, McKinsey–Envision, UBS–Warburg–Paine Webber, Credit Suisse–DLJ, Celltech–Medeva, SKB–Glaxo, NationsBank–Bank of America, Vivendi–Universal, Pfizer–Warner Lambert, Nestlé–Purina, and Deutsche Telekom–Voice Stream. Although global economic and market conditions move up and down, the future appears ripe for a continuation of international merger and acquisition activity.

In a merger, two companies agree to join their operations together to form a new company in which they participate as equal partners. In an acquisition, one firm buys controlling or full interest in another firm with the understanding that the buyer will determine how the combined operations will be managed. The majority of acquisitions are friendly – that is, the acquired firm solicits bids and enters into an acquisition voluntarily. Sometimes, however, a firm becomes a takeover target. Although mergers and acquisitions are technically different, it's common to refer to all these means for combining the operations of two firms as mergers and acquisitions, or just M&As (Charman, 1999; Deogun and Scannell, 2001).

Some observers argue that the increased pace of international mergers and acquisitions is a major driving force behind the development of multi-government agreements and rules for business conduct (Tyson, 2001). IM&A deals can have enormous economic and social consequences. They can quickly put the major competitors within a country out of business, and they can determine whether, how and where people work. Gaining government approval for international M&As is sometimes difficult, but the initial step of gaining approval usually proves to be far easier than successfully managing the new entity.

As is true for international joint ventures, international mergers and acquisitions unfold through many stages. At each stage, success requires effectively managing many HR issues, identifying the issues and their implications for HRM activities.

# The role of human resource management

Human resource management (HRM) refers to all of the dedicated activity that an organization uses to affect the behaviours of all the people who work for it. Because the behaviours of employees influence profitability, customer satisfaction and a variety of other important measures of organizational effectiveness, managing human resources is a key strategic challenge for all companies, and particularly so for those engaged in cross-border alliances (CBAs).

Every organization, from the smallest to the largest, engages in a variety of HRM activities, including formal policies and everyday practices for managing people. Policies are statements regarding how people will be managed; for example, there may be a policy to reward employees for their performance to the organization. HRM practices then take the next step and offer a more specific statement of how people will be managed to this end. For example, the practice of paying commissions based on individual sales performance is a practice that would be consistent with an HRM policy of rewarding employees for performance, as would offering team-based incentives that are tied to the performance of a team against stated team goals.

The more systematically HRM policies and practices are matched to the company, the more effective the company is likely to be (Becker *et al.*, 2001). This principle is as true for the successful management of CBAs as is it for organizations in general. And, as is true for business in general, the stakes are high. Successful CBAs may create new jobs, improve the economic conditions of a community, and produce wealth for shareowners. Conversely, failed CBAs may mean lost jobs, loss of tax revenue, declining share values, and even the eventual demise of companies. In order to develop a better understanding of the reasons for success and failure in CBAs, in the remainder of this chapter we describe some of the HR issues that arise in them and discuss their implications for a variety of HRM activities.

# International joint ventures

International joint ventures (IJVs) are legally and economically separate organizational entities created by two or more parent organizations that collectively invest financial as well as other resources to pursue certain objectives. IJVs are typically used when the required integration between the partners is high, and the venture business is characterized by uncertainty and decision-making urgency (Doz and Hamel, 1998). Although an overwhelming majority of IJVs involve only two parent firms (one from a foreign country and the other from the local country), some ventures may consist of multiple participants. Joint ventures that are launched by home-country-based (foreign) and host-country-based (local) firms are the dominant form of joint venture partnership. Because the creation of an IJV involves establishing an independent organization, the need to establish effective HR practices is particularly evident in this type of CBA.

## Reasons for forming IJVs

International joint ventures have become a major form of entry into global markets (Harrigan, 1986; Barkema *et al.*, 1997; Evans *et al.*, 2002), but there also are many other reasons that companies form IJVs. The most common reasons cited in the literature are:

- to gain technical and administrative knowledge, to learn, and to transfer that knowledge (Cyr, 1995; Lei, Slocum and Pitts, 1997; Mudambi, 2002)
- host-government insistence (Shenkar and Zeira, 1987; Gomes-Casseres, 1989)
- to gain rapid market entry and catch more customers (Shenkar and Zeira, 1987b; Harbison, 1996; Sparks, 1999)
- to capture increased economies of scale (Newburry and Zeira, 1997)
- to gain local knowledge and local market image and channel access (Lasserre, 1983; Gomes-Casseres, 1989; Harbison, 1996)
- to spread the risks (Shenkar and Zeira, 1987; Pucik, 1988)
- to improve competitive advantage in the face of increasing global competition (Porter, 1990)
- to support company strategies for internationalization (Evans *et al.*, 2002).

Of these, the reasons that appear to gaining substantial momentum are learning and knowledge-sharing and transfer (Child and Faulkner, 1998; Shenkar and Li, 1999; Reid *et al.*, 2001; Foss and Pedersen, 2002). In many industries, increasing global competition and unabated technological advancement have resulted in a wide range of cross-border collaborative partnerships intended to access knowledge, skills and resources that cannot be internally produced by organizations in a timely or cost-effective fashion. Organizational learning has long been considered a key building-block and major source of competitive advantage (Badaracco, 1991). A global alliance is not only a means by which partners trade access to each other's skills but also a mechanism for actually acquiring a partner's skills. In bringing together firms with different skills, knowledge bases and organizational cultures, IJVs create unique *learning opportunities* for the partner firms. By definition, alliances involve a sharing of resources, and this access can be a powerful source of new knowledge that, in most cases, would not have been possible without the formal structure of an IJV. As such, IJVs are no longer a peripheral activity but a mainstay of competitive strategy, forging new knowledge-transfer pathways across both technologically and traditionally linked positions.

Using and relying on external learning and knowledge transfer is challenging and complex (Barkema *et al.*, 1997; Mudambi, 2002). A fundamental impediment to interpartner learning and knowledge transfer originates from the nature of knowledge involved. Codified *explicit* knowledge is generally transparent and readily accessible and transferable, but many elements of knowledge transferred between IJV partners are tacit. *Tacit* means that the knowledge is deeply embedded in organizational routines (for example structure, rules and policies) and difficult to codify and teach. In organizations, tacit knowledge involves intangible factors embedded in personal beliefs, experiences and values. It is also stored organically in team relationships. If two firms seek transfer of the knowledge that is explicitly codifiable (for example patents), they normally choose international licensing instead of the IJV. When the knowledge is tacit, thus uncodifiable in the license contract, the IJV becomes a better device for transferring or sharing this type of knowledge.

Certainly, behaviours and styles of managers in organizations have a significant impact on the ability and willingness of a firm to learn (Frayne and Geringer, 2000). For example, learning requires managers to be open and willing to suspend their need for control. While firms and individuals need the ability and willingness to learn as they enter into the IJV formation process, they also need to be transparent so that others may learn as well (Hamel, 1991; Child and Faulkner, 1998). Thus both partners need to have similar qualities that support learning if the partnership is to have longer-term success (Lyles, 1987; Pucik, 1988; Hamel, 1991; Parkhe, 1991; Doz and Hamel, 1998). Because learning capability can quickly lead to attaining competitive advantage (Prahalad and Hamel, 1990), asymmetry in learning capability can soon lead to partnership instability and dissolution.

# A four stage model of IJVs

As noted earlier, the organizational and human resource issues in IJVs are clearly very extensive (Child and Faulkner, 1998), but they can be further refined and categorized into several stages, beginning with the development of the IJV itself (Lorange, 1986; Pucik, 1988; Lei *et al.*, 1997; Makhija and Ganesh, 1997; Schuler, 2001; Evans *et al.*, 2002). The four stages of the IJV process include:

1 **Formation**: the partnership stage;
2 **Development**: the IJV itself;
3 **Implementation**: the IJV itself;
4 **Advancement**: the IJV and beyond.

These four stages include activities that begin even before the IJV itself is formed, and conclude with the relationship among the three entities – two partners and one IJV. The HR issues in each stage of the IJV process are numerous as illustrated in Box 10.1. These HR issues and their implications for HRM policies and practices are more fully developed in the following sections.

## Box 10.1 Four-stage model of HR issues in international joint ventures

**Stage 1** Formation: the partnership

- Identifying the reasons for forming the IJV
- Planning for the utilization of its potential benefits
- Selecting a manager for new business development
- Finding potential partners
- Selecting the partner(s)
- Understanding control, building trust, managing conflict
- Negotiating the arrangement

**Stage 2** Development: the IJV itself

- Locating the IJV and dealing with the local community
- Establishing the appropriate structure
- Getting the IJV management team

**Stage 3** Implementation: the IJV itself

- Establishing the vision, mission, values, culture and strategy
- Developing the HRM policies and practices
- Dealing with unfolding issues
- Staffing the IJV

**Stage 4** Advancement: the IJV and beyond

- Learning between partners
- Transferring the new knowledge to the parents
- Transferring the new knowledge to other locations

*Source*: Schuler, Jackson and Luo (2004) *Managing Human Resources in Cross-Border Alliances*. London: Routledge; used with permission.

# Managing human resources in IJVs

As summarized in Box 10.1, the formation and operation of an IJV raises many HR issues that have implications for how the partners (the IJV parents and the IJV itself) manage their human resources. Many of these implications are grounded in the assumption that IJV parents and the IJV itself are all interested in learning (Parkhe, 1991). Watkins and Marsick (1993) put it this way:

> The learning organization is one that learns continuously and transforms itself. Learning takes place in individuals, teams, the organization, and even the communities with which the organization interacts. Learning is a continuous, strategically used process-integrated

with and running parallel to work ... The learning organization has embedded systems to capture and share learning. (1993: 8–9)

With these structural elements in place, organizations can further support knowledge flow, sharing and transfer by ensuring that their employees possess and exhibit:

- Openness
- Systemic thinking
- Creativity
- Self-confidence
- Empathy.

The parent and the IJV benefit from HRM practices that support and reinforce these role behaviours (McGill *et al.*, 1992; Jackson and Schuler, 2000, 2003). Next, we offer several propositions to guide these efforts.

## Managing human resources during stage 1 of IJVs

**Proposition 1:** When learning is important to the IJV parents, the IJV is more likely to succeed if HRM activities are used to identify and develop the absorptive capacity of the parents.

Absorptive capacity is the ability to acquire, assimilate, integrate and exploit new knowledge, skills, culture and ideas (Buckley and Casson, 1988; Inkpen, 1995; Luo, 1998). Absorptive capacity results from organizational experience and insight and from individual skills, knowledge and ability (Shenkar and Li, 1999). HRM activities that support these qualities include relevant training and development, and systematic selection practices (Pucik, 1988; Cyr, 1995; Barkema *et al.*, 1997).

Learning theory suggests that IJV relationships are more likely to be stable if the partner's absorptive capacities are similar. As Inkpen and Beamish (1997), Shenkar and Li (1999) and Badaracco (1991) have suggested, with equal absorptive capacities, partners are able to learn at equal rates. Unequal rates of learning create instability in the relationship, threatening the long-term viability and success of the IJV. Consequently, capacity analysis and development needs to be planned for early on – that is, during the formation stage of the IJV process (Pucik, 1988; Evans *et al.*, 2002).

**Proposition 2:** IJVs are more likely to be successful when HRM activities contribute to ensuring that there is a high degree of fit between potential partners.

One way that HR professionals can improve the degree of fit between IJV partners is to participate in assessing organizational fit, but this is not their only contribution. Even when the degree of fit is found to be suboptimal, a potential relationship may not be forever shelved. HRM activities may play a critical role in increasing some aspects of fit, particularly those associated with organizational criteria. For example, HRM activities can play a significant part in increasing a firm's absorptive capacity (Pucik, 1988) and thereby improve a partner's organizational criteria.

**Proposition 3:** HRM activities that build trust between the potential partners will increase their ability to resolve the potentially divisive issues related to control.

Finding a satisfactory solution to the problem of control is a major challenge for potential IJV partners (Inkpen and Currall, 1997). Partners who know little about each other are likely to exhibit lower trust towards each other and each is likely to seek ways to remain in control. As potential partners learn more about each other, they can begin to establish a relationship based more on trust. In other words, trust can become the mechanism (or substitute) for control. Trust diminishes the transaction costs associated with monitoring a partner's behaviours. Thus, by facilitating learning between potential partners, HRM activities can promote the development of trust and thereby diminish the divisiveness and the transaction costs associated with formal control mechanisms (Frayne and Geringer, 1990). For example, HR professionals in the potential parent firms might collaborate to conduct formal assessments and evaluations of their cultures and workforce capabilities. Another means by which HR professionals can promote the development of trust between potential partners is by ensuring that the manager for new business development (who often plays a key role during stage 1 of the IJV process) is capable and appropriately motivated.

**Proposition 4:** HRM activities that promote effective conflict resolution will increase the likelihood of the IJV success.

Because of the nature of the IJV process, conflicts or disagreement are almost inevitable, even among the most compatible partners. Learning about and developing trust in the partner may reduce conflict, but it will not eliminate it completely. Thus, potential IJV partners must be able to productively manage and resolve conflict to ensure that it does not create a divisiveness that eventually destroys the partnership (Child and Faulkner, 1998). During contract negotiations between the potential IJV partners, an integrative, problem-solving approach establishes an open dialogue. This in turn facilitates the discussion and resolution of issues that arise in later stages of the IJV process. HRM activities that help establish a context for effective conflict resolution include participating in the selection and training of people involved in IJV negotiations, and promoting effective communications among other managers and professional working within the potential partner firms.

## Managing human resources during stage 2 of IJVs

**Proposition 1:** When deciding where to locate the IJV, to assess the needs of all primary stakeholders promotes long-term IJV success.

Making a decision about where to locate the IJV is likely to be one of the major objectives during stage 2 development. Regardless of where the IJV is eventually located, the establishment of this new business will have implications for many constituencies (stakeholders). In order to ensure that the concerns of these stakeholders are addressed satisfactorily, their concerns must be identified and considered in the day-to-day operations of the IJV. Support or resistance from any major stakeholder group may determine the location decision and the IJV's longer-term operating success. In this entire process of stakeholder characteristics identification and assessment, the HRM department can play a vital role (Evans *et al.*, 2002; Jackson and Schuler, 2003).

> **Proposition 2:** The long-term success of an IJV is greater when state-of-the-art HR policies and practices are used to ensure that a high-quality IJV management team is recruited and retained.

The relationship between the parents and the IJV provides the context for learning among the partners (Child and Faulkner, 1998; Doz and Hamel, 1998). When this relationship is characterized by a high degree of autonomy for the IJV, the stage is set for the IJV to learn. Conversely, when control over the IJV is great, there is less opportunity for the IJV to learn the most effective means of operating within the local situation. Unless the parents feel confident that the IJV management team can succeed on its own, they will be reluctant to provide the team with the autonomy it needs to try new things, make mistakes and learn from those experiences. Subsequently, the parents also will reap fewer benefits, as their won ability to learn to be effective in the local conditions of the IJV is constrained. HRM activities that may help to ensure that the IJV management team is of top-quality include management job design, selection, development and retention.

## Managing human resources during stage 3 of IJVs

> **Proposition 1:** The chances of long-term success for an IJV are increased if the IJV develops its own vision, mission, values, culture and strategy.

The success of the IJV depends upon its being locally responsive and yet globally linked with its parents. Institutional theory suggests the importance of attending to the objectives of the IJV's multiple stakeholders, and on this point who better to know the local stakeholders than the IJV itself, even within the same country as one of the parents? Indeed, who needs to be more concerned and responsive to the needs of the multiple stakeholders other than the IJV itself? With a well-selected IJV top management team, there is a good likelihood that the vision, mission, values, culture and strategy will be crafted to fit the IJV's local circumstances (Thompson and Strickland, 1998).

While having the ability to do this is important, it is not a sufficient condition; the top team members need to be motivated as well. The parents' demonstration of trust via minimal control of their top managers will be an important incentive to motivate those IJV managers. Performance evaluations that highlight and reward the intents of both parental and IJV criteria will further enhance the motivation of the top team to establish local responsiveness while at the same time linking the IJV to the vision, mission, values, culture and strategy of the parents (Schuler, Dowling and De Cieri, 1992). Thus, establishing a vision, mission, value, culture and strategy that supports, encourages and recognizes learning and sharing will be in the interests of both the IJV and the parents (Pucik, 1988; Evans *et al.*, 2002), as more of those behaviours will occur.

> **Proposition 2:** If *tacit* knowledge is to be learned and transferred, HRM activities should reflect a long-term orientation. Conversely, if *explicit* knowledge is of primary concern, HRM activities that reflect a short-term orientation may be more effective.

Tacit knowledge is invisible; it resides in the minds of the people and the processes they have created (Inkpen and Beamish, 1997; Child and Faulkner, 1998). According to the human capital perspective, this knowledge can be more effectively retained and transferred through human resource activities that foster loyalty and commitment to the organization (Pucik, 1988; Cyr, 1995; Lei *et al.*, 1997). Such activities include values that emphasize loyalty, commitment and the importance of long-term relationships; extensive socialization and career development programmes; performance-appraisal criteria that emphasize the process through which results are achieved, as well as output; and compensation that rewards longer-term success and team-based activities (Fay, 1989; Lei *et al.*, 1997). Parents may attempt to maintain expatriates in the IJV for longer assignments in order to help transfer the tacit knowledge back to the parent. In this respect both parents and the IJV may have to recognize and reward the individual for developing a dual loyalty.

Explicit knowledge is that which can be modified, stored in data files and seen by others (Pucik, 1988; Lei *et al.*, 1997). Such knowledge is less-dependent upon the capabilities and motivations of specific individuals, and it is easily conveyed and transferred between units and individuals (Inkpen and Currall, 1997). Consequently, long-term relationships become less important and HRM activities may appropriately focus on supporting behaviours that are instrumental in the shorter term. Less investment in career development programmes is required, and appraisal criteria and compensation practices can reflect immediate results and individual output (Schuler and Jackson, 1987). Expatriates, or even project managers may be sent by the parents for short-term assignments with the express purpose of gathering explicit knowledge. One benefit of this approach may be that it is less costly, but the downside is that it fails to establish a relationship based on trust and diminishes chances of success if a long-term relationship is sought (Harbir and Zollo, 1999). Thus, it should only be used when the parents do not intend to maintain a long-term relationship with the IJV (Doz and Hamel, 1998).

# Managing human resources during stage 4 of IJVs

**Proposition 1:** If IJV partners continually assess and calibrate their learning capabilities to ensure learning symmetry is maintained, the likelihood of long-term IJV success increases.

Because learning symmetry is critical to the stability of the partner's relationship, it needs to remain in balance; such a condition can be facilitated by assessment of each partner. As the IJV matures, adjustments may be needed to reduce any differentials, and because learning capability is influenced by HRM activities, it is reasonable to regard this process of assessing and recalibrating the partner's absorptive capacity to ensure learning symmetry as an important HRM activity. As part of the process, other HRM activities such as appraisal, compensation and development need to be examined because these support and encourage the continued use and enhancement of existing learning capabilities (Child and Faulkner, 1998; Harbir and Zollo, 1999).

**Proposition 2:** As the IJV matures, investments in improving formal and informal communication will increase the likelihood of knowledge flow and learning among partners.

As partners learn more about and from each other, they develop more trust and willingness to share, and they become less protective of their knowledge (Inkpen and Currall, 1997). Trust alone does not ensure learning, however; also needed are appropriate channels for formal and informal communication among the partners (Makhija and Ganesh, 1997). Utilization of joint task forces, temporary assignments of employees from one partner to another and investments in improved cross-cultural communication all assist in formal and informal transmission of communication and information.

**Proposition 3:** Continuous evaluation and adjustment of all HRM activities is required to ensure the IJV's long-term success.

Like any organizational system, an HRM system that is static will soon outlive its usefulness. Because conditions in the environment and within the organization are constantly changing, managing people effectively demands vigilance and flexibility. Reviewing and re-evaluating HR policies and practices begins with understanding the objectives of the existing HR system – for example, was it designed to support long-term relationships or short-term relationships? Was it intended to promote learning between the parents or only between the IJV and the parents? A complete review and evaluation should consider all major stakeholders, and even if not formerly included in the evaluation processes, their voices are likely to be heard one way or the other. The results of the evaluation process serve as input into decisions about whether to revise the existing HR system, but it may also alert managers to new strategic issues.

Ongoing evaluation and review of the HR system is essential for continuous organizational learning and improvement. Where deficiencies are found, the HR professionals must assess whether these are due to poor implementation of a good HR plan, or whether the original plan was itself flawed. Appropriate HR practices may be foiled by managers and subordinates who fail to implement them. For example, when the IJV seems to be struggling for its very survival, managers in the parent organizations may find it difficult to allow IJV managers the autonomy they initially agreed to. In response, IJV managers may become suspicious of the parents' intentions and begin to question their commitment to the parents' objectives. Performance reviews, compensation decisions and a variety of monitoring activities can all send signals which suggest that the relationships among the partners have begun to drift away from the original intent. An HR review might also detect whether professionals in the organization feel that learning and knowledge transfer are truly valued and rewarded. Finally, even if an initial evaluation reveals that HR policies and practices are achieving the intended results, continuous evaluation should become part of the management routine, because changes in the parents' and IJV's objectives may require changes in their approaches to managing their human resources.

*   *   *

As this discussion suggests, there are many HR issues to manage in IJVs. Although the relevant body of research on these topics is small, we have stated our views about how to manage IJVs effectively in the form of propositions. These propositions are not hard-and-fast rules, however; rather, they reflect informed judgments that are consistent with both theory and the experiences of several IJVs. As additional research and insights accumulate, these general propositions will surely be modified and refined.

## Managing human resources in IM&As

'It's clear that you cannot stay in the top league if you only grow internally', says Vasella. 'You cannot catch up just by internal growth. If you want to stay in the top league, you must combine.' (Daniel Vasella, Chairman and CEO of Novartis in Herper, 2002)

International mergers and acquisitions represent the end of the continuum of options companies have in combining with each other. Representing the least intense and complex form of combination is licensing; next come alliances and partnerships and then joint ventures; mergers and then acquisitions conclude the combination options. In a merger, two companies come together and create a new entity. In an acquisition, one company buys another and manages it consistent with the acquirer's needs.

During the past two decades, cross-border acquisitions have exploded. According to W. T. Grimm's *Mergerstat Review*, there were only 197 cross-border acquisitions in 1985, and by 1999 there were 957. In the United States, for example, cross-border acquisitions of US companies accounted for 19 per cent of all takeovers during 1999, which compared to only 6 per cent in 1985. Despite all the challenges associated with IM&As, recent studies suggest that the combined firms are often valued more highly than the uncombined firms would ever have succeeded in creating (Seth *et al.*, 2002). Thus, longer-term, the future appears to be ripe for a continuation of international merger and acquisition (IM&A) activity, even though a temporary cooling off of the economy is also nearly inevitable.

---

## Box 10.2   HR issues in three stages of IM&As

**Stage 1**   Pre-combination
- Identifying reasons for the IM&A
- Forming the IM&A team/leader
- Searching for potential partners
- Selecting a partner
- Planning for managing the process of the IM and/or A
- Planning to learn from the process

**Stage 2**   Combination and integration

- Selecting the integration manager
- Designing/implementing teams
- Creating the new structure/strategies/leadership
- Retaining key employees
- Motivating the employees
- Managing the change process
- Communicating to and involving stakeholders
- Deciding on the HR policies and practice

**Stage 3**   Solidification and assessment

- Solidifying leadership and staffing
- Assessing the new strategies and structures
- Assessing the new culture
- Assessing the new HRM policies and practices
- Assessing the concerns of stakeholders
- Revising as needed
- Learning from the process

*Source*:   Schuler, Jackson and Luo (2004) *Managing Human Resources in Cross-Border Alliances.* London: Routledge, used with permission.

---

Many companies seem to be confronted with the need to carry out mergers and acquisitions, yet the odds of doing so successfully are relatively low. These odds can be increased, however: firms that have gained more experience and that take a systematic approach to learning from experiences in their deal-making are more likely to be successful (Arndt, 2000; Ashkenas *et al.*, 2000; Fendt, 2002a). As part of their systematic approach to completing successful IM&As, managers pay attention to HR issues that exist at each stage of the process. On the other hand, because there are more IM&As overall, there are more inexperienced executives, too, who are often less proactive, tend to underestimate HR issues and therefore not to involve HR or only late in the process (Fendt, 2002a; Levinsohn, 2002).

The key HR issues that arise in IM&As vary somewhat depending on the specific circumstances or type of IM&A under consideration. Some mergers are 'mergers of equals', examples being the merger between Citicorp and Travellers forming Citigroup; and between Ciba-Geigy and Sandoz forming Novartis. Other mergers take place between firms that are clearly unequal – at least in total size and market value. Similarly, there are various types of acquisitions such as those that involve both acquisition and integration, as typically made by GE, Siemens and Cisco Systems; and those that involve acquisition and separation such as between Unilever and Bestfoods. There are also friendly acquisitions and hostile acquisitions, although cross-border hostile acquisitions are relatively rare (Evans *et al.*, 2002). Acknowledging the different types of mergers and acquisitions is necessary in order to understand the many different HR issues that arise in IM&As. For example, a merger of equals often compels the two companies to share in the staffing implications, whereas a merger of unequals results in the staffing implications being shared unequally (Kay and Shelton, 2000). In this chapter, we can only briefly touch on the HR issues associated with the different types of IM&As (for a more complete discussion, see Schuler *et al.*, 2004).

In addition, the HR issues to be addressed in IM&As may differ depending on the objectives behind the deal. Among the numerous reasons for companies to merge or acquire are:

- the promotion of growth
- to manage technology
- as a response to government policy
- to take advantage of exchange rates
- as a response to political and economic conditions
- to reduce labour costs and/or increase productivity
- to follow clients
- to diversify and manage risk
- to achieve greater vertical integration
- as a response to shareholder and/or analyst pressure for growth, innovation, internationalization, and so forth.

In recent years, people-related reasons have become more common and with industrialized countries' dramatically aging population until 2020, this motive is likely to increase in significance. For example, engineers and scientists are in high demand worldwide, and as this demand will increase, the supply will decrease (Prognos, 2001). In industries where intellectual capital is critical to business success, as it is for semiconductor and optical networking firms, technically skilled employees are seen as more valuable than the company's product. Some banks even make dollar estimates of the value of a firm's employees, for example by applying metrics like price-per-engineer. When Broadcom bought chipmaker SiByte, it can be said to 'have paid $18 million per engineer' (Creswell, 2001a). Of course, such deals can only be successful if the employees in the target firm agree to stay after the deal is completed, but retaining talent after any merger or acquisition can be difficult. It may be even more difficult when employees in the target firm are expected to shift from working for a well-regarded domestic firm to working for a foreign-owned company, which may have less status or prestige, or is simply unknown.

Next, we describe a simple three-stage model of the IM&A process and use it to outline several HR issues that arise during IM&As. This model will again provide the foundation for developing propositions regarding how effective HRM can contribute to IM&A success.

# A three-stage model of mergers and acquisitions

Box 10.2 summarizes the HR issues to be addressed in three stages of the IM&A process: (1) pre-combination; (2) combination and integration of the partners; and (3) solidification and advancement of the new entity (Habeck *et al.*, 1999; Evans *et al.*, 2002). These three stages are applicable to most of a firm's business functions (finance, marketing, distribution, IT, manufacturing, and so on), but we highlight here only the issues that are most closely associated with managing human resources.

## Stage 1: pre-combination

The pre-combination stage includes all of the activities that occur before the IM&A is completely legally. Thus it includes the process of determining the reasons for becoming involved in a merger or acquisition (as a buyer or a target), searching for possible partners (whether domestic or international), evaluating the alternatives, selecting and negotiating with a specific partner, and planning for the eventual implementation of the deal. In many respects, these activities are quite similar to those conducted during the formation stage of an IJV.

The activities in stage 1 establish a foundation for stages 2 and 3. For example, in order for stage 2 to be effective, it is important that the partners have already carefully planned and prepared for it during stage 1. According to some estimates, lack of integration planning is found in 80 per cent of the IM&As that underperform (Habeck *et al.*, 1999).

A key HR activity in stage 1 is the performance of HR due diligence. This process should assess the human capital of an organization, but it is often carried out by lawyers and financial experts who focus on financial costs and contractual obligations. If HR is involved in this process it will go beyond to give insight into how much a business is supported by its human capital, what culture drives the company and how it impacts on performance, what added value is the human capital capable of creating in a merger, and how can it best be released and developed (Daniel and Metcalf, 2001; Devine, 2002).

## Stage 2: combining and integrating the companies

This stage begins after a merger or an acquisition is announced and pre-combination activities are completed. The general approach used to integrate and combine IM&A firms can be characterized as fitting one of four approaches: portfolio, blending, new creation, and assimilation.

In the portfolio approach, managers in the two companies retain a great deal of autonomy. Although the alliance creates legal and economic interdependencies, the top management team assumes that the two organizations will continue to operate more or less as they had operated prior to the IM&A. Presumably, the strategic value of the alliance does not lie in the integration of the separate organizational systems, so differences are 'managed' by maintaining segregated organizations. This scenario often occurs when one firm acquires another firm as a pure investor or in order to diversify into another business or region and then allows the acquired firm to operate as a relatively autonomous subsidiary.

The blending scenario arises when top managers intend the two organizations to come together or merge into a new organization that retains the best aspects of the original partners. In this scenario, the intent is to manage diversity through integration, with members of each organization adapting to the procedures and culture of their alliance partner. The blending approach is perhaps most common in IM&As that occur within an industry, and between firms that are believed to complement each other's strengths and offset each other's weaknesses.

> But surely management style, organization, and market share could have been improved without a merger? 'No,' Vasella replies. 'The merger was the trigger we needed to rethink our focus and re-challenge ourselves. We needed to create a whole new corporate culture. The creation of a new company with a new name committed to innovation gave us a competitive advantage.' (Hanes, 1999)

A third scenario arises when the partners agree to create a new firm that is truly different from either of the original partners. As we have already seen, this is typically what partners agree to do when then enter into a joint venture, especially if the IJV is located in a country other than the countries of the parent firms. Creating a new organization is the goal of some mergers also, although it seems to be less common. One indication that an IM&A is intended to form a new creation is that the resulting firm takes on a completely new name. Novartis, which was created through a merger of Sandoz and Ciba-Geigy, is one example. Although it is not strictly speaking an international M&A, cultural differences of these two global life-science players were important. As Vasella (CEO of Novartis) comments:

> We [Ciba-Geigy and Sandoz] had very different corporate cultures even though we were in the same town, separated only by a river. Companies can have substantial differences even if they are physically very close in proximity. Of course, there are also national differences. For example, one of my colleagues (a German in the U.S.) went with another colleague to a football game. His colleague was coaching and the gentleman's son was shooting the ball and couldn't score. My colleague thought, 'What a poor shot!' while the American said, 'Great try, Johnny!' I felt that this was such a wonderful example of the difference in attitude that I saw between Americans and Germans: one focuses on the effort and the possibilities for the next time, while the other thinks first about critique. (Fuld, 2000)

Having experienced a merger of similar size in 1970 with Ciba and Geigy and having seen that for two decades people tended to blame 'those of Ciba' or 'those of Geigy', the merging partners set out to do it right this time. They focused strongly on culture from the start and spared no effort to create a totally new culture from day one. The name Novartis, describing the innovation focus of the new organization and bearing no association with either of the previous names, would be its symbol. No energy would be lost with turf wars; rather, all efforts should be focused on the common project: ' … is like having a child: Each parent looks for resemblances in the eyes and face. But the child has its own identity. Both sides will need to step back a bit and not impose their own culture on it' (Smith, 2000).

Finally, in some acquisitions, the buyer clearly intends to take over and control the target; typically, General Electric and Siemens do this with many of their acquisitions (Javidan, 2002). Such experienced integrators use proven integration processes which they regard as critical growth competencies, consequently investing time on people and resources to develop the processes, functions and responsibilities, checklists and full-time integration managers long before IM&As occur (Bogan and Symmers, 2001). The target firm may be an attractive candidate for an acquisition because it has some valuable assets, yet for various reasons it is clear that it cannot survive on its own. In this scenario, the expectation is that the target firm will lose its identity and adopt the management practices of the acquiring firm. In other words, the target firm is expected to assimilate into the acquirer, as happened when Deutsche Bank acquired Bankers Trust (Atlas, 2002), and in Pfizer's hostile takeover of Warner-Lambert. When

Pfizer acquired Warner-Lambert, they adopted a few of Warner-Lambert's practices, but observers say that little of the Warner-Lambert culture remains today. Not surprisingly, most of Warner-Lambert's top-level managers have left the firm.

Regardless of the specific approach, all acquisitions require some degree of integration of systems and processes in order to achieve key synergies. Successful integration is a key challenge in stage 2 of IM&As. If the firms don't succeed in integrating their activities, the results are predictable; according to recent studies, poor integration accounts for declining productivity, leadership attrition, low employee morale and failure to meet financial goals (Bobier, 2000).

Because Johnson & Johnson engages in so many mergers and acquisitions, they have been able to study their own experiences and learn from their successes and failures. This company's research clearly indicates that a systematic, explicit integration process is at the heart of successful mergers or acquisitions. Furthermore, J&J has learned the importance of tailoring decisions about how to approach the task of integration to take into account the specific strengths and weaknesses of the acquired company. J&J has also learned that stage 2 should proceed as quickly as possible – the sooner the process begins, the better. Ideally, decisions about the management structure, key roles, reporting relationships, layoffs and restructuring should be announced within days of signing. Creeping changes, uncertainty and anxiety that last for months are debilitating and drain value from an acquisition (Bobier, 2000).

## Stage 3: solidification and assessment of the new entity

As an IM&A takes shape, it faces issues of readjusting, solidifying and fine-tuning. These issues take on varying degrees of intensity, although not importance, depending upon the approach to integration that the firms adopt. The intensity can be quite high for an international merger of equals that is intended to lead to the creation of a new entity, and failure to address the HR issues effectively is likely to mean that the intended strategy is never successfully implemented. For DaimlerChrysler, stage 3 lasted more than two years (Muller *et al.*, 2001), during which time they grappled with all of the HR issues listed under stage 3 in Box 10.2.

Like IJVs, effectively managing international mergers and acquisitions requires dealing successfully with many significant HR issues. Each stage of the IM&A process presents new challenges as well as new opportunities to create value by managing people effectively. Next, we turn to a more detailed discussion of the HR issues that arise in each of the three stages of IM&As.

## Managing HR issues during stage 1 of IM&As

**Proposition 1:** When a key objective is to develop the organization's IM&A capabilities, long-term success with IM&As will be improved by adopting HR practices that support organizational learning.

Building upon the learning-theory perspective, it becomes apparent that HR issues will be particularly important for firms that want to build their IM&A capabilities. Used singly, but increasingly in bundles, HRM practices such as recruiting, work systems design or training and development can help the new alliance be more competitive (Pfeffer, 1996). If learning about the IM&A process is among the objectives that managers have articulated, the role of managing human resources is more likely to be recognized as central to a successful IM&A process. Firms with little IM&A experience that anticipate using IM&As as a long-term strategy may recognize that their early IM&A activities will be learning experiences, but this does not guarantee that managers will make learning a key objective against which their success will be evaluated.

To ensure that learning is *intentional* and *directed*, as a starting point everyone in the organization needs to understand that learning about how to manage IM&As is a key objective for the organization. As is true for other business objectives, the learning objective will become salient to the extent that the organization develops measures for assessing learning and adopts practices intended to facilitate learning. In addition to encouraging managers to adopt a long-term learning mindset, adjustments in the current HR policies and practices may be needed in order to encourage employees to share and disseminate what they have learned.

In knowledge creation as well as knowledge transfer, HRM practices play a vital role (Pucik, 1988; Evans *et al.*, 2002; Jackson and Schuler, 2000, 2003). For example, if developing the firm's IM&A capabilities is an important long-term objective, managers with prior IM&A experience (perhaps in a previous job) should be identified early in stage 1 and encouraged to participate in the various planning teams and taskforces that are created at this stage. In addition, training programmes for employees throughout the company should begin to incorporate basic educational modules to inform employees about the legal, financial, operational and human issues associated with IM&A activity. Employees who understand the legal and financial constraints that managers face in the early stages of the IM&A process will be less likely to impute negative motives to executives who have not been completely open and forthcoming about their intentions to engage in an IM&A. Later, when the nature of the deal becomes public, educated employees will be in a better position to understand the implications of the deal for them. When a merger or acquisition is announced, uncertainty about the implications of the deal is one of the greatest sources of stress among employees. Although uncertainty cannot be completely eliminated, it can be reduced. For example, employees who understand the different reasons for IM&A activity will be less likely to simply assume that layoffs are certain to follow the announcement of a deal. Instead, they can understand that some deals may have almost no consequences for their own job security, while other types of deals are almost certain to result in layoffs. In either scenario, uncertainty is reduced and employees are empowered by their improved understanding of the situation.

**Proposition 2:** IM&As are more likely to be successful when HRM practices focus on the retention of key talent.

Having capable senior management in place for IM&As is as important as it is for IJVs. Effective leadership increases the possibilities of a successful international merger and acquisition. In the best firms, HR policies and practices that support the development of excellent leaders will already be in place long before stage 1 of a particular IM&A deal. When strong leadership talent is already available, effective retention practices can help ensure that qualified existing managers remain after the merger or acquisition is completed (Atlas, 2002). Conversely, it is best to identify the managers who will be let go as soon as possible and begin to plan for their exit.

**Proposition 3:** The long-term success of IM&As is enhanced by identifying employees who will serve as team leaders in stage 2 (integration) and involving them in many stage 1 activities.

With the possible exception of IM&As that will be managed using the portfolio approach, teamwork will be essential to successful integration. Furthermore, the work of the integration teams is likely to be facilitated by early involvement of those team leaders in the IM&A process. Therefore, stage 1 is the appropriate time to select and begin developing the team leaders who will be essential to success in stage 2.

**Proposition 4:** IM&A success is enhanced through a due diligence process that includes an analysis of the cultures of the partners, the HR policies and practices of the two firms, the financial liabilities associated with HR policies and practices, and the financial risk associated with potential loss of key talent.

When two firms are seriously interested in pursuing an IM&A, they typically sign an agreement that outlines the information that each party will be allowed to gain access to prior to the deal's close, and that provides a time frame for completing the review. Experienced firms realize the importance of gaining access to information about a wide variety of HR issues during this review process. Conducting a thorough due diligence assessment in the IM&A requires a complete assessment of the HR environment of the partner firms.

The term 'soft due diligence' is sometimes used to refer to assessment of the HR issues associated with IM&As, and perhaps this is why HR issues often receive too little attention during the due diligence process. Although widely used, the term soft due diligence is misleading. Assessing the cultures of the two firms is the softest element of a complete HR due diligence process, but appropriate analyses of the many other HR issues that are important to IM&A success are anything but 'soft'. To capture the importance of both hard and soft due diligence, Johnson & Johnson executives prefer to use a single concept that incorporates both terms: a discovery process (Bobier, 2000). This should include the following:

*Culture assessments.*   In cultural audits and assessments, perceptions and opinions are the primary source of 'data'. Being dependent on soft data does not mean that assessments of culture are unsystematic, however. Cultural assessments for IM&As are especially complex due to the interplay between corporate culture, country culture and industry culture (Shenkar and Yan, 2002; Jackson and Schuler, 2003). On the other hand, the importance of conducting a cultural assessment seems to be more easily grasped when a cross-border alliance is involved and thus may receive more attention in IM&As than in some domestic IM&As (Numerof and Abrams, 1998).

Cultural assessments involve describing and evaluating the two companies' philosophies and values regarding such issues as: leadership styles; time horizons; relative value of stakeholders; risk tolerance; and the value of teamwork versus individual performance and recognition (Numerof and Abrams, 1998). In the DaimlerChrysler combination, the importance of company cultural differences, initially downplayed, became the reason for allowing the business units to function as they wished as long as they achieved their goals (Andrews and Bradsher, 2000; Tierney, 2000). In addition to company cultural assessments, firms entering into IM&As may need to assess differences in industry cultures and country cultures.

*HR policies and the financial liabilities associated with them.*   Ideally, the due diligence process includes a complete assessment of the commonalities and differences between the HR policies in the firms entering into an IM&A. In other words, approaches to staffing, performance measurement, career development, training, compensation, and provisions to ensure due process should all be assessed. In actuality, however, the elements of HRM that are most likely to receive attention are those with clear financial or legal implications.

Because employee benefits plans can have significant long-term financial consequences, they are quite likely to receive scrutiny. When employees are represented by unions, labour contracts are also likely to receive scrutiny. In fact, union representatives may participate in the due diligence process to ensure that issues associated with possible job loss, retraining and outplacement are fully anticipated.

*Financial risks associated with loss of talent.*   Clearly, when acquiring talent is a key objective, then the deal will not be successful if most of the talent chooses to leave after the deal is announced. Even when talent acquisition is not a major objective, however, too much loss of talent can reduce the chances of an IM&A, success. Departures and early retirement of key executives can be financial costly, depending on the terms and conditions of their employment or retirement contracts. Executive departures may also have other costs, however. In addition to losing their managerial expertise, the firm may also lose a valuable source of social and political connections. In industries that depend heavily on 'star' talent for success (such as entertainment), the loss of star talent may diminish the firm's stock. Similarly, loss of key technical talent may mean that important and irreplaceable knowledge is lost. If this talent and knowledge migrates to competitors, the firm's competitive advantage may be significantly damaged. Thus, in addition to making plans for retaining key talent, it also becomes necessary to assess the probability of losing key talent and assess the costs associated with such losses. Unfortunately, the science of assigning value to intangibles, including human capital, is still in its infancy, although, in recent years some progress has been made in this area (see for example Becker *et al.*, 2001; Boudreau, 2003). Firms that are serious about assessing the financial risks associated with talent loss recognize the value of systematically estimating such risks even if they know their estimates are fallible.

## Managing HR issues during stage 2 of IM&As

Of all the HR issues that arise during the IM&A process, perhaps the most critical issue for the success of stage 2 is selection of the integration manager and the leader(s) for the new business (Ashkenas and Francis, 2000).

> **Proposition 1:** IM&As are more likely to succeed when the firms involved create a position dedicated to managing the integration process and clearly define the duties of this position.

When Johnson & Johnson analysed its experiences with mergers and acquisitions, it found that successful combinations were those guided by an effective integration manager. The most effective integration managers were able to retain a higher percentage of the acquired companies' leaders, retain a higher percentage of the total employees, and achieve business goals earlier. Furthermore, their research indicated the following:

- Successful integration managers focused exclusively on the particular acquisition or merger. This task was *not* one of many others for which they were responsible.
- Successful integration managers were *not* the same people who were running the business. Presumably, this made it easier for the integration manager to be, and to be perceived as, capable of fairly assessing the strengths and weaknesses of both partners involved in the deal.
- Successful integration managers provided continuity between the deal team and management of the new company. They understood the company, felt a sense of ownership, and were passionate about making the new organization work.
- Successful integration managers participated as members of a steering committee that included other top executives. The steering committee shared responsibility for defining the integration manager's role, establishing the objectives and process of the integration, and overseeing the progress of the various teams involved in all related projects (Bobier, 2000).

For deals that are clearly acquisitions, the job of an integration manager should be managing the integration process, *not* the business. His or her duties including assisting *both* partners as they move through the integration process.

**Proposition 2:** The value of a dedicated integration manager will be greater to the extent that he/she has competencies needed for this unique position, and performance management practices that are aligned with the performance expectations for the position.

An integration manager must have a variety of skills to be effective, at times needing to step into the following roles:

- Project manager
- Communicator; information-gatherer
- Advisor
- Advocate
- Relationship builder
- Facilitator
- Ombudsperson
- Negotiator.

Because the job of IM&A integration manager is somewhat unique, it is not one that is likely to be understood by employees who may have the required competencies. Even if the job duties *are* understood, the position may not be viewed as highly desirable, as it is clearly a temporary position. As a consequence, filling this position with the best available talent may require making a significant investment in the recruitment and selection process. Prior to choosing from among a set of candidates, the position itself must first be 'sold' as desirable. In firms with a history of IM&A activity, the rewards associated with serving as an integration manager may already be recognized by employees (of course, the risks will also be more apparent). For firms with little prior experience, however, this position is likely to be perceived as risky – and indeed that perception may be accurate. Thus, to convince the best talent to sign on to this job, the firm may need to offer appropriate support and assurances of the value the firm places on developing competencies to support future IM&A activity. Certainly plans for continued utilization of this integration competency and knowledge are imperative for further deals and for knowledge sharing. Having such plans in place may also be essential to convincing the best people to consider taking the position of integration manager.

**Proposition 3:** The success of IM&As is improved to the degree that effective HRM practices are used to establish and manage an integration team, whose role is to address each system or process that is key to creating value in the new business.

Assisting the integration manager are integration teams (Marks and Mirvis, 2000; Taylor, 2002). In almost every IM&A, there are numerous systems and processes that must be integrated in order to support efforts to attain synergies. Examples are sales reporting systems, certain IT systems, the global e-mail network and the distribution chain. Until these are integrated, day-to-day functioning may seem all but impossible. DaimlerChrysler created over 100 integration teams; specific teams were assigned to various functional areas and organizational levels within the two companies (Charman and Carey, 2000).

While there may be an endless number of differences in the systems and processes being merged together, the Johnson & Johnson study found that the most effective integration teams focused their attention on those that were essential to creating value. Not all forms of synergy are equally important. As one J&J executive stated: 'We only attacked things that would bring benefits to the business. We did not integrate just for the sake of integrating.' Once key value-drivers are identified, a team should be assigned to creating synergy and tracking the progress of integration (Bobier, 2000).

Of course the need for integration teams and the tasks that are most important for them to tackle differ according to the integration approach used. If the portfolio approach is adopted, the integration teams may focus primarily on developing shared understandings about the systems and processes in use at the various locations and establishing communication practices for people in the different facilities to use when coordination is required. If the blending approach is adopted, the integration teams will need to do much more than help the units develop an understanding of each other – they also will assess the strengths and weaknesses of the alternative systems and make choices about which to retain, which to discard, and where to make modifications. The new creation approach to integration may present an even greater challenge for the integration teams, for with this approach the expectation is that the best elements of systems in both firms will be reflected in new systems designed specifically to meet the needs of the new organization.

**Proposition 4:** Restructuring should be carefully planned and done early, fast, and only once.

When an IM&A plan includes significant restructuring and downsizing, the process of integration can be especially painful. Historically, the problem has been that executives tend to restructure slowly and to rely heavily on downsizing rather than on redesigning structures and processes (Ashkenas *et al.*, 2001).

As with other major organizational change efforts, the planning phase of a restructuring or layoff should involve the staff who will be affected by the change to help ensure their understanding and cooperation. A schedule for the change process should be developed and the changes should be conducted according to the plan. Given the importance of managing such changes, expertise in change management is an essential competency that must be present within the IM&A integration team(s). The HR staff can address this need by assessing change-management competencies when the integration team is being created, and/or by providing training and change-management services to the teams after they are formed.

Facing the threat of job loss and seeing others lose their jobs can be a traumatic and bitter experience. This is one reason why many excellent companies do everything possible to avoid layoffs, even after an acquisition. Despite their best intentions, however, even the most employee-friendly companies may conclude that some workforce reduction is necessary in order to eliminate redundant positions following an international merger or acquisition. In such situations, governmental policies and labour contracts may partially determine the layoff practices that are permitted. Nevertheless, the way a firm approaches reductions in the workforce can have long-ranging implications for employee loyalty and turnover.

**Proposition 5:** When talent retention is a key objective, achievement of this goal is more likely if the performance of upper-level managers is assessed against clearly stated talent-retention goals.

As we have already explained, stage 1 of the IM&A process is the appropriate time to identify key talent. As the deal becomes more certain, specific plans for retaining that talent should be developed; such planning may begin near the end of stage 1 or early in stage 2. Either way, it is during stage 2 that the retention plans will ultimately succeed or fail. Watson Wyatt's research on IM&As found that retention of key talent was among the top-three issues that needed to be addressed by an HRM integration plan (Yang, 2001).

Given that everyone seems to understand the importance of retaining key employees, why do so many firms seem to stumble when it comes to meeting their objectives? One likely explanation is that the identification of key talent occurs too late – sometimes not until the person has already left the firm. Another cause of talent loss is that responsibility for talent retention is pushed down to lower-level managers, when a better approach would be to involve executives at the very top. Retention of key talent begins with communication. Employees whose talents are needed must understand that they are valued and the firm wishes to retain them. This message is most effectively carried by managers positioned two or more levels above the employees of interest who themselves feel secure about their post-IM&A roles. These higher-level managers may also be more persuasive than the immediate supervisor of the person targeted for retention.

Giving managers the authority to offer cash or other incentives to workers who stay through a merger or until a specific project is completed is one way to improve their ability to retain people. Another tactic is to alter the severance agreements of employees to provide an incentive for those employees who may worry about pending layoffs and depart prematurely. Because the best talent is also the most mobile, finding ways to forestall voluntary turnover should be a high priority during stage 2.

**Proposition 6:** The success of IM&As is greater to the extent that communication about the ongoing process is frequent proactive and accurate.

It is impossible to communicate too much or in too many ways. Well-managed communications are valuable tools for retaining and motivating key employees, as well as for managing the many types of change that occur during combination and integration. Effective communication is difficult under most circumstances, but the communication challenge is especially great during IM&As. Thus, it pays to use as many ways to communicate as possible. Thoughtful use of the internet, internal company intranets and e-mail is one way to dispel rumours and keep employees updated about impending changes. Electronic communications should supplement, not replace, face-to-face discussions, however.

Managers in the acquiring firm have but one chance to extend a warm and convincing welcome to employees of a target firm, and that chance comes at the beginning of stage 2. For this communication, personal contact with a lower-level manager is likely to be more effective than electronic contact with the top executive. Personal contact should also be used to convey complex information, so employees can ask questions and get clear answers immediately.

Effective communication anticipates employees' need for information: it does not merely provide answers to questions asked. Perhaps even more important than timely information is accurate information. For example, using the term *merger* to describe a deal that will be managed using the portfolio or assimilation approach to integration can cause unnecessary confusion and misunderstanding. Likewise, using the term *acquisition* to describe a deal that will be managed as a new creation or blended organization can send the wrong signal to employees and may create more resistance to change than is necessaries.

Communication also facilitates knowledge sharing and helps ensure that lessons learned during the IM&A integration process are spread quickly throughout the organization. As J&J found, many of the same lessons were learned repeatedly across the business units, and these lessons were not always shared. Learning is a natural part of the integration process, and the need for some trial and error is unavoidable. Nevertheless, sharing problems as they are encountered and sharing solutions as they are found is one way to improve learning efficiencies. Large decentralized firms seem more prone to inefficient learning related to routine processes and procedures because there is no natural central hub for information to flow through. For example, in a decentralized firm, staffing activities are typically conducted locally, with little or no central oversight. Consequently, each unit is likely to make the same mistakes as they gain experience in managing layoffs. In a centralized firm, the benefits of such learning accumulate more quickly. This is one of the reasons why an integration team should be established for every important process within the organization – including HR processes. In decentralized firms, such integration teams provide an efficient mechanism for the rapid transfer of learning.

## Managing HR issues during stage 3 of IM&As

Once the international merger or acquisition has progressed through the stage of combination and integration, of whatever form, there remain several HR issues that need attention during solidification and assessment. Indeed, one danger at this stage is thinking that the IM&A process is finished and that issues addressed in stage 2 no longer require attention. But this is seldom true.

> **Proposition 1**: Premature disbanding of integration teams lowers the likelihood of long-term success. Integration teams should be disbanded slowly and only after the targets of their integration activity are completely stabilized.

Leadership and staffing issues that may seem to have been resolved earlier may continue to unfold for quite some time. In the DaimlerChrysler example, during the two years after the combination was announced Daimler made several leadership changes in the Chrysler Group, as the unit of DaimlerChrysler is now called (Tierney, 2000). At the beginning of 2001, Dieter Zetsche, a veteran Daimler executive, took over Chrysler's leadership, replacing a former Chrysler head James Holden. Zetsche in turn created his own top-management team composed of one Daimler veteran and five Chrysler veterans. All these changes were made because the earlier top-management team of former Chrysler veterans failed in its efforts to stop the 'breathtakingly fast decline of the bottom line' (Tierney, 2000). Thus the process of solidifying leadership may result in assessing and replacing the existing leadership. The need for new leadership may be due to inappropriate selection, or changed conditions, or both.

Just as the leadership at DaimlerChrysler had to be revised, the strategy and structure had to be assessed and revised. The new top management was given more control over the Chrysler Group largely because a senior Daimler executive was running it. He and his team developed a new strategy of cost-cutting by reducing supplier costs and reducing product offerings. Instead of running the Chrysler Group as a cash-rich growth business, management began to manage it as a turnaround. Consequently, staff reductions were also needed, and thus HRM practices for evaluation and outplacement became critical.

Along with the changes in leadership and strategy, the culture changed. Zetsche and his team were much more equalitarian than their predecessors. According to one observer, 'They [ate] in the employee cafeteria rather than the executive dining room at the headquarters in Auburn Hills, Michigan' (Muller *et al.*, 2001). To support this new culture, strategy and structure, changes were made in the performance appraisal and compensation systems, which clarified the new priorities of cost-cutting, supplier management, flexibility and improving employee morale.

DaimlerChrysler CEO Jürgen Schrempp, reflecting on these changes in the postcombination stage of the acquisition, estimated that recovery and solidification would take two to four years. Initially, back in 1998 upon purchasing Chrysler, Schrempp discussed immediate global synergies and probability. Perhaps the earlier success in its acquisition of Freightliner gave him the confidence that the Chrysler acquisition would be as successful. The contrasting experiences provided DaimlerChrysler with excellent opportunities for learning (Vlasic and Stertz, 2000; Taylor, 2001).

**Proposition 2:** Regardless of whether the IM&A process has been declared a success or a failure, the knowledge created during the process should be captured and secured for future use.

For firms that will be engaging in future IM&As, capturing and consolidating the learning and knowledge that has been generated throughout the IM&A process is perhaps the most important activity during stage 3.

As we have already suggested, retaining an integration manager is an objective that should be anticipated as early as stage 1. The importance of retaining the integration manager is that other executives will claim credit for that success. They may point to their skill in making strategic decisions, their cunning in negotiating the deal, and so on. Alternatively, if the deal seems to have failed, changes in business conditions or the partner's lack of candour during due diligence are likely to be blamed. Under either scenario, it is likely that the important role played by the integration manager will receive little attention. Similarly, the lessons everyone has learned throughout the ordeal may fade from memory, become distorted with time, or simply disappear. Ensuring that the lessons learned are retained requires intentional effort in stage 3. In addition to retaining the integration manager and key players (such as integration team leaders and members), everyone in the organization should be encouraged to reflect on what they have learned that could be useful for creating success in a future IM&A deal. These insights should be systematically surfaced, shared and recorded for future reference.

# Conclusion

As with IJVs, there are a significant number of HR issues in international mergers and acquisitions. Although different issues take priority during the three stages of IM&As, a common objective in all stages is to anticipate and manage change, and to learn from experience. In addition, although it has not been a central theme in this chapter, managing cultural differences is also a key HR issue for IM&As, as it is for any CBA. These issues and many others associated with managing human resources in IM&As and IJVs are described in greater detail elsewhere (Schuler *et al.*, 2004).

With the vast number of HR issues involved in IM&As and IJVs, the HR profession has a great opportunity to make significant contributions to the organization. The value and effectiveness of these contributions are likely to be greatly enhanced through a partnership between the HR professionals, line managers, employees and all other significant stakeholders (Jackson and Schuler, 2003).

## References

Andrews, E. and Bradsher, K. (2000) 'This 1998 Model is Looking More Like a Lemon', *New York Times*, 26 November, section 3: 1–11.
Apfelthaler, G., Muller, H.J. and Rehder, R.R. (2002) 'Corporate Global Culture as Competitive Advantage: Learning from Germany and Japan in Alabama and Austria?', *Journal of World Business*, 37:108–18.

Arndt, M. (2000) 'Let's Talk Turkeys', *Business Week*, 11 December: 44–8.

Ashkenas, R.N. and Francis, S.C. (2000) 'Integration Managers: Special Leaders for Special Times', *Harvard Business Review*, November–December: 108–14; Delta Consulting Group Study.

Ashkenas, R.N., DeMonaco, L.J. and Francis, S.C. (2000) 'Making the Deal Real: How GE Capital Integrates Acquisitions', *Harvard Business Review*, January–February: 165–78.

Atlas, R.D. (2002) 'How Banks Chased a Mirage: Costly Acquisitions of Investment Houses Proved a Bad Fit', *New York Times*, section 3.

Badaracco, J.L. (1991) *The Knowledge Link*. Boston: Harvard Business School Press.

Barkema, H.G., Shenkar, O., Vermeulen, F. and Bell, J. (1997) 'Working Abroad, Working With Others: How Firms Learn to Operate International Joint Ventures', *Academy of Management Journal*, 40(2): 426–42.

Becker, B.E., Huselid, M.A. and Ulrich, D. (2001) *The HR Scorecard: Linking People, Strategy, and Performance*. Boston: Harvard Business School Press.

Bobier, S. (2000) 'Personal Communication', in company seminar for J&J, 7 November.

Bogan, Ch. and Symmers, K. (2001) 'Marriages Made in Heaven?', *Pharmaceutical Executive*, January, 21(1): 52–60.

Boudreau, J.W. (2003) 'Strategic Knowledge Measurement and Management', in S.E. Jackson, M.A. Hitt and A.S. DeNisi (eds), *Managing Knowledge for Sustained Competitive Advantage: Designing Strategies for Effective Human Resource Management*. San Francisco: Jossey-Bass, 360–96.

Boudreau, J.W. and Rynes, S.L. (1985) 'Role of Recruitment in Staffing Utility Analysis', *Journal of Applied Psychology*, 70 (2): 354–66.

Buckley, P.J. and Casson, M. (1988) 'A Theory of Cooperation in International Business', in F. Contractor and P. Lorange (eds), *Cooperative Strategies in International Business*. Lexington, MA: Lexington Books, 31–53.

Charman, A. (1999) 'Global Mergers and Acquisitions: The Human Resource Challenge' *International Focus*. Alexandria, VA: Society for Human Resource Management.

Charman, A. and Carey, D. (2000) 'A CEO Roundtable on Making Mergers Succeed', *Harvard Business Review*, May–June: 145–54.

Child, J. (1977) *Organization*. New York: Harper & Row.

Child, J. and Faulkner, D. (1998) *Strategies of Cooperation*. Oxford: Oxford University Press.

Creswell, J. (2001a) 'When a Merger Fails: Lessons from Sprint', *Fortune*, April 30: 185–7.

Creswell, J. (2001b) 'First Cold Front', *Fortune*, February 5: 26.

Cyr, D.J. (1995) *The Human Resource Challenge of International Joint Ventures*. Westport, CT: Quorum Books.

Daniel, T.A. and Metcalf, G.S. (2001) *The Management of People in Mergers and Acquisitions*. Westport, CT: Quorum Books.

Deogun, N. and Scannell, K. (2001) 'Market Swoon Stifles M & A's Red-Hot Start, But Old Economy Supplies a Surprise Bounty', *Wall Street Journal*, 2 January: R4.

Devine, M. (2002) *Successful Mergers*. London: Profile Books.

Dowling, P.J., Welch, D.E. and Schuler, R.S. (1999) '*International Human Resource Management 3*'. Cincinnati, OH: Southwestern Publishing.

Doz, Y. (1996) 'The Evolution of Cooperation in Strategic Alliances: Initial Conditions or Learning Processes?', *Strategic Management Journal*, 17: 55–83.

Doz, Y.L. and Hamel, G. (1998) *Alliance Advantage: The Art of Creating Value Through Partnering*. Boston: Harvard Business School Press.

Doz, Y., Hamel, G. and Prahalad, C.D. (1986) 'Strategic Partnerships: Success or Surrender?', Paper presented at the Conference on Cooperative Strategies in International Business, The Wharton School and Rutgers University.

Doz, Y. and Prahalad, K. (1981) 'Headquarters Influence and Strategic Control In MNCs', *Sloan Management Review*, 23(1): 15–29.

Evans, P., Pucik, V. and Barsoux, J.-L. (2002) *The Global Challenge: Frameworks for International Human Resource Management*. Boston, MA: McGraw-Hill.

Fendt, J. (2002a) 'Learnings about Learning in M&A Transitions', *International Journal of Business and Economics*, 2002, 2(1).

Fendt, J. (2002b) 'M&A and Management Andragogy: Seeking Synergy in Two Core Drivers of Executives', *Global Competitiveness With the Zurich Genetic Living Case*, Worldwide Comparative Education Forum on Economic Globalization and Education Reforms October 2002, Zurich, Switzerland.

Foss, N.J. and Pedersen, T. (2002) 'Transferring Knowledge in MNCs: The Role of Sources of Subsidiary Knowledge and Organizational Context', *Journal of International Management*, 8: 49–67.

Frayne, C.A. and Geringer, J.M. (1990) 'The Strategic Use of Human Resource Management Practices as Control Mechanisms in International Joint Ventures', *Research in Personnel and Human Resource Management*, suppl. 2: 53–69.

Frayne, C.A. and Geringer, J.M. (2000) 'Challenges Facing General Managers of International Joint Ventures', Unpublished paper.

Freidheim C.F., Jr (1998) 'The Trillion-Dollar Enterprise: How The Alliance Revolution Will Transform Global Business'. (Reading, MA: Perseus Books).

Fuld, L. (2000) 'Ask Dow Jones, Competitive Intelligence Center, CEO Interview with Daniel Vasella' (2000) http://askdj.dowjones.com/fuld/vasella.asp.

Geringer, J.M. and Herbert, L. (1989) 'Control and Performance of International Joint Ventures', *Journal of International Business Studies*, Summer, 20: 235–54.

Geringer, J.M. and Herbert, L. (1991) 'Measuring Performance of International Joint Ventures', *Journal of International Business Studies*, 22: 253–67.

Gomes-Casseres, B. (1989) 'Joint Ventures in the Face of Global Competition', *Sloan Management Review*, Spring 30: 17–26.

Green, S.C. and Welsh, A. (1988), 'Cybernetics and Dependence: Reframing the Control Concept', *Academy of Management Review*, 13(2): 287–301.

Greenlaugh, L. (2000) 'Ford Motor Company's CEO Jac Nasser on Transformational Change, E-Business, and Environmental Responsibility', *Academy of Management Executive*, January, 14(3): 46–51.

Habeck, M.H., Kroger, F. and Tram, M.R. (1999) *After the Merger*. New York/London: Financial Times/Prentice Hall.

Hambrick, D.C., Li, J., Xin, K. and Tsui, A.S. (2001) 'Composition Gaps and Downward Spirals in International Joint Venture Management Groups', *Strategic Management Journal*, 22: 1033–53.

Hamel, G. (1991), 'Competition for Competence and Inter-Partner Learning Within International Strategic Alliances', *Strategic Management Journal*, 12, (special issue), 83–104.

Hamel, G. (2001). 'Avoiding the guillotine', *Fortune*, 2 April: 139–44.

Hanes, K. (1999), 'Making Synergies Work', *Financial Performance*, 13(3): 42–5.

Harbir, S., Zollo, M. (1999) 'Post-acquisition Strategies, Integration Capability and the Economic Performance of Corporate Acquisition', http://www.management.wharton.upenn.edu/singhh/hightech/files/AcquisitionPerformance.pdf.

Harbison, J.R. (1996) *Strategic Alliances: Gaining a Competitive Advantage*. New York: Conference Board.

Harrigan, K.R. (1986) *Managing for Joint Venture Success*. Boston: Lexington.

Hergert, M. and Morris, D. (1988), 'Trends in International Collaborative Agreements', in F. Contractor and P. Lorange (eds), *Cooperative Strategies in International Business*. Toronto, Canada: Lexington Books, 1–28.

Herper, M. (2002) Interview with Daniel Vasella for Forbes.com on July 7th: 2002.

Huselid, M.A., Jackson, S.E. and Schuler, R.S. (1997) 'Technical and Strategic Human Resource Management Effectiveness as Determinants of Firm Performance', *Academy of Management Journal*, 40: 171–88.

Inkpen, A. (1995) *The Management of International Joint Ventures: An Organizational Learning Perspective*. London: Routledge.

Inkpen, A.C. (1995) 'Believing Is Seeing: Joint Ventures and Organization Learning', *Journal of Management Studies*, 32(5): 595–618.

Inkpen, A.C. and Beamish, P.W. (1997) 'Knowledge, Bargaining Power and International Joint Venture Stability', *Academy of Management Review*, 22: 177–202.

Inkpen, A.C. and Currall, S. (1997) 'International Joint Venture Trust: An Empirical Examination', in P.W. Beamish and J.P. Killing (eds), *Cooperative Strategies: North American Perspectives*, San Francisco: New Lexington Press, 308–34.

Jackson, S.E. (1992) 'Team composition on organizational settings: issues in managing an increasingly diverse work force', in S. Worchel, W. Wood and J.A. Simpson (eds), *Group Process and Productivity*. Newbury Park: Sage, 204–61.

Jackson, S.E. (1996) 'The Consequences of Diversity in Multidisciplinary Teams', in M.A. West (ed.), *Handbook of Workgroup Psychology*. New York: Wiley, 53–76.

Jackson, S.E. and Schuler, R.S. (1995) 'Understanding Human Resource Management in the Context of Organizations and Their Environments', in M. Rosenweig and L. Porter (eds), *Annual Review of Psychology*. Palo Alto, CA: Annual Reviews, Inc.: 237–64.

Jackson, S.E. and Schuler R.S., (2000) '*Managing Human Resources: A Partnership Perspective*'. Cincinnati, OH: Southwestern Publishing.

Jackson, S.E. and Schuler R.S., (2003) '*Managing Human Resources: A Partnership Perspective*'. Cincinnati, OH: Southwestern Publishing.

Javidan, M. (2002) 'Siemens CEO Heinrich von Pierer on Cross-border Acquisitions', *Academy of Management Executive*, 16(1): 13–15.

Kay, I.T. and Shelton, M. (2000) 'The People Problems in Mergers', *McKinsey Quarterly*, 4: 29–37.

Kroger, F. and Tram, M.R. (2000) *After the Merger: Seven Rules for Post Merger Integration*. New York, London: Prentice Hall.

Lasserre, P. (1983), 'Strategic Assessment of International Partnership in Asian Countries', *Asia Pacific Journal of Management*, 72–8.

Lei, D., Slocum, J.W. Jr., and Pitts, R.A. (1997) 'Building Cooperative Advantage: Managing Strategic Alliances To Promote Organizational Learning', *Journal of World Business*, 32(3): 202–23.

Levinsohn, A. (2002) 'Capturing Elusive Value in M&A', *Strategic Finance*, Montvale, May: 83(11).

Liebeskind, J.P., Oliver, A.L., Zucker, L. and Brewer, M. (1996) 'Social Networks, Learning, and Flexibility: Sourcing Scientific Knowledge in New Biotechnology Firms', *Organization Science*, 7: 428–43.

Lorange, (1986) 'Human Resource Management in Multinational Cooperative Ventures', *Human Resource Management*, 25: 133–48.

Luo, Y. (1998) 'Joint Venture Success in China: How Should We Select A Good Partner', *Journal of World Business*, 33(2): 145–66.

Luo, Y. (2002) 'Capability Exploitation and Building in a Foreign Market: Implications for Multinational Enterprise', *Organization Science*, 13(1): 48–63.

Luo, Y. and Tan, J.J. (1998) 'A Comparison Of Multinational and Domestic Firms in an Emerging Market: A Strategic Choice Perspective', *Journal of International Management*, 4(1): 21–40.

Lyles, M.A. (1987) 'Common Mistakes of Joint Venture Experienced Firms', *Columbia Journal of World Business*, 22(2): 79–85.

Makhija, M.V. and Ganesh, U. (1997) 'The Relationship Between Control and Partner Learning In Learning Related Joint Ventures', *Organizational Science*, 8(2): 508–24.

Marks, M.L. and Mirvis, P.H. (2000) 'Creating an Effective Team Structure', *Organizational Dynamics*, Winter: 35–47.

McGill, M.E. (2002) 'Mr. Ackermann expects', *The Economist*, 70.

McGill, M.E., Slocum, J.W. Jr and Lei, D. (1992) 'Management Practices in Learning Organizations', *Organizational Dynamics*, Summer: 5–17.

Mudambi, R. (2002) 'Knowledge Management in Multinational Firms', *Journal of International Management*, 8: 1–9.

Muller, J., Green, J. and Tierney, C (2001) 'Chrysler's Rescue Team', *Business Week*, 48–50.

Newburry, W. and Zeira, Y. (1997) 'Implications for Parent Companies', *Journal of World Business*, 32(2): 87–102.

Numerof, R.F. and Abrams, M. (1998) 'Integrating Corporate Culture from International M and A's'. *HR Focus*, 75(6): 11–12.

Parkhe, A. (1991) 'Interfirm Diversity, Organizational Learning, and Longevity in Global Strategic Alliances', *Journal of International Business Studies*, 22: 579–602.

Parkhe, A. (2000) 'Performance Measurement During Mergers and Acquisitions Integration'. New York: Conference Board.

Pfeffer, J. (1996) 'When It Comes to "Best Practices"- Why Do Smart Organizations Occasionally Do Dumb Things?', *Organizational Dynamics*, Summer: 56–67.

Porter, M. E. (1990) *Competitive Advantage of Nations*. Boston: Harvard Press.

Prahalad, C.K. and Hamel, G.C. (1990) 'The Core Competence of the Corporation', *Harvard Business Review*, May-June, 68: 79–91.

*Prognos World Report* (2001) Consistent, comparable data on the future of 70 countries, www.prognos.com.

Pucik, V. (1988) 'Strategic Alliances, Organizational Learning and Competitive Advantage: The HRM Agenda', *Human Resource Management*, 27(1): 77–93.

Reid, D., Bussier, D. and Greenway, K. (2001) 'Alliance Formation Issues for Knowledge-Based Enterprises', *International Journal of Management Reviews*, 3(1): 79–100.

Schmidt, J.A. (ed.) (2002) 'Making Mergers Work: The Strategic Importance of People', *Society for Human Resource Management*, Atlanta.

Schneider, S.C. and Barsoux, J. (1997) *Managing Across Cultures*. London: Prentice Hall.

Schuler, R.S. (2001) 'HR Issues in International Joint Ventures', *International Journal of Human Resource Management*, February: 1–50.

Schuler, R.S., Dowling, P.J. and De Cieri, H. (1992) 'The Formation of an International Joint Venture: Marley Automotive Components Ltd.', *European Management Journal*, September, 304–09.

Schuler, R.S. and Jackson, S.E. (1987) 'Linking Competitive Strategy and Human Resource Management Practices', *Academic Management Executive*, 3: 207–19.

Schuler, R.S. and Jackson, S.E. (1999) *Strategic Human Resource Management: A Reader*. London: Blackwell Publishers.

Schuler, R.S. and Jackson, S.E. (2001) 'HR Issues and Activities in Mergers and Acquisitions', *European Management Journal*, June, 59–75.

Schuler, R.S., Jackson, S.E., Dowling, P.J. and Welch, D.E. (1991) 'The Formation of an International Joint Venture: Davidson Instrument Panel', *Human Resource Planning*, 15(1): 50–60.

Schuler, R.S. and van Sluijs, E. (1992) 'Davidson-Marley BV: Establishing and Operating An International Joint Venture', *European Management Journal*, 10(4): 28–37.

Schuler, R.S., Jackson, S.E. and Luo, Y. (2004) *Managing Human Resources in Cross-border Alliances*. London: Routledge.

Seth, A., Song, K.P. and Pettit, R.R. (2002) 'Value Creation and Destruction in Cross-Border Alliances: An Empirical Analysis of Foreign Acquisitions of U.S. Firms', *Strategic Management Journal*, 23: 921–40.

Shenkar, O. and Li, J. (1999) 'Knowledge Search in International Cooperative Ventures', *Organizational Science*, 10(2): 34–44.

Shenkar, O. and Yan, A. (2002) 'International Joint Venture Issues', Paper presented at the Academy of Management Annual Meetings, 10 August.

Shenkar, O. and Zeira, Y. (1987) 'Human Resource Management In International Joint Ventures: Direction For Research', *Academy of Management Review*, 12(3): 546–57.

Slocum, J.W. and Lei, D. (1993) 'Designing Global Stategic Alliances: Integrating Cultural and Economic Factors', in G.P. Huber and W.H. Glick (eds), *Organizational Change and Redesign: Ideas and Insights for Improving Performance*. New York: Oxford University Press, 295–322.

Smith, K.W. (2000) 'A Brand-new Culture for the Merged Firm', *Mergers and Acquisitions*, Philadelphia, June, 35(6): 45–50.

Sparks, D. (1999) 'Partners', *Business Week*, 5 October: 106.

Taylor, A. (2001) 'Can the Germans Rescue Chrysler?', *Fortune*, 30 April: 106–12.

Taylor A., III (2002) 'Can J&J Keep the Magic Going?', *Fortune*, 117–22.

Thompson, A.A. and Strickland, A.J. (1998) *Crafting and Implementing Strategy*. New York: McGraw-Hill.

Tierney, C. (2000) 'Defiant Daimler', *Business Week*, 7 August: 89–93.

Tyson, L. D. (2001) 'The New Laws of Nations', *New York Times*, 14 July: A15.

Vaara, E. (2002) 'On the Discursive Construction of Success/Failure in Narratives of Post-merger Integration', *Organization Studies*, Berlin.

Vlasic, B. and Stertz, B.A. (2000) 'Taken for a Ride', *Business Week*, 5 June. 84–92.

Watkins, K.E. and Marsick, V.J. (1993) *Sculpting the Learning Organization: Lessons in the Art and Science of Systemic Change*. San Francisco, CA: Jossey-Bass.

Watson Wyatt Survey (2000, December 19) http://www.watsonwyatt.com/homepage/eu/res/Surveys/MergersandAquisitions/0600/page.

Yan, A. and Luo, Y. (2000) *International Joint Ventures: Theory and Practice*. Armonk, NY: Sharpe.

Yang, C. (2001) 'Show True for AOL Time Warner', *Business Week*, 15 January: 57–64.

# 11

# Western business expatriates in China: adjusting to the most foreign of all foreign places

*Jan Selmer*

## Introduction

China is an important current and potential market for Western and other international business firms, further accentuated by China's entry into the World Trade Organization. The Chinese government has estimated that China in the next few years will need more than $70 billion in investments (Wang and Ralston, 2000) and foreign firms can make substantial contributions to that end. However, establishing operations in China may constitute more than a financial challenge to Western companies, since China is distinctly different from most other countries. From a Western perspective, China is frequently regarded as the most foreign of all foreign places; Chinese culture, institutions and people may appear completely baffling (Chen, 2001). This makes China a challenging destination for Western business expatriates and there seems to be a need for substantial cross-cultural adjustment. Westerners have to deal with a very different way of life on the Chinese mainland than in their own country, and they have to perform in an unfamiliar work context. Trying to adjust to the new cultural context could be a stressful experience and not everyone can cope successfully with the new life on a foreign assignment. This chapter deals with the crucial issue of how business expatriates adjust to work and life in China.

The first part delineates the concept of international adjustment. International adjustment is a vital area of study as research has showed that premature return rates of business expatriates are significant and that each failure gives rise to substantial direct and indirect costs to both the individual and the corporation involved. Furthermore, many expatriates remaining on their foreign assignments are considered ineffective by their parent organizations and such underperformance may result in substantial direct and indirect costs (Hilltrop and Janssens, 1990; Black, Gregersen and Mendenhall, 1992). Although the often quoted high expatriate failure rates measured as premature returns to the parent country have been challenged to have little empirical evidence, it can easily be argued that expatriates who cannot adjust but remain on their assignments and fail to perform adequately, could be even more damaging to the company than those who return prematurely (Harzing, 1995; Forster, 1997).

Secondly, the relationship between sociocultural and psychological adjustment is examined. The magnitude of this relationship may be dependent on the context. An individual's need, capacity or opportunity for integration with the host culture may determine the strength of the association between sociocultural and psychological adjustment. The greater the reliance on the host culture as the principal context for interaction, the stronger the positive relationship between the two aspects of international adjustment could become (Ward and Kennedy, 1993a, 1993b). This is an important topic to study since it suggests that improving sociocultural adjustment by acquiring relevant social skills of the host culture may promote the psychological adjustment of an individual. Additionally, the relationship between sociocultural and psychological adjustment may vary with the magnitude of cross-cultural change; the relationship could be more pronounced for small than large cross-cultural transitions. After all, it seems quite reasonable to assume that large mental adjustments take longer and are more difficult to bring about than small ones. This study was carried out in China, including the Hong Kong Special Administrative Region (SAR). Hong Kong has developed into a modern international business metropolis, but despite a common cultural origin and recent fast economic and social developments, many locations on the Chinese mainland still represent a very different context from the Hong Kong SAR.

Thirdly, this chapter also examines the time pattern of adjustment of Western expatriates on the Chinese mainland in order to establish whether there are any signs indicating a culture-shock experience. The academic literature on international adjustment has for sometime discussed the concept of the U-curve hypothesis which suggests that the adjustment of sojourners can be described as a succession of phases or stages of which an initial sudden drop in the degree of adjustment is referred to as a culture shock. However, this view is heavily contested and recent empirical studies have not given much support to the U-curve hypothesis and the culture-shock concept. The U-curve hypothesis will be explained in detail in a later section of this chapter. This study of the time pattern of adjustment is important for several reasons. In academic terms, more research is needed about international adjustment and culture shock concerning business expatriates. Despite an abundant literature on sojourner adjustment in general, empirical studies on expatriate managers' culture shock are not very common in the literature. Elsewhere, the popular business press is brimming with anecdotal stories about the dangers of culture shock for international managers but, with some notable exceptions (see for example Feldman and Tompson, 1993; Janssens, 1995), few rigorous empirical investigations have dealt with the culture shock of business expatriates, and especially not in China. This study deals with the encounter of two very different cultural realms, where one would expect Western expatriate managers to initially experience a U-shaped adjustment process tantamount to culture shock. In this respect, the study can also be regarded as a test of the U-curve hypothesis.

# International adjustment

At least two aspects of international adjustment have been identified, psychological adjustment and sociocultural adjustment (for example Searle and Ward, 1990; Ward and Searle, 1991; Ward and Kennedy, 1992). Although conceptually interrelated, the former deals with subjective well-being or mood states (for example depression, anxiety, tension and fatigue). The latter relates to the ability to 'fit in' or to negotiate interactive aspects of the host culture as measured by the amount of difficulty experienced in the management of everyday situations in the host culture (Ward and Kennedy, 1996). The concept of psychological adjustment is based on a problem-oriented view focusing on attitudinal factors of the adjustment process. The sociocultural notion of adjustment is based on cultural learning theory and highlights social behaviour and practical social skills underlying attitudinal factors, consistent with the distinction made by Jun et al. (1997) separating behavioural from attitudinal acculturation.

Black et al. (1991) argued that the degree of cross-cultural adjustment should be treated as a multidimensional concept, rather than a unitary phenomenon as was previously the dominating view (Oberg, 1960; Gullahorn and Gullahorn, 1962). In their proposed model for international adjustment, Black et al. (1991) made a distinction among three dimensions of in-country adjustment: (1) adjustment to work; (2) adjustment to interacting with host nationals; and (3) adjustment to the general non-work environment. This theoretical framework of international adjustment covers sociocultural aspects of adjustment and it has been supported by a series of empirical studies of US expatriates and their spouses (Black and Stephens, 1989; Black and Gregersen, 1990, 1991a, 1991b). McEvoy and Parker (1995) also found support for the three dimensions of expatriate adjustment.

The theoretical concept of subjective well-being, corresponding to the psychological aspects of international adjustment, has been well-developed, especially in relation to work and work environment characteristics (see for example Kornhauser, 1965; Caplan et al., 1975; Karasek, 1979). In connection with the adjustment of expatriate business managers, the concept of subjective well-being has been applied in several instances (Arnetz and Anderzen, 1992; Nicholson and Imaizumi, 1993; Forster, 1997).

# Sociocultural versus psychological adjustment

It has been argued that the magnitude of the relationship between sociocultural and psychological adjustment is dependent on the context (Ward and Kennedy, 1993a, 1993b). An individual's need, capacity or opportunity for integration with the host culture may determine the association between sociocultural and psychological adjustment. The greater the reliance on the host culture as the principal context for interaction, the stronger the relationship between the two aspects of international adjustment. For example, individuals preferring the seclusion of 'expatriate ghettos' having minimum exposure to and interaction with host nationals are unlikely to exhibit a strong relationship between psychological well being and culture-specific competence. Obviously, their potential satisfaction is not generated by a great familiarity with social skills of the host culture. On the other hand, for expatriates who are well-integrated into the host culture, the relationship between culture-specific social skills and psychological adjustment in the new culture is likely to be much stronger. This presumed relationship between sociocultural and psychological adjustment received some empirical support by a study of a small sample of Malaysian and Singaporean students in New Zealand (Ward and Kennedy, 1996). However, it is not clear whether these results also hold for business expatriates. Furthermore, in an expatriate business setting, psychological adjustment has been identified as more voluntary than sociocultural adjustment (Jun *et al.*, 1997) as it is based on deep-seated attitudinal factors. It is conceivable that, especially Western, business expatriates in Asia are less impressionable than Southeast Asian students studying abroad. Therefore, it is necessary to test the generality of the discussed findings in a business setting. The following proposition is suggested:

> **Proposition 1:** The magnitude of the relationship between sociocultural and psychological adjustment will be greater the better socioculturally adjusted the Western business expatriates are.

Related to the discussion above, Ward and Kennedy (1996) also found that the relationship between sociocultural and psychological adjustment was greater for students who made a small cross-cultural transition as compared to those who entered a host culture with a more different cultural context. As Hong Kong would probably entail a less unfamiliar cultural environment than the Chinese mainland for most Western business expatriates, the mentioned finding is also put to a test in a business context. The following proposition is offered:

> **Proposition 2:** The magnitude of the relationship between sociocultural and psychological adjustment for Western business expatriates will be greater in Hong Kong than on the Chinese mainland.

# Method

The data for this study was extracted from an investigation involving a mail questionnaire to Western business expatriates on the Chinese mainland and the Hong Kong SAR. The two samples were comparable on all background variables. Expatriates from the USA, France and Britain were the largest nationality groups in both samples. With little difference between the two samples, the overwhelming majority of all respondents were male and married, which is consistent with other investigations of business expatriates. Also for both samples, most of the respondents were CEOs or occupied other managerial positions, whereas only a few respondents were non-managerial staff.

Sociocultural adjustment was measured using the scale developed by Black (1988) and Black and Stephens (1989), which covers all three dimensions: adjustment to work, adjustment to interacting with host nationals, and adjustment to the general non-work environment. Respondents answered 14 questions covering to what degree they were adjusted or not adjusted to Hong Kong and the Chinese mainland. Psychological adjustment was measured by the General Health Questionnaire (GHQ-12) (Goldberg, 1972). Although it is a widely used measure of minor psychiatric symptoms, this instrument has also been used to assess the subjective well-being of expatriates (Arnetz and Anderzen, 1992; Nicholson and Imaizumi, 1993; Forster, 1997). The GHQ-12 asks the respondents to think about how they have been feeling over the past few weeks.

# Results

The mean scores for the three sociocultural adjustment variables were all above the mid-level point depicted as 'somewhat adjusted', indicating that the expatriates overall were quite comfortable with their respective cultural context after having spent an average of at least four years in their current assignment. However, the mean score for interaction adjustment was noticeably lower than for the two other sociocultural adjustment variables. The mean score of psychological adjustment was also above the mid-level point.

The first proposition, that the magnitude of the relationship between sociocultural and psychological adjustment will be greater the better socioculturally adjusted the Western business expatriates are, was tested by means of multiple regression. As displayed in Table 11.1, this proposition is partly supported since two of the three dimensions of sociocultural adjustment display positive and statistically significant relationships with psychological adjustment. General and work adjustment are significantly and positively associated with psychological adjustment, but not interaction adjustment.

The second proposition, that the magnitude of the relationship between sociocultural and psychological adjustment for Western business expatriates will be greater in Hong Kong than on the Chinese mainland, was also examined by multiple regression.

*Table 11.1*  The effects of sociocultural adjustment on psychological adjustment

| Independent variables | Psychological adjustment |
|---|---|
| General adjustment | .10 |
| Interaction adjustment | .05 |
| Work adjustment | .20 |
| $R^2$ | .09 |
| Adjusted $R^2$ | .08 |
| $F$ | 15.82 |

*Table 11.2*  The effects of sociocultural adjustment on psychological adjustment in the Hong Kong SAR and the Chinese mainland

| Independent variables | Hong Kong SAR psychological adjustment | Chinese Mainland psychological adjustment |
|---|---|---|
| General adjustment | .16* | .01 |
| Interaction adjustment | .02 | .07 |
| Work adjustment | .15* | .28** |
| $R^2$ | .08 | .11 |
| Adjusted $R^2$ | .07 | .09 |
| $F$ | 9.55*** | 6.20*** |

$^*p < .05$; $^{**}p < .01$; $^{***}p < .001$.

Table 11.2 shows partial support for this second proposition. For Hong Kong, both general and work adjustment are positively and significantly related to psychological adjustment, whereas the Chinese mainland only displays one such relationship in the case of work adjustment.

## Discussion

For all the three dimensions of sociocultural adjustment the Western business expatriates felt, on average, at least 'somewhat adjusted' to their current assignments in the Hong Kong SAR and the Chinese mainland. However, it is interesting to note the relatively low score for interaction adjustment which seems to suggest that the managers suffered from language problems. Not being able to interact with the host-country nationals in daily life outside work makes expatriates ignorant about local thinking and character, which influences their ability to assess work situations, sometimes leading to incorrect assumptions about people they are managing. In daily life, it could be difficult to try to rely on English either in the Hong Kong SAR or on the Chinese mainland. The spoken national language of the Chinese mainland is Mandarin which is used in daily life together with the local dialect. Although the official language in Hong Kong, both before and after the handover, is both English and Chinese, the dialect used pervasively by local Chinese is Cantonese, an almost impenetrable form of spoken Chinese, at least to most Western business expatriates, due to its complex tonality.

One of the main findings is that some empirical support was found for the argument that the magnitude of the relationship between sociocultural and psychological adjustment will be greater the better socioculturally adjusted the expatriates are. This suggests that acquiring social skills promotes the psychological adjustment of an individual. This is especially the case for work adjustment, which seems intuitively justified since the ultimate reason for the expatriate assignment is to perform certain work tasks. However, the multiple regression did not indicate any statistically significant relationship between interaction adjustment and psychological adjustment. This suggests that interacting with host nationals neither facilitated, nor discouraged psychological adjustment. Again, this may be caused by language problems, effectively separating the business expatriates from the daily life of host nationals. This seems to be the case especially in China where expatriate compounds and blocks of housing only available to expatriates are quite common (Björkman and Schaap, 1994).

The findings seem to contradict previous suggestions by Jun et al., (1997) who suggested that behavioural changes (sociocultural adjustment) may have to be adopted involuntarily due to existing circumstances while attitudinal changes (psychological adjustment) are likely to be more voluntary. Furnham and Bochner (1986) have also suggested a similar argument proposing that the expatriate does not necessarily have to undergo a basic shift in deeply held values to conform to a new set of cultural norms abroad. It is sufficient merely to learn new social and cultural skills, in much the same way as one learns a foreign language. These new practices need not become part of the permanent repertoire and can be discarded when they are no longer useful, for example when meeting fellow-nationals or after repatriation. In trying to resolve this apparent inconsistency, it would be useful to refer to the literature on acculturation (for example Berry et al., 1986; Berry and Kim, 1988; Berry, 1990). It seems that attitudinal changes could take place over extended periods of time, typically longer than the regular period of expatriate assignment. As the expatriates studied in these samples had considerably longer assignments than the average three years reported in the literature (Brewster, 1991; Selmer and Lee, 1994; Harvey, 1997), it can be speculated that they were more affected psychologically than the typical business expatriate.

Another main finding is that there was partial support for the contention that the relationship between sociocultural and psychological adjustment is greater for small rather than large cross-cultural transitions. It seems quite reasonable to assume that large mental adjustments take longer and are more difficult to bring about than small ones. Again, work adjustment seems important to facilitate the psychological adjustment of the expatriates, and especially so on the Chinese mainland.

There are several practical implications of the findings. Cross-cultural training and preparations for expatriate assignments are activities identified in the literature both as being essential for successful adjustment as well as being badly neglected (see for example Earley, 1987; Black and Mendenhall, 1990; Brewster, 1995). This is particularly true regarding language training for business expatriates (Dolainski, 1997). Despite the unmistakable fact of the importance of such training for Western expatriates assigned to China, it is seldom provided (Björkman and Schaap, 1994). Whether departing for the Chinese mainland or Hong Kong, expatriates should realize that learning the basics of Chinese should be viewed as part of the assignment (Dolainski, 1997).

The importance of work adjustment to promote psychological adjustment also indicates the need for more cross-cultural preparations in this respect. Training primarily aimed at facilitating work adjustment is not very commonly provided to expatriate managers by international firms (see for example Tung, 1982; Early, 1987; Brewster and Pickard, 1994). On the other hand, efficient cross-cultural job skills are essential for maintaining and developing the competitive strength of international firms (Bartlett and Goshal, 1989; De Cieri and Dowling, 1995). Equipping expatriate managers with cross-cultural training concerning the job context in China and the Hong Kong SAR, in order to enhance their interaction skills, enables them to function independently without knowing all the facts about the culture, because skills training focuses on 'learning how to learn' in the new cultural setting (McCaffery, 1986). Hence, providing Western business expatriates with cross-cultural job skills training to facilitate their work adjustment in China would be a highly recommended course of action for companies assigning them there, probably not only enhancing their work efficiency, but also their psychological adjustment and the firm's competitiveness. If this training is administered post-arrival, which has been advocated as enhancing efficiency (Selmer, 1997; Selmer et al., 1998), training activities could try to facilitate the whole change process (Schein, 1980) of unfreezing (creating the motivation to change), changing (developing new attitudes and behaviours based on new information and cognitive redefinition), and re-freezing (stabilizing the changes). Again, this is presumably easier to accomplish in a post-arrival situation where many of the factors contributing to this change process are in place in the new cultural context.

# Culture shock and adjustment over time

## The U-curve hypothesis

The traditional view of international adjustment is that it can be described as a succession of phases or stages. Oberg (1960) described four stages of adjustment – honeymoon, crisis, recovery and adjustment – whilst Adler (1975) saw the adjustment of the sojourner as a transitional experience implying a movement from a low to a high state of self- and cultural awareness through five phases – contact, disintegration, reintegration, autonomy and independence. Three-stage and nine-stage similar adjustment processes have also been proposed (Lesser and Peter, 1957; Jacobson, 1963; Garza-Guerrero, 1974).

Grove and Torbiörn (1985) and Torbiörn (1982) have offered an explanation of adjustment from a perspective of cognitive and motivational psychology. In Torbiörn's (1982) study this proposition is empirically supported in some crucial aspects by a large-scale survey of Swedish expatriate managers, suggesting that adjustment follows four phases: a tourist phase (a period of euphoria, often experienced by people immediately after they enter a new culture); a culture-shock phase (mental and physiological stress resulting from overstimulation and overuse of the body's coping mechanisms); a conformist phase (progressive recovery from culture shock); and an assimilation phase (completion of the adjustment process).

Most of the above-mentioned stage or phase theories of cultural adjustment presume some kind of a U-curve to depict the stages that individuals go through. This curve indicates the change over time in the degree of adjustment to the alien environment. The U-curve of adjustment depicts the initial optimism and euphoria in the host culture, the subsequent dip or trough in the level of adjustment, followed by a gradual recovery to higher adjustment levels. Previously, the U-curve has usually been connected to some kind of subjective adjustment, measuring satisfaction and well-being, which gradually declines but then increases again. Other studies have extended the U-curve to cover trends in attitudes and social interaction patterns and favourability of images of the host culture. The U-curve has also been extended to a W-curve, indicating the re-entry shock that sojourners often undergo when they return to their home culture and which is similar to what they experienced abroad, making up two consecutive Us, that is a W (Lysgaard, 1955; Gullahorn and Gullahorn, 1962; Church, 1982; Furnham and Bochner, 1986).

## Culture shock

The concept 'culture shock', like that of 'jet-lag', is now part of the popular vocabulary. Both terms are used to explain, or at least label, some more unpleasant consequences of travelling. However, being more of a generic expression, it connotes much, but signifies little.

> If there is a medical or illness analogy for culture shock, the common cold is probably the best malady to consider. Like the common cold, there is no way to prevent culture shock and one can 'catch it' over and over again. Each time we adjust to another culture or readjust to our own culture, we go through culture shock. (Weaver, 1986)

Culture shock originated with the anthropologist Oberg (1960) who referred to the distress experienced by the sojourner as a result of losing all the familiar signs and symbols of social interaction. He mentioned at least six aspects of culture shock:

1 Strain due to the effort required to make necessary psychological adjustments;
2 A sense of loss and feelings of deprivation in regard to friends, status, profession and possessions;
3 Being rejected by and/or rejecting members of the new culture;
4 Confusion in role, role expectations, values, feelings and self-identity;
5 Surprise, anxiety, even disgust and indignation after becoming aware of cultural differences;
6 Feelings of impotence due to not being able to cope with the new environment.

The concept has generated a substantial research interest since it was introduced by Oberg. Juffer (1986) scrutinized more than 35 definitions of culture shock found in research literature and categorized the prevailing definitions, causes and effects of culture shock as follows:

1 Culture shock is caused by confronting a new environment or situation;
2 Culture shock is caused by ineffectiveness of intercultural or interpersonal communication;
3 Culture shock is caused by a threat to the emotional or intra-psychic well-being of the sojourner;
4 Culture shock is caused by the need to adequately modify behaviour to regain positive reinforcement from the new environment; and
5 Culture shock is caused by growth experience.

Most researchers since Oberg have viewed culture shock as a normal process of adjustment to cultural stress, involving such symptoms as anxiety, helplessness, irritability and a longing for a more predictable and gratifying environment. Anxiety may result in such behaviour as excessive preoccupation with the drinking water, the food, minor pains, excessive fears of being cheated or robbed, fits of anger towards or avoidance of local people, and the desire to be with home nationals (Juffer, 1986; Furnham, 1993). Others have attempted to improve and extend the original definition and concept of culture shock. Hence, the following phenomena related to, but not identical with, the concept of culture shock have been suggested: culture fatigue, language shock, role shock, pervasive ambiguity, transition shock, uprooting (see for example Smalley, 1963; Byrnes, 1966; Ball-Rokeach, 1973; Guthrie, 1975; Zwingmann and Gunn, 1983). More recently, Anderson (1994) further underscored the normality of the culture-shock experience by pointing out the striking resemblance between the distress reactions humans display whenever confronted with major disruptive changes and the culture-shock syndrome. She argues that far from being culture-specific, culture-shock is simply a frustration-reaction symptom. Being alive at home or abroad means having to cope with disruptive events, and real-life adjustments involve working towards a fit between person and environment.

However, to get through the culture-shock phase of adjustment may be very painful for many sojourners, so painful for so long that some of them simply never get through. Some of them adopt an extremely hostile and critical attitude towards host nationals ('fight'), others retreat to the safety of an expatriate community or even prematurely return home ('flight'), and yet others rapidly and uncritically abandon their former identities and try to imitate host nationals in every possible way ('going native'). These coping patterns, as well as various psychological symptoms of sojourners such as rationalization, projection, withdrawal, overidentifying and other defensive mechanisms, should not necessarily be regarded as harmful. Although they distort reality, they may be functional to the newcomer, enabling him to cope. These mechanisms slow down the entry of cognitive elements from the host culture and support the strength of cognitive elements brought from the home culture, inhibiting an abrupt collapse of the frame of reference. All of these defensive coping mechanisms require substantial mental efforts, explaining why culture shock should be understood as a type of exhaustion. From a clinical psychological point of view, the coping mechanisms of culture shock become a serious mental health problem only to the extent that they come to dominate the sojourner's interaction with the environment, or when they completely break down and leave the individual susceptible to extreme anxiety, psychosomatic disorders, alcoholism, drug abuse, and so on (Grove and Torbiörn, 1985).

Countering the problem-oriented view presented above, an alternative approach to culture shock is to regard it as an experience of intercultural learning and growth. This view is outlined as follows:

> Culture shock is thought of as a profound learning experience that leads to a high degree of self-awareness and personal growth. Rather than being only a disease for which adaptation is the cure, culture shock is likewise at the very heart of the cross-cultural learning experience. It is an experience in self-understanding and change. (Adler, 1987)

Consequently, the culture-shock process is viewed as fundamental in that the sojourner must somehow confront the social, psychological and philosophical differences found between his or her own cultural perceptions and that of the new environment. Hence, the cross-cultural learning experience is regarded as a transitional experience, improving one's own self- and cultural awareness (Adler, 1987). The concept of cultural learning has been further elaborated and extended by several researchers. These models regard cross-cultural exposure as a learning experience and, instead of therapy for the sojourner, they prescribe a programme of preparation, orientation and the acquisition of culturally appropriate social skills (for example Klineberg, 1982; Furnham and Bochner, 1982, 1986; Bochner, 1986; Black and Mendenhall, 1991; Furnham, 1993). The models imply that the major task facing the sojourner is not to adjust to a new culture, but to learn its important characteristics. There are many examples in life when it becomes necessary, or at least advisable, to learn a practice even if one does not approve of it, and then abandon it later when circumstances change.

Consequently, people who acquire and selectively utilize behaviours, attitudes and values of a second culture add to themselves, just as people who learn a second language add to themselves. It is important to note that this is in sharp contrast to the traditional anthropological assumption which often takes for granted the loss and replacement of a person's first or traditional culture, when that person is exposed to and starts to use a new culture's ways. The traditional culture is thought to be 'subtracted' from the individual's repertoire as the new one is mastered. But, according to the analogy between language acquisition and developing new cultural skills, bilinguals do not give up one language to learn another; they add a second language to the first and learn to use each appropriately. Given the close links that have been shown to exist between culture and language, there seem to be important parallels between the acquisition of a second language and becoming a multicultural individual (Furnham and Bochner, 1986; Saltzman, 1986).

## Little empirical support

There is not much conclusive or generalizable empirical support for the culture-shock experience as indicated by a U-curve process of adjustment. Not all sojourners start out with a 'honeymoon phase' or with a period of euphoria and optimism, and although depression occurs with some frequency, it is far from universal. A few substantial literature reviews have examined the existence of culture shock as suggested by the U-curve hypothesis (Church, 1982; Furnham and Bochner, 1986; Black and Mendenhall, 1991). Church (1982) argues that support for the existence of a culture-shock phase in international adjustment must be considered weak, whilst Furnham and Bochner (1986) also fail to support the U-curve hypothesis and further argue that this hypothesis is too vague and too generalized to be of much use. Based on a review of 18 studies, Black and Mendenhall (1991) conclude that, due to the lack of methodological rigour in many of the investigations, it is not reasonable to either accept or reject the U-curve hypothesis. More recently, Janssens (1995) did not find any evidence of culture shock; based on the relationship between intercultural interaction, one of the dimensions of sociocultural adjustment, and length of time spent in the host country, he found that the overall pattern of intercultural interaction over time in the host country was mostly linear and increasing. This indicates that the longer the expatriate managers stayed in the host country, the more knowledgeable they became about the new culture and the more local friends they made. Similarly, Ward *et al.* (1998) studying a sample of Japanese students in New Zealand were unable to find any support for the U-curve hypothesis in either psychological or sociocultural adjustment.

## Adjustment to the Chinese mainland

From the growing literature on business management practices and policies on the Chinese mainland, one may speculate that Western expatriate managers assigned there would have to make considerable sociocultural adjustments to their roles at work (for example Child, 1994; Warner, 1995; Goodall and Warner, 1997; Selmer, 1998). This is also supported by the emerging literature dealing with work adjustments of expatriate managers on the Chinese mainland. Björkman and Schaap (1994) discussed some problems encountered by expatriates in Chinese–Western joint ventures and suggested practical ways to handle these issues. Davidson (1987) examined effective intercultural interaction in Chinese–US joint ventures, where American and Chinese board members and top managers must work together to run the company. Rimington (1996) examined the management process of developing a Sino–British joint venture and Weldon and Jehn (1996) studied intercultural conflicts in bicultural teams in US–Chinese joint ventures. Sergeant and Frenkel (1998) interviewed expatriate managers about managing people in China. The findings touch upon problems in recruitment, training, rewards, retention, performance management, management–employee relations, and expatriate management relations. Their conclusions echo other researchers in this area (for example Selmer 1998), finding major challenges in motivating employees, specifically in the design of performance management and reward systems, and that the management of expatriate relations could be considerably improved. The expatriates received little training in business customs and practices in China; managers at headquarters did not see the need to modify expectations of the expatriate managers to a different business environment where establishing and maintaining personal relationships are salient; and the lack of a common language may be a serious impediment as could bureaucratic obstacles. The final impression was that the expatriate managers were more or less left to their own devices and most organizations did not capture, systematize, disseminate and update the knowledge gained by their expatriate managers in China (Sergeant and Frenkel, 1998).

The two other sociocultural adjustment dimensions, 'interaction adjustment' and 'general adjustment', have attracted a substantial amount of research over the years and are reviewed in the literature on sojourner adjustment (see for example Church, 1982). However, only a few authors have specifically dealt with expatriate business managers. Lee and Larwood (1983) investigated the cultural socialization of US expatriate managers in Korea and found that when they adjusted their attitudes towards the host culture it resulted in more work satisfaction. Mendenhall and Oddou (1985) also supported the significance of non-work roles by analysing and pointing out the importance of expatriate acculturation gained through effective interactions with host-country nationals. Selmer (1992) and Selmer and de Leon (1989), studying Swedish expatriate managers in Southeast Asia, found non-work socialization to be difficult, due to high language and/or cultural barriers, and of little importance, resulting in a low degree of socialization in the society.

Although subjective well-being has been used in connection with outcomes of expatriate adjustment, no such study is known from the Chinese mainland. In a large-scale, longitudinal study of Swedish expatriates worldwide, examining both medical/physiological and psychological outcomes of living and working abroad, the expatriates, subjective well-being was measured (Arnetz and Anderzen, 1992).

Nicholson and Imaizumi (1993) studied the adjustment of Japanese expatriates in the United Kingdom and made a distinction between their work-related and non-work-related well-being. Aryee and Stone (1996) investigated the psychological well-being of expatriate employees in Hong Kong as represented by a quality of life concept, and found that the expatriates expressed an average positive degree of quality of life well above the mid-point of the bipolar scales used. However, despite a common cultural heritage, there are considerable societal differences between the Hong Kong SAR and the Chinese mainland (Ralston *et al.*, 1992, 1993; Selmer and Shiu, 1999), and this finding may not be generalizable beyond the limits of Hong Kong.

## Results

Using the same data-set from the Chinese mainland of Western business expatriates, the same scale was used to measure sociocultural adjustment (Black, 1988; Black and Stephens, 1989). Likewise, psychological adjustment was also measured by the General Health Questionnaire (GHQ-12) (Goldberg, 1972). The cross-sectional data for the three dimensions of sociocultural adjustment and of the subjective well-being of individual respondents was mapped over time, and to analyse the trend the data were smoothed by the technique of moving averages (Picconi *et al.*, 1993). The results are shown in Figures 11.1 to 11.4. As can be seen from the first three figures, for all three dimensions of sociocultural adjustment there seems to be a U-curve pattern starting to appear after 17–18 months' stay on the Chinese mainland, indicating a typical culture-shock experience. After that, a generally increasing trend is noticed (discounting very long assignments due to infrequent observations). In comparison, there is no such clear U-curve of the time pattern of psychological adjustment as

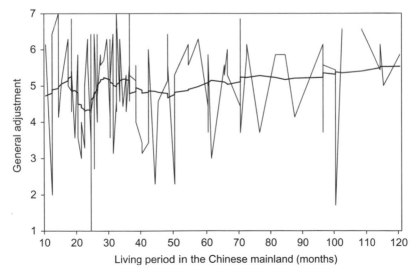

*Figure 11.1*  General adjustment over time: original data and trend

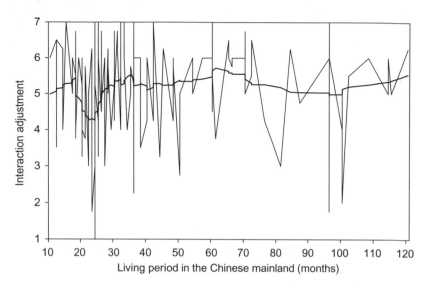

*Figure 11.2* Interaction adjustment over time: original data and trend

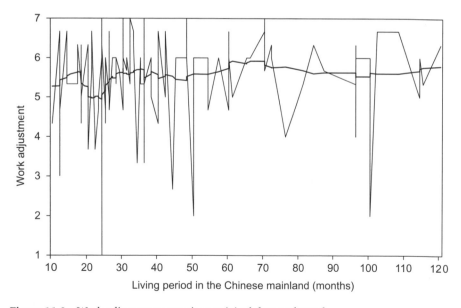

*Figure 11.3* Work adjustment over time: original data and trend

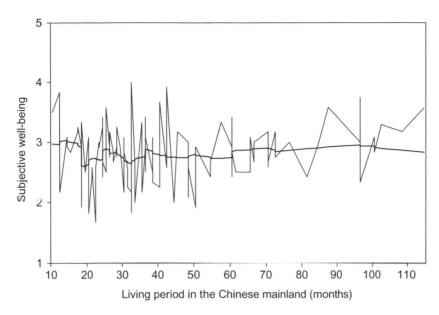

*Figure 11.4*  Subjective well-being over time: original data and trend

measured by subjective well-being (Figure 11.4); instead, this trend has two initial lightly accentuated troughs after which an almost constant level appears.

## Discussion

Plotted over time, there was clear evidence of a U-curve pattern in all the three dimensions of sociocultural adjustment, indicating a typical culture-shock experience. In terms of psychological adjustment, contrary to the case of their sociocultural adjustment, no clear U-curve pattern could be found corresponding to culture shock.

The differing trends of sociocultural and psychological adjustment are not unexpected. It may be speculated that the adjustment of psychological variables is more difficult to achieve than sociocultural adjustment, since the former involves more fundamental and deeply held attitudinal structures than the latter. Also, progress in sociocultural adjustment, as far as social skills are concerned, does not necessarily mean that the expatriate has to develop more positive attitudes at the same time (Tsai, 1995). Very much like the new language acquisition analogy discussed above, the new social skills need not become part of a permanent repertoire of the expatriate and will not be used when they are not functional, as for example when the person is among fellow-nationals or after repatriation (Bochner, 1986; Furnham and Bochner, 1986).

Although there is little empirical support for the U-curve hypothesis and the occurrence of culture shock as mentioned above, our results concerning Western expatriates assigned to the Chinese mainland seem to differ from the few other studies that have identified a culture-shock phase. The time period before culture shock sets in from our study is generally longer than previously reported. For example, in a large-scale study, of Swedish expatriates worldwide, Torbiörn (1982) found that the U-curve pattern already began to appear after 0–3 months, and in their substantive literature review of the U-curve hypothesis Black and Mendenhall (1991) depicted the culture-shock phase as starting after 0–2 months. Likewise, Ward and Kennedy (1996), investigating Malaysian and Singaporean students in New Zealand, reported a drop in both psychological and sociocultural adjustment already from 1 month. As reported above in our study however, the expatriates did not start to experience any culture shock until after 17–18 months, indicating a delayed effect when on assignment on the Chinese mainland. It is not evident why this discrepancy occurs, but it might be speculated that many Western expatriates on the Chinese mainland are to a certain degree barred from sociocultural interactions with host nationals, thus delaying their culture shock. Few expatriates can master the language well enough for any useful interactional purposes, and they often live in virtual expatriate 'ghettos', as in hotels or compounds exclusively designated for expatriates (Björkman and Schaap, 1994). In fact, most sociocultural interactions with local people probably take place at work, which our findings also seem to support since the earliest, yet most shallow, culture-shock trough occurred for work adjustment.

A general implication of our results for Western expatriate managers on the Chinese mainland, and for companies assigning Western managers there, is that all possible means should be engaged to facilitate the adjustment process on the Chinese mainland, since that could help them to avoid/shorten the period of culture shock. Cross-cultural training and preparations, including language training, as well as careful selection of candidates for expatriate assignments, are areas identified in the literature both as being essential for successful adjustment as well as being badly neglected by international business firms (Black and Mendenhall, 1990; Brewster, 1995; Aryee, 1997).

As opposed to the traditional pre-arrival cross-cultural training, post-arrival cross-cultural training has been promoted as an especially effective tool to facilitate international adjustment of expatriate managers (Selmer et al., 1998). For maximum effectiveness, the training should be given when the trainees are most motivated to learn. People in homogenous cultural environments, without travelling experience, may benefit little from training given prior to departure. On the other hand, people who have travelled enough, who have experienced contact with other cultures, are more likely to be aware of the need for training and, hence, motivated to learn. This suggests that the timing of cross-cultural training is also connected to the needs and characteristics of the trainees. Besides, in all pre-departure training there is a general problem of relating training experiences to the frame of reference of the trainee, since his or her concept of the normal is still firmly attached to the home culture. The trainee may find the topics of the course unrealistic, exotic, or simply picturesque. At the end of the course, trainees could simply end up with a set of stereotyped ideas about the host culture. The duration of most training programmes is also generally too short to achieve any fundamental and permanent changes in cultural norms. Most pre-departure training programmes probably resemble the experience of the very first period in the host country, labelled the tourist phase. (Torbiörn, 1982, 1994; Grove and Torbiörn, 1985; Triandis, 1986).

Post-arrival training need not necessarily take place immediately upon the sojourner's arrival; some training may have its maximum effect if it is delayed until the sojourner tries to cope with culture shock. Hence, such training could start about three to six months after arrival in the host country. Preferably, such training should focus on structures and relationships in the culture of the host country, world view, mentality, values, living patterns and social structure; the purpose being more of providing the sojourner with a 'grammar' rather than a 'vocabulary'. At that time, it can be assumed that the sojourner has a large amount of unstructured detailed information from his or her own experience, which could be patterned and given meaning by the structure offered by the training programme. Providing the sojourners with interaction skills enables them to function independently without knowing all the facts about the culture, because skills training focuses on 'learning how to learn' in a new cultural setting (McCaffery, 1986).

It should be observed, however, that pre- and post-arrival cross-cultural training programmes are not mutually exclusive, but rather complementary. Sequential training has been suggested as most effective if started prior to the trainee's departure from their home culture, and continued periodically during their sojourn in the host culture (Selmer et al., 1998).

To establish a basis for the cross-cultural training and create an organizational rationale for initiating an individual and organizational learning process, managers should continuously report to headquarters during the assignment in China and there should be a comprehensive debrief upon completion of the stay. This may involve examining problems experienced, practical solutions applied, and important lessons learned, as well as candid feedback on the process of managing expatriates. If possible, data could also be gathered from local employees on how they view the outgoing expatriate manager to make new expatriate managers aware of local values and perceptions. Also, experienced managers repatriated from China could take a more active role in managing and supporting current expatriates in China (Sergeant and Frenkel, 1998), as coach/mentors (Chao et al., 1992) at headquarters. Using an overlap period where the expatriate predecessor and successor are both present at the location in China to facilitate information exchange could also be useful (Selmer, 1995; Selmer and de Leon, 1997). Furthermore, giving headquarters directors more exposure to China through frequent brief visits may increase their awareness of the special circumstances meeting Western expatriate business managers in that country and pave the way for a concerted learning process to deal with the problem of culture shock in China (Sergeant and Frenkel, 1998).

# Conclusions: Western business expatriates in China

The relatively lower score on interaction adjustment than the other dimensions of sociocultural adjustment, suggests a language barrier, leaving expatriates ignorant about local thinking and character. This could influence their ability to assess work situations, with the possibility of making wrong assumptions about their subordinates.

The better adjusted expatriates are, socioculturally, the stronger is the relationship between psychological and sociocultural adjustment, especially work adjustment. This is not surprising since the reason for the expatriate to be located abroad is to perform certain work tasks. On the other hand, interacting with host nationals did not affect expatriates psychological adjustment, maybe due to language problems.

The relationship between sociocultural and psychological adjustment is greater for small than for large cross-cultural transitions. Again, work adjustment seems to be the key element to facilitate the psychological adjustment of the expatriates, and especially so on the Chinese mainland. All dimensions of adjustment plotted over time showed clear evidence of cultural shock, except psychological adjustment. This kind of adjustment may be more difficult to bring about than sociocultural adjustment due to its more fundamental and permanent change. Like a new language, the acquired social skills will only be used when they are needed and not otherwise. The time before culture shock occurs is generally longer than previously reported. Instead of within three months, culture shock did not occur until after 17–18 months in China. Difficult sociocultural interactions with host nationals could explain the delayed effect; most exchanges with locals probably take place at work, in which context also the earliest culture shock appears.

The general lesson for expatriates and their firms could be that it may be a good idea to try to facilitate the adjustment process. Cross-cultural training may be a worthwhile preparation for business expatriates destined both for the Hong Kong SAR and the Chinese mainland, and learning basic Chinese should be viewed as part of the assignment. The importance of cross-cultural training to ease work adjustment is also emphasized. Such training is not very common, but could enhance both expatriates' work efficiency and their psychological adjustment. Preferably, this training could be administered post-arrival to enhance its effect.

Upon completion of assignments, firms should debrief repatriates concerning problems experienced, practical solutions applied, and important lessons learned, as well as seeking candid feedback on the practices of managing expatriates. Additional information on the expatriates leaving may also be sought from local employees. In addition, previous expatriates could actively support current expatriates, perhaps as coaches/mentors at headquarters. Overlap periods between expatriate predecessors and successors might also be useful, and giving executives at headquarters more exposure to China might increase their awareness of potential problems in that country.

## Discussion questions

1  Imagine that you have been assigned to China as a business expatriate, how would you prepare yourself for such an assignment?
2  How can you tell if you yourself experience culture shock? What are the symptoms? How can you tell if somebody else suffers from culture shock?
3  Despite your best efforts in preparing yourself, suppose that you would anyway experience a bad case of culture shock. What would you do?

## Further reading

Chen, M.-J. (2001) *Inside Chinese Business: A Guide for Managers Worldwide*. Boston, MA: Harvard Business School Press.
Fang, T. (1999) *Chinese Business Negotiation Style*. London: Sage.
Selmer, J. (ed.) (1998) *International Management in China: Cross-Cultural Issues*. London: Routledge.
Warner, M. (ed.) (1999) *China's Managerial Revolution*. London: Frank Cass.

## References

Adler, P.S. (1975) 'The Transitional Experience: An Alternative View of Culture Shock', *Journal of Humanistic Psychology*, 15: 13–23.
Adler, P.S. (1987) 'Culture Shock and the Cross-cultural Learning Experience', in L.F. Luce and E.C. Smith (eds), *Toward Internationalism*. Cambridge: Cambridge University Press.
Anderson, L.E. (1994) 'A New Look at an Old Construct: Cross-cultural Adaptation', *International Journal of Intercultural Relations*, 18(3): 293–328.
Arnetz, B.B. and Anderzen, I. (1992) 'The Internationalization of Work. Optimizing Adaptation of Employees to a Global Economy. A Multidisciplinary Study of the Expatriation and Repatriation Process', in J. Selmer (ed.), Proceedings of the First International Conference on Expatriate Management. Hong Kong: Hong Kong Baptist College.
Aryee, S. (1997) 'Selection and Training of Expatriate Employees', in N. Anderson and P. Herriot (eds), *Handbook of Selection and Appraisal*. London: Wiley.
Aryee, S. and Stone, R.J. (1996) 'Work Experiences, Work Adjustment and Psychological Well-being of Expatriate Employees in Hong Kong', *International Journal of Human Resource Management*. 7(1): 150–64.
Ball-Rokeach, S.J. (1973) 'From Pervasive Ambiguity to a Definition of the Situation', *Sociometry*, 36: 3–13.
Bartlett, C. and Goshal, S. (1989) *Managing Across National Borders: The Transnational Solution*. Boston: Harvard University Press.
Berry, J.W. (1990) 'Psychology of Acculturation: Understanding Individuals Moving Between Cultures', in R.W. Brislin (ed.), *Applied Cross-Cultural Psychology*. London: Sage.
Berry, J.W. and Kim, U. (1988) 'Acculturation and Mental Health', in P. Dasen, W.J. Berry and N. Sartorius (eds), *Health and Cross-Cultural Psychology*, London: Sage.
Berry, J.W., Trimble, J. and Olmeda, E. (1986) 'The Assessment of Acculturation', in W.J. Lonner and J.W. Berry (eds), *Field Methods in Cross-cultural Research*, London: Sage.
Björkman, I. and Schaap, A. (1994) 'Outsiders in the Middle Kingdom: Expatriate Managers in Chinese–Western Joint Ventures', *European Management Journal*, 12(2): 147–53.
Black, J.S. (1988) 'Work Role Transitions: A Study of American Expatriate Managers in Japan', *Journal of International Business Studies*, 19: 277–94.
Black, J.S. and Gregersen, H.B. (1990) 'Expectations, Satisfaction and Intentions to Leave of American Managers in Japan', *International Journal of Intercultural Relations*, 14: 485–506.
Black, J.S. and Gregersen, H.B. (1991a) 'Antecedents to Cross-cultural Adjustment for Expatriates in Pacific Rim Assignments', *Human Relations*, 44(5): 497–515.
Black, J.S. and Gregersen, H.B. (1991b) 'When Yankee Comes Home: Factors Related to Expatriate and Spouse Repatriation Adjustment', *Journal of International Business Studies*, 22(4): 671–94.

Black, J.S. and Gregersen, H.B. and Mendenhall, M.E. (1992), *Global Assignments: Successfully Expatriating and Repatriating International Managers*. San Francisco: Jossey-Bass.

Black, J.S. and Mendenhall, M. (1990) 'Cross-Cultural Training Effectiveness: A Review and Theoretical Framework for Further Research', *Academy of Management Review*, 15: 113–36.

Black, J.S. and Mendenhall, M. (1991) 'The U-curve Adjustment Hypothesis Revisited: A Review and Theoretical Framework', *Journal of International Business Studies*, 22(2): 225–47.

Black, J.S. Mendenhall, M. and Oddou, G. (1991) 'Toward a Comprehensive Model of International Adjustment: An Integration of Multiple Theoretical Perspectives', *Academy of Management Review*. 16(2): 291–317.

Black, J.S. and Stephens, G.K. (1989) 'The Influence of the Spouse on American Expatriate Adjustment in Overseas Assignments', *Journal of Management*, 15: 529–44.

Bochner, S. (1986) 'Coping with Unfamiliar Cultures: Adjustment or Culture Learning?', *Australian Journal of Psychology*, 38(3), 347–58.

Brewster, C. (1991) *The Management of Expatriates*. London: Kogan Page.

Brewster, C. (1995) 'Effective Expatriate Training', in J. Selmer, (ed.), *Expatriate Management: New Ideas for International Business*, Westport, CT: Quorum Books.

Brewster, C. and Pickard, J. (1994) 'Evaluating Expatriate Training', *International Studies of Management and Organization*, 24(3): 18–35.

Byrnes, F.C. (1966) 'Role Shock: an Occupational Hazard of American Technical Assistants Abroad', *Annals of the American Academy of Political and Social Science*, 368: 95–108.

Caplan, R.D., Cobb, S., French, J.R.P., Van Herrison, R. and Pinneau, S.R. (1975) *Job Demands and Worker Health*. Washington, DC: National Institute for Occupational Safety and Health.

Chao, G.T., Waltz, P.M. and Gardner, P.D. (1992) 'Formal and Informal Mentorships: A Comparison on Mentoring Functions and Contrast with Nonmentored Counterparts', *Personnel Psychology*, 45: 619–36.

Chen, M.-J. (2001) *Inside Chinese Business: A Guide for Managers Worldwide*. Boston, MA: Harvard Business School Press.

Child, J. (1994) *Chinese Management During the Age of Reform*. Cambridge: Cambridge University Press.

Church, A. (1982) 'Sojourner Adjustment', *Psychological Bulletin*, 91(3): 540–77.

Davidson, W. (1987) 'Creating and Managing Joint Ventures in China', *California Management Review*, 29: 77–94.

De Cieri, H. and Dowling, P. (1995) 'Cross-Cultural Issues in Organizational Behavior', *Trends in Organizational Behavior*, 2: 127–45.

Dolainski, S. (1997) 'Are Expats Getting Lost in the Translation?', *Workforce*, February, 32–9.

Earley, P.C. (1987) 'Intercultural Training for Managers: A Comparison of Documentary and Interpersonal Methods', *Academy of Management Journal*, 30(4): 685–98.

Feldman, D.C. and Tompson, H.B. (1993) 'Entry Shock, Culture Shock: Socializing the New Breed of Global Managers', *Human Resource Management*, 31(4): 345–62.

Forster, N. (1997) 'The Persistent Myth of High Expatriate Failure Rates': A Reappraisal', *International Journal of Human Resource Management*, 8(4): 414–33.

Furnham, A. (1993) 'Communicating in Foreign Lands: The Cause, Consequences and Cures of Culture Shock', *Language, Culture and Curriculum*, 6(1): 91–109.

Furnham, A. and Bochner, S. (1982) 'Social Difficulty in a Foreign Country: An Empirical Analysis of Culture Shock', in S. Bochner (ed.), *Cultures in Contact – Studies in Cross-cultural Interaction*. Oxford: Pergamon.

Furnham, A. and Bochner, S. (1986) *Culture Shock: Psychological Reactions to Unfamiliar Environments*. London: Methuen.

Garza-Guerrero, A.C. (1974) 'Culture Shock: Its Mourning and the Vicissitudes of Identity', *Journal of the American Psychoanalytic Association*, 22: 408–29.

Goldberg, D. (1972) *The Detection of Psychiatric Illness by Questionnaire*. London: Oxford University Press.

Goodall, K. and Warner, M. (1997) 'Human Resources in Sino–Foreign Joint Ventures: Selected Case Studies in Shanghai Compared with Beijing', *International Journal of Human Resource Management*, 8(5): 569–94.

Grove, C.L. and Torbiörn, I. (1985) 'A New Conceptualization of Intercultural Adjustment and the Goals of Training', *International Journal of Intercultural Relations*, 9: 205–33.

Gullahorn, J.E. and Gullahorn, J.R. (1962) 'An Extension of the U-Curve Hypothesis', *Journal of Social Issues*, 3: 33–47.

Guthrie, G.M. (1975) 'A Behavioral Analysis of Culture Learning', in R.W. Bochner and W.J. Lonner (eds), *Cross-cultural Perspectives on Learning*. New York: Wiley.

Harvey, M. (1997) 'Dual-career Expatriates: Expectations, Adjustment and Satisfaction with International Relocation', *Journal of International Business Studies*, 28(3): 627–58.

Harzing, A.-W.K. (1995) 'The Persistent Myth of High Expatriate Failure Rates', *International Journal of Human Resource Management*, 6(2): 457–74.

Hilltrop, J. and Janssens, M. (1990) 'Expatriation: Challenges and Recommendations', *European Management Journal*, 18(1): 19–27.

Jacobson, E.H. (1963) 'Sojourn Research: A Definition of the Field', *Journal of Social Issues*, 19(3): 123–29.

Janssens, M. (1995) 'Intercultural Interaction: A Burden on International Managers?', *Journal of Organizational Behavior*, 16: 155–67.

Juffer, K.A. (1986) 'The First Step in Cross-cultural Orientation: Defining the Problem', in R.M. Paige (ed.), *Cross-Cultural Orientation: New Conceptualizations and Applications*. Lanham, MD: University Press of America.

Jun, S., Lee, S. and Gentry, J.W. (1997) 'The Effects of Acculturation on Commitment to the Parent Company and the Foreign Operation', *International Business Review*, 6(5): 519–35.

Karasek, R.A. (1979) 'Job Demands, Job Decision Latitude and Mental Strain: Implications for Job Redesign', *Administrative Science Quarterly*, 24: 285–308.

Klineberg, O. (1982) 'Contact Between Ethnic Groups: A Historical Perspective of Some Aspects of Theory and Research', in S. Bochner (ed.), *Cultures in Contact: Studies in Cross-cultural Interaction*. Oxford: Pergamon.

Kornhauser, A. (1965), *Mental Health of the Industrial Worker: A Detroit Study*. New York: Wiley.

Lee, Y. and Larwood, L. (1983) 'The Socialization of Expatriate Managers in Multinational Firms', *Academy of Management Journal*, 264: 657–65.

Lesser, S.O. and Peter, H.W. (1957) 'Training Foreign Nationals in the United States', in R. Likert and S.P. Hayes (eds), *Some Applications of Behavioural Research*. Paris: UNESCO.

Lysgaard, S. (1955) 'Adjustment in a Foreign Society: Norwegian Fulbright Grantees Visiting the United States', *International Social Bulletin*, 7: 45–51.

McCaffery, J.A. (1986) 'Independent Effectiveness: A Reconsideration of Cross-cultural Orientation and Training', *International Journal of Intercultural Relations*, 10(2): 159–78.

McEvoy, G.M. and Parker, B. (1995) 'Expatriate Adjustment: Causes and Consequences', in J. Selmer (ed.), *Expatriate Management: New Ideas for International Business*. Westport, CT: Quorum Books.

Mendenhall, M. and Oddou, G. (1985) 'The Dimensions of Expatriate Acculturation: A Review', *Academy of Management Review*, 10(1): 39–47.

Nicholson, N. and Imaizumi, A. (1993) 'The Adjustment of Japanese Expatriates to Living and Working in Britain', *British Journal of Management*, 4: 119–34.

Oberg, K. (1960) 'Culture Shock: Adjustment to New Cultural Environments', *Practical Anthropologist*, 7: 177–82.

Picconi, M.J., Romano, A. and Olson, C.L. (1993) *Business Statistics: Elements and Applications*. New York, NY: Harper Collins.

Ralston, D., Gustafson, D.J., Cheung, F.M. and Terpstra, R.H. (1992) 'Eastern Values: A Comparison of U.S., Hong Kong, and PRC Managers', *Journal of Applied Psychology*, 77: 664–71.

Ralston, D., Gustafson, D.J., Cheung, F.M. and Terpstra, R.H. (1993) 'Differences in Managerial Values: A Study of U.S., Hong Kong and PRC Managers', *Journal of International Business Studies*, 24(2): 249–75.

Rimington, R. (1996) 'The Management Process of Developing a Sino–British Joint Venture', in J. Child, and Y. Lu, (eds), *Management Issues in China: Volume II – International Enterprises*. London: Routledge.

Saltzman, C. (1986) 'One Hundred and Fifty Percent Persons: Guides to Orienting International Students', in R.M. Paige (ed.), *Cross-Cultural Orientation: New Conceptualizations and Applications*. Lanham, MD: University Press of America.

Schein, E.H. (1980), *Organizational Psychology*. Englewood Cliffs, NJ: Prentice Hall.

Searle, W. and Ward, C. (1990) 'The Prediction of Psychological and Socio-Cultural Adjustment During Cross-Cultural Transitions', *International Journal of Intercultural Relations*, 14: 449–64.

Selmer, J. (1992) '*Cultural Preparation of Expatriate Top Managers: An Exploratory Study of Swedish CEOs in Southeast Asia*', Working Paper Series no. MS91080, Business Research Centre, School of Business, Hong Kong: Hong Kong Baptist College.

Selmer, J. (1995) 'Expatriate Executive Succession', in J. Selmer, (ed.), *Expatriate Management; New Ideas for International Business*. Westport, CT: Quorum Books.

Selmer, J. (1997) 'Cross-Cultural Training for International Managers', in R.J. Stone (ed.), *Readings in Human Resource Management*, vol. III. Brisbane: Wiley.

Selmer, J. (1998) 'Strategic Human Resource Management: Expatriate Managers in China', in J. Selmer, (ed.), *International Management in China: Cross-cultural Issues*. London: Routledge.

Selmer, J. and de Leon, C.T. (1989) '*Never the Twain Shall Meet*', Research Report no. R1989:9, Department of Business Administration. Stockholm University: Sweden.

Selmer, J. and de Leon, C.T. (1997) 'Succession Procedures for Expatriate Chief Executives', *Human Resource Management Journal*, 7(3): 80–8.

Selmer, J. and Lee, S. (1994) 'International Transfer and Assignment of Australian and European Business Executives', *Asia Pacific Journal of Human Resources*, 32(3): 1–12.

Selmer, J. and Shiu, L.S.C. (1999) 'Coming Home? Adjustment of Hong Kong Chinese Expatriate Business Managers Assigned to the People's Republic of China', *International Journal of Intercultural Relations*, 23(3): 447–65.

Selmer, J., Torbiörn, I. and de Leon, C.T. (1998) 'Sequential Cross-cultural Training for Expatriate Business Managers: Pre-Departure and Post-Arrival', *International Journal of Human Resource Management*, 9(5): 832–40.

Sergeant, A. and Frenkel, S. (1998) 'Managing People in China: Perceptions of Expatriate Managers', *Journal of World Business*, 33(1): 17–34.

Smalley, W. (1963) 'Culture Shock, Language shock, and the Shock of Self-discovery', *Practical Anthropology*, 10: 49–56.

Torbiörn, I. (1982), *Living Abroad: Personal Adjustment and Personnel Policy in the Overseas Setting*. New York: Wiley.

Torbiörn, I. (1994) 'Dynamics of Cross-cultural Adaptation', in G. Althen (ed.), *Learning Across Cultures*. Washington, DC: NAFSA Association of International Educators.

Triandis, H.C. (1986) 'Approaches to Cross-cultural Orientation and the Role of Culture Assimilator Training', in R.M. Paige (ed.), *Cross-Cultural Orientation: New Conceptualizations and Applications*. Lanham, MD: University Press of America.

Tsai, H.-Y. (1995) 'Sojourner Adjustment: The Case of Foreigners in Japan', *Journal of Cross-cultural Psychology*, 26(5): 523–36.

Tung, R.L. (1982) 'Selection and Training Procedures of US, European and Japanese Multinationals', *California Management Review*, 25(1): 57–71.

Wang, X. and Ralston, D. (2000) 'Strategies for Small and Medium-Sized U.S. Businesses Investing in China: Lessons From Taiwanese Companies', *Thunderbird International Business Review*, 6: 677–701.

Ward, C. and Kennedy, A. (1992) 'Locus of Control, Mood Disturbance and Social Difficulty During Cross-cultural Transitions', *International Journal of Intercultural Relations*, 16: 175–94.

Ward, C. and Kennedy, A. (1993a) 'Psychological and Socio-cultural Adjustment During Cross-cultural Transitions: A Comparison of Secondary Students Overseas and at Home', *International Journal of Psychology*, 28(2): 129–47.

Ward, C. and Kennedy, A. (1993b) 'Where's the Culture in Cross-cultural Transition? Comparative Studies of Sojourner Adjustment', *Journal of Cross-Cultural Psychology*, 24(2): 221–49.

Ward, C. and Kennedy, A. (1996) 'Crossing Cultures: The Relationship Between Psychological and Socio-cultural Dimensions of Cross-cultural Adjustment', in J. Pandey, D. Sinha and D.P.S. Bhawuk (eds), *Asian Contributions to Cross-cultural Psychology*. New Delhi: Sage.

Ward, C., Okura, Y., Kennedy, A. and Kojima, T. (1998) 'The U-Curve on Trial: A Longitudinal Study of Psychological and Sociocultural Adjustment During Cross-Cultural Transition', *International Journal of Intercultural Relations*, 22(3): 277–91.

Ward, C. and Searle, W. (1991) 'The Impact of Value Discrepancies and Cultural Identity on Psychological and Socio-cultural Adjustment of Sojourners', *International Journal of Intercultural Relations*, 15: 209–25.

Warner, M. (1995) *The Management of Human Resources in Chinese Industry*. London: Macmillan.

Weaver, G.R. (1986) 'Understanding and Coping with Cross-cultural Adjustment Stress', in R.M. Paige (ed.), *Cross-cultural Orientation: New Conceptualizations and Applications*. Lanham, MD: University Press of America.

Weldon, E. and Jehn, K.A. (1996) 'Conflict Management in US–Chinese Joint Ventures', in J. Child and Y. Lu (eds), *Management Issues in China: Volume II – International Enterprises*. London: Routledge.

Zwingmann, C.A.A. and Gunn, A.D.G. (1983) *Uprooting and Health: Psycho-social Problems of Students from Abroad*. Geneva: World Health Organization, Division of Mental Health.

# 12

# International HRM in developing countries

*Pawan S. Budhwar and Yaw A. Debrah*

## Introduction

The developments in the fields of HRM and international HRM (IHRM) are now well-documented (see for example, Legge, 1995; Poole and Warner, 1998; Dowling *et al.*, 1999; Schuler and Jackson, 1999; Sisson and Storey, 2000; Schuler *et al.*, 2002). However, the principal focus of research on HRM and IHRM developments have been on organizations in advanced Western industrial societies. As relatively very little work on HRM research in developing countries has been done, recently some researchers have highlighted the need for cross-national HRM studies involving developing countries (Clark *et al.*, 1999; Budhwar and Debrah, 2001a, 2001b).

This is all the more important because major developments are taking place in developing nations which have in recent years liberalized their economies and opened their doors to foreign investors. It is, thus, essential for practitioners to know about the pattern of HRM systems prevalent in such countries. Moreover, focusing on developing nations would add a new impetus to HRM studies and allow researchers to go beyond the current predominant emphasis on research in developed countries. As a large number of multinational companies are now investing in developing countries (such as China, South Africa and India), it would be useful for researchers to examine the extent to which management practices from the headquarters of multinational companies in developed countries can be transferred to their subsidiaries in developing countries (Schuler *et al.*, 2002). It will also enable researchers to examine the 'convergence–divergence hypothesis' in the context of developing countries. The influence of a 'convergence hypothesis' has now waned in developed parts of the world as sufficient evidence has been gathered against it (Hofstede, 1993). However, McGaughey and De Cieri (1999) argue that organizations are becoming more similar in terms of macro-level variables (convergence), but are maintaining their culturally based dissimilarities in terms of micro-level variables (divergence). Thus the question arises, to what extent can this be applied to developing countries? An examination of this and other issues discussed earlier can contribute significantly to the fields of both HRM and IHRM. Considering such developments, it is important to investigate the patterns of HRM systems in developing countries.

There are three principal aims of this chapter. First, it highlights the need to understand HRM in developing countries in the context of globalization. Second, it highlights the main challenges to examining HRM in developing countries. Finally, it makes key suggestions for both practitioners and researchers regarding how to efficiently manage HR issues and conduct research in such countries.

## Globalization and the need to examine HRM in developing countries

This section further highlights the need to examine the scenario of HRM in developing countries, and has three main aims. First, to introduce the concept of developing countries. Second, to discuss the main reasons as a result of which developing countries have become important and why it has now become an imperative to study issues pertaining to HRM in developing countries. Third, to highlight the need to examine HRM in developing countries in light of increased globalization.

The term 'developing countries' in this chapter is used in a broad generic sense and to represent all countries other than advanced industrialized societies, which we refer to as developed countries. Some authors have used other terms such as 'less- developed countries', 'newly industrialized countries', 'third-world countries', 'emerging nations', 'emerging markets', and 'transitional economies' interchangeably for developing countries (Austin, 1990; Kiggundu, 1989; Warner, 2000). For us, developing countries are the ones which are in their early growth stages of economic development and are in the process of industrializing or are non-industrialized (see, Budhwar and Debrah, 2001b; Napier and Vu, 1998). This is an ideal-type description as all developing countries are at different stages of economic development.

The existing literature shows that apart from a few single-country journal articles and the work of a few researchers (see Kiggundu et al., 1983; Austin, 1990; Jaeger and Kanungo, 1990; Kanungo, 1995; Warner, 2000; Budhwar and Debrah, 2001b), relatively very little has been written about HRM in developing nations. This has probably been due to the limited number of researchable topics in mainly small economies with small companies and small wage employment sectors. However, over the past two decades, foreign direct investment (FDI) has increased to the developing parts of the world bringing its share from 23 per cent in the mid-1980s to 37.2 per cent in 1997 (United Nations 1998: 9). Though this amount decreased to 28 per cent in 1998 due to the financial crisis in Asia, FDI to Latin American countries has been rising continuously and is projected to rise in Asia (UNCTAD, 1999). As a consequence, of 53,000 multinational corporations (MNCs) with 450,000 affiliates operating around the world, a total of 230,696 affiliates are now based in developing countries (United Nations, 1998). As a result of such developments, there is now a growing research interest in management in developing countries (see Budhwar and Debrah, 2001b; Das, 2002) and a number of major journals have devoted special issues in this regard (see, special issues of *Academy of Management Journal*, 2000, vol. 43, no. 3 and *Journal of International Business Studies*, 2001, vol. 32, no. 1).

Further, a majority of the world's population now live in developing countries. Apart from this, developing countries also act as:

1  Significant '*buyers*': out of a total world population of 5.5 billion, only 800 million live in the developed world, the rest live in the developing countries. The majority of exports from developed countries go to developing countries. For example, Mexico alone consumes over 20 per cent of total American exports and is growing fast.

2  Important '*suppliers*' of different resources: apart from cheap human resources, developing countries also supply a large number of natural resources important for production in developed countries. Lately, a significant number of services (for example via call centres) and both software and hardware are also supplied by some developing countries to the rest of the world.

3  '*Competitors*' to developed countries, with lower labour costs. A very good example of this is the creation of a large number of call centres in India and the Philippines. The annual salaries of graduates working in call centres in Ireland, Singapore and the Philippines is $19,500, $16,000, and $2,900 respectively. In India, it is around $2,400 (for details see Chengappa and Goyal, 2002).

4  '*Strategic regional centres*' for expansion of MNCs: a very significant number of MNCs are now operating in developing countries; this will be discussed further later in this chapter.

5  '*Production sites*' for MNCs: very often we hear that some important manufacturer or service provider from developed countries has moved to a developing country. This is mainly due to the comparative advantage of producing products or providing services (see Hill, 2001).

6  '*Capital users*': such as from private creditors like the international banks and foreign official governmental assistance (for more details see Garten, 1996; Napier and Vu, 1998; Kanungo, 2000; Budhwar and Debrah, 2001b; Hill, 2001).

These factors highlight the great extent to which both developed and developing countries have now become interdependent of each other. This is also evident from the creation of various economic international trading blocs and '*growth triangles*' (Debrah *et al.*, 2000). However, it is important to recognize that best-management practices and techniques which are dictated by unique configurations of different cultural and institutional factors evolved in the context of Western cultural values, cannot be uncritically adopted in developing countries (Mendonca, 2000).

Therefore, there is a growing need to research and understand what kind of HR policies and practices are relevant for developing countries.

The case for the above-mentioned investigation is further strengthened considering the increased level of globalization of business and the competitive pressures being created by businesses from developing countries. Globalization, of all other things, has reduced barriers between countries and is encouraging closer integration of economic, political and social activity (Frenkel and Peetz, 1998). Globalization is moving at a high speed and one of the main forces behind its movement is the economic expansion in developing countries and the associated worldwide wave of economic globalization, including the lowering of tariff and other barriers to international trade. It is asserted that the increased capital flows across international borders have heightened the demand and growth of FDI resulting in rapid growth in world trade, especially, involving developing countries (see Budhwar and Debrah, 2001b).

However, it is important to keep in mind that economic globalization and its associated international competitive pressures have the potential to change HRM in developing countries. While globalization unearths some challenges for HRM in developing countries, it also offers possibilities for the transformation of personnel management (PM) into HRM in the developing world. The existing literature suggests that globalization has also ushered in new forms of management in developing countries (see Debrah and Smith, 2000a). The global competitive environment has forced governments in developing countries to shed their public enterprises or subject them to private-sector management practices. Some public enterprises have been privatized in recent years and are competing vigorously in global markets. Thus, it can be deduced that globalization is one of the key driving force behind the new developments in HRM in developing countries (Debrah and Smith, 2000a, b).

Therefore, for the development of appropriate theory and practice, it has now become important for researchers to understand how HR issues are managed and what key factors determine HRM in developing countries. However, there are a number of challenges in this regard.

# HRM in developing countries: issues and perspectives

Much of the existing literature on HRM and international management has highlighted the extent to which external environmental factors and internal work cultures influence both micro and macro-level organizational policies (Kiggundu, 1989; Jaeger and Kanungo, 1990; Budhwar and Sparrow, 2002). The predominant emphasis in this area has been on the external environment as an impediment to successful management in developing countries (Kiggundu et al., 1983; Kohn and Austin, 2000). It is suggested that the forces of instability and uncertainty in developing countries' external environment make it an imperative for managers to develop appropriate approaches to managing human resources (Kamoche, 1993). Indeed, the constant changes in the external environment of organizations tend to dictate both the pace and direction of developments in HRM policies and practices at the firm level. Nevertheless, internal factors can be equally important in shaping any firm's HRM policies and practices and, hence, need serious consideration. The main challenge, then, in examining HRM in developing countries is to highlight which factors and variables significantly influence HRM in a particular region or country. This task becomes all the more difficult considering the 'context-specific' nature of IHRM (see Schuler *et al.*, 2002).

In this regard, while reviewing the impact of the main factors on HRM in 13 developing countries, Debrah and Budhwar (2001) identify three models of influences: (a) religious influences (Islam, Hinduism, Buddhism, and traditional beliefs in spirits, fetishes and gods); (b) traditional cultural beliefs (for example Confucianism, African traditional practices and institutions, caste in India, and so on); and (c) Western colonial and modern influences. For example, the existing patterns of HRM in Iran, Pakistan, Saudi Arabia and Algeria show the influence of Islamic religion on HRM in those countries, and that, arguably, of the Islamic influence is probably the dominant factor. Moreover, regardless of the presence of unique influencing factors in the various countries, there is some commonality in the way Islam permeates organizational life in each country.

Similarly, the analysis of HRM in the sub-Saharan African countries reveals that, perhaps with the sole exception of South Africa, which essentially exhibits Western culture in organizations, traditional African culture exerts a strong influence on HRM. In Ghana, Nigeria, Kenya and elsewhere in Africa, people in organizations still place a lot of emphasis on traditional beliefs such as spirits, witchcraft, fetishes and gods (see Gardiner, 1996), traditions and institutions, customs and sociocultural issues (Debrah, 2000). In Kiggundu's (1989) view, these traditional practices tend to have negative effects on organizational performance. In particular, they compromise the integrity and efficiency of formal bureaucratic systems, injecting an element of subjectivity into HR functions such as recruitment and selection, performance appraisal, promotion, demotion and compensation. In addition, Ghana, Nigeria and Kenya are all former British colonies, and hence there are more similarities than differences in organizational management practices and systems as they all inherited similar administrative structures from the British colonial administration. In this sense, India and Pakistan also inherited some similar administrative practices from the British.

Like other developing countries, HRM in both India and Nepal is significantly influenced by both national culture and national institutions. Hinduism is the dominant religion in both countries. Budhwar (2001) and Adhikari and Muller (2001) suggest that HRM practices in these two countries are governed largely by social contacts, based on one's caste, religion, economic status and political affiliation. There is also still a strong influence of British colonial traditions in India and Nepal in the form of extensive legislation and a red-tape-ridden bureaucratic system. Again, in common with the African countries, the provisions of labour laws are not seriously implemented and moreover the uncooperative and disruptive nature of unions reduces the efficiency of organizations. However, all this is now challenged and is slowly changing due to the pressures created by the liberalization of the economy and increased competition.

There is also some commonality in the way national culture and traditions influence HRM in the Far East, for example in Taiwan, South Korea and China. In discussing the key characteristics of Korean companies, Chen (1995) mentions the profound influence of Confucianism on the values, attitudes and behavioural patterns of Koreans. Confucianism instils a belief of hierarchy and order in society as well as harmonious interpersonal relations. Buddhism is also practised in Korea and as such also influences management practices, albeit it to lesser extent than Confucianism. In addition there are American and Japanese influences on Korean management. Chen (1995) contends that in spite of the combined effects of these influences, a distinctive style of management has emerged in Korea, known as 'K-type management', and its main features include top-down decision-making, paternalistic leadership, clan management, *inhwa* (harmony-oriented cultural values), Korean flexible lifetime employment, personal loyalty and compensation based on seniority and merit-rating. Won-Woo (2001), however, discusses the rapid changes in the Korean business environment and the growing pressures on organizations to move away from the traditional values and organizational structures.

Warner (2001) highlights the 'Chinese characteristics' of bureaucratic systems in China. In both China and Taiwan just as in Korea, Confucian values have found their way into management. As such, *guanxi* ('relational networking' based on interpersonal connections, which acts as a coordination mechanism), *mianzi* (face, that is the impression of someone in public) and *renqing* (obligations) reinforce the social bonds which make the Chinese system function smoothly, and are some of the means of regulating interpersonal relationships in Chinese organizations. Although it is evident that there are some differences in the management practices in the three East Asian countries, some traditional cultures have similar, if not the same, impacts on management in all three.

The above discussion and examples in general reinforce our understanding of the impact of national factors (for example national cultures, work-related values and the external environment) on HRM in developing countries. They also highlight the influential role of national institutions as well as social institutions such as family, socialization and internalization practices on HRM in developing countries. Further, they show how these external factors in turn influence internal HR practices.

Apart from the above-mentioned national culture and national institutions, a dynamic business environment is also known to influence HRM in developing countries. For example, the analysis of Debrah and Budhwar (2001) suggests that in many developing countries enhancing international competitiveness in the globalized era has become a national priority. As a result, economic liberalization, deregulation and privatization feature prominently in many developing countries' restructuring programmes. Such features, brought on by globalization, have in turn initiated changes in HRM policies and practices.

Fundanga (1995), for example, asserts that many of the developing countries that have resorted to privatization share a common historical background and environmental factors. For instance, for most sub-Saharan African countries the first two decades after independence were characterized by rapid economic growth. Moreover, they enjoyed favourable terms of trade and high levels of public expenditure in infrastructure and services. The development of import-substituting industries brought in the rise of parastatal companies, and, furthermore, many governments moved to nationalize existing foreign companies in their countries and set up state enterprises to carry out various production functions as well as providing services. By the 1980s, however, most of the parastatals were in financial crisis as a result of corruption and mismanagement. The associated inefficiencies rendered most of them unprofitable and a burden on the government purse; hence the introduction of structural adjustment programmes (see Debrah and Budhwar, 2001).

The structural adjustment programmes spearheaded by the International Monetary Fund (IMF) and the World Bank were made conditional on the achievement of some specific objectives: (a) the liberalization of the economy by subjecting it to both local and international competition; (b) liberalization of domestic trade and commerce; (c) reform of physical policy; (d) reform of the financial sector; (e) reform of agriculture and industry; and (f) the reduction of physical deficit. The implementation programme has had significant impact on the management of human resources in many developing countries including those in sub-Saharan Africa. In particular, state-owned enterprises have been either closed/liquidated or privatized resulting in a substantial reduction in the number of employees and consequent job insecurity. Some other measures have been introduced to commercialize the provision of services in the public sector and have also ushered in new forms of managing employees. Many of these initiatives have found their way into HRM in the private sector in sub-Saharan Africa.

With the exception of China, perhaps, India is the country where the greatest strides have been made in recent years regarding liberalization of the economy (for details see Budhwar, 2001). The liberalization of economic policies has in turn a significant impact on HRM policies and practices. Many more countries such as Pakistan, Nepal, Iran, Saudi Arabia and Algeria have also initiated liberalization of their economic policies, and in the same way East Asian countries such as China, Taiwan and South Korea are currently undergoing restructuring.

In summary, the above discussion and examples help to identify how and why competitive pressures force firms in developing countries to restructure. This form of restructuring involves cutting costs through workforce reduction, the introduction of flexible HR strategies, downsizing, and employment restructuring. Again, the main stimulus for such HR changes is the globalization of business. As economies and firms are increasingly operating in a global market, firms have found it imperative to develop strategies to respond to competitive pressures. Hence, it is fair to conclude that globalization is indeed influencing, if not changing, the way human resources are managed in some developing countries (Debrah and Smith, 2000a).

The discussion, so far, highlights the impact of a number of factors and variables on HRM in developing countries. However, the main challenge in examining HRM in developing countries is how to delineate the impact of different factors and variables on HRM in each country. From the existing literature, the integrative framework developed by Budhwar and associates (see Budhwar and Sparrow, 1998, 2002; Budhwar and Debrah, 2001a, 2001b) to analyse HRM practices in a cross-national context can be useful in this regard. The framework asserts that the nature of HRM tends to be 'context-specific', and as such there is considerable diversity in the way 'culture-bound' and 'culture-free' factors impact on, and determine the nature of HRM systems in different countries. Consequently, in an attempt to illuminate our understanding of HRM practices in different countries, it is important to identify and analyse the main factors and variables that impinge on HRM in that country.

In brief, Budhwar and associates have identified three levels of factors and variables which are known to influence HRM policies and practices and which are worth considering for cross-national examination (see Figure 12.1). These are:

1    National factors involving national culture, national institutions, business sectors and the dynamic business environment;
2    Contingent variables including age, size, nature, ownership, life-cycle stage of the organization, presence of trade unions and HR strategies and interests of different stakeholders;
3    Organizational strategies such as the ones proposed by Miles and Snow (i.e., 'prospectors', 'analysers', 'defenders' and 'reactors') and Porter (i.e., 'cost-leadership', 'product differentiation' and 'market focus'); and policies related to primary HR functions and internal labour markets.

Budhwar (2001) has successfully adopted this framework to examine empirically HRM in the Indian context.

## Managing human resources in developing countries

The increasing globalization trend means the workplace of the twenty-first century will continue to witness the impact of global economic restructuring and liberalization. This has implications for the organization of work, employment, labour

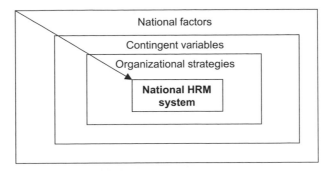

*Figure 12.1*   Factors influencing national patterns of HRM
*Source.* Budhwar and Debrah (2001b).

markets and employee/industrial relations (Chaykowski and Giles, 1998). The trend towards global integration of production and financial markets is already having immense impacts on the workplace and as a result the way human resources are managed. For instance, the recent Asian economic crisis led to some job losses not only in Asia but in other parts of the world, as Asian MNCs had to scale down, close their overseas operations or relocate operations in their home countries. Such events have serious implications for IHRM.

This is also an indication that production and employment are no longer permanently anchored to a particular physical location. As part of the process of internationalization of production, MNCs can now locate production sites at various locations around the globe and production can be relocated easily to suit company objectives (Chaykowski and Giles, 1998). Companies are now increasingly making conscious efforts to design their production and distribution systems as well as their employment strategies to meet the demands and changes in the global economy. These factors precipitate the frequent shifts in the location of employment as existing economic activities change locations and new activities are set up in such places (Peel, 1999). Thus, IHRM managers need to keep themselves updated with the scenario of HRM in different regions of the world and about the main factors which significantly influence HRM in such contexts.

Further, advances in technology have made it easier for managers to make decisions pertaining to the location of production. The internet for instance, provides avenues for organizations to create more worldwide business opportunities (Chengappa and Goyal, 2002). For instance, in order for companies located in the developed world to take advantage of lower costs they may set up accounts processing offices in developing countries or subcontract some information-processing functions to companies in developing countries (for example, India) which have advanced information technology and the necessary skilled human resources (Lamb, 2000). To be successful in such contexts, IHRM managers then need to understand the local/national dynamics (such as the social, cultural, political, legal and economic environment and the kind of internal labour markets) prevalent there that dictate the nature of HRM functions.

Moreover, globalization is making it difficult for organizations to shape employee relations policies solely in terms of a national or sub-national government jurisdiction, as some international pressure groups can exert a lot of pressure on governments to regulate some areas of employment. A case in point is the pressure on governments in some developing countries such as Pakistan to control child labour in the carpet and garments industries. Thus, with the intensification of the globalization process we are witnessing major shifts in employee relations in many developing countries (Smith and Debrah, 2000). Increasingly, these types of concerns need to be addressed by IHRM managers while developing their HR policies and practices for a specific region or a developing country.

As indicated earlier, globalization and its associated liberalization and deregulation have precipitated changes to labour markets in developing countries just as in developed countries. In the advanced economies, some writers claim there has been the near 'demise' of permanent employment with the rise of an 'insecure workforce' and the disappearance of the standard forms of employment (Heery and Salmon, 2000). Moreover, the emergence of the service economy and electronic commerce and the increasing ascendancy of information technology in the workplace have resulted in an increase in contingent workers, teleworking and other forms of the non-traditional work patterns even in developing countries (see Bezuidenhout, 2002). Thus, in developing as well as in developed countries the concept of the traditional workplace is undergoing tremendous changes both in terms of work systems and the traditional spatial ties to worksites (Chaykowski and Giles, 1998). However, the existing literature provides a far from comprehensive picture of such developments in developing countries; it is still not clear whether it is only the deregulation/liberalization of economies which is forcing such changes, or if there are other contributing factors (Debrah and Budhwar, 2001).

The pressures for change in developing countries as a result of globalization and international competitiveness require organizations to adopt strategic and proactive approaches to HRM (as happened in the USA and the UK). But, with the exception of countries such as Taiwan, South Korea and to some extent India, where HR departments are involved in the formulation of business strategies and HR is closely linked to business strategy, there is no clear evidence regarding a movement in this direction in the majority of developing countries (see Debrah and Budhwar, 2001). This is not very surprising as most developing countries have not fully embraced an integrated and focused approach to HRM. Still in the majority of developing countries, personnel management (PM) and HRM are used interchangeably (this is the kind of scenario which existed in the USA and the UK in the 1980s), but often implying a bureaucratic PM system. This is particularly more so in the public sector than in the private sector, where the traditional role of administration is prevalent. Within the private sector the MNCs are more inclined to adopt a strategic HRM approach than local firms (see Venkata Ratnam, 1998, for an example of this in the Indian context). In the few local firms that have made attempts towards adopting an HRM approach, the whole function has been broadened but not fully integrated into corporate strategy. However, the status and profile of the HR role is being elevated and brought to par (now HR is also represented at the board level along with other functions) with other business areas such as finance or production. For example, Khilji (2001) asserts that this is happening in Pakistan. Similarly, some organizations in Pakistan have adopted 'pay-for-performance', 'management-by-objectives' and 'open appraisal systems'.

These progressive developments are in sharp contrast to what exists in Algeria. According to Branine (2001), the management of employees in Algeria can best be described as personnel administration rather than HRM. This is because at present there is no clear evidence of personnel managers' involvement in strategic decision-making or in policy formulation in Algeria. Consequently, the formal role of the personnel department does not go beyond the administration of employees' files and record-keeping and the monitoring of complicated bureaucratic procedures.

Kamoche (2001) paints a similar picture with respect to his discussion of the lack of strategy in HRM in Kenyan organizations. In particular, he mentions the perceived reluctance of Kenyan managers to engage in long-term strategic planning, which he attributes to the entrenched nature of a short-term bureaucratic personnel management tradition in sub-Saharan Africa. In this respect, what is happening in Kenya is not very different from what is happening in Ghana and Nigeria. The South African case, however, is a bit unconventional in African terms because large organizations can claim to be practising HRM whilst the local enterprises cannot do so.

In China, Warner (2001) asserts that PM is basically a bureaucratic device to run the large state-owned enterprises. It is basically concerned with 'bread-and-butter' activities of recruitment and selection, reward systems, disciplinary procedures, and so on. He adds that this older form of PM practices is still more common in Chinese enterprises and in other organizations where a decidedly conservative air continues to permeate the administration of personnel. Moreover, PM is still more widely relied on in many joint ventures (JVs), whilst is mainly only in the large JVs and wholly-owned MNCs in China, particularly those with expatriate HR managers, that elements of an HRM approach are present.

On the other hand, in India the nature of the HRM function seems to be changing at a much more rapid pace, mainly due to the pressures created by the liberalization of economic policies (see Budhwar, 2001). HRM is playing a noticeable role in bringing about change in Indian organizations, but, unlike the West, human resource development (HRD) is the preferred term for the personnel function. The rapid growth and usage of the term HRD in India is an outcome of the pressures created by foreign operators (who are equipped with better resources) on local organizations. There is, thus, a strong emphasis on the development of human resources (Sparrow and Budhwar, 1997).

It is clear from the above discussion that economic globalization has created significant opportunities for some developing countries, many of which have a comparative advantage in terms of labour costs, land costs, and overall operating costs (Zimmerer *et al.*, 1998). In developing countries, MNCs and FDI create employment opportunities. However, although like local firms they are a vital source of employment, because of increasing economic globalization and the ease with which firms can relocate their production plants, they can also quickly put workers at a particular location out of jobs. Thus, foreign firms operating in developing countries need to develop proactive policies in order to tap the benefits of globalization to workers and to minimize its detrimental effects on employment. Essentially, organizations must respond proactively to the external environmental pressures by developing internal HR policies and practices capable of tapping the benefits of globalization. Based on evidence from India (see Budhwar, 2001) and Taiwan (see Huang, 2001), we argue that organizations in other developing countries have a greater chance of doing so if they move away from traditional PM practices and embrace HRM.

This is necessary because liberalization and structural adjustment policies are aimed at increasing productivity, reducing costs, improving quality and reducing overmanning (downsizing). Further, globalization and its associated international competitive pressures have forced the implementation of a number of new work systems into developing countries. These include the introduction of flexibility of operations, contingent reward systems and lean-production methodologies to underpin efficiency. All these are leading to new challenges for the HR function in general and with regard to industrial relations policy and practice in particular in developing countries (see Veersma, 1995). Still, it will not be sensible to generalize such developments to all developing countries, as the level of economic growth and developments in the HR function are at different stages in different countries. Moreover, the interplay of the main factors and variables which are known to influence HRM in different contexts (see Figure 12.1) also varies from country to country (see Budhwar and Sparrow, 2002). For example, the response of unions to common competitive pressures (such as the introduction of new production technologies, large-scale restructuring and re-engineering of organizations and pressure to increase work flexibility) varies across different countries. However, the discussion of the above issues is useful to both researchers and practitioners in the field of IHRM as it indicates the direction in which things are moving in developing countries.

Moreover, the rapid developments and the increased reliance on IT in organizations means that HR managers working in developing countries should be ready to develop appropriate HR strategies to cope with the subsequent deskilling, reskilling and multiskilling problems, workforce reduction and retention as well as career development (see for example James, 2002). These have significant implications on the management of employees and require organizations to adopt strategic initiatives and policies and to integrate HR strategies into their overall business strategies. With the current bureaucratic PM practices which prevail in most developing countries, it is unlikely that organizations can effectively utilize their human resources to achieve competitive advantage. Developing countries, then, must transform their PM into HRM. MNCs with established HRM systems can play and are playing a significant role in this regard by transferring such practices to developing countries (Luo, 2001). However, to be more successful they need to consider seriously the local context while implementing such systems.

Looking at the way national factors impact on HRM, the above discussion reveals that in some situations common or similar national factors impact in almost the same way on HRM practices in different developing countries. Of interest here is the manifold impact of religion and traditional cultures on HRM in developing countries. This is a useful note for IHRM researchers and practitioners The framework discussed in this chapter (Figure 12.1) covers various aspects of national factors which can be adopted to examine their impact on HRM in developing countries.

Moreover, employee-relations practices within present-day organizations including internal labour market (ILM) structures in most developing countries are dictated by factors such as social and cultural values, religious beliefs, caste/ethnic-based stratification, political affiliation and economic power. Such types of ILMs result in a decrease in organizational performance and breeds corruption and red-tapism. In the context of the changes taking place in most developing countries in terms of privatization and structural adjustment programmes, there is now a strong need for HRM systems in those countries to be consistent with rationalized, objective and systematic employment systems. This is already happening in some countries such as India, but there is a strong need to speed up the process in other countries.

Most developing nations have established legal structures in the form of relevant labour laws to safeguard the interests of employees. However, in many cases the provisions of the labour laws are not at all seriously implemented which results in the exploitation of employees. Child labour and minimum-wage laws are typical examples. Relevant law-enforcing agencies in developing countries need to ensure serious implementation of such provisions. Moreover, many developing countries do not actively promote equal opportunities hence the existence of disadvantage on the grounds of ethnicity, gender and age. It would be useful for IHRM managers to develop policies accordingly to tackle these problems.

Moreover, as the global economy expands and competition intensifies, unions in developing countries (for example, Africa) need to shed their confrontational attitude, which served them well in the independence struggles during the colonial period, and adopt a more positive and cooperative role. There is also the need for governments in developing countries to curtail if not uproot political influence on trade unions. Trade unions need to be strategic partners with business and industry in order to enhance the competitiveness of their organizations. IHRM managers, especially from developed countries, are aware of the benefits of such alliances in helping to build trust between the key actors of the firm.

There is also a need to make amendments in the existing labour laws in developing countries, some of which, as in India, are less relevant for the current business environment. With the privatization and structural adjustment programmes in place, there is a need to downsize organizations, but the existing labour laws do not allow such a transition. Moreover, there are no established policies for early retirements to facilitate the process of rationalizing the workforce in many developing countries. All such issues create massive challenges for HRM in those countries.

---

### Box 12.1  Globalization and the human resource development of professionals: the case of the construction industry in Tanzania*

Globalization and international competitive pressures are not new, but a new spate of economic liberalization in sub-Saharan Africa is perhaps an indication of the far-reaching effects of globalization and its accompanying international competitiveness (Turner and Holman, 2000). Since the early 1980s, the World Bank and the International Monetary Fund (IMF) have been urging sub-Saharan African governments to develop and implement structural adjustment programmes (SAPs) to turn around their near-bankrupt economies.

One country which has achieved positive results from SAPs is Tanzania. Since 1986, Tanzania has pursued an economic reform and recovery programme aimed at restoring macro-economic stability. The SAPs were initially focused on market liberalization, exchange-rate adjustment and the elimination of fiscal imbalances, but in recent years the structural reforms have been broadened with a view to accelerating economic growth and to lay the foundations for reducing poverty (Mbaku, 1999).

The Tanzanian case is all the more interesting because of its past history of socialism. In the grand economic transformation programme, the private sector has replaced the public sector as the engine of growth. Equally, socialism has given way to a market economy. The Tanzanian economic liberalization (including privatization) programme is considered successful by informed observers (IHT, 1997; *Financial Times*, 2000), and Tanzania is apparently beginning to emerge as a potential role model in economic restructuring for sub-Saharan Africa. In the words of Turner (2000: xiii):

*Once the standard-bearer of African Socialism, Tanzania's leadership today embraces foreign investors and is rapidly selling off public companies.*

Similarly, the African Development Bank (ADB) praises Tanzania's economic liberalization and development achievements. According to the ADB (1999), the reform

*Continued*

---

* This case study has been prepared from notes arising from research fieldwork conducted by George Ofori and Yaw A. Debrah (Ofori and Debrah, 2002). Fictitious names and positions (posts) have been used, and the names of the Tanzanian organizations that participated in the study have been changed to preserve confidentiality.

programme has largely succeeded in restoring macro-economic equilibrium, making it possible for Tanzania to continue to attract much needed donor support and foreign direct investment (FDI).

The initiation of the economic liberalization programme was due not only to IMF and World Bank pressure, but also to other external environmental pressures that created a fierce competitive environment for Tanzanian organizations. One source of such pressure has been the recently re-established East African Community (EAC), the aim of which is to promote a people-centred economic, political, social and cultural development in all member states. The EAC is actively involved in trade promotion, reduction of trade imbalances and the establishment of a single market and investment area. Tanzania is also a member of the Southern African Development Community (SADC), the aim of which is to foster closer economic and monetary ties through joint infrastructure projects, the harmonization of fiscal, monetary and investment policies, and the creation of a customs union (EADB, 1999).

Quite apart from these, the end of socialism has ushered in opportunities for major global or transnational organizations to do business in Tanzania. Thus, the globalization and regionalization activities in East and Southern Africa pose both threats and challenges for organizations in Tanzania. Tanzanian organizations need to develop strategies to deal with the threats and respond to the challenges but they feel that they cannot do so effectively without the help of government. On this issue, the ADB comments that:

> the challenge is for Tanzania to exploit fully the opportunities presented by regional integration by improving its competitiveness which would in turn enhance its capacity to compete in global market. 1999: 16

One way to improve the competitiveness of companies is to develop effective HRM strategies and, in particular, to equip the people with the skills and competencies needed to exploit the emerging opportunities. In the Tanzanian construction industry, however, there is apprehension that professionals such as architects, quantity surveyors and engineers do not have the skills, knowledge and competencies to enable their companies to compete with international firms. Professionals provide the driving force in the efforts of firms to create and sustain competitive advantage, but in the case of Tanzania the ability of personnel to contribute to organizational effectiveness is being threatened by the rapidity of technical, social and economic changes and, consequently, the obsolescence of their knowledge, competencies and skills. Francis Mapunda, the Chief Executive of the National Construction Industry Development Board, a strong advocate of effective HRD programmes for construction workers in general, but professionals in particular, is determined to tackle this problem.

Mr Mapunda points out that the construction industry in Tanzania plays an important role in the economy as well as in national development. However, he laments the lack of a systematic and sustainable HRD programme for professionals. This is in spite of the impact of competitive pressures arising from globalization, regionalization, increased domestic competition, technological changes, economic liberalization and restructuring, commercialization and privatization of public enterprises in the Tanzanian construction

*Continued*

industry. The existing HRD programmes are: fragmented (each profession and trade organization has its own programme); lack overall strategy and continuity; lack coordination; lack sustainable funding; are dependent on funding by foreign donor agencies; and lack accreditation or national recognition systems. Consequently, professionals in the industry face many challenges relating to the practitioners' lack of preparedness to work in a dynamic environment (Ofori and Debrah, 2002).

A direct result of this is that, in recent years, Tanzanian construction consultancy firms are facing an uphill battle in competing with foreign firms for contracts in Tanzania. With the opening-up of Tanzanian markets, professional construction firms from South Africa, Kenya, Europe, China and further afield have increased their operations in Tanzania and, as such, Tanzanian firms are facing increasing competition. In many instances the foreign firms win tenders for projects and this has led Tanzanian professionals to assess their unfavourable competitive position.

A report recently prepared by a consultant for the Commonwealth Secretariat attributes the uncompetitiveness of Tanzanian firms to their lack of experience in operating in a market economy. It asserts that during the years of socialism many professionals worked in state-owned enterprises, but with the dismantling of socialism, the implementation of SAPs and the liberalization of the economy, and the privatization of public enterprises, many professionals lost their jobs in the public sector, subsequently setting up consultancies to provide professional services. It is further asserted that although many of these professionals possessed the necessary technical qualifications, they were ill-equipped for the competitive world of private enterprise. It is argued that for these professionals to compete effectively in a market economy, they need to acquire managerial skills in marketing, financial management, business management, time management, quality management, contract management and information technology among others. Mr Alfred Nyanza, Chairman of the Tanzanian Association of Construction Industry Consultants, also argues that there is a need for professionals to have a post-qualification training programme to improve their performance, update their skills and avoid technological and managerial obsolescence.

It is against this background that the NCIDB is advocating for the institution of a mandatory structured Continuing Professional Development (CPD) programme in Tanzania. In addition, the NCIDB is exploring the possibility of government assistance in setting up a sustainable funding mechanism and framework for a post-qualification HRD programme for professionals in the industry. There is a general consensus in the industry that such a programme is necessary to enhance the competitiveness of Tanzanian professional consultancy firms in the era of globalization.

# Conclusion

This chapter has argued that there is a dearth of literature on IHRM in developing countries, and in view of this has provided some compelling arguments why HRM academics and practitioners need to know more about HRM issues in such countries. In particular, the chapter has highlighted the HRM implications of the increase in FDI in developing countries in recent years. It has also illuminated our understanding of the levels of globalization of businesses and the accompanying international competitiveness in developing countries which are putting pressures on managers to develop appropriate HRM responses.

In line with this view, it is asserted that globalization and its accompanying economic liberalization have been the driving force behind the transformation of HRM in developing countries. Just as in developed countries, globalization is a double-edged sword. It provides opportunities for managers to overhaul their antiquated HRM practices and adopt modern ones that are capable of dealing with the threats and opportunities in the organizational environment. But at the same time globalization can spell doom for employees as organizations react to competitive pressures by cutting jobs, restructuring and thus creating insecurity in the workplace. Such an environment has the potential to undermine employee commitment and loyalty, particularly in instances where there are constant violations of psychological contracts. It is therefore argued that organizations in developing countries need to adopt a strategic HRM approach which seeks to balance employee well-being against the interest of the organization. In other words, managers in developing countries should develop an environment where issues of trust and organizational justice are taken seriously.

## Discussion questions

1 Discuss the main reasons why both IHRM researchers and practitioners need to examine HRM in developing countries?
2 Highlight the possible factors and variables, which can influence HRM in developing countries? Provide examples of some developing countries and the main factors which are known to determine HRM systems in those countries.
3 What are the key messages coming from this chapter for both IHRM researchers and practitioners regarding managing human resources in developing countries? Identify and discuss.

## Further reading

Budhwar, P. and Debrah, Y.A. (eds) (2001) *Human Resource Management in Developing Countries*. London: Routledge.
Budhwar, P. and Sparrow, P. (2002) 'An Integrative Framework for Determining Cross National Human Resource Management Practices' *Human Resource Management Review*, 12(3): 377–403.
Jaeger, A.M. and Kanungo, R.N. (eds) (1990) *Management in Developing Countries*. New York: Routledge.
Warner, M. (ed.) (2000) *Regional Encyclopaedia of Business and Management: Management in the Emerging Countries*. London: Thomson Learning Business Press.

## References

*Academy of Management Journal* (2000) Special Research Forum on Emerging Economies, 43(3).
Adhikari, D. and Muller, M. (2001) 'Human Resource Management in Nepal', in P. Budhwar and Y. Debrah (eds), *Human Resource Management in Developing Countries*. London: Routledge, 91–101.

African Development Bank (1999) 'United Republic of Tanzania: Country Strategy Paper 1999–2001', ADB, Abidjan: Côte d'Ivoire.

Austin, J.E. (1990) *Managing in Developing Countries*. New York: Free Press.

Branine, M. (2001) 'Human Resource Management in Algeria', in P. Budhwar and Y. Debrah (eds), *Human Resource Management in Developing Countries*. London: Routledge, 155–73.

Bezuidenhout, A. (2002) ' "What we do" or "Who we are"? Trade Union Responses to Globalization and Regionalization in South Africa', in Y.A. Debrah and I.G. Smith (eds), *Globalization, Employment and the Workplace: Diverse Impacts*. London: Routledge, 85–114.

Budhwar, P. (2001) 'Human Resource Management in India' in. P. Budhwar and Y. Debrah (eds), *Human Resource Management in Developing Countries*. London: Routledge, 75–90.

Budhwar, P. and Debrah, Y. A. (2001a) 'Rethinking Comparative and Cross National Human Resource Management Research', *International Journal of Human Resource Management*, 12(3): 497–515.

Budhwar, P. and Debrah, Y.A. (2001b) (eds) *Human Resource Management in Developing Countries*. London: Routledge.

Budhwar, P. and Sparrow, P. (1998) 'National Factors Determining Indian and British HRM Practices: An Empirical Study', *Management International Review*, 38, Special Issue 2, 105–21.

Budhwar, P. and Sparrow, P. (2002) 'An Integrative Framework for Determining Cross National Human Resource Management Practices', *Human Resource Management Review*, 12(3): 377–403.

Chaykowski, R. and Giles, A. (1998) 'Globalisation, Work and Industrial Relations', *Relations Industrielles – Industrial Relations*, 53(1): 3–12.

Chen, M. (1995) *Asian Management Systems: Chinese, Japanese and Korean Styles of Business*. London: Routledge.

Chengappa, R. and Goyal, M. (2002) 'House Keepers to the World', *India Today*, November: 18–48.

Clark, T., Gospel, H. and Montgomery, J. (1999) 'Running on the Spot? A Review of Twenty Years of Research on the Management of Human Resources in Comparative and International Perspective', *International Journal of Human Resource Management*, 10(3): 520–44.

Das, S.P. (2002) 'Foreign Direct Investment and the Relative Wage in a Developing Economy', *Journal of Development Economics*, 67(1): 55–77.

Debrah, Y.A. (2000) 'Management in Ghana, in M. Warner (ed.), *Management in Emerging Countries*. London: Thomson Learning, 189–97.

Debrah, Y.A. and Budhwar, P. (2001) 'Conclusion: International Competitive Pressures and the Challenges for HRM in Developing Countries, in P. Budhwar and Debrah, Y. (eds), *Human Resource Management in Developing Countries*. London: Routledge, 75–90.

Debrah, Y. A., McGovern, I. and Budhwar, P. (2000) 'Complementarity or Competition: The Development of Human Resources in a Growth Triangle', *International Journal of Human Resource Management*, 11(2): 314–35.

Debrah, Y.A. and Smith, I.G. (2000a) 'Globalization and the Changing Nature of Employment', *International Journal of Manpower*, 21(6): 446–51.

Debrah, Y.A. and Smith, I.G. (2000b) 'Introduction: Work and Employment in a Globalized Era', *Asia Pacific Business Review*, 7(1): 1–20.

Dowling, P.J., Welch, D.E. and Schuler, R.S. (1999) *International Dimensions of Human Resource Management*, 3rd edn. Cincinnati, OH: Southwestern College Publishing.

EADB (1999) 'East African Development Bank, Annual Report and Accounts', Kampala: Uganda EADB.

*Financial Times* (2000) '*Financial Times* Survey: Tanzania', July 24.

Frenkel, S. and Peetz, D., (1998) 'Globalisation and Industrial Relations in East Asia: A Three Country Comparison', *Industrial Relations*, 37(3): 282–311.

Fundanga, C.M. (1995) *Privatization of Public Enterprises: Theory and Practice*, London: Cassel.

Gardiner, K. (1996) 'Managing in Different Cultures: The Case of Ghana, in B. Towers (ed.), *The Handbook of Human Resource Management*. Oxford: Blackwell, 488–510.

Garten, J.E. (1996) 'The Big Emerging Markets', *Columbia Journal of World Business*, Summer, 7–31.

Heery, E and Salmon, J. (2000) 'The Insecurity Thesis', in E. Heery and J. Salmon (eds), *The Insecure Workforce*. London: Routledge.

Hill, C.W.L. (2001) *International Business*. New York and London: Irwin McGraw-Hill.

Hofstede, G. (1993) 'Cultural constraints in Management Theories', *Academy of Management Executive*, 7(1): 81–94.

Huang, T.C. (2001) 'Human Resource Management in Taiwan', in. P. Budhwar and Y. Debrah (eds), *Human Resource Management in Developing Countries*. London: Routledge, 56–74.

IHT (1997) 'Tanzania', *International Herald Tribune*, 8 December: pp. 12–13.

Jaeger, A.M. and Kanungo, R.N. (1990) (ed.) *Management in Developing Countries*. New York: Routledge.

James, J. (2002) 'The Human Development Report 2001 and Information Technology for Developing Countries: An Evaluation', *International Journal of Technology Management*, 23(6): 643–52.

*Journal of International Business Studies* (2001) 'Symposium: The Impact of Developing Economies and Economies in Transition of the Future of International Business', 32(1).

Kamoche, K. (1993) 'Towards a Model of HRM in Africa', in J. B. Shaw, P. S. Kirkbride and K. M. Rowlands (eds) *Research in Personnel and Human Resource Management*. Supplement 3, Greenwich, CT: JAI Press.

Kamoche, K. (2001) 'Human Resource Management in Kenya', in P. Budhwar and Y. Debrah (eds), *Human Resource Management in Developing Countries*. London: Routledge, 209–21.

Kanungo, R.N. (1995) (ed.) *Employee Management in Developing Countries*. Greenwich, London: JAI Press.

Kanungo, R.N. (2000) 'Business Culture, The Emerging Countries', in M. Warner (ed.), *Regional Encyclopaedia of Business and Management: Management in the Emerging Countries*. London: Thomson Learning Business Press, 60–7.

Khilji, S. (2001) 'Human Resource Management in Pakistan', in P. Budhwar and Y. Debrah (eds), *Human Resource Management in Developing Countries*. London: Routledge, 102–20.

Kiggundu, M.N. (1989) *Managing Organizations in Developing Countries*. West Hartford CT: Kumarian Press.

Kiggundu, M.N., Jorgensen, J.J. and Hafsi, T. (1983) 'Administrative Theory and Practice in Developing Countries: A Synthesis', *Administrative Science Quarterly*, 28, 66–84.

Kohn, T.O. and Austin, J.E. (2000) 'Management in Emerging Countries', in M. Warner (ed.) *Management in Emerging Countries*. London: Thomson Learning, 9–25.

Lamb, J. (2000) 'Recruiters Turn to India for IT Expertise as Skills Crisis Bites', *People Management*, August.

Legge, K. (1995) *Human Resource Management: Rhetorics and Realities*. Chippenham: MacMillan Business.

Luo, Y. (2001) 'Determinants of Local Responsiveness: Perspectives from Foreign Subsidiaries in an Emerging Market', *Journal of Management*, 27(4): 451–77.

Mbaku, J.M. (1999) 'A Balance Sheet of Structural Adjustment in Africa: Towards a Sustainable Development Agenda', in J. M. Mbaku (ed.), *Preparing Africa for the Twenty-First Century: Strategies for Peaceful Coexistence and Sustainable Development*. Aldershot: Ashgate, 119–49.

McGaughey, S.L. and De Cerie, H. (1999) 'Reassessment of Convergence and Divergence Dynamics: Implications for International HRM', *International Journal of Human Resource Management*, 10(2): 235–50.

Mendonca, M. (2000) 'Human Resource Management in the Emerging Countries', *Regional Encyclopaedia of Business and Management: Management in the Emerging Countries*. London: Thomson Learning Business Press, 86–94.

Napier, N.K. and Vu, V.T. (1998) 'International Human Resource Management in Developing and Transitional Economy Countries: A Breed Apart?' *Human Resource Management Review*, 8(1): 39–77.

Ofori, G. and Debrah, Y.A. (2002) *Establishing a Sustainable Funding Mechanism for Training Professionals in the Construction Industry in Tanzania*. Report Submitted to the Commonwealth Secretariat, London.

Peel, Q. (1999) 'Walls of the World Come Tumbling Down', *Financial Times Survey: The Millennium – Part 1*, Monday, 6 December: 1.

Poole, M. and Warner, M. (1998) (eds) *The IEBM Handbook of Human Resource Management*. London: International Thomson Business.

Schuler, R.S., Budhwar, P. and Florkowski, G.W. (2002) 'International Human Resource Management: Review and Critique', *International Journal of Management Reviews*, 4(1): 41–70.

Schuler, R.S. and Jackson, S.E. (1999) (eds.) *Strategic Human Resource Management*. London: Blackwell.

Sisson, K. and Storey, J. (2000) *The Realities of Human Resource Management*. Buckingham: Open University.

Smith, I.G. and Debrah, Y.A. (2000) 'Conclusion: Globalization, Work and Employment in the Asia-Pacific Region', *Asia Pacific Business Review*, 7(1): 239–54.

Sparrow, P.R. and Budhwar, P. (1997) 'Competition and Change: Mapping The Indian HRM Recipe Against World Wide Patterns', *Journal of World Business*, 32(3): 224–42.

Turner, M. (2000) 'Tanzania: A sub-Saharan Success Story', *Financial Times*, World Economy (Africa), 23 September, XIII.

Turner, M. and Holman, M. (2000) 'Coming Out of the Shadows', *Financial Times* Survey: Tanzania, 24 July, 1.

UNCTAD (1999) *World Investment Report 1999*. http//www.unctad.org

United Nations (1998) *World Investment Report 1998: Trends and Determinants*. New York: United Nations.

Veersma, O. (1995) 'Multinational Corporations and Industrial Relations', in A. Harzing and J. Van Russeyveldt (eds), *International Human Resource Management*. London: Sage, 318–36.

Venkata Ratnam, C.S. (1998) 'Multinational Companies in India', *International Journal of Human Resource Management*, 9(4): 567–89.

Warner, M. (2000) (ed.) *Regional Encyclopaedia of Business and Management: Management in the Emerging Countries*. London: Thomson Learning Business Press.

Warner, M. (2001) 'Human Resource Management in the People's Republic of China', in P. Budhwar and Y. Debrah (eds), *Human Resource Management in Developing Countries*. London: Routledge, 19–33.

Won Woo, P. (2001) 'Human Resource Management in South Korea', in P. Budhwar and Y. Debrah (eds), *Human Resource Management in Developing Countries*. London: Routledge, 34–55.

Zimmerer, T.W,, Alavi, J and Yasin, M.M (1998) 'Developing Countries' Strategic Opportunities', *Thunderbird International Business Review*, 40(3): 315–31.

# part 4

# Emerging issues in international HRM

# 13

# Shaping history: global leadership in the twenty-first century

*Nancy J. Adler*

We have a responsibility in our time, as others have had in theirs, not to be prisoners of history, but to shape history ... (Former US Secretary of State Madeleine K. Albright, 1997)

Shaping history; that is the challenge of global leadership – creating a twenty-first century in which our organizations and the societies in which they operate enhance, rather than diminish, civilization. For global leaders, economic viability is necessary, but no longer sufficient for organizational, let alone societal, success.

Success; none of us can claim that the twentieth century exited at the level of success we might aspire to, a success defined by peace, prosperity, compassion and sustainability. As we ask ourselves which of the twentieth century's legacies we wish to pass on to the children of the twenty-first century, we are humbled into shameful silence. Yes, we have advanced science and technology, but at the price of a world torn asunder by a polluted environment, cities infested with social chaos and physical decay, an increasingly skewed income distribution that condemns large portions of the population to poverty (including people living in the world's most affluent societies), and rampant physical violence continuing to kill people in titularly limited wars and seemingly random acts of aggression. No, we did not exit the twentieth century with pride. Unless we collectively learn to treat each other and our planet in a more civilized way, it may soon become blasphemy to even consider ourselves a civilization (Rechtschaffen, 1996).

## Entering the twenty-first century

As the twentieth century becomes history, do the events of the opening years of the twenty-first century encourage us? Unfortunately, no. If anything, many economic and societal trends appear to be heading in the wrong direction. We need look no further than the events of September 2001 to be humbled into silence, if not despair. Review just a few of the facts from that tragic month.

September 2001 opened with the UN-sponsored World Conference Against Racism in Durban, South Africa.[1] As the world watched with high expectations, the conference drowned in a cacophony of intolerance, expressed by official delegates from more than 160 countries as well as by thousands of representatives of non-governmental organizations. 'The meeting, which was intended to celebrate tolerance and diversity, became an international symbol of disiveness ... (Swarns, 2001: A1)'. According to the world press, the results reflected 'less a new international unity than a collective exhaustion' (Slackman, 2001: A1).

One week later, on 11 September, terrorists destroyed the World Trade Centre and parts of the Pentagon, killing over 3,000 people. In the immediate aftermath, while stockmarkets plummeted, public rhetoric and behaviour became increasingly susceptible to simplistic definitions of good and evil and calls for large-scale military retaliation. The escalation of ignorance-based hatred attempting to pit the Western world against Islamic communities and nations became palpable. Perhaps the danger, absurdity and pain can be best symbolized by the fate of a woman living far from both Durban and the World Trade Centre. As the woman, a Montreal doctor, made her usual hospital rounds the week after the terrorist attacks, she was strangled. Why? Strictly because she was Muslim. Her status as a physician and good citizen, working daily to save the lives of her fellow human beings, was obliterated in the eyes of her attacker solely because she practiced a religion he failed to understand.

Hate and intolerance, optimism reduced to hopelessness, compassion eclipsed by anger, ignorance motivating senseless action: is this the scenario that will define the twenty-first century; that will define our children's future? Possibly, but hopefully not. Hope for a better outcome rests largely with the quality of business, political and societal leadership offered by women and men worldwide.

Although from the perspective of September 2001 it seems otherwise, the twenty-first century need not become just a time of terrorism, intolerance, fear and deteriorating economic conditions. It also could herald an era of unprecedented global communication, global contact and global commerce; led in large part by global companies and organizations (Friedman, 2000). The ability of global companies to work successfully across cultures, however, while better than the track record of participants at UN-racism conferences, remains humbling. Historically, three-quarters of all international joint ventures fail.[2] One wonders, at times, why societies choose to continue to become more globally interconnected and companies to continue to expand beyond their borders, when the track record of global cross-cultural relations remains so dismal.[3] Weaving the peoples of the world together, whether in companies or in society at large, is clearly not easy. Our current approaches beg for new – or perhaps ancient but forgotten – perspectives. Is it not possible to imagine a world defined by peace and prosperity in the twenty-first century; to imagine a global civilization that we could bequeath with pride to our children and our children's children? Would not our wisest global leaders know how to guide us in creating such a world. Naïvely idealistic? Perhaps, but not historically. Such visionary leadership only appears naïve from the parochial perspective of the last 9,000 years.

As archaeologists and other scholars have observed, there have always been legends and writings about an earlier, more harmonious and peaceful age (Eisler, 1987).[4] The Bible, for example, tells us of the Garden of Eden. But many, if not most people assume that these are only idyllic fantasies, expressing universal yearnings for seemingly impossible goals. Only now, thanks to new scientific dating methods and specific findings, are archaeologists exposing the actual facts, rather than the myths and fantasies, of our distant past (Gimbutas, 1991).

New excavations reveal that these supposed legends derive not from idealistic fantasies, but from folk memories about real flesh and blood people who organized their societies along very different lines from our own. At Chatal Huyuk and Hajilar, for example, both located in modern-day Turkey, archaeologists date communities to 7,000 BC, 90 centuries ago. These communities were located in the middle of fertile plains, not in defensible positions against stone cliffs or atop mountains, nor surrounded by moats, walls or other defense systems. Their art, moreover, shows no sign of either individual or community-level violence. Excavations reveal only minimal indications of hierarchy.

Just as Columbus' discovery that the world was not flat made it possible for our ancestors to 'find' a world that, in fact, had been here all along, the archaeologists' new findings allow us to rediscover prosperous communities that were organized peacefully and cooperatively with their neighbours (Eisler, 1987). Their recent findings allow us to ground supposedly naïve, unattainable idealism in the reality of history. Perhaps not coincidentally, women led most of these communities.

## Is such a world possible again?

What would it take to remarry such idealism with contemporary global realities? First, we would need to again believe that prosperity and a civilized way of living together on this planet are possible; that twenty-first century humanity is capable of success, broadly defined. To that end, the archaeologists' findings are crucial. We know that we achieved such success once; the only question is if we can achieve it again in this century. Second, we would need to believe that change is possible; that society is capable of moving from a world organized around war and violence, the extremes of poverty and wealth, and an overall mentality of scarcity to one organized around peace, prosperity, compassion and abundance. And third, we would need to move from discrete local perspectives to broadly encompassing global perspectives. We would need to move away from divisiveness and return to more unifying images and strategies. For humanity to embrace each of the beliefs needed to create a healthy, economically vibrant and sustainable global society, we would need approaches to leadership that differ quite markedly from those offered by most leaders in recent history.

Where are we to find leaders to guide us towards such beliefs that differ so distinctly from those of the recent past? While most societal commentators continue to review men's historic patterns of leadership in search of models for twenty-first century success, few have begun to recognize, let alone appreciate, the equivalent patterns of historic and potential future contributions of women leaders. What could the world's women leaders bring to society? Have we begun to enter an era in which both male and female leaders – rather than just men alone – will literally and symbolically 'shape history'?

## Women leading countries and companies: no longer men alone

While rarely recognized or reported in the media, the trend towards women joining men in senior leadership began in the twentieth century and now, in the twenty-first century, has become inescapable. The pattern is easiest to see when observing leaders of countries. Whereas in the past almost all political leaders were men, the number of women selected to serve as president or prime minister of their country in the last half century has increased markedly, albeit from a negligible starting point. As highlighted in Figure 13.1, no women presidents or prime ministers came into office in the 1950s, just three came into office in the 1960s, five in the 1970s, eight in the 1980s, and 31 in the 1990s. The number of women serving their country at the highest level of political leadership has increased by almost 100 per cent in just the last decade. As listed in Table 13.1, countries as dissimilar as France, India, and Rwanda have all selected women to lead them. While the increase is impressive, the total is not. Given that there are more than 185 countries in the world, many with both a president and a prime minister, and each with multiple leaders over the past 50 years, a total of 47 women in a half century is neither a large nor impressive number.

Are the increasing numbers a new trend? Yes. Among the 47 women leaders, 85 per cent are 'firsts,' the first woman whom their particular country has ever selected to lead them. Take Ruth Dreifuss, for example, who became President of Switzerland in 1999 after a 700-year history of male-led democracy. Among the women who are not 'firsts' – those who followed another woman into office – all seven took office in just the last decade. As can be gathered from Table 13.1, the countries that have selected a second woman to lead them (and, to date, no country has ever selected more than two women) represent a culturally, geographically and economically very diverse group of nations; including Bangladesh, Bermuda, Haiti, Ireland, New Zealand and Sri Lanka.[5]

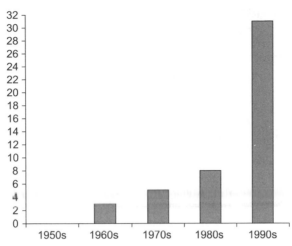

*Figure 13.1*   Increase in women political leaders in the last half of the twentieth century

*Table 13.1*   A chronology of women political leaders

| Country | Name/Date | Office |
|---|---|---|
| Sri Lanka | Sirimavo Bandaranaike<br>1960–65; 1970–77, 1994–2000 | Prime Minister |
| India | Indira Gandhi<br>1966–77; 1980–84 | Prime Minister |
| Israel | Golda Meir<br>1969–75 | Prime Minister |
| Argentina | (Maria Estela [Isabel]<br>Martínez de Perón)<br>1974–76 | President |
| Central African Rep. | Elizabeth Domitien<br>1975–76 | Prime Minister |
| Netherlands Antilles | Lucinda da Costa Gomez<br>Matheeuws<br>1977 | Prime Minister |
| Portugal | Maria de Lourdes Pintasilgo<br>1979 | Prime Minister |
| Bolivia | Lidia Gueiler Tejada<br>1979–80 | Interim President |
| Great Britain | Margaret Thatcher<br>1979–90 | Prime Minister |
| Dominica | Mary Eugenia Charles<br>1980–95 | Prime Minister |
| Iceland | Vigdís Finnbógadottir<br>1980–96 | President |
| Norway | Gro Harlem Brundtland<br>1981; 1986–89; 1990–96 | Prime Minister |

*Table 13.1*   *Continued*

| Country | Name/Date | Office |
|---|---|---|
| Yugoslavia | Milka Planinc 1982–86 | Prime Minister |
| Malta | Agatha Barbara 1982–87 | President |
| Netherlands Antilles | Maria Liberia-Peters 1984; 1989–94 | Prime Minister |
| The Philippines | Corazon Aquino 1986–92 | President |
| Pakistan | Benazir Bhutto 1988–90; 1993–96 | Prime Minister |
| Lithuania | Kazimiera-Danute Prunskiene 1990–91 | Prime Minister |
| Haiti | Ertha Pascal-Trouillot 1990–91 | President |
| Burma (Myanmar) | Aung San Suu Kyi 1990–** | Opposition Leader** |
| East Germany | Sabine Bergmann-Pohl 1990 | President of the Parliament |
| Ireland | Mary Robinson 1990–97 | President |
| Nicaragua | Violeta Barrios de Chamorro 1990–96 | President |
| Bangladesh | Khaleda Zia 1991–96 | Prime Minister |
| France | Edith Cresson 1991–92 | Prime Minister |
| Poland | Hanna Suchocka 1992–93 | Prime Minister |
| Canada | Kim Campbell 1993 | Prime Minister |
| Burundi | Sylvia Kinigi 1993–94 | Prime Minister |
| Rwanda | Agatha Uwilingiyimana 1993–94 | Prime Minister |
| Turkey | Tansu Çiller 1993–96 | Prime Minister |
| Netherlands Antilles | Susanne Camelia-Romer 1993; 1998–99 | Prime Minister |
| Bulgaria | Reneta Indzhova 1994–95 | Interim Prime Minister |
| Sri Lanka | *Chandrika Bandaranaike Kumaratunga 1994–* | Executive President and former Prime Minister |
| Haiti | Claudette Werleigh 1995–96 | Prime Minister |

***Table 13.1*** *Continued*

| Country | Name/Date | Office |
|---------|-----------|--------|
| Bangladesh | *Hasina Wajed 1996–* | Prime Minister |
| Liberia | *Ruth Perry 1996–* | Chair, Ruling Council |
| Ecuador | Rosalia Artega 1997 | President |
| Bermuda | Pamela Gordon 1997–98 | Premier |
| Ireland | *Mary McAleese 1997–* | President |
| New Zealand | Jenny Shipley 1997–99 | Prime Minister |
| Guyana | Janet Jagan 1997–99 | Prime Minister, President |
| Bermuda | *Jennifer Smith 1998* | Premier |
| Lithuania | Irene Degutienë 4–18 May 1999 | Acting Prime Minister |
| Mongolia | Nyam-Osorily Tuyaa 22–30 July 1999 | Acting Prime Minister |
| Switzerland | Ruth Dreifuss 1999 | President |
| Latvia | *Vaira Vike-Freiberga 1999–* | President |
| Panama | *Mireya Moscoso 1999–* | President |
| New Zealand | *Helen Clark 1999–* | Prime Minister |
| Finland | *Tarja Halonen 2000–* | President |
| Philippines | *Gloria Macapagal Arroyo 2001–* | President |
| Senegal | *Madior Boye 2001–* | Prime Minister |
| Indonesia | *Megawati Sukarnoputri 2001–* | President |

( ) = No longer living.

\* = In office as of December 2001.

\*\* = Party won 1990 election but prevented by military from taking office; Nobel Prize laureate.

© Nancy J. Adler, 2003

Given these trends, there is no question that more women will be leading countries in the twenty-first century than have ever done so before. Already in the opening years of this century, four additional women have been selected to lead their countries: Tarja Holonen in Finland, Gloria Macapagal Arroyo in the Philippines, Madior Boye in Sengal, and Megawati Sukarnoputri in Indonesia. Arroyo is the second woman to assume the presidency in the Philippines.

## Women leading companies

Are there similar increases in the number of women leading major corporations (see, among others, Adler and Izraeli, 1994; Adler, 1997a, 1997b, 1999b, 2002)? Whereas the patterns among business leaders are not as clear as those among political leaders, surveys suggest an increasing number of women leading global companies. The initial numbers, however, are very small. Even including executives who had held positions below the number-one position in their company, women still held less than 5 per cent of the most senior management positions in the United States and less than 2 per cent of all senior management positions in Europe at the end of the last century.[6] Moreover, not until the late 1990s did either the *Fortune* top 30 or the *Financial Times* (FT-SE) 100 include a woman among their lists of leading CEOs.[7]

Contrary to popular belief, however, women's scarcity in leading major corporations does not reflect their absence as leaders of global companies. Unlike their male counterparts, most women chief executives either create their own entrepreneurial enterprises or assume the leadership of a family business (for a discussion of women who are global entrepreneurs, see Adler, 1999a, 1999c).

## Women leading: a global trend, not a local oddity

As Box 13.1 highlights, similar to women-led countries, women-led businesses are distributed worldwide. They are not clustered in the few countries considered to be female-friendly – those countries providing women with equal property rights, equal access to education, healthcare and employment, and equal protection under law. The women leaders come from some of the world's largest and smallest countries, some of the world's richest and poorest countries, and some of the world's most socially and economically advantaged and disadvantaged countries. They come, moreover, from every geographical region, represent all six of the world's major religions, and lead companies in a wide range of industries. The changing trend towards women's leadership is a broad-based, worldwide phenomenon, not a trend limited to a few particularly pro-women countries, a few particularly pro-women industries, or one particular region of the globe.

Moreover, most major corporations that select women as senior business leaders are not those that have implemented the most advanced female-friendly policies (such as those providing day-care centres and flextime). Among the 61 American *Fortune* 500 companies employing women as chairmen, CEOs, board members, or

# Box 13.1 Global women business leaders

How many of us recognize the names of the world's women business leaders? All of the women included on the following list lead or have led companies with current revenues over US $1 billion, or for banks, with assets over US $1 billion:

**Ernestina Herrera de Noble, Argentina, $1.2 billion**; President and editorial director of Grupo Clarin, the largest-circulation Spanish newspaper in the world.

**Francine Wachsstock, Belgium, $2.25 billion**; President of the board of administrators, La Poste, Belgium's state-owned post office and largest employer.

**Beatriz Larragoiti, Brazil, $2.9 billion**; Vice-President (and owner) of Brazil's largest insurance company, Sul America S.A.

**Maureen Kempston Darkes, Canada, $18.3 billion**; President and General Manager of General Motors of Canada.

**Ellen R. Schneider-Lenne, Germany, $458 billion in assets**; Member of the Board of Managing Directors, Deutsch Bank AG, responsible for operations in the UK (deceased).

**Nina Wang, Hong Kong, $1–2 billion in assets**; Chairlady of Chinachem Group, property development.

**Tarjani Vakil, India, $1.1 billion in assets**; Chairperson and managing director, Export-Import Bank of India, highest ranking female banking official in Asia.

**Margaret Heffernan, Ireland, $1.6 billion**; Chairman, Dunnes Stores Holding Company, largest retailing company in Ireland.

**Galia Maor, Israel, $35.6 billion in assets**; CEO of Bank Leumi le-Israel.

**Gloria Delores Knight, Jamaica, $1.86 billion in assets**; President and managing director, The Jamaica Mutual Life Assurance Society, largest financial conglomerate in English-speaking Caribbean (deceased).

**Sawako Noma, Japan, $2 billion**; President of Kodansha Ltd., largest publishing house in Japan.

**Harumi Sakamoto, Japan, $13 billion**; Senior Managing Director, The Seiyu, Ltd., a supermarket and shopping-centre operator expanding throughout Asia.

**Khatijah Ahmad, Malaysia, $5 billion**; Chairman and managing director, KAF Group of Companies, financial services group.

**Merce Sala i Schnorkowski, Spain, $1.1 billion**; CEO of Renfe, Spain's national railway system, currently helping to privatize Colombian and Bolivian rail and selling trains to Germany.

**Antonia Ax:son Johnson, Sweden, $6 billion**; Chair, The Axel Johnson Group, retailing and distribution, more than 200 companies.

*Continued*

**Elisabeth Salina Amorini, Switzerland, $2.8 billion**; Chairman of the Board, managing director, and chairman of the group executive board, Societe Generale de Surveillance Holding S.A., the world's largest inspection and quality control organization, testing imports and exports in more than 140 countries.

**Emilia Roxas, Taiwan, $5 billion**; CEO, Asiaworld Internationale Groupe, multinational conglomerate.

**Ellen Hancock, USA, $2.4 billion**; Executive Vice-President and co-chief operating officer, National Semiconductor Corp.

The list includes most other countries of the world when companies are included with revenues over a $250 million, including such women business leaders as:

**Donatella Zingone Dini, Costa Rica, $300 million**; Zeta Group, fifth largest business in Central America, conglomerate.

**Nawal Abdel Moneim El Tatawy, Egypt, $357 million in assets**; Chairman, Arab Investment Bank.

**Colette Lewiner, France, $800 million**; Chairman and CEO, SGN-Eurisys Group, world's largest nuclear fuels reprocessing company.

**Jannie Tay, Singapore, $289 million**; Managing director, The Hour Glass Limited, high-end retailer of watches.

**Aida Geffen, South Africa, $355 million**; Chairman and managing director, Aida Holdings Ltd., residential commercial real estate firm.

**Ann Gloag, United Kingdom, $520 million**; Stagecoach Holdings Plc; Europe's largest bus company.

**Linda Joy Wachner, United States, $1.1 billion** (combined); Chairman of The Warnaco Group ($789 million) and Authentic Fitness Corporation ($266 million).

**Liz Chitiga, Zimbabwe, $400 million**; General Manager and CEO, Minerals Marketing Corporation of Zimbabwe; in foreign currency terms, the biggest business in Zimbabwe.

*Source*:   Kelly, C. (1996) '50 World-Class Executives', *Worldbusiness*, 2(2): 20–31.

one of the top five earners, for example, only three are the same companies that *Working Woman* identified as the most favourable for women employees.

As can be seen, the trends among political and business leaders appear similar. More women are leading global firms than has ever been true in the past, with the vast majority being the first woman that their particular firm has ever selected to hold such a position. Based on such increases, we can easily predict that women's voices will become a more common, and therefore more important, addition to the world's global leadership dialogue in the twenty-first century. Change is not only possible, it has already begun to happen.

# Global leadership: numbers are not enough

Increasing the number of women in leadership positions is certainly a necessary condition for equity, but it is not a sufficient condition for shaping history. The fundamental challenge is not simply to get more women into senior leadership. Rather, it is to get the type of leadership in the world that will foster global society's survival and prosperity.

Based on research observing women managers, many people have predicted that women leaders would exhibit the new sought-after twenty-first century leadership style; including incorporating new, more inclusive, trustworthy, and humanistic approaches. They base their predictions on the many researchers crediting a disproportionate number of women with many, if not all, of the following qualities:

> empathy, helpfulness, caring, and nurturance; interpersonal sensitivity, attentiveness to and acceptance of others, responsiveness to their needs and motivations; an orientation toward the collective interest and toward integrative goals such as group cohesiveness and stability; a preference for open, egalitarian, and cooperative relationships, rather than hierarchical ones; and an interest in actualizing values and relationships of great importance to community. (See, among others, summary of traits in Fondas, 1997: 260)

By contrast, traits that have been culturally ascribed to men include:

> an ability to be impersonal, self-interested, efficient, hierarchical, tough minded, and assertive; an interest in taking charge, control, and domination; a capacity to ignore personal, emotional considerations in order to succeed; a proclivity to rely on standardized or 'objective' codes for judgment and evaluation of others; and a heroic orientation toward task accomplishment and a continual effort to act on the world and become something new or [different]. (Fondas, 1997: 260)

To date, however, no research focused on senior leaders (rather than employees or managers) exists to support or refute claims that women would make more effective twenty-first century leaders than men. Not surprisingly, similar to men, women exhibit a wide range of leadership visions, approaches and levels of effectiveness (Adler, 2002). One need look no further than the ouster on corruption charges of Turkey's former Prime Minister, Tansu Ciller, or the demise of Sotheby's former CEO Diana Brooks (indicted, along with Sotheby's former Chairman, Alfred Taubman, on criminal conspiracy and price-fixing charges) to know that women leaders, like their male counterparts, are neither perfect nor a universal solution to the world's or any particular company's problems.[8]

Do some women exhibit exemplary styles of leadership? Yes; not all women, but certainly many give us reason for hope, especially those not mimicking the style of leadership of most twentieth-century male leaders. Ireland's first woman President, Mary Robinson, for example, brilliantly took her commitment to human rights into the presidency of Ireland, transforming the position from one of ceremony to one of substance. She then let go of the presidency – a typically feminine use of power, 'letting go' – in order to continue her human rights agenda on a broader, worldwide scale at the United Nations. Aung San Suu Kyi, the legally elected leader of Burma (Myanmar) was incarcerated in her own home by the military for more than six years. While under house arrest, the military dictatorship even denied her the right to see her husband one last time before he died of cancer. Given her situation, does Suu Kyi advocate annihilating the military dictatorship that has imprisoned her and her people for so long? No, to this day, she fearlessly advocates dialogue – words, not guns – a unity strategy typically attributed to what many consider to be a more feminine approach to leadership.

Agatha Uwilingiyimana, the former Prime Minister of Rwanda, similarly exemplifies the courage it takes to break with traditional leadership approaches and use unifying strategies – strategies many attribute to a more feminine approach. By 1993, the level of violence in Rwanda had forced the Hutus and Tutsis to seriously consider signing a peace agreement. But who would have the courage to sign such a paper with the sworn enemy? No one relished the risk, as extremists on both sides considered those who would sign as traitors. At that crucial moment in Rwanda's history, no man accepted the risk of becoming a peace-making Prime Minister. In July 1993, it was Uwiligiyimana, in the name of peace and unity, who agreed to serve her country as Prime Minister. Less than a month later, the peace agreement was signed. Less than a year later, extremist Hutus began hunting down and killing Tutsis and moderate members of the Hutu government. Agatha Uwilingiyimana, a moderate Hutu, was one of the first murdered. Although reported as a Tutsi murder in the Western press, Agatha was killed by her own people, by extremist Hutus who rejected her attempts at unity and peace.

Is the situation in Rwanda so extreme that it would be inappropriate for the rest of the world to attempt to learn anything from Uwiligiyimana's story? The answer is a resounding no. Think for a moment of some of the other women leaders with whom we are perhaps more familiar. Former President of the Philippines, Corazon Aquino, like Uwiligiyiama, also believed in building coalitions with the opposition. She invited members of both her own and the opposition party to join her presidential cabinet. The world press, viewing her leadership through the obsolete lens of divisive twentieth-century perspectives, labelled her invitation to the opposition as the naïve act of a housewife who doesn't know what it means to be President. In response, Aquino explained that she never again wanted political differences resolved by murder. She wanted to preclude the possibility that any person would to have to watch the political assassination of their spouse as she had had to witness when her husband, Benigno Aquino, the then opposition leader, was murdered upon his return to the Philippines. In her cabinet, animated discussion replaced murder as the accepted form of political discourse.

Aquino, similar to Robinson in Ireland, refused to run for a second term because she believed that democracy, not her longevity as President, was more important.

Having lived through years of Marcos' dictatorship, she believed that Filippinos deserved to choose a new President after she had served her initial six-year term. Each of these leaders went outside of the patterns of history and said 'Enough!' There has to be a better way.'

Are the stories of more inclusive leadership all stories of political leaders? Of course not. Rebecca Mark, for example, as CEO of Enron Development Corporation, negotiated the first major commercial agreement among the Arabs and Israelis following the Oslo Peace Accords.[9] Rebecca Mark saw coalition-building – including across groups that the world had always viewed as enemies – as a smart business practice. Did people question her judgement? Of course. Did she do what hadn't been done before? Yes. As Rebecca Mark's decisions show, true leadership, by definition, is not the act of the usual.

As both business and political leaders, women regularly challenge conventional wisdom and practice in their leadership approaches. Britain's Anita Roddick, founder and former CEO of The Body Shop, for example, challenged conventional practice in the beauty and healthcare industry, in her product design (for example, by not allowing animal testing), in her marketing (by not promising unattainable beauty), in her organization design, and in her strategic intent (for example, by tying societal commitments to product strategies). Sweden's Antonia Ax:son Johnson, CEO of the fourth-generation, 200-company family business, The Axison Johnson Group, eliminated all war- and violence-related toys from the company's department stores. Although the toys would have increased revenues, they were not consistent with her concept of 'the good company.'

## People's aspirations: hope, change and unity

To understand the dynamics of the twenty-first century, we must go beyond strictly attempting to assess if, or how, women's approaches to leadership differ from those of their male counterparts. We know that they differ in some cases, but certainly not in all, or may be most, cases. Given the absence of consistently substantiated differences and, at the same time, the rapid increase in the number of women leaders (especially in the last decade), we must ask why countries and companies worldwide – for the first time in modern history and after so many years of male-dominated leadership – are choosing (often for the first time) women to lead them. It appears that people worldwide may want what all women symbolize, but what only some women leaders exhibit.

### Leadership symbolism: the possibility of change

Perhaps the most powerful and attractive symbolism of women leaders is the possibility of significant change. When a woman is chosen to become president, prime minister or CEO – when no other woman has ever held such an office and when few people thought she would be selected – people begin to believe that other, more sub-stantive and less symbolic changes are also possible. The combination of a woman being an outsider at senior leadership levels previously controlled by men, and of her beating the odds, provides powerful public imagery supporting the possibility of broad-based societal and organizational change. The fact that most women, to date, are the first women to assume senior leadership positions, underscores the beginning not just of symbolic change, but of real change. Mary Robinson's presidential accept-ance speech captures the unique event of Ireland electing its first woman president coupled with the possibility of national change:

> I was elected by men and women of all parties and none, by many with great moral courage who stepped out from the faded flags of Civil War and voted for a new Ireland. And above all by the women of Ireland … who instead of rocking the cradle rocked the system, and who came out massively to make their mark on the ballot paper, and on a new Ireland.[10]

The fact that the women who become leaders are perceived to differ from their male counterparts (whether or not they actually do) fosters the sense that change is possi-ble. In Kenya, for example, when Charity Ngilu became the first woman to run for the presidency, many Kenyans saw her as representing 'a complete break with [the] divisive tribal politics of the past' (McKinley, 1997: section 1, p. 3). As one Kenyan observed, 'Charity is talking about unity, and this unity will unite both men and women … If we vote for a man, there will be no change. With a woman, there will have to be a big change' (*ibid.*).

The symbolism supporting the possibility of change is almost identical in the business world, where most women CEOs are 'firsts'; not only the first woman, but also often the first outsider that the company has selected to lead them. Notable examples include Marjorie Scardino, the first woman, first outsider, and first American to become CEO of Britain's Pearson plc, as well as the first woman to lead a *Financial Times* (FT-SE) 100 firm; Carly Fiorina, the first woman and first outsider to lead Hewlett Packard and a *Fortune* top-30 firm; and Charlotte Beers, the first woman and the first outsider that Ogilvy & Mather Worldwide had ever brought in to lead their worldwide advertising business.

## Leadership symbolism: the possibility of unity

In addition to the possibility of change, women also symbolize unity – and women leaders are no exception. Nicaragua's former President Violetta Chamorro, for exam-ple, became a symbol of national unity following her husband's assassination. Chamorro even claimed 'to have no ideology beyond national "reconciliation"' (Benn, 1995). Chamorro's ability to bring her four adult children (two of whom were prominent Sandinistas while the other two equally prominently opposed the Sandinistas) together every week for Sunday dinner achieved near legendary status in war-torn Nicaragua (Saint-Germain, 1993: 80). Chamorro gave symbolic hope to the nation that it, too, could find peace based on a unity that would bring all Nicaraguans together. That the behaviour of a woman leader led to family unity becoming a symbol for national unity is neither surprising nor coincidental.

On the basis of similar dynamics, Pakistan's former Prime Minister Benazir Bhutto and the Philippines former President Corazon Aquino each came to symbolize unity for their strife-torn countries. As the scope of governments' influence and companies' operations expand to encompass the world, the desire and need for unifying strategies increase. Currently, women symbolize the hope for unity within multinational and multicultural constituencies.

The hope that women leaders will foster unity and inclusiveness is heightened by the ways in which women gain access to power. In contrast to many of their male counterparts, most women leaders develop and use broad-based popular support, rather than relying primarily on traditional, hierarchical political party or corporate structural support. This broad based inclusiveness, often seen as a precursor of other hoped-for unifying strategies, has been particularly apparent among the aspiring women political leaders who are often not seriously considered as potential candidates by their country's main political parties. They are consequently forced to gain support directly from the people (which, of course, is a profoundly democratic process).

Mary Robinson, for example, campaigned in more small communities in Ireland than any previous presidential candidate before either her party or the opposition took her seriously. The opposition later admitted that they did not seriously consider Robinson's candidacy until it was too late to stop her (Finlay, 1990). Similarly, Corazon Aquino, whose campaign and victory were labelled the People's Revolution, held more than 1,000 rallies during her campaign, while incumbent Ferdinand Marcos held only 34 (Col, 1993). Likewise, Benazir Bhutto, who succeeded in becoming Pakistan's first woman and youngest Prime Minister, campaigned in more communities than any politician before her. Only later did her own party take her seriously (Weisman, 1986; Anderson, 1993).

In business, the disproportionate number of women who choose to start their own companies echoes the same pattern of broad-based support. Rather than attempting to climb the corporate ladder and to break through the glass ceiling into senior leadership positions in established corporations, these entrepreneurial women build their success directly in the marketplace. The types of broad-based support developed by women political leaders and entrepreneurs differ only in their source, with the former enjoying support directly from the electorate whereas the latter gains support directly from the marketplace. In both cases, the base of support is outside of the traditional power structure and therefore more representative of new and more diverse opinions and ideas. Their sources of support, and therefore of power, more closely reflect the flattened network of emerging twenty-first century organizations and society than they do the more centralized and limited power structures of most twentieth century organizations.

# Shaping history

As President of the Czech Republic Vaclav Havel (1994: A27) has said, the world is 'going through a transitional period, when something is on the way out and something else is painfully being born', it is not surprising that people worldwide are attracted to women leaders' symbolic message of bringing change, hope and the possibility for unity. The interplay of women's and men's styles of leadership will define the contours and potential success of twenty-first century society. The risk is in encapsulating leaders, both women and men, in approaches that worked well in the twentieth century but foretell disaster for the twenty-first century. The challenge is in the urgency and complexity. As poet David Whyte (1994) enjoins us:

> The journey begins right here, in the middle of the road, right beneath your feet. This is the place. There is no other place, there is no other time.

This chapter is reproduced from R.J. Burke and C.L. Cooper (eds) (2004) *Leading in Turbulent Times: Managing in the New World of Work*, Blackwell Publishing Ltd., with permission.

## Notes

1  The official title of the UN Conference was the United Nations' World Conference Against Racism, Racial Discrimination, Xenophobia and Related Intolerance.
2  A.T. Kearney's study reported in Haebeck *et al.* (2000) and in Schuler and Jackson (2001). The same study, as cited by Schuler and Jackson, concludes that 'only 15 per cent of mergers and acquisitions in the U.S. achieve their objectives, as measured by share value, return on investment and post-combination profitability'. For research on the instability of international joint ventures, see the summary by Yan and Zeng (1999). Although the definitions (complete termination versus significant change of ownership) and overall results vary, numerous studies have reported substantial international joint venture instability, including 55 per cent termination reported by Harrigan (1988), 49 per cent termination reported by Barkema and Vermeulen (1997); and 68 per cent instability through termination or acquisition reported by Park and Russo (1996). Also see Gary Hammel's classic 1991 article.
3  For a notable exception, see the description of the Norway-based global company, Norske Skog, in Adler (2003).
4  This section is excepted and adapted from Riane Eisler's insightful 1987 book (see book jacket).
5  Countries with two-women presidents and prime ministers include: Bangladesh with Khaleda Zia (1991–96) and Hasina Wajed (1996–present), Bermuda with Pamela Gordon (1997–98) and Jennifer Smith (1998–present), Haiti with Ertha Pascal-Trouillot (1990–91) and Claudette Werleigh (1995–96), Ireland with Mary Robinson (1990–97) and Mary McAleese (1997–present), New Zealand with Jenny Shipley (1997–99) and Helen Clark (1999–present), and Sri Lanka with Sirimavo Bandaranaike (1960–65; 1970–77; 1994–2000) and Chandrika Kumaratunga (1994–present).
6  United States' statistics based of the research of Catalyst as originally published by Wellington (1996). European statistics reported in Dwyer *et al.* (1996).
7  Carly Fiorina, CEO of Hewlett-Packard and Marjorie Scardino, CEO of Pearson plc.
8  For a description of the case against Sotheby's former chairman, A. Alfred Taubman, on criminal conspiracy charges for a price-fixing scheme with arch-rival auction house, Christie's, see the business press in November–December 2001, including the *New York Times* reporting (see, for example, Blumenthal and Vogel, 2001).
9  Note that this was long before the demise in 2001 of Enron, under the leadership of Chairman Kenneth L. Lay. Among many other business articles covering Enron's downfall, see Oppel and Atlas (2001).
10  Speech in the Royal Dublin Shaw grounds, Dublin, 9 November 1990 as reported in Finlay (1990: 1).

# References

Adler, N.J. (1997a) 'Global Leaders: A Dialogue with Future History', *International Management*, 1(2): 21–33.
Adler, N.J. (1997b) 'Global Leadership, Women Leaders', *Management International Review*, 37(1): 171–96.
Adler N.J. (1999a) 'Global Entrepreneurs: Women, Myths and History', *Global Focus*, 11(4): 125–34.
Adler, N.J. (1999b) 'Global Leaders: Women of Influence', in G. Powell (ed.), *Handbook of Gender and Work*. Thousand Oaks, CA: Sage, 239–61.
Adler, N.J. (1999c) 'Twenty-First-Century Leadership: Reality Beyond the Myths', in A.M. Rugman (series ed.) and R. Wright (volume ed.), *Research in Global Strategic Management*, vol. 7, in series *International Entrepreneurship: Globalization of Emerging Business*. Greenwich, CT: JAI Press, 239–61.
Adler, N.J. (2002) 'Women Joining Men as Global Leaders in the New Economy', in M. Gannon and K. Newman (eds), *Handbook of Cross-Cultural Management*. Oxford, England: Blackwell, 236–49.
Adler, N.J. (2003) 'Global Companies, Global Society: There is a Better Way', in M. Goldsmith, J. Belasco and L. Segil (eds), *The Leader As Partner*. New York: AMACOM, 223–30.
Adler, N.J. and Izraeli, D. (eds) (1994) *Competitive Frontiers: Women Managers in a Global Economy*. Cambridge, MA: Blackwell.
Albright, M.K. (1997) Harvard Commencement Address as reported in the *New York Times*, 6 June: A8.
Anderson Fix, N. (1993) 'Benazir Bhutto and dynastic politics: Her father's daughter, her people's sister', in M. A. Genovese (ed), *Women as National Leaders*. Newbury Park, CA: Sage, 41–69.
Barkema, H. and Vermeulen, F. (1997) 'What Differences in the Cultural Backgrounds of Partners are Detrimental for International Joint Ventures'?, *Journal of International Business Studies*, 28(4): 845–64.
Benn, M. (1995) 'Women who rule the world', *Cosmopolitan*, February.
Blumenthal, R. and Vogel, C. (2001) 'Trial Prosecutor Depicts Ex-Chief of Sotheby's as Price Fixer', *New York Times*, 4 December: A20.
Col, J.M. (1993) 'Managing softly in turbulent times: Corazon C. Aquino, President of the Philippines', in M. A. Genovese (ed.), *Women as National Leaders*. Newbury Park, CA: Sage, 13–40.
Dwyer, P., Johnston. M. and Lowry, L. (1996) 'Europe's Corporate Women', *Business Week*, 15 April: 40–2.
Eisler R. (1987) *The Chalice and the Blade: Our History, Our Future*. San Francisco: Harper & Row.
Finlay, F. (1990) *Mary Robinson: A President with a Purpose*. Dublin, Ireland: O'Brien Press, 1.
Fondas, N. (1997) 'The Origins Of Feminization', *Academy of Management Review*, 22(1): 257–82.
Friedman, T.L., (2000) *The Lexus and the Olive Tree: Understanding Globalization*. New York: Anchor Books.
Gimbutas, M. (1991) *The Civilization of the Goddess: The World of Old Europe*. San Francisco: Harper San Francisco.
Haebeck, M.H. Kroger F. and Trum, M.R. (2000) *After the Mergers: Seven Rules for Successful Post-Merger Integration*. New York: Prentice Hall/FT.
Hammel, G. (1991) 'Competition for Competence and Inter-Partner Learning Within International Strategic Alliances', *Strategic Management Journal*, 12(1): 83–103.
Harrigan, K.R. (1988) 'Strategic Alliances and Partner Asymmetries', in F. Contractor and P. Lorange (eds.), *Cooperative Strategies in International Business*. Lexington, MA: Lexington Books, 205–26.
Havel V. (1994) 'The New Measure Of Man', *New York Times*, 8 July: A27.
Kelly, C. (1996) '50 World-Class Executives', *World business*, 2(2): 20–31.
McKinley, J.C., Jr (1997) 'A Woman to Run Kenya? One says, 'Why Not?' *The New York Times* world late edition, 3 August Section 1: 3.
Oppel R.A. Jr. and Atlas, R.D. (2001) 'Hobbled Enron Tries to Stay On Its Feet', *New York Times*, December 4: C1 and C8.
Park, S.H. and Russo, M.V. (1996) 'When Competition Eclipses Cooperation: An Event History Analysis of Joint Venture Failure', *Management Science*, 42(6): 875–90.
Rechtschaffen, S. (1996) *Timeshifting*. New York: Bantam Doubleday Dell Audio.
Saint-Germain, M.A. (1993) 'Women in power in Nicaragua: Myth and reality', in Michael A. Genovese (ed.), *Women As National Leaders*. Newbury Park, CA: Sage, 70–102.
Schuler, R.S. and Jackson, S.E. (2001) 'Seeking An Edge in Mergers and Acquisitions', *Financial Times*, Special Section, Part Two: 'People Management', October: 22.
Slackman, M. (2001) 'Divisive U.N. Race Talks End in Accord', *Los Angeles Times*, 9 September: A1.
Swarns, R.L. (2001) 'Race Talks Finally Reach Accord On Slavery and Palestinian Plight', *New York Times*, 9 September: A1.
Weisman, S.R. (1986) 'A Daughter Returns To Pakistan To Cry For Victory', *New York Times*, 11 April: 12.
Wellington, S.W. (1996) *Women in Corporate Leadership: Progress and Prospects*. New York: Catalyst.
Whyte, D.(1994) *The Heart Aroused*, New York: Currency Doubleday, 27.
Yan, A. and Zeng, M. (1999) 'International Joint Venture Instability: A Critique of Previous Research, A Reconceptualization, and Directions for Future Research', *Journal of International Business Studies*, 30(2): 397–414.

# 14

# International HRM in the twenty-first century: crossing boundaries, building connections

*Sully Taylor and Nancy K. Napier*

Just as individuals, organizations and societies evolve and change over time, so too do professional disciplines. The field of personnel and labour relations evolved to human resource management (HRM) in the late 1970s, and as the importance of international and global organizations emerged in the following decades, international human resource management (IHRM) has become an important part of the field. Both practitioners and academics increasingly point to IHRM as a critical element for the success of multinational corporations (MNCs), necessary for global competitiveness. In particular, the growing dispersion of key talent throughout the MNC's network (Nohria and Ghoshal, 1997) combined with the emergence of the human organization as key to competitiveness (Becker and Huselid, 1998; Ulrich, 1998; Pucik *et al.*, 1992) and the role of the IHRM function and manager (see for example Napier *et al.*, 1995) makes IHRM an exciting and crucial area to study and to practice.

The coming decades are likely to further emphasize the importance and centrality of the IHRM field for HRM practitioners, organizational managers, scholars and students who wish to pursue the discipline. This chapter outlines reasons for IHRM's importance and provides a basic framework in which to think about IHRM in the future. We have three aims. First, because the emphasis in this book is on what students of management need to understand about this burgeoning and stimulating field, we discuss macro trends that we think will become increasingly important in the work lives of people whose careers will span the next 20 to 30 years of this century. Second, we discuss what such trends might mean for those who carry out the IHRM discipline in terms of its mandate or roles and responsibilities. Finally, we examine possible impacts on the IHRM function and practices/policies. The selection of global trends is, of necessity, somewhat arbitrary, based on our individual, and hence idiosyncratic, knowledge. Nevertheless, we have sought to identify trends that would affect organizations and workers in settings beyond the typically discussed industrialized countries in North America, Europe and Japan. It is a cliché to say that world is becoming a small place, but indeed it is – for several of the reasons many pundits have raised and which we discuss below.

## Global Trends

Numerous books, journal articles and magazines offer ideas of key trends that have or will affect the way people live and work in the next decades (for example Rosen, 2000; Govindarajan and Gupta, 2001; Evans *et al.*, 2002). We have chosen four major trends that will affect organizations, as well as individuals, and that will affect the IHRM discipline and activities within organizations: (1) the changing profile of MNCs; (2) growing global interdependencies; (3) increasing global fragmentation; and (4) the psychic-shock syndrome, our term for the dramatic and often overwhelming shifts occurring in the ways societies and individuals operate.

# A profile of MNCs and their activities

Three trends relating to multinational corporations appear to be developing in the early years of the century. First, more MNCs are emerging from countries other than the traditional sources. Second, the places where MNCs are conducting business and placing their investments are shifting. Third, there is growing interdependence among the operations of MNCs, both with regard to task interdependence and knowledge flows.

## Who are the players?

The majority of MNCs dominating global economic activity from the 1960s to the early 1990s were based in industrialized countries, particularly North America and Europe, or from the Asian countries of Japan and South Korea. In 1980, 100 per cent of the world's largest 100 firms were from these countries (Hjelt, 2002). By 2002, the percentage had dropped to 95 per cent (Hjelt, 2002), and given recent global economic trends will continue to drop over the next few decades. As economies in Asia, for example, have strengthened in the last two decades, so too have their business organizations, creating some leading MNCs in the process. Companies in Taiwan, China, Thailand and Singapore – companies such as Acer and Legend – are now some of the world's fastest growing. Firms from Mexico, such as Vitro, are also gaining in international strength and reach. Thus, the traditional global MNC leaders will increasingly find themselves in a world with new competitors. These competitors may have business strategies, cultures and approaches to management that are quite different from what the industrialized-country-based MNCs have pursued.

## Where are MNCs doing business?

A second trend relating to MNCs is that even the traditional powerhouses are beginning to pursue business in locations that are new and culturally divergent for them. Throughout the 1980s and early 1990s, most foreign direct investment (FDI) by the traditional industrialized-country-based MNCs was among themselves (Dicken, 1998); that is, within countries that were highly developed and, except for Japan/Korea, often not too dissimilar culturally. Many US firms set up operations in Ireland and continental Europe, for example. German firms moved into Eastern Germany and the other former Soviet bloc countries post-1989. While those countries were economically weaker, their history and cultural backgrounds were nevertheless somewhat linked to Germany's.

Beginning in the 1990s, however, that pattern began to change. Foreign direct investment increasingly goes to developing and emerging economies and to locations where cultures are significantly different from the MNCs' home countries Those same German firms that moved into Eastern Europe started moving into Vietnam and China, for instance. China became, in fact, the largest recipient of FDI in 2002 worldwide, with over $50 billion in approved investments (*Business China*, 3 March 2003). While Taiwan had dominated investment in China during the 1980s and 1990s, increasingly MNCs from North America and Europe began to move into China as well. Like China, Malaysia, Poland and Thailand ' ... consistently attract foreign direct investment worth more than 3 per cent of their annual GDP' (Lodovico *et al.*, 2001: 49). Thus, a key global trend facing MNCs is that their competition is changing and that they must learn to succeed in developing countries that diverge culturally from them.

## How are the MNCs doing business?

Bartlett and Ghoshal (1989) in *Managing Across Borders* identified what they called the emerging 'transnational' organization. The key components of a transnational are the ability to simultaneously balance pressures for localization and integration, as well as capitalize on knowledge-creation from its diverse foreign activities. While not all MNCs follow a transnational strategy, the globalization of markets – both consumer and labour – as well as the increase of market-based economies, has nurtured a tendency towards greater complexity of operations overall and increased resource flows among subunits (Birkinshaw and Hood, 1998: Gupta and Govindarajan, 2000). Effectively dealing with the complexity of operations and the interdependencies among the units requires a great deal of knowledge flow across units.

# The MNCs on many levels

Along with the increasingly complex environments facing MNCs is the growing awareness of global interdependence and attendant pressures on them (Singer, 2002). In particular, two issues emerge: (1) connections across many levels, and the implications of actions by one country or region on others, and (2) the notion of sustainability, or looking at many stakeholders in determining MNC contribution and performance.

## Connections across many levels

Singer (2002) argues that we are tied together by atmosphere, economics, law (or lack of it) and community (defined broadly). At its most basic level, this global interdependency means that actions taken by an organization, individual or group on any given level (for example physical/environmental, health and social, economic, political or military, business) can influence other entities, locally, regionally or globally. The terrorist movement offers a recent and vivid example of such interdependencies.

The growing anti-globalization movement, as evidenced by the strident protests in Seattle in 1999, is a backlash against these growing interdependencies, arising when protesters feel that their cultural or economic sovereignty is threatened. Recently this movement has raised its stakes with attacks on well-known targets such as McDonalds and Nestlé, and on world economic forums such as Davos. The protests in Europe and elsewhere against a US-led war on Iraq also show the growing sense that one country cannot take unilateral action that may have dire consequences for the world community. The attitude that a country will (or can) focus only on its own citizens' needs (for example oil for Americans) and not realize its actions influence other parts of the world is increasingly viewed as unacceptable and naïve.

## Sustainability

Related to such connections is the idea that firms and organizations need to consider a wide range of stakeholders in their actions and measures of contribution and performance. Loosely termed 'sustainability,' the expectations that corporations must address environmental and social results as well as financial performance have grown exponentially over the last decade. Sustainability is defined as ' ... meeting the needs of present generations without compromising the ability of future generations to meet their own needs' (Phillips and Claus, 2002: 6). Companies concerned about sustainable contribution often adopt the 'triple bottom line' of economic, environmental and community results to measure their performance. Such corporate social responsibility ... 'can be a reconciling mechanism between global and anti-globalization forces, government regulations and self-regulation, and a tool for the global HR professional in balancing the needs of the company with those of its multiple stakeholders' (Phillips and Claus, 2002: 2). European firms, in particular, have pushed for greater adoption of corporate social responsibility practices. The movement has led to the creation of ISO 140001 (specifies a framework of control for an environmental management system against which an organization can be certified by a third party), adoption of product life-cycle regulations, and 'dematerialization,' or reducing the amount of raw materials used to produce goods (Holliday *et al.*, 2002). The increased scope of the performance results that MNCs are embracing, and the resultant wider definition of relevant stakeholders, is an important global trend that will impact IHRM.

# Fragmentation

Ironically, the increased awareness of global interdependence has been accompanied with growing fragmentation or fractionalization on a number of planes. This global fragmentation appears as a breakdown of traditional and long-standing expectations and values, with little respect for national geographic borders. Few countries or groups are immune and some face these breakdowns to a greater extent than others. At least four areas have emerged: (1) the dispersion of talent, (2) the rise of religious and ethnic militancy, (3) the technological divide, and (4) the erosion of social capital.

## Dispersion of talent

Several scholars and practitioners point to a trend where people with special talents or characteristics show little loyalty to country or region. Rather, such people of similar skills and talents tend to relate more to one another than to a country, regardless of setting or ethnic background. Kanter (1995) described this new global élite as 'cosmopolitans', people who because of their wealth, connections and worldview have more in common with others who have similar experiences, assets and viewpoints than with the majority of their fellow citizens. Iyer (2000) uses the term 'global souls' to portray people who see the world as their workplace, entertainment source or market. Zacharay (2000) refers to 'hybrids', or persons who intermarry, live outside the countries of their birth, and are comfortable crossing cultural and geographic boundaries.

The trend of more cosmopolitans and people who are comfortable crossing boundaries brings with it an inevitable 'talent divide'. As employees with technical or managerial skills form cadres spanning national borders, there is, at the same time, a pool of people within their home countries who may wish to be part of the global-souls cadre, but are unable because of discrimination or lack of access to education and subsequent careers. In addition, while the increase in education of, and competition for, cosmopolitans continues to grow worldwide, access to education and lucrative and challenging careers remains a dream for many in developing countries.

## The rise of religious and ethnic militancy

Fragmentation is occurring in other ways as well. Within countries and regions, as well as across borders, religious ideology creates increasing fragmentation, from the conservative Christian movement in the USA to the radical Islamics that spurred Osama Bin Laden and al Qaeda, to the orthodox Jews in Israel (Huntington, 1998). Recent events in Nigeria and the Ivory Coast point to the ongoing national divisiveness created by religious and ethnic differences, turning countries such as the Ivory Coast that had enjoyed a prolonged period of post-colonial national cohesiveness into divided societies.

## The technological divide

Fragmentation also appears to be resulting in a technological divide, with many countries, particularly those in Africa and South America, falling further behind in developing the technological infrastructure and labour-market skills that permit participation in the global economy. Technological change 'increases inequality between highly skilled workers, who can make use of the new technologies, and unskilled workers, whose labor the new technologies may make redundant' (Singer, 2002: 89). Such disparity may also relate to overall income levels, further increasing differences among rich and poor nations.

## Erosion of social capital

One final trend connected to fractionalization is the erosion of social capital that is occurring worldwide (Putnam, 1993; Fukuyama, 1995). Specifically, social capital is 'an asset embedded in relationships – of individuals, communities, networks, or societies' (Leana and Van Buren III; 1999: 538–9). Social capital supports the creation of mutual goals and trust that helps communities and organizations achieve their objectives. Putnam (1993) describes how participation in civic organizations helps to create the networks and mutual trust that are crucial to people cooperating together on wider community issues, such as bond levies.

As people become more mobile, more focused on narrow personal interests and with less time to engage in civic activities, social capital declines, leading to both a decrease in the ability to support community goals and an inability to create large business organizations that rely on organizational social capital in order to function (Fukuyama, 1995). In essence, erosion of social capital means that people build fewer links within a community (or organization), feel less connected to those communities and as a result, tend to give back less to them over time.

Likewise, as employees hold less loyalty to organizations (and as organizations focus less on building such loyalty), those employees will remain fewer years and feel less committed to the organization, making it harder for managers to pull people together to work towards organizational goals. As we discuss later, such organizational social capital is of increasing importance to MNCs, making this global trend a worrisome one for IHRM professionals.

## The psychic shock syndrome

We also see a fourth, largely unnamed, global trend that has implications for IHRM. We call this trend the 'psychic shock syndrome', and define it as the increasingly fast and sharp shifts in the realities with which people and organizations must deal (Bell, 2002/2003). Several examples have emerged in the last 15 years. First, a paradigm shift occurred when 12 planned economies of the Soviet bloc, China and Vietnam, decided to move towards market economies. This change affected over 1.6 billion people – more than 360 million East Europeans and Russians and over one billion Chinese, Vietnamese and Mongolians – about 30 per cent of the world's total population and about 7 per cent of the global GDP in 1990.

Another major shift occurred when the dot.com internet businesses and stock markets of major industrialized countries collapsed in the late 1990s. For the previous two decades, US economic growth and involvement of individuals in the stockmarket was unprecedented. The sharp upswings in economic growth and the status of technical wonderkids of the 1990s in the USA screeched to a halt with the downturn, shattering expectations and beliefs. Many in the USA had never had such experiences. Young people had no personal understanding of economic cycles and hardship. When the economies of the USA, Japan and Europe slid, the impact on middle-class participants, in particular, was devastating. The economic shocks suffered in Mexico over the last two decades, and most recently in Argentina, have also caused wrenching changes in the expectations of the middle class. The rapid rise of China in the world economy has likewise shifted the economic landscape sharply over the last decade.

Furthermore, rapid shifts in demographic profiles of many countries have been dramatic. Many European countries and Japan face rapidly aging populations with their attendant problems (for example social security, healthcare, and finding employees for needed jobs). As medical advances increase life expectancy, those challenges will face other countries as well. The USA anticipates a population soon to be dominated by immigrants or second-generation young people – Hispanics, Asians and other people with a non-European background. Hispanics are now the largest minority in the USA, surpassing African-Americans for the first time (*New York Times*, 22 January 2003). Finally, countries such as China face uneven gender balances – China's one-child policy encouraged families to abort or put female babies up for adoption, in favour of the preferred boy child, skewing the balance of men to women in later years. The result is that those young boys will grow up in a world where they must compete for the limited number of women, or find other women from other countries to be their wives.

Discoveries in science will more often challenge our long-held views of a mechanistic world and force us to deal with 'facts' that can shift depending on the observer (Wheatley, 2001). Combined with these attacks on accepted 'truisms', information of every sort, desired or not, bombards people globally and locally. This mountainous barrage of information is increasingly difficult to absorb. The internet, satellite television, voice and text messages on mobile phones, 24-hour TV, electronic mail, advertisements on sports players, or speciality magazines – all offer an overload of information, causing psychic shock for those seeking to deal with it all.

Finally, the psychic shock of overextension – obligations at work, home and play – put pressure on employees, customers and suppliers that tax their abilities to succeed. At work, lower-level employees take on more tasks, often without the authority to complete them with autonomy. Senior managers face increasing accountability – stemming from the recent corporate mismanagement of such firms as WorldCom, Enron and Arthur Andersen – to the demands to 'do more with less' that firms face as competition across countries grows. Particularly for those whose jobs are connected to the global economy, the work pressures have increased (Schor, 1991, 1999; Kanter, 1995), with no relief or reduction in sight. The cumulative physical and emotional effects of these 'psychic shocks' are an important aspect of the global workforce that the IHRM profession must recognize and address.

These trends affect such issues as the types of employees that will be available to MNCs, their motivation and expectations, and the management approaches that firms will need to employ to achieve the performance they seek. For example, as some countries' labour supply declines, firms may have to redefine the recruiting inducements they use – perhaps adding better financial, quality of life or health-related benefits. Likewise, as individuals become increasingly overextended, their capacities for creative thinking and acting may fall, putting firms in jeopardy of long-term research and development outputs, the ability to identify and pursue strategic directions, or to see and address future shifting trends.

While many more global trends exist, these represent a range of impacts – from psychic to economic to environmental, to the splitting up of people and ideas – that may affect the nature and manner in which organizations pursue IHRM. As we discuss below, global trends affect the future evolution of IHRM in different ways, with some trends having little impact on certain aspects of IHRM. To provide some overview and guidance, we created a matrix of these differential effects that is presented in the Appendix A.

## International HRM dimensions

Many scholars have proposed various frameworks for thinking of the human resource discipline (Ulrich et al., 1997; Evans et al., 2002). While they differ in language and some aspects, fundamentally practitioners and scholars face the same three issues: deciding upon the goals or mandate of the human resource area within an organization; determining the way to structure and carry out activities that fall under the umbrella of HRM; and finally, specifying the particular HRM activities, policies or actions that are appropriate for the organization. Here, we focus on the IHRM aspects of organizations, rather than those that affect the domestic side of employees within a single country.

# The IHRM mandate and the impact of global trends

All MNC leaders must decide upon the mandate or mission and goals of an international HRM area. The mandate covers what the IHRM area is responsible for, what it should focus on, and how its success is measured. In the early days of IHRM, the mandate's main component was to oversee and coordinate activities relating to expatriate managers of internationalizing companies. The days of focusing on sending home-based executives abroad to manage wholly owned subsidiaries have ended; as MNCs' structures, missions, operations and measurements become more complex, IHRM has had to adjust. It is also becoming more important for IHRM's mandate and purpose to be clear not only to those who carry out its activities (that is, HR personnel as well as managerial employees), but also to those affected by the activities.

### Diversity of MNCs and their home countries

Several of the trends mentioned above dramatically affect the mandate of IHRM and will continue to do so for the foreseeable future. The increasing numbers of MNCs based in countries outside Western countries, South Korea and Japan means that IHRM's mandate and methods will become more diverse, and the knowledge of how to effectively manage IHRM must be expanded.

For instance, we must consider more specifically how economic systems may influence IHRM systems in various countries and regions. In a study of how different forms of capitalism influence employee practices, Redding (2001) claimed that various forms may act as a proxy for home bases of MNCs. For instance, Redding (2001) argued that there are six configurations of capitalism, each of which suggests differences in ownership, coordination and HR practices (Evans *et al.*, 2002). The types and basic goals include:

- *Individualism* form (North America, UK), focuses on providing return to shareholders
- *Communitarian* form (European large-scale), focuses on commitments and obligations to a broader set of stakeholders (e.g., communities, employees)

- *Industrial-district* form (European, family-owned firms in Italy and Scandanavia) optimizes interests of family owners and senior managers
- *Keiretsu*, the Japanaese form, emphasizes the provision of stable employment
- The Korean *chaebol* form seeks to fulfil a national economic plan for development
- *Chinese capitalism* uses family-owned firms, dispersed throughout Asia (especially Hong Kong, Taiwan and Singapore) to build wealth of family owners.

Each form will influence the mandate for IHRM – ranging from finding the best people to achieve quick financial goals that increase share value, to finding loyal employees who will look after a family's best interests, to developing practices that maintain ongoing and long-lasting employment, which may mean employees accepting lower salaries in exchange for long-term firm commitment. In short, the underlying context and HRM philosophy may influence the way that an MNC conceives of its IHRM mandate. Interestingly, though, some of the other trends mentioned above may force reevaluation of the mandates. For example, as Japan's economic slump continues, the notion of lifelong employment as an IHRM mandate is eroding, as can be seen in the recent layoff of 10 per cent of worldwide employees at such traditional *keiretsu* stalwarts as NEC (*New York Times*, 22 January 2003).

The increasing diversity of the underlying mandate of IHRM in MNCs is significant for several reasons. First, since much of the research on IHRM has been driven by researchers from primarily the USA and Europe studying firms in those regions or in Japan and Korea, the mandates common for firms in those countries may have biased the research in some way. As more non-Western and non-Japanese or Korean MNCs emerge – and as scholars in those regions begin to conduct indigenous research – increasing diversity of the mandates for IHRM will likely emerge. This could well affect research results, particularly with regard to identifying what IHRM should concern itself with and how it should measure its success. Moreover, if the profile of MNCs begins to draw from a wider array of countries, there will likely be a growing divergence in the mandates that IHRM professionals are given. For example, in MNCs headed by overseas Chinese, where the HRM function is usually seen as minimalist, the IHRM professional will have a very different mandate than if functioning within a Japanese MNC. An IHRM professional in a Chinese MNC may have little or no mandate for identifying and developing global leadership – since many top positions are held by family members – or the criteria for selecting leaders may be simplified and heavily based on the amount of loyalty shown to the head of the firm.

## Need for individual leaders and learning organizations

In addition to the influence of the underlying form of capitalism affecting the IHRM mandate of a global firm, there is growing evidence that the mandate of IHRM, particularly at the corporate level, is being influenced by two key strategic needs: the need to ensure global leadership talent, and the need to leverage learning throughout the organization (Scullion and Starkey, 2000). The growing interdependencies found in modern MNCs pressures them to identify the core competencies needed by global managers to effectively interact across borders, and the excentralization of key resources means that learning is likely to occur anywhere in the network (Bartlett and Ghoshal, 2000).

> ... (T)he main role for corporate HR in the international firm concerns the management of senior managers and high-potential people who are identified as strategic human resources and seen as vital to the company's future and survival'. (Scullion and Starkey, 2000: 1065)

In their study, Scullion and Starkey (2000) found that international UK firms identified senior management development, succession planning and development of a cadre of international managers as their main agenda items. At the same time, Kamoche (1997) has persuasively argued for the necessity of managers in international assignments to leverage the learning that occurs during the assignment. This underscores the role IHRM must play in building processes and procedures that help a global firm's human resources to share, pool and leverage the learning that occurs throughout the network (Taylor *et al.*, 1996; Stroh and Caligiuri, 1998; Bartlett and Ghoshal, 2002).

## Sustainability and the communities where MNCs operate

Another aspect of the richer and more diverse mandates for IHRM we are likely to see in the future concerns the impact of global firms adopting more sustainability-oriented strategies. As we mentioned above, the notion of sustainability is rapidly gaining a foothold among corporations, leading to a focus on greater numbers and types of stakeholders. In essence, MNCs may be faced with the question of what is global leadership – not only for the organization but also for the broader environment (Kiger, 2002; Wilson, 2002). As a focus on sustainability grows, we anticipate the mandate of IHRM to include more expectations for how MNCs can and should operate within the various communities with which they interact: from using hiring practices that support various communities and various ethnic groups, to developing employees in ways that allow them to contribute both to the firm and also to the broader community (for example allowing time off for family and civic participation), as well as to also prepare employees to address the question of what sort of community they want to live in.

Osland *et al.* (1999) utilize the Natural Step approach to sustainability to examine how HRM's mandate will be affected by sustainability goals. Its focus has been mostly used to examine the sustainability of natural resources, but it is argued that it could be used to examine the sustainability of human resources: 'In protecting the general environment, a steward within an organizational context is responsible for ensuring the health, well-being, and enhancement of the firm's human resources' (Osland *et al.*, 1999: 178). Osland *et al.*, contend that human resources must not be depleted faster than they can be reinvigorated, or at a faster rate than society's support mechanisms. Further, they maintain that demands placed on human resources must not surpass the development and regenerative capacities of employees and supporting social systems, and that human resources must be treated fairly (*ibid.*: 182–3).

By following the first maxim – not depleting human resources faster than they can be reinvigorated – companies must examine the balance between work, family and community sustainability, and recognize that communities where employees work and live are important sustainers of the ongoing vitality of the firm's human resources. This applies to any location – in the home country or abroad. In such a situation, the IHRM mandate must include explicit attention to the various communities in which a firm operates and consider how it contributes to the betterment of those communities. For example, Holcim's Columbian subsidiary, Cementos Boyaca, ... 'developed a project to help improve the living standards of rural communities within the area of influence of the cement-manufacturing facility in Nobsa' (Holliday *et al.*, 2002: 118).

In addition, the IHRM area may need to address the issue of inequality in skills within the communities in which it works. Terranova, a GrupoNueva forestry products company, ... 'has created a development training center to offer training in various trades to adults in the community of Cabrero, in the south of Chile', where many adults had not finished their schooling and needed more skills to find a job (*ibid.*: 116).

Thus, a key challenge of sustainability is the pressure on IHRM to understand which communities the firm is responsible to and for. How far 'out' should the circle of responsibility go? Are the communities of major suppliers also part of its mandate? As Nike found in the early 1990s, defining the scope of responsibility too narrowly can lead to significant public-relations problems, at the very least. The company was chastised for instance, because of the poor working conditions and employee practices used by some of its Korean subcontractors in Vietnam.

## Organizational social capital

The IHRM mandate will also encompass a growing need to create organizational social capital on a global basis. Two main factors drive this. First, the high degree of interdependence of subunits within MNCs and the attendant knowledge flows that these require, pressure MNCs to create the global social capital to nurture these flows. Because social capital leads to a greater commonality of goals, as well as mutual trust, employees are more likely to put narrow interests aside to achieve wider organizational goals. In addition, they are more likely to trust one another with information and knowledge that they might previously have hoarded (Leana and

Van Buren, 1999; Kostova and Roth, 2003):

> High levels of social capital are reflected in a motivation for social actors to maintain ...
> relationships, ... reciprocate past favors of the other social actors, an expectation that the
> other actors will also reciprocate, a psychic comfort in asking ... for resources and in ...
> the perceived likelihood of providing, receiving, and asking for, help from the other social
> actors. (Kostova and Roth, 2003: 301)

They go on to note that the existence of social capital as a public good supports an
array of cooperative and proactive behaviors. An example of such behavior in the
MNC context is described by Kao's chairman Yoshio Maruta, who says that his objective is to create a company, where 'if anything goes wrong in one department, those in
other parts of the organization should ... help without being asked'. (Ghoshal and
Bartlett, 1995: 92)

Similarly, recognizing the high interdependence between its units, ABB promotes
informal exchanges to create a system which works 'when a quality manager in
Sweden feels compelled to telephone or fax the quality manage in Brazil with a problem or an idea' (Taylor, 1991: 97)' (Kostova and Roth, 2003: 302).

Increasing fragmentation also affects the creation of global organizational social
capital. The fractionalization along religious, technological, and talent lines make it
necessary for global firms to nurture social capital to overcome conflict and divergence with a global workforce. Since divisions in religion, ethnicity or culture are
likely to be exacerbated in the short term (Huntington, 1998), the ability of an MNC
to create social capital and reap its benefits in higher internal trust and sharing of
mutual goals becomes even more crucial.

The IHRM area enters uncharted waters when it accepts as part of its mandate the
creation of global social capital. Initial work in the USA suggests that 'high performance work practices' (for example long-term employment, high investment in
employee training and development, egalitarian work environment) are most often
linked with high social capital (Leana and Van Buren, 1999). Even with ongoing
research in this area (Taylor et al., 2003), effective practices to nurture global organizational social capital are far from being firmly established. Finally, IHRM must also
deal with the fact that social capital on a societal level has been observed to be in
decline (Putnam, 1993; Fukuyama, 1995), making the task of creating organizational
social capital that much more difficult.


## Dealing with psychic shock

We also anticipate that the IHRM mandate will, given the increasing severity and
frequency of psychic shock effects as well as the interdependencies described above,
include a greater emphasis on being a change agent (Evans et al., 2002). IHRM will
increasingly have the responsibility of identifying how environmental changes

interconnect with changing business strategies and pressures, and to prepare and guide organizations and employees for such upcoming changes. For example, Hewlett-Packard's outsourcing of its printer manufacturing to Asia has left mostly a research and development function in its Vancouver, Washington, site. The IHRM role now is to ensure a smooth transfer of technological knowledge to the new sites as well as minimize the disorientation of the remaining workforce in the 'old' sites.

Anticipating and dealing with the psychic-shock effects of large demographic shifts will also become part of IHRM's mandate. In Europe, for example, the precipitous decline in birthrates and the simultaneous rise in immigrants and refugees from culturally distinct countries puts stresses on society and organizations. Asylum-seekers, illegal immigrants and legal immigrants put huge pressures on social services and, even when they are legitimately in a country, are often viewed as a negative influence (Figure 14.1).

IHRM will thus increasingly have to cooperate with the domestic IIR function to help prepare local 'native' employees to work effectively with these immigrants, sharing their knowledge on effective intercultural working relationships with national units faced with a new and growing workforce diversity. Similarly, international mergers and acquisitions also require IHRM to tackle the challenges of merging organizational cultures that are often highly influenced by their national backgrounds, such as in the acquisition of Chrysler by Daimler Benz. Given the increased importance of the effective functioning of the human organization to global competitiveness (Pucik *et al.*, 1992), IHRM's role in creating successful international mergers, acquisitions and alliances has become crucial, and in other large organizational changes such as shifts in global strategies or shifts in demographics.

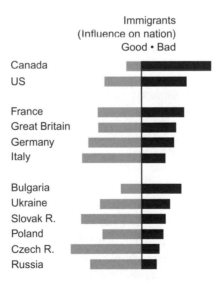

*Figure 14.1*   Citizens' views of the perceived influence of immigrants

*Source*:  The Pew Research Center for The People & The Press, © 2002, reproduced with permission.

As we suggest through the issues raised in this section, one of the IHRM professional's most critical future tasks will be to assess what are its responsibility areas and what its measures of success will be. The increasing diversity in the country of origin of MNCs, combined with pressures to move towards sustainable global business strategies, a focus on building organizational social capital and dealing with the incessant psychic shocks employees are subjected to, will stretch the imagination and skills of IHRM experts in the years to come. Each of these issues will influence the ways in which MNCs will carry out IHRM, as discussed in the next section.

## The IHRM function and activities

The IHRM function refers to the structure for implementing the area's mandate. Any MNC has several structural IHRM decisions to make: whether the function will be centralized or spread throughout the organization, whether it will be in the form of a network with shared responsibility across the organization, whether the firm will create a consistent IHRM function across borders or an integrated corporate culture globally (Wellins and Rioux, 2000). Interestingly, while researchers in the field call for more understanding of the function and its relationship to strategy (for example Walsh, 1996; Marschan et al., 1997), there has been little in terms of clear-cut approaches and their link to performance.

Thus, we continue to learn from practice, which suggests that as the mandate changes over time, the nature of the structure could, in fact, change dramatically. For example, as firms reduce costs and find the best IHRM practices and personnel globally, they may seek to outsource parts of the IHRM function. They may, for instance, use international recruiting or compensation consulting firms (Cuthill, 2000; Wilson, 2002) rather than conduct their own recruiting or manage compensation internally. On the other hand, the decisions may vary based upon the nature or home country of MNCs. Hong Kong-based, primarily family-owned MNCs may choose to remain small in terms of revenues rather than expand so large that non-relatives would be forced to play a large role; likewise, they may be less apt to outsource than would an American or European firm that has more options available and whose management is more familiar with the concept of using outsiders to do critical IHRM tasks.

Furthermore, as interdependence becomes more the norm at a macro and societal level, so too does the need for interconnectedness of tasks and information that must flow within an MNC. The result will be a need for greater IHRM integration/coordination. The balance is one that scholars have examined (for example Taylor et al., 1996) and practitioners have tried to implement for several years. The coordination of the function becomes even more important as its function takes on the change-agent role within firms as well. Given such requirements, the need to harmonize across borders grows.

Finally, interdependence and across-border coordination of information also means a more coordinated approach to developing talent and, in particular, in the ways to develop global leaders within MNCs. While we might, then, assume that links between MNC strategy and IHRM function should become closer (see for example Scullion and Starkey, 2000), other forces may enter the picture in terms of how the function will be carried out. For example, purely locally focused training may no longer suffice. Firms, with their IHRM functions, will develop programmes that develop leaders within many regions to be able to manage, understand and lead firms in a complex global environment. Yet, conversely, fragmentation may drive a push towards more localization/decentralization, as religious or ethnic considerations force considerations of the particular over the integrated whole. The balancing act – how much integration and coordination versus local or decentralized management – requires careful consideration and flexibility to address needs – or demands – in different areas of an MNC's world.

One of the final trends, psychic shocks, will further complicate the IHRM function's role, emphasizing the need for vigilant monitoring of employee health (mental and physical), as well as the need to communicate effectively throughout the organization to anticipate shared trends that will affect HR activities that will in turn affect employees. Again, though, the diversity of MNCs may influence the extent to which such monitoring may (or can) occur or the degree to which MNC management shares information. In transition-economy firms, where information was viewed as power in state-owned enterprises, the willingness to share information by management may be difficult to instill. Likewise, privacy laws may limit the amount of monitoring that firms are able to conduct within certain societies or countries. Thus, one of the demands facing IHRM professionals is to be more aware of and know how to handle such trends or shocks that emerge from globalization.

All of these changes in the HRM function will require greater international experience and knowledge of IHRM professionals. One way to ensure this is to increase the diversity in the backgrounds of the IHRM professionals, a move many companies have already taken. Yet as Black and his colleagues found in the late 1990s, in spite of the high priority MNCs place on IHRM tasks such as global leadership development as key to their future competitiveness, the majority of the firms they studied felt that their IHRM function was not up to the task (Black et al., 1999). The hiring and development of IHRM managers will become a key challenge for many MNCs.

Just as the IHRM mandate and functions require re-evaluation in an environment of dramatic trends, so too do the IHRM activities and practices need reassessment. For example, when employees work in regions with major terrorist activity (such as the Middle East, Latin America, Southeast Asia), the IHRM professionals of an MNC may need to develop practices and policies that help to address physical danger. For the future, however, the IHRM activities may need to include 'crisis policies' for areas currently not in danger but potentially vulnerable. With regard to specific IHRM practices, the firm faces decisions such as who to recruit and place in such regions, what obligations it has to employees who work there, and whether and how it balances those regions, the employees it hires to work there, and the responsibilities the MNC has to the community.

With regard to the trends mentioned earlier, the fragmentation issues raise questions such as how much HRM policy replication a firm can have in global settings. For example, while Disney Japan was based very closely on the long-successful American model, Disney Europe fared less well. Disney Europe, based outside Paris, faced uncomfortable problems with French employees who resisted long-existing Disney policies, for example regarding hair length or behaviour expectations, and who had expectations about fewer working hours per week than the USA or Japan has.

In addition, given the costs, dangers and national government requirements for more local employees to be hired, MNCs are increasingly using what we call 'global suitcase employees', or employees who work in a variety of regions for short-term (that is under one year) assignments. Rather than being expatriates, with the time to learn and understand a culture (and the expensive costs related to expatriates), these workers become more like 'chameleons', learning about a new setting, culture and expectations quickly. Such a group raises new issues for IHRM functions and the related policies.

## Conclusion

The IHRM professional's job in the next two decades will be one of the most challenging within the global business environment. Balancing a firm's requirements and goals with global trends and pressures makes it an extremely difficult but exciting profession, requiring the skills of a diplomat, the knowledge of a hard-headed business person, and the empathy of a psychologist.

In this chapter, we sought to stimulate thinking about what future IHRM specialists need to address, rather than to provide pat answers. We discussed several key trends that we anticipate will affect the role, function and activities of IHRM, and four key trends emerged in our discussion:

- The changing profile of multinational corporations (for example more from developing and non-North American, European or Japanese home countries)
- Growing global interdependencies in terms of the links across economics, politics, social, technological and environmental factors affecting MNCs, as well as the increasing realization of the need for sustainable development within communities
- Increasing global fragmentation stemming from rivalries in ethnic, religious and social/moral diversity
- Psychic-shock syndrome where individuals become overwhelmed with the shifts and changes occurring in their societies and the world at large.

These trends will probably influence the mandate (or role and responsibilities) of the IHRM area, in terms of how a firm and the IHRM area views its communities, what it should contribute and how it should be measured, and the nature and types of employees it will need, train and keep. Likewise, the functions and activities will vary depending upon such trends, as the home-country approaches and culture may come into play as well.

The mandate, function/structure and activities of IHRM that will be common in 2030 are not yet clearly visible to anyone. In this chapter we have tried to argue that it is becoming the duty of the students who wish to become IHRM professionals to learn how to look at the wider environment in order to anticipate what they will need to successfully meet their firms' challenges in the future. As IHRM professionals in the future, students will need to learn how to follow trends, not only in the industry in which their firms compete, but also in the social, scientific, political and environmental areas, and deal with the many contradictions they see between the trends, such as those between growing interdependence and growing fragmentation.

While the trends we have discussed as particularly important to IHRM in the future may not be the complete or even the correct set, we hope the discussion has shown how IHRM professionals of the future will need to become very savvy about the wider world on many levels in order to be effective strategic partners with the management teams of the MNCs. Learning to identify and track such trends, and think through what the implications for IHRM might be as students, is good preparation for being global managers of IHRMs for the year 2005, 2010 or 2030.

## Discussion questions

1 What elements of psychic shock have you experienced in the last 12 months? What new evidence has emerged recently that was not included within this chapter (for example dealing with a new fast-spreading virus)?
2 Give the differences among multinational firms, how might the mandates for IHRM vary among them (for example along what dimensions)?
3 In your reading of newspapers and business journals, find three examples of the tension between integration and coordination faced by multinationals, and explore how the tensions might affect IHRM in the firm.
4 Which IHRM-related issues, if any, will be particularly salient to small and medium-sized firms in Europe, North America and Japan, and how?

# Appendix: Overview of effects of global trends on the future IHRM mandate, function and policies

| Global trend | IHRM mandate | Effect on:<br>IHRM function | IHRM policies |
|---|---|---|---|
| Changing profile of MNCS | • Growing diversity of home countries of MNCs, leading to increasing diversity of mandates<br>• Increasing focus on global talent development | • Greater international experience and background diversity of IHR personnel | • Increasing policies to address physical danger<br>• Policies to deal with increasing number of 'global suitcase employees' |
| Growing global interdependencies | • Greater emphasis on mandates of learning and sustainability<br><br>• More of a change agent<br>• More of a creater of social capital | • Growing outsourcing of certain aspects of IHRM<br>• Growing interdependence and coordination of IHR function | • Growing number of locales globally with 'critical' employees |
| Global psychic shocks | • Creator of global social capital<br><br><br>• Become a global change agent<br>• Proactively anticipate shocks and take appropriate steps | • Need to devolve authority to local operations that need responsiveness | • Need for greater localization of policies<br><br>• Create policies regarding outsources, 'shocks' employees globally |

# Further reading

Dicken, P. (1998) *Global Shift*, 3rd edn. New York: Guilford.
Holliday, C., Jr, Schmidheiny, S. and Watts, P. (2002) *Walking the Talk: The Business Case for Sustainable Development*. San Francisco: Berrett-Koehler.
Scullion, H. and Starkey, K. (2002) 'In Search of the Changing Role of the Corporate Human Resource Function in the International Firm', *International Journal of Human Resource Management*, 11(6): 1061–81.
Wheatley, M. (2001) *Leadership and the New Science: Discovering Order in a Chaotic World*. San Francisco: Berrett-Koehler.

# References

Bartlett, C. and Ghoshal, S. (1989) *Managing Across Borders*. Cambridge, MA: Harvard
Bartlett, C. and Ghoshal, S. (2002) 'Building Competitive Advantage Through People', *Sloan Management Review*, 43(2): 34–41.
Becker, B. and Huselid, M. (1998) 'High Performance Work Systems and Firm Performance: A Synthesis of Research and Managerial Implications', *Research in Personnel and HRM*, 16: 53–101.
Bell, C. (2002/2003) 'Normative Shift', *National Interest*, Winter, issue 70: 44–54.
Birkinshaw, J. and Hood, N. (1998) 'Multinational Subsidiary Evolution: Capability and Charter Change in Foreign-Owned Subsidiary Companies', *Academy of Management Review*, 23: 773–95.
Black, J.S., Gregersen, H.B., Mendenhall, M.E. and Stroh, L.K. (1999) *Globalizing People through International Assignments*. Reading, MA: Addison-Wesley.
*Business China* (2003) 'Changing Currents', 3 March: 3–9.
Cuthill, S. (2000) 'Managing HR across International Borders', *Compensation and Benefits Management*, Summer: 43–5.
Dicken, P. (1998) *Global Shift*, 3rd edn. New York: Guilford.
Evans, P., Pucik, V. and Barsoux, J.-L. (2002) *The Global Challenge: International Human Resource Management*. Boston: McGraw-Hill.
Fukuyama, F. (1995) *Trust: The Social Virtues and the Creation of Prosperity*. New York: Free Press.
Ghoshal, S. and Bartlett, C. (1995) 'Changing the Role of Top Management: Beyond Structure to Processes', *Harvard Business Review*, Jan./Feb.: 89–96.
Govindarajan, V. and Gupta, A.K. (2001) *The Quest for Global Dominance*. San Francisco: Jossey-Bass.
Gupta, A.K. and Govindarajan, V. (2000) 'Knowledge Flows within Multinational Corporations', *Strategic Management Journal*, 21: 473–96.
Hjelt, P. (2002) 'Fortune Global 5 Hundred', *Fortune*, 22 July, 2002.
Holliday, C., Jr, Schmidheiny, S. and Watts, P. (2002) *Walking the Talk: The Business Case for Sustainable Development*. San Francisco: Berrett-Koehler.
Huntington, S. (1998) *The Clash of Civilizations and the Remaking of World Order*. New York: Touchstone Books.
Iyer, P. (2000) *The Global Soul: Jet Lag, Shopping Malls, and the Search for Home*. New York: Knopf.
Kamoche, K. (1997) 'Knowledge Creating and Learning in the International Firm', *International Journal of Human Resource Management*, 8(3): 213–25.
Kanter, R.M. (1995) *World Class*. New York: Touchstone.
Kiger, P. (2002) 'How Deloitte Builds Global Expertise', Workforce.com, June.
Kostova, T. and Roth, K. (2003) 'Social Capital in Multinational Corporations and a Micro-Macro Model of its Formation', *Academy of Management Review*, 28(2): 297–317.
Leana, C. and Van Buren III, H. (1999) 'Organizational Social Capital and Employment Practices', *Academy of Management Review*, 24(3): 522–37.
Lodovico, A., Lewis. W., Palmade, V. and Sankhe, S. (2001) 'India – From emerging to surging', *McKinsey Quarterly*, Special Edition, Issue 4: 28–51.
Marschan, R. Welch, D. and Welch, D. (1997) 'Control in Less Hierarchical Multinationals: The Role of Personal Networks and Informal Communications', *International Business Review*, 5(2): 137–50.
Napier, N.K., Tibau, J., Janssens, M. and Pilenzo, R. (1995) 'The Role of the International Human Resource Manager: Managing from the Outside and the Inside', in G. Ferris (ed.), *Hand Book of Human Resources Management*. Oxford: Basil Blackwell, 217–42.
*New York Times* (2003) 'Hispanics Now Largest Minority, Census Shows', 23 January: A1.
*New York Times* (2003) 'NEC Uses Vacancy at Top to Reaffirm Shift', 22 January: C4.

Nohria, N. and Ghoshal, S. (1997) *The Differentiated Network: Organizing Multinational Corporations for Value Creation*. San Francisco: Jossey-Bass.

Osland, J., Drake, B. and Feldman, H. (1999) 'The Stewardship of Natural and Human Resources', in C. Dempsey and R. Butkus (eds), *All Creation is Groaning*. Minneapolis, MN: Liturgical Press: 168–202.

Phillips, R. and Claus, L. (2002) 'Corporate Social Responsbilitity and Global HR: Balancing the Needs of the Corporation and its Stakeholders', *International Focus*, Society for Human Resource Management.

Pucik, V., Tichy, N. and Barnett, C. (1992) *Globalizing management: Creating and leading the competitive organization*. New York: Wiley.

Putnam, R. (1993) *Making Democracy Work: Civic Traditions in Modern Italy*. Princeton, NJ: Princeton University Press.

Redding, G. (2001) 'The Evolution of Business Systems', *Euro-Asia Centre Report No. 72*. INSEAD, Fontainbleau and Singapore.

Rosen, R. (2000) *Global Literacies*. New York: Simon and Schuster.

Schor, J. (1991) *The Overworked American*. New York: Basic Books.

Schor, J.B. (1999) *The Overspent American*. New York: Perennial Books.

Scullion, H. and Starkey, K. (2000) 'In Search of the Changing Role of the Corporate Human Resource Function in the International Firm', *International Journal of Human Resource Management*, 11(6): 1061–81.

Singer, P. (2002) *One World: The Ethics of Globalization*. New Haven, CT: Yale University Press.

Stroh, L. and Caligiuri, P. (1998) 'Increasing Global Competitiveness through Effective People Management', *Journal of World Business*, 33(1): 1–16.

Taylor, W. (1991) 'The Logic of Global Business: An Interview with ABB's Percy Barnevik', *Harvard Business Review*, March-April: 91–105.

Taylor, S., Beechler, S. and Napier, N.K. (1996) 'Toward an Integrated Theory of International Human Resource Management', *Academy of Management Review*, 21(4): 959–85.

Taylor, S., Boyacigiller, N., Beechler S. and Levy, O. (2003) 'The Human Organization of MNCs and its Effect on Global Competitiveness', Working Paper. Portland, OR: Portland State University.

Ulrich, D. (1998) Intellectual capital = competence × commitment. *Sloan Management Review*, Winter, 39(2): 15–27.

Ulrich, D., Losey, M. and Lake, G. (eds) (1997) *Tomorrow's HR Management*. New York: Wiley.

Walsh, J. (1996) 'Multinational Management Strategy and Human Resource Decision Making in the Single European Market', *Journal of Management Studies*, 33: 633–48.

Wellins, R. and Rioux, S. (2000) 'The Growing Pains of Globalizing HR', *Training and Development*, May: 79–85.

Wheatley, M. (2001) *Leadership and the New Science: Discovering Order in a Chaotic World*. San Francisco: Berrett-Koehler.

Wilson, F. (2002) *A Global Vision*. www. Peoplemanagement.co.uk. 12 September.

Zachary, P. (2000) *The Global Me*. New York: Publicaffairs.

# Index

United States – *continued*
  goal setting 95
  human resource function 32
  immigrant population 304
  industrial relations 166, 174, 175
  number of expatriates 115
  repatriation 142
  staffing 56–7, 58–9, 63
  trade unions 160, 161, 165
  training and development 75
  women managers 182
Uwilingiyimana, Agatha 286, 292

Van Buren III, H. 303, 310
Van de Vliert, E. 136
Van Gennep, A. 14, 136–7, 138
Van Maanen, J. 137
Van Ruysseveldt, J. 6, 7, 160, 167
Vasella, Daniel 215, 220
Veersma, O. 270
Venkata Ratnam, C.S. 269
Vermeulen, F. 207
Vernon, R.G. 24–5
Vietnam 304
Vinnicombe, S. 196
Visser, J. 160, 167
Vlasic, B. 230
Von Glinow, M. 22
Vu, V.T. 261

Wachter 117
wages *See* compensation
Wally, S. 62
Walsh, J. 196, 312
Waltz, P.M. 253
Wang, X. 236
Ward, C. 237, 238, 239, 247, 252
Warner, M. 248, 260, 264, 269
Watkins, K.E. 209
Watts, P. 302
Weaver, G.R. 244
Weisman, S.R. 295
Welch, D. 4, 24, 48, 78, 109, 312
Welch, L. 78
Weldon, E. 248
Wellins, R. 312
West, M. 134, 135
Westwood, R.I. 181, 183
Wexley, K.N. 95, 97, 100
Wheatley, M. 305
White, B. 186, 189, 197
Williams, S. 92, 105
Williamson, O. 49, 115, 116, 117, 122
Williamson, P. 60
Wilson, F. 308, 312
Wilson, M. 22, 52
Windolf, P. 166
Womack, J. 157
women 36, 37, 145–6, 181–97, 242, 243, 252

barriers to progress 181–2, 183, 185–7, 188–9, 197
  organizational and structural 189–92
business leaders 288–9
and careers 186–9
and dual career issues 187–9
equality legislation 171–2
and families 186, 187, 190, 191, 193
and formal policies 189–92
and future civilisation 293–6
and future unity 291–3
glass ceiling 187, 191, 295
leadership 17–18, 283, 284–96
  global 288–90
  roles 291–3
management style 184–5
and masculine ethic 182, 184, 197
mentoring 192, 194, 195–7
myths about 183
networking 192–4
occupational segregation 186
and old-boy network 193–4
participation in management 37
political leaders 284–7, 291–3
qualities of 291
and quasi-expatriation 150
repatriation 144–6
share of expatriates 182–3
stereotyping 181, 184, 185, 188, 192
tokenism 145
traditional attitudes to 181–2, 185–6, 191
Won-Woo, P. 264
Woodward, S. 116, 117, 120
Works Councils 164, 166, 168, 175
World Conference Against Racism 282
World Trade Centre 282
world trends 282, 299, 304–5
  change in 283–4, 293–6
worldwide functional management 39–40
Worm, V. 109
Wraner, M. 160
Wright, P. 51, 115, 116, 117

Xiucheng, F. 9

Yan, A. 119, 125, 126, 128, 203, 224
Yang, C. 228
Yeager, M. 184
Yip, G. 7
Yli-Renko, Autio A. 9
Yong, M. 84
Young, S. 7

Zachary, P. 302
Zander, U. 9
Zeira, Y. 207
Zimmerer, T.W. 270
Zollo, M. 213, 214
Zucker, L. 203
Zwingmann, C.A.A. 245